GOMPERS IN CANADA

Samuel Gompers

ROBERT H. BABCOCK

Gompers in Canada:
a study in American
continentalism before the
First World War

UNIVERSITY OF TORONTO PRESS

© University of Toronto Press 1974
Toronto and Buffalo
Printed in Canada

ISBN 0-8020-2142-5 (cloth)
ISBN 0-8020-6242-3 (paper)
LC 74-78507

Because reading every letter was out of the question, I drew up a checklist of important Canadian labour leaders before using these sources. All letters to Canadian organizers whose names are listed in the AFL's *List of Affiliated Organizations* [vol. 1 (1902-17), AFL-CIO Archives] were scanned. I examined references to P.M. Draper, J.A. Flett, the Federation Executive Council, and to random numbers of international union heads and secretaries of Canadian city central bodies. No doubt some important letters were overlooked by this research technique.

A relatively small proportion of incoming letters are on microfilm in the National Union Files and in the Samuel Gompers Files at AFL-CIO archives. The latter also preserve useful press releases, speeches, and conference proceedings touching upon Canadian labour matters. Collectively these letters reveal the motives, attitudes, and concerns of American labour leaders upon Canadian affairs that were ordinarily disguised in the published proceedings.

In Canada the papers of the Trades and Labor Congress for this period have not survived, and the *Proceedings* of the annual conventions are lamentably brief. Quite by accident I discovered that detailed accounts of convention debates usually could be found in the pages of the *Toronto Globe* and occasionally in other Canadian newspapers. It was then possible to discover the crucial issues at each session and determine the positions taken by various Canadian labour leaders on controversies with the AFL .

The AFL-CIO denied me permission to use the minutes of the Federation Executive Council meetings for this study; I relied upon abstracts of them printed in the *American Federationist*, supplemented by material gained elsewhere in their archives. Until the full minutes are made available to all scholars, many assessments of AFL intent and purpose will remain more hypothetical than otherwise might be the case.

This project began as a doctoral thesis at Duke University. Professor Richard L. Watson, Jr, directed the thesis and provided valuable advice and encouragement. Professors Richard A. Preston and R. Taylor Cole put their knowledge of Canada and Canadians at my disposal and lent a helping hand at every stage. My research was made easier by the skills and kindnesses of the following: E. Logan Kimmel, records administrator at the AFL-CIO, and his library staff; Dr J.P. Després, assistant deputy minister, Canada Department of Labour, who permitted me to draw upon his collection of materials on the history of Quebec labour; Mrs Phyllis Andrews of the Wells College library; and Mrs Dawn Dobson of the Canadian Labour Congress library. Miss Marjorie Robertson of the Canada Department of Labour library anticipated my questions, showered me with materials, and went far beyond the call of duty in locating the pictures of Canadians which appear in this volume through the courtesy of her library. The two photographs of Samuel Gompers, alone and with members of his Executive

Council, are reproduced courtesy Culver Pictures. I am indebted to the staffs of the Library of Congress and the Public Archives and National Library of Canada for assistance, and to Wells College for a grant to aid typing costs. The book has been published with the aid of the Social Science Research Council of Canada using funds provided by the Canada Council.

At various stages the manuscript benefited greatly from the comments of Eugene Forsey, Ramsay Cook, I.M. Abella, R.I.K. Davidson, and Patricia Lagacé. Nearly all the statistics on the size of trade unionism in Canada up to 1902 were provided by Senator Forsey, who graciously permitted me to draw upon part of his manuscript study of Canadian unions in the nineteenth century. Indeed, at every stage of the research and writing of this work I enjoyed the wit and wisdom of Senator Forsey. While all these people influenced my thinking, I remain responsible for any errors and omissions.

Two people offered constant encouragement when the whole idea was just a dream. My old boss, Frank Andreone, knew better than anyone how to help a teacher to grow. And my wife, Rosemary, to whom this book is lovingly dedicated, sacrificed her own professional interests and assumed many of my family responsibilities during months of graduate study, research, and writing.

RHB

Patrick M. Draper (TLC *Official Book* 1901)

John A. Flett (TLC *Official Book* 1901)

James Simpson (Allied Trades and Labor Association *Souvenir Labor Day Programme* 1925)

Samuel Gompers and some members of the AFL Executive Council. From left to right, seated, James Duncan of the Stonecutter's Union, Samuel Gompers, Frank Morrison, secretary of the AFL; standing, Max Morris of the Retail Clerks, John B. Lennon of the Tailors, and John Mitchell of the United Mine Workers

GOMPERS IN CANADA

1
Introduction

For many years Canadians have debated whether their country should have its own trade-union movement. One of the earliest and most dramatic rehearsals of the perennial arguments on both sides of that question reverberated from the crimson and gold furnishings of the Canadian Senate on 29 April 1903. The chamber's brilliant decor offered plush quarters for a group of men whose presence there climaxed successful years in politics or business. It contrasted sharply with the dingy union halls and sooty factory stairways where Canadian workers debated the same questions. The senators gathered on that day to take up the second reading of a bill providing two years' imprisonment for any American citizen coming to Canada to assist striking workers.[1] It was no secret that many Canadian miners, railway labourers, and factory workers had been joining locals of American trade unions in hopes of bettering their lot. But strikes had come to Canada, and the senators believed them to have been imported from the United States. The bill before them promised to go a long way toward separating Canadian trade-union locals from their parent organizations south of the border.

Senator James Lougheed, a middle-aged lawyer and Conservative who had moved in his youth to the West and had become a leader of the Calgary bar, sponsored the measure. Conditions were different in Canada, he began. 'We know very well that certain classes of labour in the United States are becoming very largely tainted through the importation of those anarchistic classes from southern Europe that have [contributed] to the very many upheavals of industrial life in that country.' This class of labour had infected the agitators who were coming into Canada to establish unions and foment strikes. He said that his proposal was not aimed at the American Federation of Labor (AFL) and 'the more responsible classes of labour organizations of an international character.' But his bill did not exempt AFL officials from the proposed ban.[2]

Other senators were well satisfied with the bill and failed to see any necessity for distinguishing between the AFL and more radical labour organizations. Senator William Gibson embraced the measure wholeheartedly. A successful businessman, he had emigrated to Canada from Scotland in 1870 and had grown affluent building bridges and culverts for the Grand Trunk Railway. Nearly every union in the country was directed from AFL headquarters in Washington, Gibson declared, 'and many of the troubles that Canada is now suffering under are not directed by our own people, nor started by our own people, but by men who are sent from Washington to organize unions.' Gibson wanted Lougheed's bill to go even further and specifically abolish all American unions in Canada.[3]

Employers in the United States faced an industrial crisis, Senator James McMullen declared. One of the Liberal party's Old Guard, the aged McMullen had come to Canada from Ireland as a boy and had risen to become a director of the Dominion Life Insurance Company and the Grand Trunk Railway. After eighteen years of faithful party service in the House of Commons, he had been appointed to the Senate in 1902. American labour organizations, McMullen said, 'claim the right to dictate how many hours a man shall work in a day. If a man is disposed to work ten hours they will declare that he shall not work more than eight, and force him to join the union and live up to its rules.' American trade unions lent strength to Canadian unions through their common affiliation. In fact, McMullen complained, Samuel Gompers was in Ottawa at that very moment and was scheduled to address a large gathering of working men in the Canadian capital. McMullen supported Lougheed's proposal because he agreed with the view that Canadian workers were competent to manage their own affairs without foreign interference.[4]

George McHugh was one of only a handful of senators who were willing to defend international trade unionism in Canada that day. 'It would be a very nice thing to have Canadian unions confined to the Canadian people alone,' he said, 'but you must understand that very often there is trouble going on between capital and labour, and capitalists do not hesitate to go outside of Canada to get capital to run their enterprises, and so long as they go outside, perhaps the labourer would have some justification for going out and amalgamating with unions outside of Canada.' McHugh failed to convince the bill's supporters, who voted their approval on second reading.[5]

About three months later the senators jumped at another chance (the third reading of the bill) to express their opinions on trade unionism in general and American organizations in particular. The bill, incidentally, had been amended by a committee to permit international union officers to enter Canada only for the purpose of settling a strike. Senator John V. Ellis, a former printer's apprentice who had become editor of a leading newspaper in New Brunswick, expanded the argument offered earlier by Senator McHugh. 'We have evidence that between monopolists in Canada and in the United States there is a constant and active organization,' he said. 'There is a constant union between them, while on the other hand, capitalists are endeavouring to prevent an organization on the part of labour.' Ellis thought the Lougheed bill went too far.[6]

William J. MacDonald, the archetype of the self-made man in the Canadian Senate, vehemently disagreed with Ellis. 'By invoking the aid of outside people,' he said, 'they declare themselves to be incompetent fools who cannot manage their own affairs.' The seventy-year-old legislator had left Britain in the service of the Hudson's Bay Company in 1851 and had managed his own affairs very well since that time. After prospering in both politics and business in British Columbia, he had become a senator when that province entered Confederation in 1871. He was utterly unsympathetic to any trade unions; *American* unions only compounded his distaste.[7]

Another senator who had once served a printer's apprenticeship, Thomas Coffey of London, Ontario, thought the bill had been framed for the exclusive benefit of employers. 'Take my own business: we will say that a printer comes from Chicago or Detroit, or Cincinnati, or some western city to Toronto and gets employment, and he happens to say to one of his fellow workingmen "I do not think you are getting enough wages in this city. You ought to agitate for an increase." This law will take hold of that man and put him in jail for simply making that assertion.' 'Serves him right!' Senator MacDonald blurted. 'Is that not interfering with the liberty of speech, of which we are so proud in Canada?' Coffey retorted. 'We know perfectly well that our Canadian young men are continually going to the United States, and if we put a law on our statute-book which is unfriendly to the United States, we must expect that that unfriendliness will revert to our own people when they go to the great republic.'[8]

After Lougheed attempted to placate Coffey and some of the other critics of his bill, Senator Gibson again led the attack upon American trade unions in Canada. 'I venture to say that before a walking delegate[9] set his foot in Canada, there was no difficulty in settling the labour disputes in our factories and workshops ...' Walking delegates crossed the border for the purpose of benefiting themselves and destroying the industries of Canada, 'so that the like industries on the other side of the line may control the markets during the time our industries are tied up.' Then Gibson attacked Gompers: '... If he could get labour organized as he wishes, he would be in a position to destroy the building trade of any country on the face of the earth ... Imagine such power in the hands of any man,' Gibson exclaimed, 'and that he may be allowed to come to Canada or send his satellites here to destroy our peace and harmony. He should never be allowed to land in the country if that is his intention.'[10]

Gibson's outcry provoked a rebuttal from Henry J. Cloran. A Montreal lawyer who had helped found that city's crafts-dominated Trades and Labor Council, Cloran had been in the Senate less than a month and thus had had no opportunity to air his views during the earlier reading. 'If this honourable House can prevent men from outside the limits of Canada coming in to assist their brother toilers, why not declare that the toilers of Quebec shall be restrained from coming into the province of Ontario? Why not localize your organizations so as to make them insipid, useless and powerless? In union there is strength, and I say this Bill is an attack on the brotherhood of man.'[11]

But the men who defended American unions in Canada were outnumbered. James Kerr, a successful Ontario lawyer, summed up the majority view. 'I am sure that if a Canadian so far forgot himself as to cross the international boundary line and set to work to stir up or incite strikes, or lock-outs, I would think the United States people would send him back where he came from.' 'He would be shot like a dog, and serve him right, too,' old Senator MacDonald interjected. Kerr continued, '... it is a sad reflection on the people of Canada that we cannot produce as good people to settle these questions here as they have in the United States. The sooner we rely upon ourselves for the settlement of our labour disputes ... the better for us.' The Senate passed Lougheed's bill and sent it to the House of Commons. The future of American trade unions in Canada hung in the balance in early 1903, and the careful and deliberate work of Samuel Gompers to build a continental labour federation seemed about to be undone.[12]

The man whom a good many Canadian senators blamed for the spread of strikes to Canada was born in a London tenement in 1850, the son of a cigarmaker whose parents had migrated from Amsterdam.[13] Young Samuel, one of five children living in a two-room apartment amidst poverty and unemployment, attended a Jewish free school for only a few years before leaving at age ten to become a shoemaker's apprentice. The noise of the machinery soon persuaded him to abandon this trade and take up cigarmaking under his father's tutelage. Three years later Gompers was again in motion. Urged on by hardships at home and news about America inspired by the Civil War, the family boarded a ship in June 1863 and sailed for New York.

For a time after settling on the East Side, Gompers worked with his father at their apartment before finding employment in a cigar factory. At seventeen he married a young working girl who came to live in the cramped Gompers household. During the next few years, despite long hours of daily toil and grinding poverty, Gompers became known among his friends for his boundless energy, his good-natured camaraderie, and his keen, absorbing mind. The young cigarmaker enhanced his skimpy formal education by attending lectures and debates at the Cooper Union, by plunging into the activities of fraternal orders, and especially by joining in the readings and discussions which flourished in cigar shops undisturbed by the clatter of machines. One of the cigarmakers always read aloud from books and magazines, his fellows paying for his time by turning over a number of their cigars. In this way Gompers, a favourite reader in the shop, discussed, debated, and digested the theories of Marx, Engels, and other European intellectuals concerned with the plight of labour.

In his youth Gompers was both a member of the Cigarmakers' Union and a socialist. Looking back much later on these years, Gompers stressed the influence that a Swedish labour theorist, Ferdinand Laurrell, had had upon his thinking. Laurrell had urged Gompers to study socialist ideas without joining the political party. 'Study your union card, Sam,' Laurrell had told him, 'and if the idea doesn't square with that, it ain't true.[14] Following Laurrell's advice, Gompers became active in the affairs of the Cigarmakers.

Trade unions served a multitude of purposes for industrial workers. Insurance schemes offered minimal economic security; elaborate rituals and initiations patterned after the fraternal orders brightened lives dulled by daily, repetitive tasks. Industrial warfare generated a mythology which bound men together in times of trial and invariably tossed up saints and martyrs to be worshipped by the rank and file. National trade unions such as the Cigarmakers were products of the expansion of industry in the latter half of the nineteenth century. A new, continental transportation system enabled factories to grow larger and more distant from their markets. More and more itinerant craftsmen rode the rails from city to city in search of work. Finally, groups of workers in the same trade united with their brethren in other cities in order to preserve a tenuous influence upon working conditions in their trade. Such unions became international in scope when they reached across the border to affiliate locals of the same trade in Canada or Mexico.[15]

The depression of 1873 took a heavy toll of American craft unions. The Cigarmakers' Union lost five-sixths of their membership and were reduced by 1877 to a thousand people spread over seventeen locals. Only eight or nine of approximately thirty national and international craft unions survived, but many locals remained alive to the advantages of a larger and more secure organization. Samuel Gompers plunged into the task of reorganizing the New York City local and, along with Adolph Strasser, persuaded his colleagues to admit other workers involved in the cigar trade. In 1875 he became president of Local 144 and supervised the continuing work of organization and consolidation. The New

York cigarmakers won their first strike in years and obtained a 15 per cent wage increase. But the manufacturers retaliated, forcing Local 144 into a protracted struggle and leaving Gompers, by then the father of five, unemployed and black-listed. Laurrell soon found him a job and Gompers again threw all his energies into union work.[16]

As Gompers rose to prominence within the national organization, he worked to establish a system of unemployment, sickness, and death benefits which became the foundation of 'business unionism.' He persuaded his brethren to place strike authority in their union officers' hands and called for a program of strike assistance. By 1881 the Cigarmakers' International Union had become the strongest, most financially secure trade union in America, and Gompers was recognized by his colleagues to be an indefatigable worker, an excellent union hall stump speaker, and a formidable opponent in union politicking.[17]

Though Gompers surrounded himself with a coterie of friends and followers, he was by no means without opponents. In the 1870s a good many workers who favoured a militant socialist political program joined any one of a number of Marxist groups in New York City. They often shared the ultimate goals of the craft unions, but they greatly differed on tactics as well as on the question of opening their ranks to middle-class reformers and intellectuals. At length the Gompers group acquired a journal to promote their trade-unionist views and called for the creation of an American national labour body modeled after the Trades Union Congress of Great Britain.[18]

Over one hundred workers gathered at Turner Hall in Pittsburgh in 1881 to establish the new federation. Gompers sat for the Cigarmakers, one of thirty craft unions represented. Asserting their mutual interests and their desire to coordinate legislative efforts, cooperate in strikes, and share their limited re-sources, the delegates launched a Federation of Organized Trades and Labor Unions of the United States and Canada. But the new national trade-union centre was hardly a success. The meteoric rise of the Knights of Labor, a reform union mixing skilled and unskilled labour, opening its ranks to the disgruntled, and pursuing policies designed to reform the entire economic order, completely overshadowed the new craft group. After the Knights began to accept workers who normally might have joined a craft union in their trade, a long, bitter conflict broke out. Craft unionists who had shared with the Knights in the formation of the Federation of Organized Trades and Labor Unions abandoned that shelter in 1886 and set up their own national centre – the American Federation of Labor. As their president they chose the 36-year-old cigarmaker from London via New York who had done so much to earn their gratitude and further the cause of business trade unionism.[19]

An able, dedicated group of craft unionists nursed the AFL through its infancy, carefully choosing realistic targets and always aiming for the long haul. Their 'dual-union' arch-enemy, the Knights, lost members in the late 1880s almost as rapidly as it had gained them in the early years of that decade, and the hollow shell of the Noble Order of the Knights of Labor soon passed into the hands of a motley group of left-wing and agrarian reformers. Hardened by its struggle with the Knights and tempered by Haymarket and Homestead, the AFL managed to survive the severe depression which struck in the 1890s.[20]

Gompers presided over an association of national and international craft unions. He was assisted by other officers and an Executive Council charged with helping organize locals in different trades, with setting up city centrals and state federations designed to influence legislation, and with establishing national unions in crafts not yet unionized. They were also expected to lobby in the halls of Congress. They had power to investigate strikes and lockouts and could appeal to AFL affiliates for money to aid union causes. At the annual convention where policies were outlined and officers selected, each craft union cast one vote for every hundred members on its roll. Affiliated unions paid the Federation one-half cent per month for each unionist, and the AFL also collected charter fees. A handful of the larger unions gradually assumed power within the Federation because they always cast the largest number of votes and paid the most dues. Invariably their officers dominated the Executive Council and thereby assured their own authority within the AFL structure. While Gompers had no obedient constituency beyond the Cigarmakers, his obvious fairness and dedication to the workers' interests, his genial manner and good will, along with his rising stature as a public figure, enabled him to wield influence beyond the powers vested in his office.[21]

Both the Federation of Organized Trades and the American Federation of Labor were supposed to include Canadian workers. American trade unions, Gompers believed, rested upon immutable economic laws. In the new continental product and labour market, no particular locality could maintain high wages by itself. Hence many of the craft unions began conducting their organizing activities on both sides of the border. The first American unions sailed to Canada at mid-century on new rivers of commerce, arriving at about the same time that Senator MacDonald had plunged into the wilderness of British Columbia to seek his fortune. When American businessmen later retreated behind a tariff wall, the British North American provinces confederated to create a new national economy. Rupert's Land was purchased, a new transcontinental railroad bound the provinces with steel, and a tariff stimulated domestic manufacturers in textiles, iron, coal, and boots and shoes. A modest growth in the size of the Canadian industrial working class fostered trade unionism of both the purely local as well as the international variety.[22]

The Iron Moulders' International Union, organized in 1859, entered Canada in the same year. Locals were chartered in Montreal, Hamilton, Toronto, Brantford, and London in the year of its founding. William Sylvis, the Moulders' President, made his first tour of the Canadian locals in 1863 and reported: 'I looked about me to ascertain what kind of people I had got among and what kind of a country I had got into, but I failed to see any difference between them and those I had left behind ... I found that the people walked upright, and spoke the same language – that the trees grew perpendicular and that the water ran downstream, and that altogether it was very much the same kind of a country I had left, and I soon began to feel at home.'[23] But Sylvis encountered obstacles. A Kingston moulder told him that workers had no right to interfere with the bosses. In Montreal he found that the employers had split the local by playing upon the religious, political, and national differences among the men. Only in Toronto was he openly welcomed. After the Civil War when Canadians began moving south to find jobs in cities such as Oswego and Syracuse, Sylvis journeyed to Canada again, and in 1868 the union convention met in Toronto. Throughout the next two decades several Canadians held important offices in the union.[24]

Periodic depressions accentuated the problem for American unions. As Senator Coffey observed during the debates on the Lougheed bill, Canadian workmen drifted across the American border in search of jobs. Since the factory centres of both countries faced each other across the Great Lakes, lines of travel and communication were plentiful. Newspapers and government reports testified to the flow of people southward. An alderman in Hamilton told Canadian government investigators about the hundreds he knew in the 1880s who had left for the United States and were making a good living there – his two brothers included. New England textile mills often hired whole French-Canadian families. No less than four steamship lines ferried scores of people from the Maritimes to Boston. By 1891 nearly one million Canadians, particularly the skilled and semiskilled, had moved across the boundary and competed with Americans in the job markets of the United States.[25]

The wave of Canadians moving southward during the 1870s and 1880s encouraged many more American craft unions to extend their operations to Canada in order to protect American members from the unorganized Canadian segment of the continental labour market. They set out to prevent Canadians from depressing prevailing wages in the United States. A Canadian who crossed the line with a union card in his pocket was obligated to work for union wages.

For the Canadian, the card opened the door to superior wage levels and working conditions in many trades. Often it served as a meal ticket in an era without food stamps or unemployment insurance.[26]

American unions encountered very few obstacles when they first extended their operations to Canada. There were no strong Canadian national unions to compete with them. Canadian locals, often scattered over vast distances, small in size and few in number, found the benefits of affiliation with larger and richer American groups quite attractive. The boundary, undefended and unmarked by road signs or immigration offices, seemed totally irrelevant to the purposes of trade unions in the nineteenth century. By the end of 1880 several other American crafts had followed in the wake of the Moulders. There were Canadian locals of the Typographers, Locomotive Engineers, Cigarmakers, Crispins (in the shoe trade), Machinists, Blacksmiths, Locomotive Firemen, Sailers, Flint Glass Workers, and Railway Conductors. Altogether about thirty-nine to forty-three Canadian locals maintained a connection with American unions in 1880; eleven more were locals of British unions. In addition between twenty-eight and forty-two purely local or regional Canadian unions flourished.[27]

A glance at life in Toronto helps explain why Canadian workers listened eagerly to American union organizers. The city's population had mushroomed from 30,000 at mid-century to over 144,000 in 1891, driving rents sky high and forcing many working-class families to share their two- or three-room apartments with boarders. Only 873 of 5181 homes surveyed by the Toronto Board of Health in 1884 had water closets; most families used 'foul privy pits' just outside the kitchen door. They existed on a steady diet of bread, oatmeal, potatoes, beans, cheese, and tea. They worked sixty or more hours a week in unsanitary, inadequately ventilated factories, amidst noisy, dangerous machines. Seasonal unemployment of males forced many women and children into the factories, where by 1891 they made up one-third of the industrial labour force in Ontario. Eaton's and other retailers successfully avoided the few government factory regulations by contracting with sweatshops. Louis Gurofsky, a Toronto tailor, went into one shop on King Street 'and could hardly breathe for steam, heat and the smell from the gas irons; I could not even see the girls.' He knew of a place 'on Elizabeth Street where you can go at 11 or 12 at night and 5 A.M. in the morning and still find them working.'[28] The first Canadian trade unions struggled to alleviate such human misery.

In 1873 a successful strike by Toronto printers had resulted in laws legalizing trade-union activities in Canada, and led to the formation of the first national trade-union centre, the Canadian Labor Union (CLU). Though it failed to survive the decade and never spread beyond the larger Ontario towns, the CLU lobbied for protective legislation and served to emphasize the fact that Canadian workers lived under a different set of laws enacted by a very different political process. Meanwhile, the Toronto Trades Assembly, a forum for various locals in the city, kept trade unionism alive in Canada.

Toronto unionists achieved sporadic success in launching a Canadian national labour movement. In 1881 the Assembly, reorganizing itself as the Trades and Labor Council, invited the International Typographical Union to hold its convention in Toronto. Two years later they convened a short-lived Canadian Labor Congress; finally in 1886 the Toronto workers launched a permanent national trade-union centre for Canada. This new group, called the Trades and Labor Congress (TLC) of Canada, held its first convention only a few weeks before the founding of the American Federation of Labor in the United States.[29]

The Trades and Labor Congress differed appreciably from its American counterpart. It unified all the various locals in Canada for legislative purposes by accepting delegates from the Knights of Labor and purely local or regional unions as well as from locals of the international crafts. Since the AFL had been organized specifically to exclude the Knights from craft-union ranks, it was far more homogeneous than the Congress. The Canadian labour centre remained bottled up in Ontario and Quebec, its affiliates most numerous in the vicinity of its most recent convention. Many Canadian locals saw no real need for a body that seemed rather ineffectual on the political front and offered no resources to aid workers in their economic struggles. Congress revenue fluctuated sharply, never rising to $1000 until after the turn of the century. The Knights of Labor exercised considerable influence within the Congress long after their brethren in the States had fallen into oblivion and had ceased to threaten the AFL. Members of the Knights served in the Congress presidency seven times between 1887 and 1895, and others were active in committees and on the convention floor. Many Canadian unionists, including Daniel J. O'Donoghue, the father of trade unionism in Canada, held cards in both the Knights and in the craft union of their trade (in O'Donoghue's case, the typos). Ruling circles in the AFL considered this to be heresy.[30]

As the American crafts' stake in Canada grew, American labour federations began to notice their brethren in the land of the maple leaf. In 1882 the Toronto Trades and Labor Council received an invitation from the Federation of Organized Trades to send delegates to the latter's convention in Cleveland that year. The convention call noted that Chinese coolies were being imported into Canada without any restrictions, and concluded that 'the interests of our Trade Union brethern [sic] north of the border demand that legislative work should be attended to in Ottawa as well as in Washington.'[31] Of course the Americans stood to benefit since many coolies were believed to be slipping across the border into the United States and competing with American labour. Though no

Canadians attended the sessions, the next year the legislative committee of the Toronto city central approved the American labour group's objectives and urged that a delegate be sent. Apparently the Canadians later decided that they could not afford it. Another effort to secure Canadian representation in 1884 came to no avail.[32]

In the late 1800s a few Canadians attended American Federation of Labor conventions as delegates of the American crafts. In 1887 John Kane of Toronto represented the United Brotherhood of Carpenters and Joiners. R.H. Metcalf, also of Toronto, was one of three who composed the delegation from the Iron Moulders' Union of North America. Metcalfe returned in 1890, 1891, and 1892, but by the latter year he had joined the exodus to the United States and was living in Cleveland. In general, contacts between Canadian and American union officials seemed infrequent. The Canadian labour leaders had not yet established any significant relationship with Gompers and the AFL, and by 1893 the spirit of continentalism was barely strong enough to prompt a few international union locals in Canada to contribute to the Homestead strikers' legal defence fund.[33]

While the AFL and the TLC remained apart, their different environments and contrasting memberships quite naturally led to the development of varying approaches to the problems facing them in the new industrial society. Craft-organized trade unions in the United States posed certain continuing problems for Federation leaders. Intricate jurisdictional lines separated the workers of one craft from another. When employers introduced new machinery or materials or procedures, jurisdictional conflicts often broke out and the lines had to be redrawn. For example, when pipes were devised to house electrical wires in building construction, did the electricians' or the plumbers' union have control over the men who installed the pipes from conduit boxes to outlets? Such disputes often blew up into power struggles that threatened to disrupt and weaken the AFL. They sometimes led to secessions and to the formation of dual unions which openly challenged the Federation and its affiliates. The conflicts arising out of the American craft structure frequently diverted Gompers' attention away from expansion of trade unionism and toward the preservation of existing prerogatives and trade boundaries.

Out of such trials Gompers built a well-defined structure and forged a philosophy of trade unionism designed above all to protect and extend his influence and ideas. Although he initially showed some sympathy for labour political action and a wide variety of reformist goals, Gompers' conflicts with the Knights of Labor and other dual-unionist rivals led him to condemn long-range reform efforts and attempts to channel the political sentiments of unionists into a labour party.[34] In order partly to define itself more sharply from the Knights of Labor and socialist labour organizations which challenged the primacy of the

AFL, the Federation embraced business unionism as an ideological creed.[35] After craft-union socialists failed to ram their platform through the Federation convention in 1895, the AFL banned partisan politics from discussion at all future conventions. By then Gompers had identified all the friends and enemies of trade unionism in general and of the AFL in particular. The 'lessons' he drew from the old struggles gave him confidence in his ability to discern unerringly the future direction of the AFL throughout North America.

The Trades and Labor Congress did not experience such fires of controversy in its early years, and its structure and philosophy remained less well defined. Craft locals in Canada appeared relatively unaffected by the presence of mixed assemblies of the Knights of Labor in the same towns. The conflict in the United States between the Knights and the crafts had little impact on Canada. In comparison to most European countries there appeared to be little class-consciousness in both Canada and the United States, but Canadian unionists seemed less fractious than Americans and more willing to cooperate with each other in the struggle for their mutual advancement. In Canada both the Knights and the crafts cooperated to seek redress through political action.[36] Knights and other unionists from Montreal to British Columbia nominated candidates for political office, and Daniel O'Donoghue became the first successful working-class candidate in Canada when he took his seat in the Ontario legislature in 1874. Though Canadian unionists may have shifted their emphasis in the 1880s and 1890s from the national to the provincial political scene, they continued to believe that political activity was vital to improvement of working conditions. The Congress passed resolutions calling for independent political action on eight different occasions between 1883 and 1899. The Knights' reformist goals and tendency toward political action paralleled British influences and gave the Trades and Labor Congress a distinctive flavour if not a philosophy. While locals of international craft unions affiliated with the AFL were numerous in Canada, they did not dominate the annual conventions of the Congress in the nineteenth century and were not able to inculcate the business unionism of the AFL and the international crafts.

In the United States Samuel Gompers had forged a homogeneous grouping of predominantly craft-oriented national unions by 1895, had declared war upon his dual-unionist enemies, and had opted for short-term objectives achievable through economic action. In contrast the Trades and Labor Congress of Canada had spread its mantle over a variety of trade-union groups – the Knights of Labor, international craft union locals, purely local and regional unions – and was struggling to find a common political denominator and break out from its base in central Canada. Separated by thousands of miles of empty space, divided by essentially regional economies, speaking two languages, and leaning toward political action, the affiliates of the Trades and Labor Congress reflected above all the many disparities rending the fabric of Canadian national life. In these circumstances the two national labour movements came into direct contact at the turn of the century.

2
First encounter

Though Samuel Gompers paid little attention to Canadian labour in the early years of the American Federation of Labor, he busied himself with international labour issues from the very start. Three years after the AFL was founded, he issued invitations to the 'organized wage workers of the world' to meet at an international congress in Chicago in 1893 during the World's Fair. The British Trades Union Congress responded favourably. But when the International Socialist Congress, an organization supported by many European labour unions, refused to accept the invitation, Gompers was forced to cancel his plans. Humiliated, he quickly blamed the European refusal on the influence of 'malicious' American socialists, and the incident helped sharpen the line in his mind between socialist labour organizations and his own business unionism. Gompers then decided to build a trade-union international grouping distinct from the Socialist International.[1]

In 1894 the AFL president set out to win the active support of British trade unionists to this scheme. In that year and the next the Trades Union Congress and the Federation exchanged the first fraternal delegates to each others' conventions, and Gompers himself represented the AFL in Britain in 1895. Though the American delegates to the British unions suggested that a 'bona fide [international] trade union congress' be convened on the initiative of the Trades Union Congress, they were unable to drum up enough enthusiasm to win English labour's support for the idea.[2]

It was during Gompers' attempts to create an international grouping of trade unions that he made his first overtures to the Canadian Trades and Labor Congress. Reporting to his Executive Council in September 1896, Gompers observed that German trade unions had promised to send a delegate to the British unions along with the AFL. 'I anticipate that we may have this interchange of fraternal delegates extended, and have been in correspondence with the executive officers of the Canadian Trade & Labor Congress, and am confident that a delegate will be elected by that body, which convenes this month.' Gompers hoped that the exchange of fraternal delegates among various national labour bodies would lead to the 'holding of bona fide International Trade Congresses every few years.'[3]

The Canadians welcomed communications from the AFL at this particular moment. George Dower, the Congress secretary-treasurer, complained to Gompers about the American alien labour law. The law had been designed to ban the importation of labour under contract and was wholeheartedly supported by the Federation. Dower evidently felt that it hindered the movement of Canadians southward into the American job market. Although sympathetic to these complaints, Gompers pointed out both the necessity for excluding oriental labour from the United States, and the difficulty of designing legislation that would stop the influx of working men coming to the United States from other countries by way of Canada. He admitted the justice of Dower's position, but told him that he hoped the Trades Congress convention that year would not take any 'ill-advised action' on the matter. 'Were it not for the fact that I have an important engagement elsewhere at that time,' Gompers added, 'I should make it my business to be in attendance.'[4]

Gompers then urged the Trades Congress to select a fraternal delegate to attend the AFL's December convention. He cautiously refrained from mentioning his proposed international trades congress to Dower. Instead, he linked the alien labour law issue to his request: 'I am sure that the selection of a fraternal delegate would help to the solution of this question and tend to establish more direct relations between the organized workers of the American Continent. More than likely,' he concluded, 'the interchange of fraternal delegates would then be made a permanent feature and would finally result in the attainment of the highest hopes entertained by earnest and thinking trade unionists.'[5]

Dower again brought up the alien labour question, but Gompers curtly dismissed him, noting instead that the Canadian had made no reference to Gompers' invitation to send a fraternal delegate. 'I do hope that this will be taken up by your Congress,' he entreated, 'and [as?] these reciprocal visitations of fraternal delegates tend to bind our fellow workers more closely together. This is certainly desirable.' Hinting at his larger purpose this time, he told Dower that the exchange would foster better understanding and a greater solidarity between wage workers of all countries. Still failing to kindle any enthusiasm among the Canadians, Gompers then sent blank credentials for the unnamed Canadian fraternal delegate, and also forwarded the names of the two prominent

British labour leaders who were expected to attend the Federation meeting. Later in the winter of 1896 the British delegation was feted, but no Canadian unionist appeared. Though Gompers referred Dower's letters to a special committee on immigration, the convention made no reference to Canadian complaints about the alien labour law.[6]

It is not clear why the Trades Congress or its leaders failed to send a delegate. Three months before the AFL gathering, Gompers' first letter had been read into the minutes of the Trades and Labor Congress convention and had been referred to a special committee for consideration. The *Toronto Globe* had thought that the spirit, at least, of Gompers' views on the alien labour issue had been 'admirable.' A Trades Congress committee had been less impressed, particularly about the call for an exchange of fraternal delegates. It had recommended that Congress leaders be instructed only 'to consider the subject ... in the said letters along such lines as may be deemed best to secure the end in view.' The Congress seemed vexed at Gompers' position on the alien labour issue. There may have been a question whether the Congress treasury could absorb the costs of sending a fraternal delegate. At the Trades Congress convention in 1897, the Canadian labour leaders took note of the Federation's inaction. They referred again to Gompers' desire to begin an annual exchange of fraternal delegates, but the convention decided it could not see its way clear to send a representative.[7]

A new and fundamental issue between the two labour groups, involving dues money, added to the Canadian convention's coolness toward the AFL. A Vancouver printer had noticed in the financial reports of the International Typographical Union that a certain sum was being paid monthly to the AFL. When Dower sent out a circular asking for contributions to keep a Congress legislative committee in Ottawa during the parliamentary session, the printer suggested instead that the per-capita dues paid by Canadian locals through their international unions to the AFL be turned over to the Trades Congress.[8] Congress leaders agreed. 'While on the subject of the American Federation of Labor,' they said in 1897, '[we] believe that your Congress is entitled to some of the money paid to the Federation by Canadian members of International Unions.' They recommended that Canadian locals follow the Vancouver printer's suggestion; it was unfair for the Federation to spend Canadian dues money on lobbying efforts in the halls of the United States Congress.[9]

The Canadian demand for a greater share of AFL per-capita income arose amidst a loud clamour by some Canadian unionists for separation from Americans. An element within the Congress wanted to transform the Trades Congress into a fully autonomous Canadian federation of labour. With power to charter unions such an organization might very well drive the American craft unions out of Canada.

This movement for greater autonomy had begun in Canadian labour circles a few years earlier. In 1894 a Trades Congress committee composed in part of veteran Canadian labour leaders D.A. Carey, P.J. Jobin, and J.W. Patterson went along with the notion that the Congress reconstitute itself as a Canadian federation with full power to issue charters and perform 'such other duties as pertain to a national organization.'[10] Subsequently Jobin was elected president of the Trades Congress. However, in his address to the convention a year later, Jobin seemed to have second thoughts. 'In dealing with this question of a Canadian Labor Federation,' he declared, 'remember, fellow-delegates, that to reach its maximum efficacy organization of labor must be universal. If means are devised whereby, without antagonizing any of the existing international bodies, it would be possible to consolidate the efforts of the toilers of our Dominion, I believe that the means already exist in and through the Trades and Labor Congress of Canada.'[11] Jobin's words reflected some hesitation on the part of Trades Congress leaders to rush down the road to autonomy. They had been unable to discuss the matter together before the Congress convened in 1895 and decided to return the question to the delegates with the 'sincere hope' that something be done to accomplish the organization of Canadian workers. Still, they suggested that the Congress keep the same name, while assuming the power to charter locals in Canada in trades without international or national charters.[12]

If the Trades Congress officers followed this procedure and granted priority to the international unions already in the field, the charter of such 'federal labour unions' would not necessarily constitute a direct threat to international union jurisdictions. But the Vancouver Trades and Labor Council urged the Congress to go a step further and begin chartering city central labour bodies in Canada. The AFL claimed this authority, although it had not yet exercised it in Canada. The delegates decided to set up a special committee to consider these recommendations and other changes in the Trades Congress constitution. The committee endorsed the proposals submitted by the Congress officers, and also urged adoption of the appellation 'Canadian Federation of Labor.' While the new name indicated the desire of the committee to create an organization that eventually would become fully autonomous, the men also agreed with the Congress officers' view that the 'CFL' should respect international union jurisdictions in Canada for the time being.[13]

Delegates to the convention of 1895 granted chartering powers to their officers, though refusing at the same time to change the name of the Congress to the Canadian Federation of Labor. More controversial to supporters of the AFL brand of international unionism that year was an amendment to the Congress constitution which admitted representatives of the Socialist Labor party to the Congress. The business unionists counter attacked, losing by a close vote their motion to bar the socialists. Because the AFL still refused to bestow recognition on groups other than trade unionists, the Trades and Labor Congress appeared to be choosing a path at some variance from that followed by the Federation. Then, in 1896, more conservative elements managed to recapture the Congress. The socialists were thrown out, while the Congress decided to retain its power to grant trade-union charters. The issue of autonomy remained unresolved.[14]

At the convention held in September 1897, the running debate over the future of the Trades and Labor Congress broke wide open. Delegate R.G. Hay, representing the Ottawa Allied Trades and Labor Association, reopened it by introducing a motion to change the Trades Congress into a federation of labour. Again the arguments of previous years were repeated, and again the direction of trade unionism in Canada seemed at stake. But the new issue concerning the per-capita tax payments made the discussions doubly fateful in 1897. If a large number of Canadian locals were sufficiently provoked by the financial issue to withdraw from the international unions, throw in their lot with the Canadian dual unionists, and transfer their allegiance to a fully autonomous Canadian federation of labour, a continental trade-union movement appeared doomed.[15]

When a committee reported adversely on Hay's motion for autonomy, he rose to defend his proposal.[16] The time had come, he said, when the labour organizations of Canada should be nationalized. It was inconsistent for labour men who believed the national flag should be flown over public schools to advocate the superiority of international unions over national ones. Delegate T.H. Fitzpatrick of the Toronto Typos believed that many Canadian workers refused to join unions because they knew their dues money would go to the United States. He saw no reason why Canadians should not have a labour association based upon the same principles as the American Federation of Labor. He did not think it vital that the Trades Congress change its name, but he thought it necessary for some labour body to issue charters and supplies to the unorganized in Canada.

Several delegates jumped up from their seats to defend international unionism. John Flett of the Hamilton Carpenters tried to dispel the notion that Canadians received nothing in return for their per-capital tax contribution. He pointed to a specific case involving a carpenters' local in his city. It had received $1200 from the union headquarters during a strike years before – an amount more than it would be able to pay back for years. While Flett thought that national limits to the labour movement were unwise, he suggested that it would be 'much better' if the Canadian Congress received its 'just proportion' of per-capita taxes for its own legislative needs. William Keys of the Montreal Knights of Labor local assembly argued that the Canadians could not afford an organization similar to the AFL. Fred Walters of the Hamilton Moulders followed Flett's tack. As treasurer of his local, he had received no less than $19,000 to support a strike of Canadian moulders. 'The [Canadian] iron moulders have received $3 for every $1 they have sent away.' Walters agreed with Flett that the per-capita tax paid by Canadians to the AFL should be handed over to the Trades Congress. Edward Williams of the Hamilton Trades and Labor Council conceded the importance of cultivating national sentiments. Nevertheless, years ago 'in the largest strike of railway men known in Canada, the strikers would have been utterly helpless had it not been for the connection with the support of the organization on the other side.'

The supporters of international unionism no doubt convinced some of their fellow delegates, though at least one man was dissuaded by them. It appeared, R. Keys of the Montreal Trades and Labor Council said, that the country could not get along without the United States for twenty-four hours. 'It was galling to him as a Canadian to hear these remarks,' the *Globe* reported him as saying, and he was going to vote for autonomy. Nevertheless, the motion for a Canadian federation of labour went down to defeat.

The supporters of international unionism in Canada were victorious, yet the problems that had provoked the debate still remained unresolved. The movement for greater autonomy was providing highly significant background to the demand first raised by the Canadians in 1896 for a share in the revenue paid by them to the American Federation of Labor. It was becoming increasingly apparent that a large number of Canadian toilers, organized into locals of international craft unions with headquarters in the United States, paid dues to essentially American organizations. A part of their contribution was forwarded to the AFL and used for legislative purposes in the United States rather than in Canada. Furthermore, Canadians thought that the American alien labour law threatened the free movement of Canadian craftsmen into American jobs and thereby nullified an important advantage possessed by Canadian holders of international union cards over other American immigrant streams. At the same time, growing numbers of Canadian industrial workers, whose jobs were the product of the early phases of a tremendous boom in the Canadian economy, needed to be organized into trade unions in order to protect wages and working conditions. Where was the money to come from? In the past Canadian toilers had been dependent upon occasional visits from the full-time organizers maintained by each international union, as well as upon the voluntary efforts of local unionists who laboured nights and Sundays to organize the crafts.[17] Charters had been obtained from the Federation or international union headquarters in the United States. As business conditions brightened in 1896 and 1897, Canadian trade-union leaders, aware of the growing number of unorganized workers in their midst, welcomed the assumption of chartering powers by the Congress. Lacking funds, though, they hoped the AFL would assist them.[18]

The Canadians had reason to be optimistic in the fall of 1896. More by accident than design the Federation president had just appointed the AFL's first general organizer for Canada. A Sault Ste Marie, Ontario, merchant, P.J. Loughrin, had told Gompers of his interest in the labour movement, and had asked him for an organizer's commission. Evidently the Canadian's earnestness had overcome Gompers' doubts about the wisdom of commissioning a business-man. He dispatched the desired document and inadvertently authorized Loughrin to act throughout the whole of Canada on behalf of the Federation.[19]

The new representative set up a federal labour union in his home town and secured an agreement whereby city authorities promised to employ only union men. Loughrin began filling Gompers' head with his plans and promises, some of which spilled over into politics and brought about a clash with the Federation president. Loughrin's brother, a Liberal, had been campaigning for a seat in the Ontario legislature, and Gompers heard allegations that Loughrin, using his authority as an organizer, was compelling every union member to vote for his brother 'or cease to belong to the union.' Although Gompers questioned Loughrin's intervention in the election, he apparently was pleased with the outcome. He wrote Loughrin that he hoped the new legislator would be 'in a position to render some good service to our cause.'[20]

It was not long before Loughrin was in hot water again. Early in 1897 Gompers began laying plans for an extensive speaking and organizing trip across North America. He asked Loughrin to correspond with union officials in several Canadian towns in order to set up a ten-day Canadian leg of the trip. Loughrin appeared to stall, offering a variety of excuses. According to him the Trades Congress leaders were 'fakes' who wanted to rule Canada. He asked Gompers to call these men into line, and promised the Federation leader that he would 'reunite the country' if Gompers would 'stand by' him. As the date of departure approached, Gompers grew impatient. After Loughrin mysteriously asked the AFL president to hold 'them' until a signal was given, Gompers, thoroughly per-plexed, wrote back that he did not understand what Loughrin was talking about. When Loughrin still failed to act, Gompers was forced to cancel the Canadian speaking dates.[21]

Loughrin left Sault Ste Marie for Toronto, telling the press that he himself was making a month-long Canadian tour 'in the interests of labor generally.' However, at labour gatherings he did not talk much about the usual trade-union organizing details, but stressed the harm being done to Canadians by American investors in Canadian forests and mines. Loughrin also circulated a manifesto to boards of trade and municipal councils in which he called for an export tariff on pulpwood and an alien labour law to match the American statute. 'It can be readily seen,' he told a reporter, 'that the pulpwood resources of the United

States must, at an early date, succumb to the enormous consumption ... and it is just a matter of a few years till we are able to dictate terms to the world for pulp and paper as well as nickel.' Both the Toronto mayor and the president of the board of trade signed Loughrin's petition.[22]

Within a short time Gompers obtained a copy of Loughrin's petition and the newspaper interview and showed the evidence to the Executive Council. 'It appears,' Gompers later told Loughrin, 'that you are not only using that commission for business purposes but to estrange the workingmen of the Dominion of Canada and the United States.' The AFL leader summarily revoked Loughrin's commission. The Canadian had failed to observe that in the US business and labour interests were intertwined.[23]

Loughrin's subsequent action highlighted the precarious state of American unions in Canada at this time. He communicated with Trades Congress leaders in Toronto and offered to affiliate some 500 men engaged in the lumber industry on the north shore of Lake Superior. Then Loughrin's local in Sault Ste Marie told Congress officers that they intended to withdraw from the AFL and asked for information regarding affiliation with the Congress. Obviously the Trades Congress, having assumed power to issue charters, was becoming an alternate organizing centre for Canadian toilers. Although Loughrin's schemes ultimately miscarried, Trades Congress leaders – too impoverished to dispatch an organizer of their own – became more conscious of the opportunities for growth that were slipping through their fingers. Some thought that money was the nub of the problem. Others still felt that the Congress needed to reconstitute itself into an autonomous labour body in order to meet the new conditions.[24]

The need for organization work was a prime topic at the Trades Congress convention in 1897. Congress officers warned the delegates that it would be expensive. They estimated that it would cost about $200 to obtain charters and other printed matter; some arrangement would have to be made until dues from new unionists covered expenses. The crucial need for revenue was also revealed after resolutions were introduced from the floor calling for the appointment of a salaried organizer. The committee on officers' reports told the delegates that they could find no way to cover the financial burden. Reluctantly, they handed down an unfavourable decision. After concluding that 'the salary and expenses of such an official would involve an outlay of five or six times the annual income of this Congress,' the committee urged that action be deferred until an appeal had been made to the AFL concerning the legislative expenses of the Trades Congress. They apparently calculated that more money would be available for organizing work if the burden of lobbying expenses was lightened. Surprisingly, the Congress refused to take the first step toward securing AFL support by sending a fraternal delegate to the Federation convention of late 1897. Some doubtless realized that such a move would forfeit any further steps toward greater autonomy for the Trades Congress.[25]

Gompers had not dispaired of creating an international trades congress through the exchange of fraternal delegates. 'Our efforts and our hopes should not be circumscribed by Cities, States, or geographical divisions of our country,' he told the AFL delegates at their convention in 1897. 'Our aim should be to unite the workers of our continent and to strive to attain the unity, solidarity, and fraternity of the workers of the world.' P.J. McGuire, a friend of Gompers and president of the United Brotherhood of Carpenters, urged that the AFL take the initiative to 'more closely cement the interests of the Trades Unions of America.' He moved to send an AFL fraternal delegate to the next convention of the Trades Congress. McGuire was well aware of the financial issue that had arisen a few months before. A number of unions in Canada paid per-capita tax to international unions in the United States, he said, and 'as we send delegates to England we should also send one to Canada.' The motion was adopted and the convention unanimously elected Thomas I. Kidd of the Woodworkers to become the AFL's first fraternal delegate to the Trades Congress. Meeting separately, the Federation Executive Council authorized Gompers to seek an adjustment with the Canadians.[26]

In late April of 1898, a few days after President McKinley had asked Congress for a declaration of war against Spain, Gompers told the Executive Council that the Canadians were ready to bargain. 'Secretary George W. Dower states that if the sum of $100.00 was set aside each year by the A.F. of L. to aid their legislative committee, the arrangement would be satisfactory and appease any dissatisfaction which may exist among the labor organizations of Canada.' Gompers proposed that the AFL make the annual grant to the Congress, and asked the Council members to vote on it.[27]

At the same time several Canadian locals were generating considerable pressure on the officers of some of the international unions for an adjustment of the dues issue. In St Thomas, Ontario, a local of the Journeymen Tailors took the ultimate step that all international union officers feared. It seceded from the international union in February 1898 and became Local 1 of the Journeymen Tailors' Union of Canada. The Canadian tailors complained that too much money flowed across the border into American coffers, and that the American alien labour law had voided the advantages of membership in an international trade union. They began spreading their views across Canada in a circular letter to other tailors' locals.[28]

It is not surprising, then, that the AFL Executive Council moved quickly to approve the $100 grant to the Trades and Labor Congress. Gompers explained to Dower that the appropriation would require the annual endorsement of the AFL convention, but he expressed no doubt of its approval. 'I am sure I express the hope of organized labor of our Continent,' he said, 'when I say that it is our earnest wish that the movement of America may be more solidified as the times goes on, and that our most sanguine expectations of success may be surpassed.' It was a typical rendering of Gompers' rather diffuse sentiments.[29]

The AFL's grant was offered at a time of triumphant American expansion into the Caribbean. The victory of American arms over Spain cast a bright, warm glow over all English-speaking North Americans, and the Canadians effused good feelings for their brethren across the line. The Trades Congress gathered at Winnipeg in September 1898 in an atmosphere which foreshadowed the subsequent rhetoric of Canadian-American relations. At a banquet tendered by city hall officials, the AFL was toasted while a brass band played 'Yankee Doodle' and 'For They Are Jolly Good Fellows.' Several speakers, including a Winnipeg alderman, lauded the American nation. Kidd's response suggested the way in which those heady days of imperial expansion were subtly influencing the nature of American labour's internationalism. Steps were being taken, Kidd asserted, to secure the harmonious working of the labour organizations of the United States, Canada, and Mexico. He believed that 'the safety of the United States, of Canada, and other countries depended upon the organization of wage workers.'[30] Federation leaders joined the ranks of industrialists and politicians who felt that American power depended upon achieving pre-eminence within the entire western hemisphere. Gompers may have been unable to counteract the influence of socialists in the European labour movement, but he was more successful in strengthening his grip upon organized labour in Canada.

The executive committee of the Trades Congress (president David Carey and secretary-treasurer George Dower) met with Kidd and discussed the AFL's grant at considerable length. Kidd promised the Canadians that if they would send to the AFL convention a petition requesting the legislative grant, he would endorse the aims and objectives of the Trades and Labor Congress in his report to the AFL delegates who were meeting in Kansas City later that year. Afterwards, in their report to the Trades Congress delegates, the two Canadians strongly recommended that the Congress not only follow Kidd's suggestions, but also send its own fraternal delegate to the coming Federation convention. Immediately following this proposal, a platform committee moved to assist Kidd's defence of Trades Congress aims. It reported on a thirteen-point draft statement of Congress objectives. The document went a long way to reassure conservative international union officers that the Trades Congress was a safe 'investment,' and that the Canadian trade-union national centre had not been infected by socialist measures aimed at the total transformation of the industrial community. The Canadians adopted the platform and proceeded to elect their president, David Carey, to be the first fraternal delegate to the AFL.[31]

At the Federation convention in Kansas City in late 1898, Kidd carefully compared the functions of the AFL with those of the Trades and Labor Congress. They were radically different bodies, he said, because the Canadian group was not concerned with jurisdictional disputes between international unions. The Trades Congress was designed to secure beneficial legislation and organize workers wherever they were able. However, the two organizations might very well become enemies, he implied.

It would be unwise to deny or ignore the fact that a feeling of antagonism obtains among many of the active workers in Canadian labor circles toward the American Federation of Labor. Many believe that it is unfair for the International unions with which they are connected to pay a per capita tax to the Federation on their account, which they claim goes toward the support of a lobby in Washington.

To the Canadians, Kidd explained, the Federation appeared to be purely an American group unconcerned with labour legislation beyond American boundaries, while the Trades Congress was essential to Canadians who lived under different institutions and dissimilar laws. Only a powerful Trades Congress could influence Canadian law-making bodies. 'As nearly all the unions affiliated with the Labor Congress are likewise affiliated with the A.F. of L.,' Kidd asserted with considerable exaggeration, 'the former thinks the Federation should aid it in trying to secure remedial legislation.'[32]

Kidd told the delegates of his meetings with the Trades Congress executive committee. He noted their desire to receive AFL assistance in organizing Canadian workers. 'There can be no question,' he concluded, 'about the wisdom of your last Convention electing a fraternal delegate to Canada. Many small misunderstandings were easily explained away, and, by continuing to send fraternal delegates misunderstandings of the same kind will, in the near future, cease to exist.' Later, convention delegates, a bit confused, endorsed the $100 grant 'in the matter of organization in Canada' (the Executive Council had considered it to be a grant for legislative purposes).[33] Thus by the end of 1898 the Trades and Labor Congress had embarked upon a new course.

The Trades Congress had been organized originally to represent the legislative interests of Canadian trade unionists, some of whom were members of international craft unions with American headquarters. In 1886 these American crafts had banded together under one banner designed to wave over the North American continent. Despite this, neither national labour centre had defined its relationship to the other. When Gompers decided to organize an international federation of labour, he turned his attention toward Canadian unions for the first time. Meanwhile some Canadian unionists realized they were paying a portion of Federation expenses without deriving any benefits, and they resented it. Uncertainty over the effect of the American alien labour law, combined with the desire of many Canadian labour leaders to begin an organizing campaign among the new industrial workers in their own towns and cities, led several Canadian unionists to advocate an autonomous labour structure. But the Trades and Labor Congress was not able to expand its activities without additional income. A Canadian federation of labour never came to pass and Congress leaders, apparently supported by most of the rank and file, finally agreed to exchange fraternal delegates with the Federation. In return the Canadians received an annual grant from the AFL for 'legislative' purposes in lieu of the per-capita contributions made by Canadian workers through their international unions to the AFL. In 1898 this grant represented about 20 per cent of Congress income. In effect this money shattered the dreams of those who wanted to create a Canadian federation of labour, and paved the way for the absorption of the Trades Congress into the American Federation of Labor. Canadian unionists were probably unaware that the AFL was acting in its own interests; Gompers and his colleagues were increasingly apprehensive about the rapid changes taking place in the North American industrial scene at this time.

3
The rise of branch plants

The first encounters between the American Federation of Labor and the Trades and Labor Congress of Canada had been made in response to Gompers' scheme to create an international fraternity of craft unions and to Canadian desires for more money for organizing and legislative efforts. After 1898 the whole rationale for the AFL's relationship with the Canadian labour movement changed, responding to new developments within the American business community. In a word, branch-plant factories begat 'branch-plant' unionism.

America's commercial expansion into Canada had roots deep in the nineteenth century. The similarity of the two cultures, the ease with which capital, labour, and raw materials could cross the border, and the complementary nature of American and Canadian resources encouraged a close relationship between the two economies. As early as 1840 American enterprise spilled over the boundary. With the advent of the National Policy, more American branch plants were set up behind the Canadian tariff wall. US companies seeking sales north of the border 'usually found it wise to build or acquire factories there,' and by 1887 there were eighty-two American branch plants in Canada.[1]

In the years just before the Spanish-American War, business journals began to talk openly of the advantages of expansion. Some feared that America's capacity to produce goods had outstripped what the domestic market could consume. Others equated the closing of the frontier with the ending of American opportunities. After the war, some became disillusioned with expansion because of the difficulty of pacifying the Philippines. Most did not: 'whatever difference of opinion may exist among American citizens respecting the policy of territorial expansion,' former Secretary of State John W. Foster wrote in 1900, 'all seem to be agreed upon the desirability of commercial expansion. In fact it has come to be a necessity to find new and enlarged markets for our agricultural and manufactured products. We cannot maintain our present industrial prosperity without them.'[2]

A wave of business consolidations at the end of the nineteenth century prepared the way for expansion into foreign markets. Some 2700 industrial combinations were formed between 1897 and 1902 in the United States, with a total capitalization of $6.5 billion. Over a thousand mergers took place in the single year of 1899 alone.[3] John D. Rockefeller assured everyone that the growth of giant businesses was 'merely a survival of the fittest ... the working out of a law of nature and a law of God.'[4] President Theodore Roosevelt agreed, adding that large-scale units were vital in order to wage effective competition in international markets. Both the mergers and the expansion of direct investment abroad were facilitated by a large-scale capital market in the United States at the turn of the century.[5]

In the nineteenth century small groups of American businessmen in states adjacent to Canada had begun to campaign for that country's annexation. Near the turn of the century a number of leaders in American politics and business revived the idea of continental union. Motivated largely by commercial objectives and sustained by Darwinist notions, Theodore Roosevelt, Chauncey Depew, Elihu Root, Paul Dana, and Thomas C. Platt, along with 700 others, formed a Continental Union League in order to promote 'industry and progress' throughout North America. Andrew Carnegie was rumoured to be willing to spend millions on the cause, and a flurry of bills was introduced in both houses of Congress to further it. The Republican party platform hopefully anticipated ultimate union of all English-speaking peoples on the continent. Part of Henry Cabot Lodge's 'large policy,' whereby the United States was expected to become the dominant power in the western hemisphere, presupposed the annexation of Canada.[6]

Anti-imperialists who were repelled by the racially heterogeneous tropics found no such objection to amalgamation with Canadians. Americans and Canadians, Andrew Carnegie said, were indistinguishable. More bluntly, Champ Clark gave Canadians the highest American accolade: 'They are people of our blood. They speak our language. Their institutions are much like ours. They are trained in the difficult art of self-government.' From his outpost of empire, even the American consul at Manila confidently expected to see the day when the Stars and Stripes would fly over Canada.[7]

Yet the political annexation movement never really fired businessmen's imaginations; it was the commercial map of Canada that was engraved on their hearts. The need for Canadian markets seemed imperative. The New York Merchants' Association called upon the State Department to settle all outstanding disputes with Canada 'so that we may be united for wider commercial relations.' The Association argued that the United States had developed so rapidly, and had so busied itself with its internal affairs, that it had not paid proper attention to pushing its products 'which now, in many instances, are being over-manufactured and for which a market must be found abroad, unless we want to have our industries glutted.'[8]

Testifying before the US Industrial Commission in 1901, a representative of the Boston Chamber of Commerce emphasized the importance of Canadian trade to New Englanders. 'We look upon Canada as fairly tributary to our market,' he said. 'We believe that the border line is largely an artificial one, and that as we are, to quite an extent, cut off from the West, we should have the right, as far as possible, to exploit the country to the north and east of us. If Canada is ever to be made a part of the United States it must be by drawing the Canadians to us with the strongest possible bands of trade.' He concluded that the United States should make overtures to Canada in regard to a reciprocity treaty.[9]

At a meeting in 1900 of the National Association of Manufacturers, two visiting Canadian businessmen were welcomed with open arms. As one American entrepreneur put it in his greeting: 'Wherever the English-speaking race is found there we can place our wares on the market and find a ready sale.'[10] Businessmen turned their attention northward and marshalled their dollars for an economic invasion of Canada. Who could predict the outcome? 'If we have closer commercial relations with Canada,' a Congressman noted, 'some day this relationship may blend the two peoples into one harmonious whole, and ... the territory lying north of us may become a part of the United States, as it should be.'[11]

A tremendous boom in the Canadian economy magnetically pulled American financial and technological resources northward. The settlement of the Canadian prairies and the growth of a wheat-export economy revolutionized the economic structure of Central Canada. Before 1900 the small and highly regional Canadian markets had engaged in little interchange of goods. But the National Policy began paying off at last when Central Canada became a manufacturer of industrial goods for the prairies. 'The demands of Manitoba and the Northwest territories are an increasing factor in the prosperity of Toronto industries,' the *Labour Gazette* noted. Growth of industry in Canada was not limited to prairie farm production. All segments of Canadian manufacturing prospered, and most classes of industrial goods doubled in value of net output between 1900 and 1910. From 1901 to 1904 alone, the index of industrial production in Canada rose by one-fourth.[12]

'Never in the history of Canada has the industrial outlook been so bright as it is to-day,' the American consul-general in Montreal reported in 1903. 'The present year promises to be made memorable by the establishment of new and immense enterprises and the extension of many existing ones.' Most of the new businesses, he added, were aided by American capital.[13] Because of the Canadian tariff, branch plants again proved to be the most effective way for Americans to break into Canadian markets. In 1909 Toronto boasted of no fewer than fifty American branch factories.[14] The steel industry in Sydney, Nova Scotia, received support from Americans. American financiers initiated formation of the Algoma Steel Company in 1901 and the Steel Company of Canada in 1910.[15] 'Look at what the International Harvester Company did,' Premier Roblin of Manitoba told a visitor. 'When they found themselves confronted with a tariff of twenty per cent on their machines entering Canada, what they did was to put up several million dollars' worth of plant in Hamilton, Ontario, where they now employ from 1200 to 1500 Canadian workers, and support a large village full of folk.'[16] Factories sprung up in the environs of Montreal, Toronto, and other Canadian cities. General Electric, Westinghouse, American Locomotive, Swift & Co., Singer Manufacturing Company, American Asbestos, Standard Oil, National Cash Register, Sherwin-Williams, du Pont, Ford, and Goodyear, among scores of others, organized Canadian branch plants.[17] According to Fred W. Field, the editor of the *Monetary Times of Canada,* the American commercial invasion applied to a lengthy list of articles, including barrels, blind rollers, buttons, carpet sweepers, corsets, condensed milk, bags, corks, carriages, couches, brass goods, billiard tables, cords, disinfectant, fly paper, files, fire extinguishers, fountain pens, gramophones, hardware, pickles, presses, pulleys, razors, rubbers, sealers, shoes, scales, typewriters, watch cases, and tobacco. By 1902 the *Globe* observed that shopwindows, 'especially in the poorer parts of our cities and towns,' were filled with 'American trash,' adding that 'it is to be condemned, not because it is American, but because it is trash.' A decade later there were about two hundred us branch factories in Canada – more than in any other nation.[18]

Hobson noted in 1906 that some of the most powerful American trusts had set up large works inside Canada. Not only did Canadians eat the 'embalmed' beef of the Chicago meatpacking trust, but they smoked with the consent of the American Tobacco combine. In the latter case, public pressure forced the Canadian government in 1904 to limit the company's restrictive trade practices.[19]

In Western Canada the American mining frontier stretched into the interior of British Columbia. The development and manufacture of heavy mining machinery in the 1880s and 1890s in the United States made it possible to work certain Canadian resources which were more readily available or richer than American mines. American capitalists constructed railroads from Spokane, Washington, the economic capital of the region, into the Kootenay and Boundary districts of British Columbia. The Heinze and Guggenheim interests poured money into British Columbia mines and smelters.[20] The president of the Canadian Pacific Railway complained in 1896 that American railway lines carried the greater part of the Canadian mining traffic southward.[21] American miners as well as American money swept into the Canadian mining camps, bringing trade-union ideas with them. By 1904 in such towns as Rossland, British Columbia, they made up nearly one-third of the population. They strengthened the belief of many observers that economic integration of the two nations was just over the horizon.[22]

Technological changes introduced by Americans were a very important force behind the economic boom in Canada after 1895. The transfer of capital, as Aitken has pointed out, reflects the level of importation of advanced technology. Steam turbines replaced huge reciprocating engines in Canada, and more power machinery with electric controls was introduced. American textile machinery began to supplant English machines. The introduction of automatic typesetting machines imported from the United States revolutionized the Canadian printing trade at the turn of the century. In Winnipeg membership in the printers' local dropped nearly 40 per cent for a time. Thus many Canadian as well as American industrial workers faced the unsettling effects of advancing American technology at the turn of the century.[23]

In the winter of 1902, thousands of Canadian families shivered in uncomfortable awareness of the growing interrelationship of the two nation's economies. The Pennsylvania anthracite strike did not affect bituminous coal users in Eastern and Western Canada, but in Ontario the price of coal went up as much as 400 per cent before coal altogether disappeared. 'Seldom has a single industrial disturbance in another country affected so closely the homes of the masses of the people in this country, or been the cause of as much widespread anxiety as the present difficulty,' the Labour Gazette said. The anthracite supply in Canada did not reach normal proportions until the winter was nearly over.[24]

By 1914 Americans had invested $618.4 million, or one-quarter of all American foreign investments, in Canadian factories and resources. The value of American investments in Canada multiplied four-and-a-half times during this period, while British investments, though larger in absolute terms, grew just three-and-a-half times. Most British capital went into portfolios, whereas almost 55 per cent of American money was in the form of direct investments in Canadian factories and mines. These direct investments resulted in the extension into Canada of American factories, business methods, and personnel.[25]

A few Canadians fretted over their country's growing dependence upon American trade and investment. 'There is no knowing where this is going to end,' Senator Francis Clemow told his colleagues. 'There is nothing to prevent United

States capitalists buying up the stock of the Canadian Pacific Railway, and what would be the result to this country if they obtained control of that great line for their own purposes? ... If they [the Canadian government] wish the whole of the business of this country to be taken over by United States capitalists it is their concern, but I do not think the people of this country will agree to it.'[26] Canadian businessmen seemed considerably less apprehensive, judging from views expressed in *Industrial Canada*. One prominent Canadian employer, replying to the toast of 'Canadian industries' at a Montreal banquet, endorsed an even higher Canadian tariff. His reason was startling; American manufacturers would find their market cut off, he said, and would gladly come over to Canada in increasing numbers. He appeared to equate Canadian prosperity with the flow of American investment.[27]

Branch plants brought other kinds of continentalist associations in their wake. At the turn of the century many Canadian and American manufacturers joined together in trade associations and negotiated market-wide agreements with trade unions. Coinciding with the rise of great trusts and business combinations, these associations were also a response to new technological and organizational innovations in the industrial system which were revolutionizing employee relations. Giant corporations depersonalized contacts between the factory owner and his operatives. Since corporate profits in the new era depended upon costs rather than upon competition, employers cooperated in order to hold the line or reduce wages. Two of the associations in the metal trades illustrate the expansion to continental proportions of major areas of the North American industrial economy during this period.[28]

The success of an organization of stove founders in the 1880s and early 1890s led to the creation of the National Founders' Association in 1898. The Association enrolled 600 firms in the United States and Canada, and proceeded to sign a continent-wide contract with the Iron Moulders' Union. The agreement set up a joint arbitration board to handle labour-management disputes. In the succeeding months at least two Canadian locals of the Moulders' Union failed to reach agreement with their employers through this pioneer industrial relations machinery and went out on strike. Both the Founders' Association and the Moulders' Union, then, were organizations for whom the forty-ninth parallel offered no barrier.[29]

The National Metal Trades Association, organized in 1899 with 325 firms in nearly all the states and Canada, signed an agreement with the International Association of Machinists in the spring of 1900.[30] Samuel Gompers prematurely labeled it a 'remarkable success' which attempted 'to preserve industrial peace and harmony by amicable discussion and interchange of views ...'[31] A year later, when the Machinists' Union failed to win the nine-hour day through bargaining, the American members struck the Association. The twenty-eight Canadian locals of the Machinists' Union continued to honour the agreement with Canadian foundries; perhaps they hoped to exert leverage on the American firms by maintaining production levels in Canada. The strike failed, but had it been successful several large Canadian companies belonging to the National Metal Trades Association would have been required to comply with the conditions demanded by the union from American firms.[32]

By 1902 most of these collective bargaining agreements between labour and management had broken down. American businessmen seemed to adopt a more militant anti-labour stand. While they still gave lip-service to rugged individualism in dealing with employees, they entered into new combinations to attack trade unions. After the collapse of its bargaining with the Machinists, the National Metal Trades Association established a pool of skilled workers to provide strikebreakers for any of its members in difficulty with a union. An employers' association founded in Dayton, Ohio, in 1900 grew into the anti-labour Citizens' Industrial Association of America under David M. Parry, later head of the National Association of Manufacturers. Parry preached against the closed shop, restrictions on output or in the number of apprentices, walking delegates, and sympathetic strikes. He called for 'full enforcement of the law.' In several American cities, businessmen organized employers' councils in response to the federation of union locals, particularly in the building trades. Other employer groups combined to set up company unions.[33]

The new aggressiveness of employers found expression in Canada. *Industrial Canada* noted 'a powerful sentiment in favor of closer union among the manufacturers in every branch of industry.'[34] The Canadian Manufacturers' Association, reorganizing in 1900, successfully lobbied through its new parliamentary committee against several union-sponsored bills. Employers in Toronto formed their own association in the same year, and by 1902 the members had pledged to protect each other against 'unjust' demands from labour unions. In the same year the president of the Toronto group closed his speech by quoting the three principles of the Metal Trades Association; the right of employers alone to determine working conditions, the refusal to arbitrate with workers on strike, and the open shop.[35] In Montreal, following a year-long struggle in which a Cigarmakers' Union strike had been smashed, the Canadian businessmen's journal drew the lesson that manufacturers, by taking united action, could successfully resist the assaults of the strongest international unions.[36] Throughout Canada employers formed new trade groups. The British Columbia Mining Association was organized in February 1903, and lumber and shingle manufacturers banded together in the following year. When Vancouver logger employers united, they based their rules and regulations on a Seattle group in the same industry. Some entrepreneurs continued to rely upon the older, paternalistic techniques in employee relations: the Cockshutt Plough Company, for example, still gave each of its employees a turkey for Christmas dinner.[37]

The stiffening of Canadian employers to union demands did not go unnoticed in labour circles. When the president of the Trades and Labor Congress discussed employers' associations in 1904, he noted that several Canadian groups had been patterned after the 'Parry type ... pursuing similar methods, having walking delegates, business agents, etc.' The Canadian Manufacturers' Association disagreed, claiming that Canadian employers wanted to prevent labour crises, whereas their American cousins were combining largely to fight trade unionism. Most trade-union leaders failed to see the distinction and viewed the aggressiveness of employers as a continental and not just a Canadian or American phenomenon.[38]

Fortunately for the North American labour movement, employer groups did not always march in a solid phalanx. The National Civic Federation, formed in 1901, brought Wall Street, labour, and public leaders into a forum that endorsed collective bargaining and model trade agreements. The Civic Federation and its most prominent leader, Mark Hanna, supported the AFL and condemned the union-busting activities of the employers' associations. 'The smashing of unions,' the Civic Federation asserted, 'has led to the development of a powerful Socialist party in Australia.' Although the president of the Trades and Labor Congress called for the formation of a similar group in Canada, nothing apparently came from his suggestion.[39]

The rise of big business and its expansion to continental proportions served both to stimulate and to justify a similar growth by American trade unions. Expansion seemed 'natural' to trade unionists. Most craft-union leaders shared the Darwinism of the business community. The labour movement was thought to be an organic, living thing which followed pre-determined laws of growth and decay. 'The law of growth in organized labor,' Gompers told the Federation in 1904, 'is as little understood by ... [labour's critics] ... as it is by others who lack the experience, or who have not had the time, opportunity, or inclination to inquire and study.' Each succeeding expansion and consolidation in the business community, he noted, had been matched by similar developments within the labour movement.[40] Governments could not control the trusts, an AFL committee declared: 'The trust is an industrial disease which can only be alleviated and finally cured by remedies taken from the industrial garden; organizations of labor, free from all anti-combination laws, given full freedom to use its own natural weapons ... will meet this evil and overcome it in the natural evolutionary way.'[41] The trusts, one labour leader wrote, were 'really due to the American genius for doing things upon a large scale, and putting natural forces to the best use.'[42] Recalling labour's experiences under the Sherman Act, Gompers felt sure that more anti-trust legislation could not help labour's cause. Any new law, he said, 'would beyond doubt react with greater force and injury upon the working people of our country than upon the trusts.' It remained for industrial workers to solve the trust issue by organizing on a scale comparable to the new business combinations. Before the American Federation of Labor could assert itself within the new continental industrial community, Canadian as well as American workers needed Gompers' attention.[43]

Gompers quickly accepted the new reality. He discussed or actually began active organizing campaigns in Canada, the Philippines, Puerto Rico, and Hawaii. He took an interest in Cuban affairs. But the AFL's thrust into Canada came earlier and easier than the later moves into Mexico and the Caribbean. 'We are more than neighbors; we are kin,' the Canadians were told. 'We speak a common language, are descendants from the same races, inhabit the same land and our labor problem with all its ideals, aspirations and ambitions is alike for both of us.'[44] It is clear that Gompers and other American union leaders were anxious to devote resources to the Canadian labour field because they feared that American employers would take too many jobs across the boundary if Canadian labour was poorly organized. As one of them put it: 'International bosses have made the welfare of a trade in one country of vital importance to the welfare of the same trade in another country.'[45]

During a speech in Toronto in 1900, Gompers referred publicly for perhaps the first time to the connection between the changes taking place in the business world and the expansion of the American labour movement into Canada. Gompers had come to Canada to support streetcar workers in London, Ontario, on strike against the American-owned traction company in their city. He declared that the time of the individual employer and the old partnership firm had passed away. The company and the trust had taken the place of the individual; in dealing with capital, trade unions also must replace individuals. He urged Torontonians to help the men in London to put down the American capitalist who had come into Canada 'to oppress' Canadian workingmen. 'When the Yankee capitalist did this it was but natural that the Yankee "agitator" should follow him.' Gompers' words remain to this day the chief justification for international unionism in Canada.[46]

Guided by its Darwinian compass, the AFL joined the northward journey of migratory American entrepreneurs and turned its attention to the organization of Canadian workers during the period of its own spectacular growth in the United States. In a few years Gompers was able to tell the Federation convention that the AFL's limits were 'no longer from Maine to California, from the Lakes to the Gulf, but we include the whole of the United States, Canada,

Hawaii, Cuba, Porto Rico, Mexico, the Philippines and British Columbia.'[47] One acute observer was apprehensive of the outcome. 'There are symptoms of the approach of an economical crisis here,' Goldwin Smith wrote from Toronto in 1901. 'The extension of the Trusts seems likely to be met by a counter-extension of unions, so that we shall have strikes for the whole continent. I suppose we shall manage to rub along, but there may be a lively quarter of an hour.'[48]

4
Organizing boom

Before the arrival of Gompers, labour in Canada was predominantly regional in organization and outlook. Handfuls of Canadian industrial workers were strung out along 3000 miles of Canadian-American border and cut off from each other by mountains, muskeg, and vast empty space. Industrialization exerted an uneven impact upon Canadian regions, and there was scarcely a 'national' economy. Ontario became the nearest Canadian counterpart to the burgeoning American industrial community. East of Ontario, manufacturing was limited largely to textiles, cigars, and shoes in Quebec, and in the Maritimes to activities connected with shipping, fishing, and construction, along with the coal mining and iron works in Cape Breton. West of the Great Lakes, Winnipeg sufficed to provide the goods and services for the sparsely settled prairies stretching toward the Canadian Rockies. On the far side of that formidable mountain barrier, small industries grew up to serve the needs of lumber and mining communities in British Columbia. Not surprisingly, then, by 1890 American international unions concentrated 146 of their 238 Canadian locals in Ontario, the province with the most factories. Quebec and British Columbia could claim only 30 and 25 locals respectively, the Maritimes had 22 locals, and Manitoba listed 11. Ontario also dominated the building trades with 29 of 55 locals spread throughout Canada. More important, nearly half (104) of the country's labour groups were locals of the railway running trades. The railways that bound Canadians together in nationhood were still their biggest industry.[1]

Although the economic boom which followed the depression years of the late 1880s and early 1890s began to integrate Canadian economic regions into a genuinely national economy, the disparities in trade-union organization remained great for a good many years. By the end of 1897, Ontario could boast of roughly 192 to 194 locals of international trade unions; Quebec, far behind with 47 locals, and British Columbia with 27 locals, remained clearly outdistanced. Nova Scotia and New Brunswick together possessed 30 labour organizations, and the Winnipeg area increased to 15 locals. Despite the renewed industrial growth, the railway running trades still accounted for about one-third of the trade union locals in Canada in 1897.[2]

In consequence the Trades and Labor Congress remained an Ontario- and Quebec-centred body. Correspondence and an occasional delegate were received from British Columbia and the Maritimes, but the majority of delegates and concerns reflected Central Canada's viewpoint. As Canadian industry expanded to national proportions at the end of the nineteenth century, the outlook of the Trades Congress broadened similarly. More attention was paid to reports from British Columbia at Congress conventions. Similarly, both Trades Congress president Ralph Smith and secretary George Dower suggested that steps be taken 'to bring about at least a friendly intercourse' with the Maritimes-based Provincial Workmen's Association.[3]

The need to organize mushrooming numbers of industrial workers throughout the whole country noticeably attracted the attention of Canadian labour leaders at the turn of the century. As early as 1895, the Trades Congress's officers in Quebec suggested that American union organizers be sent to the 'Lower Provinces' (the Maritimes), but little was done.[4] When a Montrealer boasted in 1898 that the labour movement in his city had grown by 4000 in three years, the gains, probably exaggerated, were largely the work of the Canadians themselves.[5] The AFL did not appoint a new Canadian organizer in the months following P.J. Loughrin's dismissal, and although several international unions selected Canadian vice-presidents and gave them organizing responsibilities, the magnitude of their task, as well as the distances to be covered, overwhelmed their efforts. By 1898 the Trades and Labor Congress appeared hopeful of taking up the burden. It had assumed the power to issue charters to Canadian central labour bodies and federal labour unions. The Congress expected to receive financial assistance from the AFL, and while avoiding a premature challenge to the international unions, seemed on the verge of becoming the Canadian national trade-union centre in fact as well as in name.

Early in the spring of 1898, a group of employees of the government-owned Intercolonial Railway organized a union at Moncton, New Brunswick, and applied to the Trades Congress for a charter. George Dower, the Congress secretary, prepared documents and forwarded them to the Moncton men, who became 'Federal Labor Union No. 1,' the first union chartered by the Canadian national labour body. At the convention later that year, the officers recommended that the Trades Congress expand its efforts and secure the affiliation of city central bodies through a grant of Congress charters. Dower and President D.A. Carey thought that it would tend to bring into the fold many local organizations that had kept aloof.[6]

Their recommendation may have been prompted by the fact that the AFL had chartered its first Canadian central body the year before. In Montreal a Central Trades and Labor Council composed of delegates from both the crafts and the Knights of Labor had been set up by the Montrealers themselves in 1885 or 1886. But some of the craft delegates had grown restive under the Knights-dominated body's control. They started a movement in 1897 to set up a new city central. Gompers told P.J. Ryan, an actor and prominent Montreal unionist, that mixed assemblies of the Knights of Labor had no place in the labour movement. At first he urged the city's craft-union leaders to convert the existing central council into a strictly craft-union organization.[7] In July he relented when the Montreal craft leaders assured him that there was no chance of working within the Central Labor Council. 'It was the consciousness of this fact that the old central body of Montreal was not conducted upon these [craft] lines ... that prompted me finally to issue the charter to you,' Gompers wrote.[8] Hereafter Montreal was blessed with two competing central labour bodies. The Federation apparently made no further incursions into Canadian territory in 1897 and 1898.

By the fall of 1899 the Trades Congress had issued charters to five more federal labour unions, although it had not provided a constitution, by-laws, ritual, stationery, or supplies for the new affiliates. Pleas from labour leaders in New Brunswick and Ontario for a full-time organizer, while recognized as urgent, were rejected once more for lack of funds.[9] Hence the Trades Congress had taken only a hesitant half-step forward on its own when the American Federation of Labor began a gigantic organizing effort that stretched across the border into Canada and soon dwarfed the Congress's endeavours.

In the early months of 1899 the AFL was spending only about $50 a month on organizing activities. But in mid-year the Executive Council authorized the appointment of the Federation's first full-time walking delegates, who were quickly dispatched to the American south and Rocky Mountain regions. Federation organizing expenses climbed rapidly; by October they totaled over $1000 a month. In that month alone eighty-two charters were issued by the AFL. Annual expenditures on organizing activities rocketed from $1257 in 1898 to $6373.66 a year later. The new Federation policy was a direct response to the tremendous number of business consolidations and trust formations that had occurred throughout 1899.[10]

The AFL's house organ, the *American Federationist,* began to chronicle the spectacular growth of the North American labour movement during these years. The continent was divided into organizing districts; each month several pages were filled with enthusiastic reports from organizers near and far. In May 1899, two Toronto trade unionists bore first witness to the impact of the Federation's efforts in Canada. Organizer Devereaux of Ingersoll, Ontario, reported the formation of a union of butchers, and expected to set up locals of iron workers and wood workers. Louis Gurofsky, the Toronto tailor, organized garment cutters, barbers, harness makers, hotel employees, electrical workers, cloak makers, carters, window shade makers, and teamsters. 'The prospects for trade unionism hereabouts are bright for the coming year,' he wrote.[11]

The AFL did not send a full-time organizer to work in Canada; instead, Gompers issued volunteer commissions to a number of prominent Canadian trade unionists, and usually paid their expenses. George Warren, a cigarmaker who had been active in Montreal labour circles for years, received his commission from Gompers in March 1899. J.W. Patterson and C.S.O. Boudreault, Ottawa printers, and George Bartley and J.H. Watson of Vancouver, a printer and a boilermaker respectively, received Federation commissions between 1897 and 1899. During the latter part of 1899, a whole corps of Canadian volunteers began to report on strikes and organizing gains from Quebec to British Columbia. The young Canadian-born secretary of the AFL, Frank Morrison, was dispatched to speak at a monster demonstration in London, Ontario, where the streetcar employees were on strike. Through correspondence with the Canadian volunteers and others, Gompers grew more enlightened about the problems and prospects of the Canadian labour movement. As he became better informed of the needs of labour in Canada, he took increased interest in organizing efforts there. He expressed regret 'that there should be any slackness of energy in any city of Ontario, where I am lead [*sic*] to believe that there is such a fruitful field for the work of organization.'[12] By the first of December 1899, the Federation claimed 10,457 Canadian members. Apparently unaware of or unconcerned with the Trades Congress' chartering moves, the AFL issued its second charter to a Canadian central body – the Revelstoke, British Columbia, Trades and Labor Council in 1899.[13]

By 1900 AFL leaders felt reasonably certain of sufficient income from their per-capita tax to assure the maintenance of a permanent staff of organizers. In February Gompers appointed John A. Flett of Hamilton, Ontario, as the Federation's general organizer for Canada. Flett had defended international unionism at the Congress convention in 1897 and had come to Gompers' attention through his energetic work and well-written reports while an AFL volunteer. The forty-year-old Canadian had been a member of one of the most powerful AFL affiliates, the United Brotherhood of Carpenters, since his apprentice days in the early 1880s. During the heyday of the Knights of Labor he had gained union leadership experience as secretary of Local Assembly no. 2225, the largest in Hamilton at the time with over 600 members. In subsequent years Flett had occupied every post in his carpenters' local, had represented his union on the Hamilton Trades and Labor Council, and had served the latter for years as chairman of its organizing committee. In 1895 the Hamilton Trades and Labor Council had chosen Flett to be one of its delegates to the Trades Congress convention in London. Although probably not a Socialist Labor party member, he had vigorously defended party representation at the Trades Congress convention, which no doubt helped him win election that year to the Ontario executive committee of the Congress. In 1898 the Winnipeg convention had elected him vice-president of the Trades Congress, and he was still occupying that post when he was added to the AFL payroll. A forceful speaker, Flett habitually created a pleasing impression on his listeners, 'and at the same time leaves the conviction that he is thoroughly in earnest and devoted to the cause of industrial liberty.'[14] Because he was no enemy of international trades unionism, the suave, witty, and walrus-moustached Canadian quickly won the trust of the Federation leaders. He became the Federation's chief agent at a critical time when the future course of the labour movement in Canada was uncertain. In succeeding years Flett exerted a profound influence on the relationship between the American and Canadian labour movements and trade-union centres.

Flett's career with the AFL began in rather spectacular fashion. In his first tour through many of the smaller towns of Ontario, he set up fourteen locals in only seven weeks. Several large manufacturing firms had reputedly located in more remote areas in order to gain immunity from wage rates won by unions in the larger Canadian cities. When employers heard of Flett's activities, they induced the press and pulpit to condemn the 'invasion,' as they put it, of a 'foreign' labour organization desirous of the poor working man's money. 'It was fortunate that I was known to be a thorough Canadian,' Flett reported, 'seeing that the general knowledge of this fact was sufficient to counteract all such misrepresentations.' It would not be the last time that employers attempted to bolster their influence over workers through an appeal to the workers' patriotism.[15]

Readers of the *American Federationist* received a graphic picture of the efforts being made by the AFL's new representative in Canada. Flett's blunt narrative laid bare both successes and failures; some obstacles he overcame and others, such as the weather, he could only endure.

Starting from Niagara Falls, and visiting such towns as St. Catharines and Merriton, addressing meetings, making personal visits to shops, and trying to get a sufficient number of a trade interested to form a union of their craft, I was reluctantly compelled to leave the Niagara peninsular [sic] without accomplishing the desired object. St. Catharines is a town strewn with the wrecks of many an assembly of the Knights of Labor, making it very difficult to successfully carry on the work of reorganization. I next visited the city of Brantford, where I found a flourishing federal labor union, and a trades and labor council. Held organization meeting of painters, barbers, and printers. The last named had a union at one time, but surrendered their charter and as a consequence were working for very low wages. I succeeded in organizing the carpenters, plasterers and sheet metal workers of that city; leaving there I went to Guelph, the weather at that time being very cold and stormy. There I found a federal labor union and a trade and labor council in rather weak condition. Passing to the towns of Berlin and Waterloo, with residents mostly German, I found three unions already there; and, after holding many meetings, the following unions were organized and charters sent for: Woodworkers, varnishers and finishers, bricklayers, carpenters, tanners and curriers, painters, broommakers, and trades and labor council. There are now 11 union[s] in those towns. From Berlin I went to Preston and organized the woodworkers, varnishers and finishers; held a meeting of iron molders, and sent in application to the international secretary for charter. Leaving Preston, I went to St. Thomas and was successful in organizing the painters and bricklayers. A federal labor union has since been organized there. Proceeding to Stratford, where I held several meetings of painters, blacksmiths and bricklayers, was only successful in organizing the carpenters, but expect to see a central council there soon. From there I visited Seaforth and held a meeting of furniture workers and secured quite a number to make application for charter. Organized the woodworkers of Goderich and also the woodworkers of Wingham — furniture manufacturing being the principal industry in these small towns ... In this city [Hamilton] I have been holding meetings nightly, with this result: We have organized the broomworkers, furniture woodworkers, and expect to send for charter for a federal labor union. We have unions of lathers, coremakers, and bicycle workers under way.[16]

Virtually everywhere he travelled Flett's organizing abilities found abundant scope for exercise. Years later, local labour leaders in Ontario often pointed to Flett's first visit when they dated the beginning of the labour movement in their community.

By the end of 1900, Flett reported much satisfaction with the gains that had been made by the AFL and international unions in Canada. The general election late in that year had distracted some workers' attention from trade-union affairs, but most towns that had had two or three locals in 1899 had central bodies with up to fifteen locals in 1900. Undoubtedly Flett was responsible for the largest share of the 140 or so international union locals chartered in Canada during 1900.[17]

Gompers himself devoted three days in May 1900 to speechmaking in Ontario cities on behalf of Canadian labour; his efforts testified to the greater attention the Federation president was devoting to AFL interests in Canada. The bitter struggle which had broken out the year before between the workers of London and the street railway company was still being waged in 1900. On May Day Gompers and W.D. Mahon, president of the union of street railway employees, spoke for an hour to a crowd of 10,000 in a London Ontario park. Only a few small boys who smashed some streetcar windows marred the otherwise peaceful gathering. At Hamilton the next evening, Gompers, his voice hoarse from earlier efforts, talked with difficulty to a small gathering arranged by Flett. The American labour leader defended the walking delegate in a manner that impressed even the local newspaper editor. At Toronto on the evening of 3 May, he was loudly cheered by an audience of 1500 who attended an open-air meeting. Gompers delivered the speech linking the presence of American unions in Canada to the activities of American businessmen. Moved by the warmth of his reception, he said it revealed the 'unity and breadth of the labor movement.' In all mankind's history, he declared, never had there been 'such an awakening in the realm of labor as the world was now witnessing.'[18]

Gompers' new attention to Canadian labour affairs was matched by that of leaders of several international unions. Their requests for assistance in órganizing Canadian workers were relayed through Gompers to Flett, who was not entirely free to map out an organizing campaign tailored to his own view of Canadian labour's needs. In November 1900, for example, the president of the Tobacco Workers' International Union asked if Flett would 'give us a helping hand to try and bring the Tobacco Workers into line.'[19] Flett had already assisted in the organization of this union's local in London weeks earlier; he may have been responsible for setting up a similar local in Toronto soon after the union head's request. In early 1901, the president of the International Association of Allied Metal Mechanics was embarrassed when the Union's Toronto local, one of whose members was third vice-president of the International, voted to disband. Gompers informed Flett of a 'special desire' that the Toronto men be reorganized as soon as possible, and asked him additionally to organize the metal mechanics in Hamilton and Brantford. Later Gompers told Flett of his deep gratification at the latter's success in carrying out these requests.[20]

At times the Canadian organizer worked under Gompers' supervision to settle disputes between battling locals in Canada. The AFL leader received a complaint from the president of the International Association of Machinists over the actions of the Kingston, Ontario, local of the Ironworkers' Helpers' Union – an AFL-chartered federal labour union. When the machinists at the locomotive works had struck for higher pay, the leaders of the federal labour union had permitted some of their members to take machinists' jobs. Gompers immediately dispatched Flett to the scene. After considerable correspondence, the conflict was resolved in the Machinists' favour when Flett was ordered to remove the AFL seals from the Ironworkers' Helpers' charter.[21]

On occasion Flett was instructed to mediate between an employer and a union. The St Catharines Laborers' Union, a local directly attached to the Federation, struck against their employers and turned to the AFL's defence fund for financial aid. The request did not arrive at Washington headquarters until after the strike had begun. Gompers reminded Flett that an AFL affiliate was precluded from striking without prior approval from the Federation Executive Council. The Canadian was sent to St Catharines with authority to seek a settlement between the workers and their employer.[22] In another case both the president and vice-president of an AFL-chartered federal labour union had lost their jobs as a result of their union activities. '... Now, this is a very serious blow to us,' the union secretary at Hespeler, Ontario, wrote to Gompers. '... Our union wants to know what to do at once, or if you think best send a man here to deal with this mill owner ... We sent a committee to see this mill owner but he refuses to talk with them. Please let us know at once.' The Hespeler workers faced combined economic and political power. 'This mill owner,' they added, 'is the Mayor of our town.' Gompers dispatched both words of encouragement and organizer Flett to the scene.[23]

Sometimes Flett became entangled in jurisdictional problems that actually delayed, albeit infrequently, the organization of Canadian locals. Flett told Toronto harbour's marine firemen to join a Buffalo local of the Marine Firemen's Union, but the American group refused to admit the Canadians. Flett asked Gompers whether the AFL might charter them if they were also refused a charter by the International Longshoremen's Association. Gompers, ever mindful of a powerful affiliate's trade boundaries, told Flett that 'so long as the Longshoremen's Association claims jurisdiction over the Marine Firemen, charter could not be granted' by the AFL. Apparently the Longshoremen did refuse to accept the marine firemen, but by 1904 there was a local of the International Marine Firemen, Oilers, and Watertenders' Union in the Toronto port.[24]

Early in 1901 Flett proposed a swing through the Maritime provinces, but hinted that he was presently weighed down with special requests which had been relayed to him from the heads of several international unions. Gompers expressed faith in Flett's judgment, yet indicated that it would be well first to dispose of the internationals' demands. The Canadian organizer bowed to Gompers' advice and serviced the craft locals in Quebec and Ontario before squeezing in two eastward journeys in the fall of 1901.[25]

Flett became the first trade unionist to unfurl the AFL banner in the Atlantic provinces. He found a need not only to organize workers, but also to bring the union label message. 'The Maritimes,' he reported, were 'the dumping ground for the products of non-union labor of Quebec and upper Canada. It is here that the scab cigars of Montreal are sold without question.'[26] In New Brunswick he organized longshoremen, cigarmakers, machinists, painters, carpenters, and bartenders, among other trades, and affiliated them with the AFL crafts. He made a quick trip to Halifax where he chatted with members of the city Trades and Labor Council at their Labour Day picnic and persuaded them to apply for an AFL volunteer organizer's commission for one of their number. Shortly thereafter, Kempton McKim, later prominent in Winnipeg labour councils, became the Federation's first Nova Scotia representative. By November, Flett had organized no less than 25 unions in the Maritimes.[27]

In the latter part of September, Flett interrupted his work in the Maritimes to attend the Trades Congress convention in Brantford. There, trade-union officials in both Nova Scotia and Prince Edward Island pointed to the crying need for an organizer in Eastern Canada. 'In the town of Sydney, where during the last two years mechanics from all parts have gone, there has not been one Union organized, nor has an organizer paid that town a visit. If it were possible to send an organizer there and also in other towns of our Province, much good to organized labor would result ...' In Prince Edward Island, a delegate from the Trades Congress-chartered Federal Labor Union no. 10, composed of railway workers, claimed that his organization was the only trade union in the entire province. 'What is most wanted first is a good man,' he added, 'who is thoroughly versed in all that pertains to the organized labor movement, and is a good organizer.' After the convention, Flett returned to the Maritimes and worked diligently for several weeks. Thus it was an American Federation representative, and not an official of the Trades Congress, who first appeared on the scene in the Maritime provinces.[28]

In Charlottetown, Prince Edward Island, Flett set up locals of the trackmen, carpenters, painters and decorators, printers, and an AFL-chartered federal labour union of iron workers. He was no doubt responsible for the appointment of Harry Corcoran as volunteer organizer on the island; Corcoran worked throughout the spring of 1902 gathering a local of teamsters and organizing labourers' unions in both Charlottetown and Summerside. He also managed to create a trades and labour council in the provincial capital, of which he became secretary. The AFL recognized the group on 27 February 1902. Once again the Federation had chartered a Canadian central body – an action which Trades Congress leaders had hoped to accomplish through their own organization.[29]

At the instigation of John Mitchell, the president of the United Mine Workers of America, the AFL followed the example of the Trades Congress in making overtures to the Provincial Workmen's Association. Mitchell asked Flett to obtain the views of the Association on amalgamation with the mine workers. 'If there were any possibility of our organization obtaining jurisdiction over the miners of Canada,' Mitchell wrote to Gompers, 'without entering into a contest with the national union now established there, we would do so; but unless they would withdraw from the field or amalgamate, we would not care to spend any money in a fight with them for control, as we have a wide field yet remaining uncovered in the United States.'[30] Flett conferred with Association secretary John Moffatt and deposited Federation literature with him shortly after his arrival in Nova Scotia. The Grand Council of the Association discussed the proposal at its meeting in Halifax on 17 September, but no definite action was taken.[31]

When Flett returned to central Canada in early 1902, he left volunteers Harry Corcoran and Kempton McKim to nurse the infant locals he had organized and to set up new ones as opportunities warranted. In his travels through Ontario and Quebec, Flett sponsored the commissioning of several unionists, many of whom worked hard for the Federation with little or no recompense. By mid-1901 the Federation could claim representation in Brockville, Hamilton, Kingston, St Catharines, Norwich, Ottawa, London, Stratford, Sault Ste Marie, and Toronto in Ontario; Montreal in Quebec; and Nanaimo, Vancouver, and Victoria in British Columbia. In addition one man worked the railway trades east and west of Moose Jaw in the North West Territories.[32]

Throughout the boom years of 1900-3, Gompers was besieged by requests from his Canadian volunteers for more organizing money. He weighed these demands with others pouring in from the four corners of the United States. Flett, for example, pressed the AFL leader to send a special organizer to Sault Ste Marie. 'I assure you I fully appreciate the situation as you describe it to exist,' Gompers wrote, 'but ... at this time, owing to the enormous expenses of the A.F. of L. as indicated, in the way of organization work, in the various sections of the country, I do not see my way clear to act favorably upon the suggestion you make ... I regret exceedingly that I cannot take advantage of the opportunity offered, but for the reasons above stated, it is absolutely out of the question.'[33] Over and over again Gompers wrote variations of the same negative refrain, many to ambitious men who sought a secure career in organized labour. Daniel Stamper, for example, tried several times to persuade Gompers to place him on the Federation payroll; he finally resigned his voluntary organizer's commission and told Gompers he was going into a business venture. Both the Federation and the international unions paid an organizer only $10 or $15 for each charter sent to union headquarters. The money was sufficient to encourage men to set up unions in the vicinity of their homes, yet it was not enough to permit them to travel or leave their employment for any length of time. Gompers did not want volunteers to take time away from their regular jobs and charge it to the Federation unless they had been specifically directed to do so by the AFL. Thus the turnover of volunteer organizers was fairly heavy, and John Flett shouldered the heaviest part of the burden of organizing Canadian industrial workers for the American Federation of Labor.[34]

Even before Flett's appointment, volunteer organizers had made some headway in the Montreal area in 1899 and 1900. 'Never since 1867 have trade unions progressed as they are progressing today,' George Warren, an AFL volunteer in Montreal, declared in 1900. 'Organization is having a real boom in this city, and it is to be hoped that the various [international union] executives will take advantage of this fact.' Warren had even made a trip to Quebec City in order to urge workers there to purchase only union-made goods.[35]

By late 1900 the growth of international unionism was sufficient to worry many employers in the province. When Quebec city boot and shoe workers, in locals unaffiliated at that time with the Boot and Shoe Workers' International Union, struck one small factory in October 1900, an employers' association locked out the toilers in the remainder of the city's shoe establishments. 'The manufacturers are decided not to open their doors until they have checked the intervention of foreign labor unions in the carrying on of their business.' a Quebec city newspaper reported.[36] Actually, the Quebec city workers had not yet been organized by AFL unions, and with no outside help available to them, they agreed after a month-long strike to submit the issues to the archbishop of Quebec. Archbishop Bégin's award provided for the creation of a permanent arbitration panel to settle future disputes and forbade workers to strike while issues were under discussion. In effect, the archbishop committed his power and prestige in a manner designed not only to minimize industrial 'disorder,' but also to counter the international unions relying on strikes in their struggle for improved working conditions.[37]

Upon his arrival in Montreal, Flett expected to achieve even greater success in Quebec than in Ontario. 'There is virgin soil here for this kind of work,' he wrote. But the challenge soon proved to be greater than he had anticipated. Flett quickly noted the virtues of Warren's bilingualism and sought his appointment to the AFL staff. Gompers demurred: 'We must husband our resources to the very best of our ability,' he told Flett. Handicapped by his inability to speak French, Flett encountered many obstacles when he began working in Quebec in early 1901.[38]

Shortly before the archbishop announced his decision in the Quebec city shoe strike, Gompers dispatched Flett to Valleyfield to assist the members of Federal Labor Union 7387 who, Gompers wrote, were 'so vilely treated by the Cotton Company of Valleyfield. It is certain that the Company has broken faith, if nothing else ...' The Federation leader sent $50 to aid in the legal defence of the workers, and asked Flett to give them 'assistance ... encouragement, advice and so on.' While in St Hyacinthe Flett visited three independent shoemakers' locals with the intention of affiliating them with the Boot and Shoe Workers' International.[39]

Meanwhile John Tobin, the president of the International Boot and Shoe Workers, came to Montreal in March 1900 to organize his trade and found another four independent shoeworkers' locals in that city. The independents refused to affiliate with the International Union, banded together to form a rival group (the Canadian Federation of Boot and Shoemakers), and resisted the International Union's blandishments. In 1901 Tobin promptly asked Gompers for Flett's assistance, and in the following weeks the two men worked their way together through Quebec shoe factories. But international unionism made slow progress beyond the cosmopolitan city of Montreal. 'When we consider the strong feeling and prejudice that exists in the province against international trade unionism, both by the clergy and laymen,' a chastened Flett reported, 'our progress is most marked.'[40]

The language barrier made the work doubly difficult. Flett expressed his indebtedness to Warren, but noted that voluntary efforts were not enough. 'Agitation now going on must be followed up by those crafts using labels, having their agitating matter printed in the French language.' The International Shoe Workers could claim only six locals in Montreal by 1903, and the predominantly French-speaking Canadian Federation of Shoe Makers had easily preserved its separate existence and had even absorbed the St Hyacinthe local. Apparently the Quebec city shoeworkers, although invited to join the International, decided to stay away from 'foreign' trade unionism.[41]

Yet the American trade unions did record some gains in 1901 and 1902. Quebec city tanners and curriers and carpenters decided to affiliate with the American Federation of Labor. Several trades were organized in Montreal and the growing influence of organized labour in that city was reflected in a resolution passed by the city council requiring all municipal printing to bear the union label.[42] Some American labour leaders were optimistic. W.D. Mahon, Gompers' friend and the president of the Street Railway Employees' Union, 'found the Frenchmen [at the Trade Congress convention in 1900] just as earnest and sincere, and, if anything, more enthusiastic than the English-speaking delegates in pushing the work of organization.'[43]

It was not easy to maintain the momentum in Quebec. When the secretary of an AFL-chartered tanners' union noted that eighteen members of his fledgling local had resigned, Gompers urged him to persevere and build up his union treasury. The Federation, he warned, could not help him financially. 'As you are aware,' he said, 'we are doing all within our power to assist our fellow workers in the Dominion of Canada ... The territory to be covered is extended; our means are limited ...'[44] In the following months Flett devoted considerable time and effort in the Montreal area on behalf of the longshoremen, cigarmakers, shoe-workers, and other trades, often to see his organizing gains dissipated by strike losses.[45]

The AFL's work in Quebec was hindered by the Anglo-Saxon biases many American labour leaders shared with their generation. Although Gompers on occasion had boasted of his linguistic ability, he bluntly told his French-Canadian correspondents to write to him in English. He was exasperated when George Warren suggested Federation endorsement of an international language, 'I find my time too fully crowded to say one half I want to say in the English language,' he retorted.[46] To sensitive Quebeckers a union message in a foreign language was not likely to win many converts. Outside of Montreal, then, where at the end of 1902 there were some 64 to 66 locals affiliated with the central body, the international unions failed to make a significant showing in Quebec. As a result the province became a centre of dual unionism.[47]

Between 1900 and mid-1903, the American Federation of Labor's general organizer for Canada concentrated most of his efforts in Ontario and in the environs of Montreal. He managed a successful tour of the Maritime provinces as well. But across the vast reaches of Canada west of Ontario, only a handful of volunteer organizers toiled on behalf of the Federation. To entreaties that Gompers appoint a full-time man to work in Western Canada, the American labour leader responded again and again that the Federation's funds simply would not permit the additional expense.[48]

Since they were forced to work at odd hours and with limited funds, the volunteers in Western Canada faced a good many obstacles and yet made significant gains on behalf of the Federation. in 1899 J.H. Watson, the chairman of the Vancouver Trades and Labor Council's organizing committee, reported having set up a local of the retail clerks. George Bartley said that the city's plasterers had expressed the intention of joining the international union of their trade.

Both men helped organize a number of other trades in the following years. Daniel Stamper, working the Canadian Pacific route in British Columbia and the North West Territories, organized the previously mentioned Revelstoke, British Columbia, Trades Council and three unions in that city. He noted that it had taken him nine months to organize the labourers there; as a boom town it was probably filled with transients. Both the Revelstoke and Vancouver central bodies endorsed AFL boycotts.[49]

The value to American unions of organization in British Columbia was well illustrated by an incident that took place in 1902, when the boiler makers in Seattle struck for the eight-hour day. The owners of a steamer in need of repairs refused to bow to the Seattle workers' demands and moved the vessel to Victoria, British Columbia, where the work-day was ten hours. The boilermakers of Victoria, however, would not work on the job for a longer period than the eight-hour day the Seattle men wanted. The international union, through its expansion into the Canadian branches of what had become a continental job market, protected the interests of its American members. And it introduced generally superior American wages and working conditions into the Canadian industrial community.[50]

Dedicated to assuring their survival through organization and expansion, American trade unions by the end of 1902 had tremendously enlarged their membership and activities in Canada. New internationals formed after 1890 had set up an estimated 339 to 350 locals in Canada between 1898 and 1902. At the same time the older international unions, no less dedicated to the expansionist ideas of that era, had picked up between 378 and 387 new locals in the country. A large number of the locals had been organized by Canadians themselves who merely sent in a request for a charter to a union headquarters. But AFL organizers had appeared responsible for the organization of over 60 locals of the 140 or so established in Canada in 1900, and about 80 of the 160 chartered in 1901. Perhaps 50 of the 270 to 290 locals chartered in 1902 had been set up by Federation representatives. No less than 57 of the 160 locals chartered in 1901 had been started by John Flett, and a year later he was given credit for most of the 50 locals set up by Federation workers. From November 1899 to October 1902 the AFL spent $6134.22 on Canadian organizing and legislative work. Eighty-eight per cent of that amount was allocated to Flett. By 1902 the Federation had allocated roughly 7 per cent of its total annual organizing expenditures to Canada and was collecting dues from over 700 AFL international union locals and 46-7 federal labour unions in Canada.[51]

While the concentration of industrial activity – and therefore of trade-union efforts – had remained centred on Ontario, all areas of the country had shared in the growth of trade unionism, as the statistics in Table 1 reveal. The

TABLE 1
Regional distribution of trade-union locals established in Canada, 1897-1902

Area	Approx. no. locals end of 1897	Percentage of total	Approx. no. locals end of 1902	Percentage of total
BC	27	8.4	137-40	13.2
Prairies	24	7.5	75-7	7.2
Maritimes	30	9.3	94-7	9.1
Quebec	47	14.6	115-19	11.0
Ontario	192-4	60.0	612-27	59.0

SOURCE: Eugene Forsey (ms) revised in a letter to the author, 19 April 1969

spectacular growth of the labour movement in British Columbia was a reflection of the mining boom and the growth of a prairie market for the coastal province's goods and services. The relative decline in Quebec's position was at least partial testimony to the extraordinary obstacles faced by organizers in that province. Ontario's predominance over other Canadian areas remained steady, yet the explosion of industrial activity in that province was reflected in the eclipse of the railway running trade locals by the building trades. In 1897 the running trades had three times as many locals as the building trades, but by 1903 the latter, with over two-thirds of their locals situated in Ontario, had clearly outdistanced the railway organizations there. Outside of Ontario and British Columbia, the running trades – along with the railway telegraphers, carmen, railway clerks, the switchmen, the trackmen, and the United Brotherhood of Railway Employees – still accounted for the most significant number of international union locals. Hence most of the gains made by the carpenters, painters, bricklayers, plumbers, tailors, woodworkers, machinists, miners, printers, barbers, bakers, moulders, street railway workers, and cigarmakers had taken place in Ontario and in British Columbia.[52] Tables 2 and 3 show the breakdown by trades and by cities.

Noting the great gains made by organized labour in Canada, one AFL volunteer declared that the general prosperity in Canada had made the work easier than usual. But the principal factor, he insisted, had been the efforts of Flett and the AFL volunteer organizers, along with the work of the officers of both the international unions and the Trades and Labor Congress.[53] There seems little doubt that the Federation made a vital contribution to the expansion of the Canadian labour movement, which numbered perhaps 60,000 to 70,000 unionists by the end of 1902.

Nevertheless, the strong need felt by American labour leaders to organize Canadian labour blinded them to the fact that American labour institutions,

TABLE 2
Distribution of international union locals
in Canada by trades, 1902

Trades	Approximate no. of locals
Railway unions	313-16
Building trades	174-8
Metal trades	149-53
Clothing trades	58-61
Printing, publishing	59
Woodworking	58-61
Transport, non-railway	48-9

SOURCE: Eugene Forsey (ms), revised in a
letter to the author, 19 April 1969

TABLE 3
Distribution of international union locals in Canada by
city and province, 1902

Ontario		Quebec	
Toronto	105-6	Montreal	64-6
Hamilton	47-8	Quebec city	13
London	37-9		
Ottawa	35-6	Manitoba	
Kingston	21	Winnipeg	36
Brantford	20-1		
Berlin	19	British Columbia	
Guelph	19	Vancouver	35
St Catharines	19	Victoria	22
Stratford	18	Nelson	17
Windsor	16		
Peterborough	16	Nova Scotia	
Smith's Falls	15	Halifax	19-22
St Thomas	14		
Brockville	13-14	New Brunswick	
Galt	12	Saint John	17
Sarnia	10-11		
Woodstock	10		
Sault Ste Marie	9-10		

SOURCE: Eugene Forsey (ms), revised in a letter to the author,
19 April 1969

methods, and objectives might not be well adapted to the Canadian workers' environment and temperament – particularly in the political realm. Although Gompers asserted that Canadian and American workers were 'one and the same in spirit, in fact, in union, with one common polity and policy; with identical principles, hopes and aspirations,'[54] a good many Canadians felt smothered by the AFL leader's verbal embrace.

5
Labour politics in Canada

There is an old tradition of independent labour political action in the Canadian trade-union movement. In the 1870s the Canadian Labor Union entertained motions calling for working men's platforms and candidates. Out of this effort came the successful election of Daniel O'Donoghue to the Ontario legislature. In the next decade the Knights of Labor in Canada offered candidates for provincial and federal legislatures in several Ontario cities and in Montreal. The Toronto Trades Council nominated or endorsed labour men in various elections. Resolutions for independent political action were frequently adopted by the Trades and Labor Congress in the last two decades of the nineteenth century.

Certainly the parliamentary political institutions of British North America encouraged political action by labour groups. Canadian unionists hoped to follow the example of the Irish contingent in England and elect enough sympathizers to obtain the balance of power in Canadian legislatures. In addition there were close personal ties between the Canadian and British trade unionists. Many Canadian labour leaders had brought British labour's ideas, including socialism and independent political action, across the Atlantic; once ensconced in Canada, these men usually kept in touch with their old friends in England. Nevertheless, most Canadian working men's campaigns for political office were fruitless. Suffrage barriers were lower in Canada than in England, and both the Grits and Tories had sunk roots within the artisan classes. The strength of the two major parties led many labour leaders to work within them.[1]

The intensity with which Canadian unionists in the late 1890s held their political opinions was revealed by Daniel O'Donoghue to W.L. Mackenzie King. The young King, about to embark on his exposé of government sweating contracts, asked the veteran labour leader for letters of introduction to Montreal unionists. O'Donoghue readily complied, adding a word of advice. 'Have nothing to say as to Canadian Party Politics – don't pretend or admit that you know anything about our parties!! ... Be an enthusiastic Political Economist – while in Montreal this time, and *nothing* more ...'[2] O'Donoghue, by the way, was known to be a staunch Liberal party supporter.

Yet the position of the two chief parties in workers' sentiment was not wholly secure. All the radical political and economic winds of the late nineteenth and early twentieth centuries, generated by the human costs of industrialism, buffeted the Canadian labour movement. Some of the winds originated in England, but a good many gusts blew over from across the Canadian-American boundary. Nationalist clubs founded upon Edward Bellamy's notion, for example, contributed to the political fervour of Canadian industrial workers and reformers. Henry George's single-tax mania quickly spread all the way to British Columbia. By 1894 several union locals favoured seating delegates from single-tax groups at Trades Congress conventions. A year later O'Donoghue advocated George's system of taxation as 'the only correct one for public purposes.' The radical panaceas of the 1880s and early 1890s broke ground for later generations of socialists and reformers to sow and reap. As a result, some trade unionists were emboldened to take political matters into their own hands.[3]

Part of the reason for their audacity was occasioned by the failure of both Grits and Tories to respond to the evils of the new industrial society with ameliorative legislation. '... This fact fully demonstrates the futility of our efforts for legislation along present lines,' a Trades Congress committee complained in 1895, 'and labor organizations should now unite for independent political action.' This particular resolution probably reflected the dominant role played by Canadian socialists at that meeting of the Trades Congress. But the cry for independent political action found growing support from the non-socialists who controlled Congress meetings in subsequent years. In 1897 the Trades Congress urged the nomination of labour candidates in all federal constituencies where there was any chance of victory. A growing political consciousness paralleled the great expansion of Canadian trade unionism in the years after 1898. No doubt the growth of the organized labour movement stiffened the resolve of unionists to force comparable gains on labour's legislative front. But it was easier for workers to agree on the necessity for political action than to reach a concensus on tactics.[4]

Economic conditions in the mountain regions fostered political unionism in British Columbia. Mining communities tended to polarize employer and worker interests into opposite camps. Dependent upon faceless companies for food, clothing, shelter, and medical care in their one-industry towns, the miners saw themselves driven into 'class wars' which seemed to confirm classic Marxian assumptions. Miners turned to political action to redress the economic imbalance. In the early 1890s miners' candidates had been elected to local offices throughout the mountain west of the United States, often on labour or populist tickets. The failure of Bryan's crusade in 1896 turned many discontented miners towards socialism. The new radicalism of American miners rode into the Kootenay district of British Columbia on the same rail lines that began hauling Canadian ores to American smelters and markets at the end of the nineteenth century.[5]

Western metal miners had organized the Western Federation Miners, a militant industrial union, at Butte, Montana, in 1893.[6] The depression of the early 1890s and mediocre leadership set the new organization off to a shaky start, but in 1896 the Miners' Union came to life under Ed Boyce, a new secretary. Boyce led the union into the AFL and into a strike at Leadville, Colorado, and appealed to the Federation for financial help. The AFL circulated the appeal to its affiliates but raised only a pittance. Boyce blamed Gompers for the failure of the miners' strike. Soon, rumours of the impending formation of a federation of labour that would rival the AFL in the mountain states reached Gompers' ear. Boyce said he no longer cared to sit and listen 'to the delegates from the East talking about conservative action when 4,000,000 idle men and women are tramps upon the highway, made so by a vicious system of government that will continue to grind them further into the dust unless they have the manhood to get out and fight with the sword or use the ballot with intelligence.' In May 1897, the miners pulled out of the AFL, and a year later they set up a Western Labor Union to charter trade unions and challenge the AFL's jurisdiction and authority west of the Mississippi.

In 1895 the Miners' Union crossed the frontier into Canada and organized a local in the new metal-mining district at Rossland, British Columbia. By 1898 the union had set up eleven more locals in both coal and metal mining areas. Spreading to the east, it attached some 200 Lethbridge coal miners to both the Miners' Union and the Western Labor Union in 1898. The miner's militancy caught the attention of the manager of the War Eagle Mining Company in Rossland, who began to complain about his 'War Eagle savages' – the Yanks who made up 85 per cent of his labour force. They were the same bunch, he said, who had kept American mining camps in constant turmoil.[7]

Gompers sympathized with the metal miners, but he did not approve of their radicalism. One of his cardinal principles required industrial workers to pledge first loyalty to the union in their trade. In Gompers' view, labour politics interfered with workers' dedication to their trade unions. He believed that independent political action, or the advocacy of socialism, often led to dual unionism.

Political unionists generally favoured industrial over craft organization, relied upon ideological cohesion rather than pride of craft, and tried to exert political as much as economic power. Clearly, the Western Labor Union fitted these generalizations, and it had already spread to Canada.[8]

As the AFL grew in size and affluence after 1898, the dangers from 'dual unionism' grew correspondingly greater to the Federation. Thousands of new trade unionists, organized at great cost and effort by the Federation and the international unions, had not been sufficiently disciplined to withstand the lure of mermaids who promised an instant utopia through political action. The new members had not yet built up a large stake in the benefit and insurance funds of unions that helped in time to bind workers to their craft group. No one could be certain if the thousands of Canadian unionists organized between 1899 and 1902 would continue to pledge their loyalty and money to their craft unions. Some were likely to take up the socialist cause, others tempted to adopt an independent political stance or work for the Grit or Tory parties. In fact, all three paths became increasingly attractive to Canadians during the years of the AFL's spectacular growth. And two of them were to issue forth eventually as dual unionist threats to the Federation.

Samuel Gompers had no doubt about the road organized labour in Canada should take. Since the rise of political unionism in Canada paralleled developments in the United States at the turn of the century, Gompers treated its manifestations in Canada and in the United States as two aspects of the same problem. Gompers' attitude was based on the fact that two of the agents of political unionism in North America – the Western Federation of Miners and the Socialist Labor Party – *were* American-based rivals of the American Federation of Labor. Equally important, the Canadian socialist movement at the turn of the century derived much of its ideology and support from across the border. Since the environment and obstacles were identical, Gompers reasoned, the philosophy and tactics of international craft unionism applied equally well to both countries.

Gompers remembered that American socialists, after barely failing to capture the AFL in 1894 and 1895, had organized a rival trade-union federation called the Socialist Trades and Labor Alliance in December of 1895. The new radical group had declared war on the AFL and had attracted about a hundred unions, mostly within the New York City vicinity.[9] These dual-unionist tactics were exported to the first Canadian branch of the Socialist Labor party set up in London, Ontario. Soon there were branches in Toronto, Hamilton, Brantford, Ottawa, Halifax, Winnipeg, Vancouver, and three in Montreal. All followed a policy of denying membership to existing trade-union officers. This action, 'together with their severe criticism of all who cannot see eye to eye with them, has made the growth of their organization almost an impossibility,'[10] and by April of 1901 there were only four cells left in Canada. Yet the Socialists had been strong enough momentarily to capture the Congress at London in 1895, where they had given it a strong shove down the road toward national autonomy and political action.[11]

The debates at the Trades Congress convention of 1896 over whether to keep Socialist party representation revealed some sympathy for, and not a little fear of, the radical party. John Flett vigorously defended socialist representation in the Congress – years before he was to enter the AFL's employ, it should be noted. In Western Canada and especially in Ontario, he said, socialism was spreading rapidly. He believed that a careful study of the Socialist platform would convince anyone of its affinity with Trades Congress objectives. But a number of prominent Congress leaders, according to the *Globe*, believed that the Socialists threatened not only the usefulness but even the life of the Congress. They wished to unseat the Socialist party at the Quebec convention in 1896. They feared socialist influence at the forthcoming Congress convention in 1897 at Hamilton, where the party was entrenched. No doubt the anti-AFL stance of Socialist Labor party members alienated many Canadian trade unionists. The *Globe* reporter noted that the Socialists sat on one side at Trades Congress conventions, while the trades unionists held aloof on the other. There was no fusion, he said, 'and there is very little hope of there ever being any.'[12]

The AFL had 'solved' its own political difficulties by amending its constitution to ban party politics, 'whether they be Democratic, Republican, Socialistic, Populistic, Prohibition, or any other,' from the floor of Federation conventions. Fortunately for Gompers, intra-party squabbling soon weakened the rival American socialist trade-union centre, the Alliance, and left it under the doctrinaire and authoritarian control of Daniel DeLeon. At the turn of the century more moderate and less Marxian socialists then decided to abandon the Socialist Labor party and infiltrate the AFL. They began to sponsor radical resolutions at Federation conventions, and harrassed Gompers by offering left-wing candidates for Federation leadership posts.[13]

The moderate socialists in both the United States and Canada were animated by a passionate humanitarianism. Even some clergymen joined the party, believing that the robber barons had offended Christian ethics. Their anti-capitalism derived more from Bellamy's *Looking Backward* than from Marx's *Das Kapital*. They read J.A. Weyland's *Appeal to Reason* (which had 15,000 Canadian subscribers) and believed with him that 'Socialism is coming. It's coming like a prairie fire and nothing can stop it ... you can feel it in the air. You can see it in the papers. You can taste it in the price of beef ... The next few years will give this nation to the Socialist Party.'[14] All socialists believed in the organization of labour along industrial rather than AFL craft lines; they differed on tactics. The conservative 'slowcialists' endorsed a tactic of 'boring from within' the AFL and urged their followers to join the Federation crafts. More radical leaders like Eugene Debs wished to confront the Federation with dual-unionist organizations and found natural allies in the Western Federation of Miners and its off-shoot, the Western Labor Union. All of these factions and forces, including the industrial unions which were assailing the AFL, soon found expression in Canada.[15]

The first moderate socialist movement in Canada, drawing its inspiration from such groups as the Single Taxers, the Nationalist clubs, the Producers' Exchange, the Anti-Poverty Society, and the Methodist church, was the Canadian Socialist League. It was founded by George Wrigley and his brother, G. Weston Wrigley, in 1899; they announced that Christ had been the first socialist. No doubt the religious overtones helped the Canadian Socialist League to establish seventeen branches throughout the country by 1901, and it began to collect money to place an organizer and lecturer in the field. Well-known American socialists such as Eugene Debs, the Canadian-born Herbert Casson, and George Bigelow stopped in Canada to lecture the faithful. In the spring of 1902 Ontario socialists prepared to participate actively in the provincial election campaign.[16]

The Canadian Socialist League, unlike the Socialist Labor party, worked in harmony with trade unions and urged their members to join the union of their trade. They were actively supported by radical clergymen in Ontario. But the election results in 1902 were disappointing to Ontario socialists. Although they made some inroads in Toronto, where the Trades and Labor Council had pledged both moral and financial support to the four League candidates, none of the nominees came close to winning. The trade-union vote had not been won over from the Grits and Tories, and the small socialist vote split between the Canadian Socialist League and the Socialist Labor party. The most 'successful' candidate received only 425 of 6051 votes polled.[17]

Still, the Canadian Socialist League took comfort in the fact that it had outpolled the Socialist Labor party. The Ontario elections served to emphasize the rapid decline of the DeLeonist party. 'Here in London, the national headquarters [of the Socialist Labor Party],' the *Industrial Banner* noted, 'it could not muster a hundred votes, in East Middlesex [county] it failed to rally a corporal's guard, in Toronto and Hamilton it came out of the contest with sadly reduced and decimated ranks ...'[18] The League's moderate approach had been more effective among trade unionists than had the abusive tactics of the Socialist Labor party. Shortly after the Ontario election, the Wrigleys felt enough confidence in the wave of the future to rename their paper the *Canadian Socialist*. But in contrast to the political situation in Ontario, socialism appeared to be a flood tide in distant British Columbia by September of 1902. The Wrigleys decided to move to Vancouver, where their newspaper became the *Western Socialist*.[19]

Socialism took root in British Columbia when Arthur Spencer of Hamilton, a Canadian Pacific Railway employee, was transferred to Vancouver. Spencer had been a member of a Socialist Labor party branch in Hamilton, and found no difficulty in organizing a socialist group in his new home in December of 1898. The Vancouver cell set up a Trades and Labor Alliance to rival existing trade-union groups, and asked for a seat on the Trades and Labor Council. As could be expected, the craft-dominated central body, whose secretary was an AFL organizer, refused to admit them.[20]

The Socialist Labor party entered British Columbia politics under particularly favourable circumstances. The metal miners in Kaslo and Slocan had combined to elect a progressive to the provincial legislature in 1898. Nanaimo coal miners had elected the secretary of their union, Ralph Smith, to the same legislative body. The two trade-union sympathizers were joined by four other pro-labour men and together they held the balance of power in the Legislative Assembly for the next two years. Suddenly the labour vote became an important factor in provincial politics, since the provincial premier was dependent upon the labourites to maintain a majority in a house characterized by fluid political groupings. The handful of labour representatives extracted five important legislative concessions in 1899, including a measure inaugurating the eight-hour day in metal mines. The flood of labor legislation 'could not fail to impress active unionists with the value of political action.'[21]

Gompers was fully aware of the rise in the political temperature of Federation affiliates in British Columbia. He told George Bartley to 'keep down the political heelers.' They more than anyone 'bring odium upon our cause, prevent its growth, impede its progress.' Political action to advance the interests of the working people, Gompers declared in an obvious gibe at the socialists, 'is a very much different thing than the political party domination by anyone ... to serve the selfish interests of the few.'[22]

By 1900, despite Gompers' views, even Bartley's Trades and Labor Council at Vancouver had begun to act as a political party. The fire in British Columbia was fanned by news from Winnipeg, where that city's trade unionists had secured the election of Arthur Puttee, the editor of a labour paper, to the House of Commons on an independent labour ticket. The Winnipeg unionists had organized a labour party in 1895 and had persuaded Puttee to run. 'You've got to, Art,' they had told him. 'Why you're the only man in the whole movement we can run without losing his job.'[23] The scent of political victory prompted the West Coast unionists to convene organization and nomination meetings, and platforms were drawn up. Some of their ideas, such as the anti-Oriental planks, had been popular in the West for years, and the single tax was still advocated by a few. Many of the newer demands pushed by the Vancouver unionists seemed to stem from the AFL's legislative platform. Yet the Coast unionists diverged from traditional Federation tactics. They set up an independent labour party to offer candidates in the forthcoming provincial elections, and were assisted by several locals of the international craft unions. Ralph Smith toured the mining towns, helped in political organization, worked for the nomination of labour men, and traded upon his prestige and influence as an MLA and as president of the Trades and Labor Congress.[24]

But labour in British Columbia did not speak with one political voice. Socialists on the Vancouver Trades Council had opposed the motion to set up an independent labour party in Vancouver. In 1900 a splinter group from the Socialist Labor party, the United Socialist Labor party, began to inject a revolutionary element into the political picture. Until then the crafts-dominated central bodies in British Columbia had worked only to curb the power of big capital. But the United Socialists proposed to abolish private ownership and substitute a Marxian collectivity. Their attacks cut into Ralph Smith's support on the Coast and on Vancouver Island. Some of the coal miners began to condemn Smith's 'political opportunism,' and only the Vancouver Trades Council, along with AFL organizer J.H. Watson, provided the Trades Congress president with continuing support. Although Smith was victorious at the polls in 1900, none of the other independent labour party or socialist candidates won a federal seat. Both the labour parties and socialists licked their wounds and prepared for the next electoral battle.[25]

The socialist faction received new support from the province's mining areas. The militant Western Federation of Miners began to spread rapidly through the Kootenay, Yale, and Boundary districts. By 1899 the union had set up a district organization, and early in 1900 the AFL organizer traveling through the area reported on the growth of the Federation's rival. He counted over 2800 members in eleven British Columbia mining towns. Rossland alone had 1400 in the Miners' Union. Not all the militant unionists were Americans, he noted; 65 per cent of the Western Federation of Miners' members in Sandon, and about 75 per cent in Whitewater, were British subjects. Fierce opposition from both Canadian and American mine owners tended to push the Miners' leadership into a more radical stance, in politics as well as in trade unionism. Unyielding corporations were a strong promoter of theoretical socialism among unionists. Although the Miners adopted several straight socialist resolutions in 1901, they did not directly endorse the socialist party. The path was still open for both the miners and trade unionists in British Columbia to unite on a common political platform.[26]

The Vancouver Trades Council suggested the creation of a broadly based political body that would attract non-unionists as well as labour men. The miners also seemed to favour an all-inclusive grouping and called for a convention of delegates from provincial labour and reform bodies to meet at Kamloops in the spring of 1902. The sixty-three delegates who gathered there on 14 April spoke for nineteen locals of the Western Federation of Miners, seven railroad unions, ten other locals, seven trades councils, three labour parties, seven socialist groups, and a single tax club. Twenty-three delegates were members of the Western Federation of Miners alone, but several coastal labour leaders were present, including George Bartley and J.H. Watson. Both these men still held their AFL organizer's commissions. A new political group, the Provincial Progressive party, was launched with a label and platform broad enough to appeal to many reformers as well as to discontented farm and small business interests.[27]

The Kamloops convention and its political offspring did not succeed in papering over the chasm between doctrinaire socialists and pragmatic politicians in British Columbia trade-union circles. The core of the Progressive party never moved far from the metal-mining districts; as the miners drifted further to the left, the political gap widened. Two months later the split became unbridgeable when the Western Federation of Miners, at its convention in Salt Lake City, formally endorsed socialism and founded the American Labor Union to challenge the AFL throughout all of North America. The American Labor Union, according to the *Miners' Magazine,* planned to 'unfurl its flag in every state in the Union' and 'force the Gompers brigade to keep step to the music of progress or eliminate this per capita tax-eating gang from the councils of organized labor.'[28] Two AFL men who had come to urge the miners' re-affiliation with the Federation were politely received. But the fiery Eugene Debs swept the miners off their feet and carried the hour in his address to the convention.

The actions at Salt Lake City doomed the Provincial Progressive party. The British Columbia vice-president of the miners opposed the resolution endorsing socialism and refused re-election after its passage. He was replaced by a socialist, and socialists in the British Columbia sections of the miners began to move slowly to strengthen their position. Debs himself took time to assist them after the convention. On a speaking tour in British Columbia in July 1902 he denounced the Provincial Progressive party. It was a haven, he said, for 'anarchists, single taxers, direct-legislationists, cast-off capitalist politicians, and many honest, but misguided men, who know little or nothing about socialism ... The party has no mission except to retard the progress of the bonafide socialist movement ... in twelve months, or less, it will have ceased to exist.'[29] At Vancouver, Revelstoke, Slocan, Nelson, Phoenix, and other towns, Debs helped to wean the socialists away from the moderate Provincial Progressive party. He was opposed by men such as Chris Foley, who endorsed independent political action. But Foley's second electoral defeat in late 1902 helped bring about the downfall of the moderate party and boosted the socialist cause.

Thus Debs's prediction came true. He advised British Columbia workers to endorse 'a straight-cut class conscious socialist party' and avoid parties that sought 'to harmonize the conflicting interests of the classes involved in the class struggle.'[30] After Debs moved on to American cities, many unionists in British Columbia remembered his words and prepared to follow his advice. Indeed, socialism did appear to be approaching flood tide in the Coast province, and it is understandable why the Wrigley brothers planted their socialist paper in such fertile ground.

Certainly the paper's circulation in the West must have exceeded its Toronto figures, because 'class-struggle' literature fell on rather deaf ears in Ontario. Trade unionists were more numerous in that province, most closely tied with international craft unionism, more generously distributed among manufacturing and building trades and less concentrated in raw materials industries. No mere handful of monopolists dominated the industrial community in Ontario. Many Eastern unionists could readily agree with *The Toiler* on the existence of 'an identity of interest between capital and labour.'[31] Yet the political and legislative victories of trade unionists in British Columbia after 1898 had a profound effect on labour in Eastern Canada.

Delegates to the Trades and Labor Congress convention at Montreal in 1899 noted the sharp contrast between the reports of labour leaders from British Columbia and those from Ontario. The former had reported 'every instance crowned with success;' the latter had told of gaining nothing from their presentations to provincial political leaders.[32] The only solution, the Ontario leaders had suggested, was to follow the example of their brethren in the West. John Flett, a member of the Ontario executive committee, promptly called for a referendum among Congress affiliates. Locals were to be asked whether they would provide moral and financial assistance to independent labour candidates. The negative reaction of the resolutions committee provoked an animated debate on the floor of the Congress. Flett told the delegates that it 'was time for the labor men to come out from the old parties and dismiss the old methods.' He urged them to stop going to the government with petitions, and 'asking it to do this or do that.'[33] The division within the ranks of Canadian labour between East and West, between opponents and supporters of political action, was evident to all. Yet for the moment at least, the West's political victories were sufficient to win Eastern trade unionists over to Flett's resolution. The motion was unanimously adopted, and the referendum vote was taken later that year.[34]

J.H. Sullivan, the AFL's fraternal delegate to the Trades Congress who had witnessed the debates and resolutions on the floor of the Canadian national trade-union centre, told the AFL convention delegates about it a few weeks later. The Canadians had adopted a resolution which called for direct labour representation in legislatures 'on lines similar to the organized workers of Great Britian, British Columbia, New Zealand and Australia.' The Canadian fraternal delegate to the AFL, D.A. Carey, also made special mention of the miners of British Columbia in his speech to the Americans. They had developed the principles of unionism to such an extent 'that they're practicing what they preach and have a miner on the floor of the legislature to make known their wants.' To many American radicals and political minded unionists, it must have appeared that the Canadians were staking out advanced ground in North American trade-union circles. In Gompers' mind it was doubtless too far advanced.[35]

On the floor of the AFL convention a 'slowcialist' printer from Cleveland introduced a motion paralleling the Canadian statement. His resolution called on the Federation to recommend that American labour bodies 'use their ballots, their political power on independent lines from the capitalistic parties, in harmony with the action of our brother trade unionists of Europe, Australia, Canada, and other civilized communities, based on their class interests as wageworkers.' The AFL rules committee remained faithful to Gompers' political principles and offered a substitute motion which urged American labour to use its political power, but only in accordance with the Federation's previous declarations. After some debate, the more radical proposal which had been inspired in part by Canadian labour's political victories was dropped, and the rules committee's substitute was adopted. The convention approved the second $100 legislative lobbying grant to the Trades and Labor Congress. Of course the money was supposed to be used to win legislative favours from the existing parties, as the AFL was accustomed to doing.[36]

By the time the Trades Congress met in convention in September of 1900, Arthur Puttee's by-election victory in Winnipeg had added more fuel to trade-union demands in Canada for independent labour political action. The Manitoba labour leaders told of the 'immense benefit' gained by them from 'experienced labor representation' in the House of Commons. 'Whatever doubts may have existed in the minds of labor men as to the wisdom of the course ... they have been entirely removed by the success which has attended the presence in Parliament of one direct representative of organized labor.'[37]

The Congress's executive committee reported on the results of the referendum called for in 1899. Only forty-four Congress affiliates, with a membership of 2932, had voted, but these men had endorsed the call for political action by an overwhelming vote of 1424 to 167. Unionists in Ottawa, Hamilton, London,

Winnipeg, and cities in British Columbia voted in favour. 'Five years ago such action would have been impossible and speaks volumes for the great advancement that is taking place ...' the *Industrial Banner* declared. But the small number of locals who participated in the poll reflected one of the obstacles which international unionism offered to labour politics in Canada. The Cigarmakers' local in Toronto, for example, had declined to vote, 'as Constitution of International is against political action of any kind.' A Congress committee noted the meagre tally of votes and declared that it did not indicate the sentiment of organized labour in Canada on the issue. Others, including John Flett, declared the vote to be sufficient to justify proceeding along independent political lines. A long discussion showed that all were anxious to promote the interests of labour, but opponents felt the move toward a labour party was advancing too rapidly. The resolution was finally approved by a vote of 38 to 22. Later, Trades Congress leaders appealed for contributions to the expenses of labour candidates in the forthcoming elections. 'Though the question whether or not the Congress should advise independent political action found the leaders divided,' the *Globe* reported, 'it was only on the ground that such a course might retard the rate of progress already attained.'[38]

There was no question where the Trades and Labor Congress of 1900 stood on socialism, even of the moderate variety. The Canadian Socialist League sent G. Weston Wrigley to the deliberations, but the Congress overwhelmingly refused to seat him. The delegates resolved that only political candidates with at least a year's membership in a trade union were eligible for selection or endorsement by the Trades Congress. Thereby, a good many 'gentlemen' socialists were denied any Trades Congress backing.[39]

It is apparent that the Trades Congress in 1900 had staked out a political position to the 'left' of the Grits and Tories, but had also spurned the advances of the moderate Canadian socialists and remained to the 'right' of that political option. At the same time organized labour in Canada was beginning to attract the attention and powerful blandishments of the reigning Liberal party. Under the guidance of Sir William Mulock, the Laurier government passed an act in 1900 authorizing the creation of boards of conciliation to facilitate bargaining in labour-management disputes. The act also established a Department of Labour to collect statistics, provide conciliation services, and publish a monthly magazine devoted to labour matters. Finally, Mulock appointed Daniel J. O'Donoghue as 'fair wages officer' to enforce payment of prevailing wages on all government contracts. At least three other prominent trades unionists found positions in the federal or Ontario government that year.[40]

At the Trades Congress convention, a few delegates expressed doubt over the government's motives; it was a 'sop' thrown to 'put off,' they alleged. But the majority felt that much had been accomplished by a government which had earnestly dealt with labour questions 'in a fair and non-partisan spirit' and had enacted laws sanctioned by public opinion. The appointment of trade unionists to government office was highly praised at the convention.[41]

The reasons for the Laurier administration's new policies were not difficult to fathom. The government faced an electoral contest a month following the labour session and was not strong in Ontario. In fact the federal Conservatives went on to win a majority of 22 in the province, and Laurier, as Sir John Willison later put it, 'never wooed Ontario again.' The Liberals kept trying, however, and their policy was quite simple. By agreeing to labour's 'reasonable' demands, the Liberals hoped that Trades Congress leaders would abandon their attempts to organize a labour party. 'It is as you know not an easy matter to keep a new political party [i.e., a labour party] in existence,' one Liberal worker wrote Laurier, 'especially where a progressive party is moving to advance its lines.' Both Laurier and Mulock put in an appearance at the closing banquet of the Trades Congress convention in 1900 to woo the labour vote. Mulock received 'a most complimentary welcome,' the *Globe* said. Laurier spoke briefly and noted 'with pleasure' the presence of labour representatives in the Commons. 'Titles do not make the man,' said Sir Wilfrid. 'If there is an aristocracy in this country, it is the aristocracy of labor, to which all belong.' His words were reminiscent of Macdonald's attempt a quarter century before to win the affections of labour by passing himself off as a 'cabinetmaker.'[42]

Even the Department of Labour's new deputy minister felt the pressure to garner votes for the Liberal party. Mackenzie King fully supported the appointment of trade unionists and labour men as correspondents for his *Gazette*. The Liberal cause was helped along in labour circles by the Canadian Manufacturers' Association's hostility to the new department and its magazine. 'The fact that the Manufacturers are so pronounced against it is certainly a testimony in its favor,' one labour paper noted.[43]

Many witnessed the new Grit tactics with varying degrees of distaste. Apparently the party readily succeeded in burrowing into the ranks of the burgeoning trade-union movement between 1900 and 1902. At any rate, D.A. Carey, upon his return from the AFL convention, advised his fellow Canadians to give less prominence to politicians and political action at Trades Congress meetings. 'I do think,' Carey concluded, 'that in the interest of all concerned it would be better for labor and its leaders in this country to follow the example of the American Federation of Labor and confine the future in a stricter sense [to] legislation for labor pure and simple.'[44]

Although supporters of independent political action had two men on the floor of the Commons, Canadian unionists still needed the Laurier government's good will. Smith and Puttee could introduce labour legislation from their newly won seats, but it took a government-led majority to enact all bills into laws. Hence the Trades Congress leaders still relied very much on a formal annual meeting with Laurier and key cabinet ministers. At these meetings, which had been the custom for several years, Trades and Labor Congress resolutions were laid before the government ministers. The AFL's legislative grant had been appropriated to subsidize this particular endeavour, and Gompers went to even greater lengths to strengthen it. Upon the Congress secretary's request, the Federation leader lent Flett's services for a week without cost. Even more important, the Federation raised its annual grant to $200. Trades Congress officers hoped to appoint a full-time lobbyist at Ottawa in 1902, but their financial weakness forced them to rely again upon an annual presentation. Flett again lent his assistance.[45]

In that year the AFL's general organizer appeared before the highest leaders of both the federal and Ontario governments to lobby on behalf of the Congress. His political views had moved several degrees closer to AFL principles since the time seven years before when he had endorsed seating the Socialist Labor party at the Trades Congress convention. In 1900 he had voted against seating even the more moderate Canadian Socialist League delegate. He still supported independent political action, but he was above all a realist. While power remained in Liberal hands, labour had to seek concessions through the Laurier government. At Ottawa in 1902, Flett presented the case for an eight-hour day for employees of government railways. He laid special emphasis 'on the hard and wearing work of railway employees, and expressed the belief that the Government only needed to have the facts pointed out to grant this request.' As was often the case, the government possessed unrevealed 'facts' which made inaction more attractive.[46]

Both the Grits and Tories had access to wealth unavailable to trade-union candidates. Labour's independent political action, like any venture into politics, needed money in large quantities. The Manitoba executive committee of the Trades and Labor Congress had pointed out in 1901 that Puttee's narrow election victory had been dearly bought by labour groups in Winnipeg. The Manitobans had called upon the Congress to raise money itself or through locals unwilling or unable to sponsor candidates. 'If definite steps along this line were taken,' they had concluded, 'it would enhance the prospects of election of many more such men as we have succeeded in sending to Ottawa.'[47]

But the Trades Congress faced the same disabilities in pursuing a course of independent political action as in organizing the unorganized. Only 135 of the 871 trade-union locals in Canada bothered to affiliate with the Congress in 1901. Most of the unaffiliated locals had been chartered by the international unions or the AFL and paid their dues to American headquarters. Benefit payments and strike funds were administered from across the line. The Trades Congress could not compel Canadian locals to affiliate or pay Congress assessments; it could only woo them into the fold by the promise of legislative benefits. Canadian trade unionists agreed on the need for ameliorative legislation; they disagreed on political tactics. Supporters of independent political action wanted to operate from a trade-union base, but found it difficult to bring together various locals whose organizational and monetary ties led southward. In some cases the political policies of Canadian locals, as the Toronto Cigarmakers' local had revealed, reflected an essentially American attitude. The very weakness of the trade-union base forced independent labour candidates to seek alliances with the Liberals, who were increasingly amenable to such agreements as organized labour grew in political potency.

Before the expansion of the AFL into Canada in the late 1890s, both the Liberal and Conservative parties had been able to siphon off the political currents within the Canadian labour movement. But more and more politically conscious wage workers were infected by radical notions that swept through North America in the wake of industrialization, and most of the panaceas demanded political action on the part of labour. In British Columbia, the concentration of the province's wealth in the hands of a few, especially in the mining industry, led unionists there to take up political weapons as well as to affiliate with the radical American union in that region, the Western Federation of Miners. In Eastern Canada only a handful of trade unionists embraced the socialist movement during those years at the turn of the century when the international crafts and the AFL gained strength in Ontario and Montreal.

Independent labour politics in British Columbia, coupled with the weakness of the closely matched political factions, paid off between 1898 and 1900 when the labour politicians held the balance of power in the provincial legislature. Then a split over tactics, augmented by the turmoil from strikes in the mining areas at that time, drove a wedge between supporters of independent political action and the socialists. The former wanted to exert leverage on the Grit party, but the doctrinaire radicals campaigned for *Der Tag*. The Provincial Progressive party made a last ditch effort to unite the two factions in a common course of political action, and failed when the Western Federation of Miners decided to ride along on Eugene Debs' 'Red Special' in mid-1902. Hence, radical labour politics in the Coast province led to a split with the Eastern-based Trades and Labor Congress, and to affiliation of elements in the labour movement of the Canadian West with the Western Federation of Miners-American Labor Union combination. By 1902, these dual unions threatened the AFL throughout the North American continent.

The success of British Columbia labour politics at the turn of the century generated shock waves throughout North American labour circles. In the United States, the AFL leadership managed to beat back 'slowcialist' challenges on the convention floor. In contrast, influential labour leaders in Canada took up the cry for independent political action, and were able to point to at least two victories – Smith's at Nanaimo, and Puttee's at Winnipeg – by the end of 1900. But independent political action in Eastern Canada was hindered by two considerable obstacles: (1) the hesitancy or inability of many international union locals to engage in politics, and (2) the moves by the Liberal party to direct labour's interests and desires into its own orbit. Smith and Puttee did not hold the balance of power in the House, and still found it necessary to deal with the Laurier government in order to secure political results. Their dependency was augmented by the fact that the Canadian trade unionists' international union tie left the Trades and Labor Congress weak and impoverished, and left labour candidates or officeholders prey to the enticements of Liberal politicians.

The saga of Ralph Smith provided a case in point. Before the federal elections in British Columbia in 1900, the Liberal party had sought an accommodation with labour forces. After Smith agreed to run for parliament in the Nanaimo constituency, he responded to Liberal overtures. 'Although I am interested in independent labor representation,' Smith told Laurier, 'I can assure you Sir that [it] is the liberal cause for which I have strong sympathy.' Laurier indicated that there would be no by-election in Smith's riding, and hinted that a general election was imminent. Smith began his campaign preparations, and won the seat on an independent labour platform. Laurier sent his 'sincere congratulations on your splendid victory as well as my thanks for the same.'[48] Clearly, Smith depended upon the Liberals for funds and patronage, and Laurier hoped to snuff out a third-party challenge to his government.

The growing split between independent labour politics and socialism in British Columbia struck Nanaimo earlier than elsewhere, and Smith found himself under attack from the left. The split within the ranks of the Nanaimo miners' association quickly grew too deep to heal. The miners turned away not only from Smith, but also from the Trades Congress of which he was president. The Nanaimo radicals charged that the Trades and Labor Congress had become a part of the Liberal political machine and that a number of its leaders were employees or favourites of the Laurier administration. The miners saw no benefits to be derived from recent Federal legislation on labour matters. Besides, the Congress had been of no help to them during strikes – it had no defence fund. In mid-1902 the Nanaimo miners repudiated their affiliation with the Congress and decided to join the Western Federation of Miners.[49] By this action Ralph Smith's trade-union supporters were swept away from him in the socialist tide of

1902, and his political future became all the more dependent upon the Grits. Politics was a risky business, and independent labour politics even more so.

In the eyes of many unionists in British Columbia, the success of Liberal tactics provided sufficient reason for them to break with the Trades Congress and establish ties with the Western Federation of Miners and American Labor Union. And as we shall see, the Liberals in Eastern Canada, with Ralph Smith's assistance as president of the Trades and Labor Congress, appear to have begun consolidating their inroads into the Canadian labour movement by moving to establish a purely national labour organization. It is apparent, then, that political unionism in both Eastern and Western Canada soon spawned dual-union threats to the American Federation of Labor and its affiliates. The new enemies emerged at a time of apparent strength, but of actual vulnerability, for the Federation. It had grown by leaps and bounds in the preceding three years, but the membership had not yet been 'digested' and was easily wooed away by siren calls of dissenting voices.

6
Dual unions

As exchanges between the Trades and Labor Congress and the American Federation of Labor on political as well as other matters grew more frenetic, a new and ambitious secretary took over the job of guiding the Congress's destiny. The retiring officer, George Dower, had initiated the correspondence with the AFL in 1896, and those missives had led first to the exchange of fraternal delegates, and later to the AFL legislative grant. But Dower apparently did not understand French and was unable to supervise the publication of the French edition of the Congress *Proceedings*. In 1900 a special committee of the Trades Congress found him negligent in this aspect of his duties. The Congress elected a new and bilingual secretary, Patrick M. (Paddy) Draper, to succeed Dower.[1]

A thirty-two-year-old native of the Ottawa valley with an Irish-Canadian background, Draper had become a compositor at the government printing bureau in 1888. He had enlisted in the Ottawa local (no. 102) of the International Typographical Union at the same time. A very popular young printer, he had served later as the local's secretary, and had been its president since 1893. In 1897 Draper had been a dominant figure in the re-organization of Ottawa's central body, the Allied Trades and Labor Association.[2] The new secretary brought ideas and vigour to the Trades and Labor Congress of Canada at a critical time in its history. Draper was a Canadian nationalist who, avoiding the fringes of the labour movement, won perennial re-election and served as secretary of the Congress for an unprecedented thirty-five years. He became president the year before his retirement. At the close of his career, friends who had often heard Draper 'call a spade a spade' affectionately presented him with a silver-plated shovel.[3]

Draper laboured to make the Trades and Labor Congress into a smoothly functioning national trade-union centre. He provided books, ordered stationery, and sent circulars to Canadian locals urging affiliation with the Trades Congress. In early 1902 he broadcast the Congress message in 5000 six-page folders, sent along with application forms to central bodies across the country. The Congress's revenue more than doubled within two years, and Draper set up a tiny office with a couple of desks and a typewriter.[4]

In one of Gompers' first letters to Draper, the AFL leader asked the new Trades Congress secretary to write a summary of the year's progress in the Canadian labour movement. Gompers wanted the information for his report to the AFL convention, since the American and Canadian labour movements, he asserted, were so closely allied in interests and organization. He told the Federation delegates later that year that 'the labor movement in Canada is part of our own; and we have endeavoured to encourage our fellow workers by advice and such practical assistance as was within our power.'[5] The Canadian fraternal delegate confirmed Gompers' assessment. 'The memberships of the Trade Unions have increased beyond every expectation during the past year,' he said, 'and it is all due to the fact of the American Federation of Labor placing a Canadian organizer [John Flett] in the field.'[6]

At a time when international economic competition and expansion was uppermost in the minds of many Americans, Gompers' public speeches reflected his growing conviction that the AFL would achieve predominance over the whole continent. Gompers still endorsed the goal of a world-wide labour movement, but this vision had receded somewhat further on the horizon. Gompers and other international union leaders became convinced of the necessity of first consolidating labour forces throughout the North American continent under AFL authority before proceeding to a marriage with European trade unions. The geopolitics of American labour statesmen began coinciding with the outlook of many American business and political leaders. Continental unification, these men believed, was both desirable and inevitable, and only time would tell whether economic expansion presaged political union.

The consequences of this kind of thinking for Canadian labour were two-fold. First, American labour leaders stressed the similarities rather than the differences between the American and Canadian labour movements. In addition they envisioned the Canadian organizations in a distinctly subsidiary role to the American groups. For example W.D. Mahon, who had represented the Federation at the Trades Congress convention in 1900, told the AFL convention later that year that workers in both countries faced the same conditions. 'They are, like us, a cosmopolitan people, having workers of all nationalities to contend with ...' Mahon then revealed what he and other international union heads had concluded from the similarity of labour conditions in both countries: he drew a parallel between the Trades and Labor Congress and state federations of labour in the United States. 'The Congress compares more nearly to our State Federations than it does to the American Federation of Labor,' he declared, 'as the object of the Congress is to secure legislation for the workers, and it does not deal with any trade disputes ...'[7] At an early date, Canadians appeared destined for 'statehood' in the North American labour world.

Draper was not an enemy of international unions in Canada, but it is clear that he hoped to transform the Trades Congress into an effective national centre with a status equivalent to that of the AFL. He noted in mid-1901 that the Trades Union Congress of Great Britain represented the working people of that country in the same manner that the American Federation of Labor personified the wage earners of the United States; he concluded that the Trades and Labor Congress of Canada was 'equally independent, important and necessary ... within its own scope and realm.' However 'scope and realm' might be interpreted, Draper envisioned the Trades and Labor Congress as something more than a state federation under AFL hegemony. Under Draper's guidance, for example, the Trades Congress immediately began to exercise vigorously the one essential power that no American state federation possessed – the power to charter unions and central labour bodies.[8]

Draper obtained an opportunity to express his views to Gompers at their first face-to-face meeting in June of 1901. Gompers had been invited to speak at the convention of the International Association of Machinists in Canada and arranged to meet both Draper and Flett in his rooms at the Palmer House in Toronto. Apparently the three men had a frank discussion 'on matters of interest affecting the relationship of the Labor movement of the United States and Canada.' At the conclusion of their talks, the AFL leader entertained Draper at the Pan-American Exposition in Buffalo. Later, in response to a request from Draper, Gompers drew up a letter requesting Canadian locals of the international unions to affiliate with the Trades Congress.[9]

Draper's first Trades and Labor Congress convention as secretary met at Brantford, Ontario, in September of 1901. John Flett returned from his organizing trip in the Maritimes to attend the gathering. For the first time in the history of the Canadian labour movement, all the provinces were represented on the floor of the convention. Delegates had been sent by thirty-four union locals, two Congress-chartered federal labour unions, three district assemblies and ten local assemblies of the Knights of Labor, two local federations of trade unions, and si· .een trades and labour councils. Into this mixed gathering the Congress president, Ralph Smith, dropped a bombshell.[10]

In all likelihood Smith had become the agent for a plan by Laurier and Sir William Mulock to nationalize the Canadian labour movement.[11] Near the end of his presidential address, he proposed the creation of a Canadian federation of labour. 'I think it is of vast importance that this Congress should adopt some method of increasing its own usefulness,' he began.

There ought to be a Canadian Federation, for whilst I believe that unionism ought to be international in its methods to meet the necessity of combatting common foes, this usefulness is only assured by the strength of national unions. A federation of American union[s] represented by a national union [the AFL], and a Federation of Canadian unions represented by a national [a CFL], each working with the other in special cases, would be a great advantage over having local unions in Canada connected with the national unions of America.[12]

The Trades Congress president also suggested that American citizens should not participate in the settlement of Canadian industrial disputes. He was not critical of their behaviour in Canada, but he was convinced 'that there are such distinctive differences in the condition of each that a presentment of Canadian matters by Canadian leaders, and vice versa by American leaders would lead to a greater success and would not in any way prevent a Federation of the national bodies.'[13]

Smith's plea had Grit politics written all over it. The remark about Canadians settling Canadian disputes nicely dovetailed with employers' condemnations of 'foreign agitators' – international union officials accused of crossing the boundary with the intent of disrupting Canadian production.[14] Smith acknowledged that labour faced a 'common foe' which had to be dealt with through 'international methods,' yet he seemed to contradict himself when he asserted that only national unions could adequately reflect the Canadian environment. His plea attempted to win over the disgruntled from both the managerial and working classes. A Trades Congress committee approached Smith's suggestion in a gingerly manner reminiscent of the way in which similar proposals had been handled six years before. A special panel was authorized to investigate and report to the Congress at the session in 1902. The Congress also chose to send Draper to the forthcoming AFL convention as its fraternal delegate.[15]

When Gompers learned of these events, he invited the Trades Congress secretary to meet the AFL executive council before the Federation convention had assembled. Upon arrival, Draper asked the Americans to increase their legislative grant. He undoubtedly used Smith's proposals to advantage in his conferences with Federation officials, and the council raised its annual gift to $300. At the AFL convention a few days later, Draper made it clear that he had no desire to see the Trades Congress become an appendage of the Liberal party. '... A very strong feeling is growing in Canada in favor of National Unions, arising out of criticisms of our opponents, who say that Yankee labor leaders are responsible for many strikes in Canada.' Draper quoted Ralph Smith's call for a Canadian national trade-union structure, and concluded his speech with a plea for action by the international unions. Later Draper was told that he had made a strong impression upon the AFL directors. But the Canadian politicians' scheme was only one of a number of challenges menacing international unions in 1902.[16]

At the same AFL convention in 1901 where Draper had spoken, a resolution was introduced which threatened the whole structure of international craft unionism. It called upon the convention to amalgamate the different crafts employed in the same industry 'so as to present a solid front and increase the solidity of all workmen irrespective of trades.'[17] The motion reflected the fact that technological advances and new machinery had brought chaos to traditional lines of jurisdiction between the crafts. It proposed that the AFL alleviate the problem by replacing the craft system with an industrial type of organization. However, Gompers and the international union heads maintained that the laws of trade-union growth dictated organization only along craft lines. They feared the instabilities and political tendencies of labour bodies which accepted all workers within a given factory. Mixing skilled with unskilled workers was 'as impractical as endeavouring to mix oil and water, for the oil will persistently seek the higher level.'[18]

The motion calling for industrial unionism was referred to a special five-man committee on trade autonomy, presided over by Gompers himself. This blue-ribbon panel handed down a report, later known as the Scranton declaration, which gave a ringing endorsement to the craft system of trade-union organization. No radical departure was made from traditional AFL practice. The panel asserted that the interests of workers throughout North America would be best advanced by 'adhering as closely to that [craft] doctrine as the recent great changes in methods of production and employment make practicable.'[19]

The Scranton declaration was laid down alongside the principle of 'voluntarism,' because one of the key AFL affiliates, the United Mine Workers, happened to be an industrial union. 'Voluntarism' meant that each trade had the right to decide its own policies and principles without outside interference. In reality it meant that powerful unions like the UMW were permitted to adopt an industrial organization, but the carpenters, machinists, and other strong crafts would not allow weaker unions to organize upon the same heretical principles.[20]

The Scranton declaration was not only a product of the impact of technology on craft unions, it was also a response to the challenge from the West. Before the Federation convention in late 1901 Gompers had sent a circular letter to all international unions in which he had called attention to the Western Labor Union's activities. The Executive Council had instructed Gompers to urge the international unions to send organizers into the mountain west 'so as to endeavor to offset the movement on the part of the Western Labor Union.' The Federation also had dispatched an organizer to the scene.[21] But these moves failed to stop the Western Federation of Miners, at its convention in May 1902, from converting the Western Labor Union into a continental challenge to the AFL (the American Labor Union). A month later the president of the Shoe Workers' International Union reported to AFL secretary Morrison that the American Labor Union (ALU) had successfully crossed the Mississippi River and had recently issued charters to shoe trade supply workers at Lynn and Haverill, Massachusetts. 'There is talk of organizing a Central Labor Union under a charter from the American Labor Union ...' he added.[22]

Eugene Debs argued that Westerners were only acting defensively against AFL threats to wipe them out. He said that the threat of dual unionism had provoked the Federation to spend more money and work harder in the West than ever before. But the Western Labor Union-American Labor Union challenge, he admitted, was based on more than feelings of neglect. 'It is certain that there is to-day a radical fundamental difference between the Eastern and Western wings of the American Labor movement and that in their present state and with their present conflicting policies and tendencies, they can not be united[;] and if they could be, factional and sectional strife would be at once engendered and disruption would be inevitable.'[23]

The West stood for industrial unionism and radical political action; the East endorsed craft organization and legislative lobbying. Across the border, radical unionists in the Canadian West looked at their relations with the Trades Congress in the same light in mid-1902, and turned from the Trades and Labor Congress to the American Labor Union. The secretary of the socialist party in Nanaimo helped lead the attack on the Trades Congress and its president. In fact, he called Ralph Smith the 'Gompers of Canada.'[24]

At the same time a new ALU-associated industrial union, the United Brotherhood of Railway Employees (UBRE), widened the continental division between Eastern and Western labour. Leaders of the UBRE set out to band together into one trade union the thousands of men employed on American railroads and on the Canadian Pacific and Canadian Northern lines. Locals had been planted in Winnipeg and Vancouver by the end of June 1902, when Winnipeg machinists decided to strike against the Canadian Northern. Although the conservative running-trade brotherhoods remained at work and Eastern unionists offered little sympathy to the strikers, the UBRE promptly joined the contest. When the new industrial union, struggling alone, failed to win a clear-cut victory, the Trades and Labor Congress bore the backlash of Western anger.[25]

The failure of Eastern trade unionists to come to the aid of the United Brotherhood of Railway Employees prompted a secessionist movement in British Columbia. The Phoenix Trades Council withdrew from the Trades Congress and endorsed the Socialist party. The Fernie central body refused to affiliate with the Congress. Then the Victoria Trades Council withdrew from the Trades Congress and took out a charter from the American Labor Union. 'The old-time [trade union] workers,' George Bartley and J.H. Watson reported later, 'have temporarily stepped aside and allowed the political socialists to run their course.'[26]

Little appeared to stand in the way of a steady march by the United Brotherhood of Railway Employees across the continent toward Ontario. The form of the challenge to the AFL, as well as some of the tactics, were revealed by the president of the United Brotherhood. He told his organizer to write articles designed to win public sentiment for industrial unionism, and split the rank and file in the AFL from its leadership. 'In this way you will constantly stimulate and augment a great public sentiment for the U.B.R.E. – for Industrial Unions, for the A.L.U., and for Socialism (but don't use the word) and against capitalism and the Gompers faction which is working in harmony with Marcus A. Hanna and the infamous civic federation to keep down the masses of the people.'[27]

Clearly, the AFL faced a real threat from left-wing dual unionism in 1902 – perhaps the biggest menace since de Leon's challenge in the 1890s. The ALU and the UBRE were contesting international craft unionism on both sides of the forty-ninth parallel. If the leftist dual unionists captured or destroyed the Trades and Labor Congress, they could then launch an attack on the international craft unions in the United States from their Canadian haven. Gompers personally wielded the power to keep these groups at bay in the United States, but he had no assurance that Draper and the Trades Congress would survive a left-wing assault.

In addition to the machinations of the Liberal party and radical unionists in Canada, the American craft unions were troubled by rumours of secession among Canadian unionists. These difficulties were linked to the rapid expansion of the craft unions in Canada during the preceding years. Some locals chafed under the new restrictions that devolved from their affiliation with international union headquarters in the United States. Others resented the high level of dues, and feared that their hard-earned money would be squandered or misspent by union officials. In the event of dishonest union officialdom, legal recourse for the Canadians was bound to be complicated. J.H. Watson, the AFL volunteer organizer who had climbed on Ralph Smith's Liberal party bandwagon, reported strong sentiment in Vancouver against the flow of union money to the AFL. 'Our local International Unions get no benefit from the American Federation of Labor,' he insisted, 'but they do get help from the Dominion Trades Congress, through legislation they get enacted for the benefit of the workers.' He declared that international union payments to the AFL on Canadian membership should be directed instead to the Trades Congress. It was the same complaint which had arisen in 1898, and which the AFL's legislative grant to the Congress had been designed to satisfy.[28]

Just as the complaints of four years before had led to secession movements within some international unions, so also did the grievances of 1901 and 1902. Dissatisfaction broke out in some of the Canadian branches of one of the most powerful AFL affiliates, the United Brotherhood of Carpenters and Joiners. Members in Nelson, British Columbia, argued that Canadian locals of the Carpenters' Union would have flourished far more if they had been directed from a Canadian headquarters. Acting on this notion, they went so far as to try to reorganize the United Brotherhood's Canadian locals into a separate national union. 'We would suggest that a convention be called to meet at some central point, say Winnipeg, Toronto or Ottawa, each organization agreeing to send delegates with instructions to do all they can to help form a central body in Canada, and to discuss other matters of importance.' The Nelson men opined that 'the membership of all organizations would be doubled in one year if all the unions should be brought under one independent Canadian head.' They called for immediate action, and then asked the Trades Congress to grant them a charter.[29]

While Draper wanted to see the Trades Congress become a full-fledged national labour centre, he refused at this point to incur the bitter wrath of the AFL by recognizing the dissident carpenters. His failure to grant this charter provoked criticism. 'I think the time has arrived,' J.H. Watson declared, 'when the Canadian Trades Congress should ... allow unions not wishing to belong to an International Union, to become Federal Labor Unions, chartered by the Congress.'[30] This was precisely what the AFL began to fear might occur. If it did happen, the Trades Congress would undermine the authority of every international union headquarters in dealings with Canadian locals. Instead of obeying a jurisdictional decision, or a dues assessment, or a contract clause, a Canadian local might be tempted to abandon its international headquarters without temerity and find refuge in the Trades and Labor Congress.

Just such a complication appeared to be arising among shoe workers' locals in the province of Quebec. TLC leaders from that province had been trying without success to amalgamate the Canadian Federation of Boot and Shoe Makers, a dual union composed predominantly of French-speaking members, with the Boot and Shoe Workers' International Union. Accepting their failure as final, they persuaded the Canadian dual union to apply for admission into the Trades Congress, and expressed the hope that the independent shoeworkers would be seated at the next convention beside representatives of the international union locals. Indeed, the Quebec labour leaders went even further and asked the Trades Congress to grant a charter to *any* local that applied for it. That suggestion, if acceded to, would have removed the deference paid by the TLC to international union jurisdictions and would have led to a plethora of dual unions throughout Canada.[31]

In Eastern as well as Western Canada, the AFL craft unions faced disruption within their ranks. Remnants of the Knights of Labor assemblies remained in control of the Central Trades Council in Montreal. Both the Central Council and the crafts-dominated Federated Council sent delegates to TLC conventions, but the Federated Council campaigned to obtain the expulsion of the Knights' representatives, partly because the presence of a competing central body in Montreal gave encouragement to secessionist movements within the international locals of that city. Moreover, the competition for new affiliates made it doubly difficult for the craft-dominated Federated Trades Council to adhere strictly to jurisdictional lines. In the fall of 1901 Gompers received a complaint that the AFL-chartered Federated Council was harbouring an independent group of lasters in violation of the AFL constitution. The Shoe Workers' International Union had affiliated three locals to the Federated Trades Council and expected to add three more, the informant stated, but their efforts were hindered by the lasters. The Federated Trades Council, it seems, had originally admitted the lasters in order to keep them from moving over to the Central Council. But instead of imbibing the international spirit, they were 'corrupting such International feelings as may have heretofore existed in the Council.'[32]

The rivalry between these two central bodies, augmented by the ancient friction between the crafts and the Knights, created a situation favourable to the Liberal party's schemes. Gompers was told that some of the locals affiliated with the Federated Trades Council were leaning toward the Canadian federation of labour 'as outlined by Ralph Smith ... at the recent session' of the TLC.[33] Then, in May or June of 1902, Congress secretary Draper put the stamp of legitimacy on the Central Trades Council when he issued that body a TLC charter.[34] Montreal now had the distinction of possessing two central councils, one holding an American and the other a Canadian charter. The situation was not very conducive to harmony between the Federation and the Trades Congress.

Draper's grant of TLC charters to Canadian central bodies provoked a confrontation with the AFL. Draper argued that Canadian city centrals, because of their legislative concerns on the municipal level, required Canadian charters. In May of 1902 he requested some thirty-five trades councils to take out Congress charters. Within a few weeks the Toronto District Council, the Windsor Trades Council, and the aforementioned Central Council in Montreal complied.[35] On the other hand, since 1897 when the AFL had issued its first charter to a Canadian central body (the Montreal Federated Trades Council), Federation organizers had set up councils with American charters in Revelstoke and Victoria, British Columbia, Brockville and Galt-Preston, Ontario, and Charlottetown, Prince Edward Island. Whereas Draper saw city centrals in terms of their legislative functions, Federation leaders considered city centrals to be vital agents enforcing AFL jurisdictional lines at a time when the latter were under great strain from shifts in technology. In order to carry out American labour leaders' orders, city centrals throughout North America were routinely expected to ostracize recalcitrant locals. If an AFL-chartered council dared refuse, Gompers invariably threatened to revoke the council's charter. But what could the AFL do if the rebellious council held a Trades Congress charter? After all, trade-union discipline has always rested upon the threat of expulsion.

In 1902 the first serious conflict to erupt from the presence of two national trade-union centres competing in the same territory broke out on Prince Edward Island. The Congress had chartered the first trade union on the Island when it had formed Federal Labor Union no. 10 from a number of railway employees. In 1901 Flett had arrived in Charlottetown and organized several locals for the AFL, and later a trades council had been chartered by the American Federation. But when the TLC-chartered local presented its credentials and asked for a seat on the council, that AFL-chartered body, acting on the advice of the Federation secretary, refused 'on the ground that they did not belong to an International Union of the American Federation of Labor and consequently could not form part of the general labor movement.' It was a very undesirable state of affairs, the secretary of FLU no. 10 told TLC officers, and he hoped the convention of 1902 would solve the issue. 'Personally,' he added, 'we are strongly of the opinion that Canadian Trade and Labor Councils should be chartered by our Trades Congress.'[36] Draper told Trades Congress delegates that the time had arrived 'when the powers, rights and privileges of this Congress, as the national organization for legislative purposes of the Canadian wage-earner, must be defined.' Until the AFL recognized Congress chartering rights, he thought it useless for the TLC to expend more time or energy on organizing endeavours. Draper believed that the Trades and Labor Congress of Canada needed, at minimum, the power to continue chartering both central bodies and federal labour unions.[37]

Similar uncertainty as to the line between TLC and AFL jurisdictions provoked an outburst from Western Canada in 1902. A Vancouver-based freight handlers' union, chartered by the Trades Congress, had embarked upon an effort to organize Canadian railway freight handlers into a national union. At the same time the International Longshoremen's Association had begun to grant charters to workers in this field. John Flett had awarded Longshoremen's charters to railway freight handlers in Ontario and the Maritimes, and the Vancouver freight handlers were furious. They 'had spent a lot of time and money in communicating with Freight Handlers in Canada, but now their time and labor are lost.' Flett could not serve two masters, the Vancouver unionists argued, and should resign either his Trades Congress vice-presidency or his AFL organizer's post. The Trades Congress was warned that it had little time left to establish a Canadian federation of labour. 'If we are going to do anything for the Trade Union movement in Canada, we must do it at once, or else all our organizations will become American organizations, which I, for one, do not wish to see.'[38]

Besides the Congress-Federation dispute over chartering authority, the two groups disagreed on a major policy issue – compulsory arbitration. The rash of strikes which accompanied the technological changes and trade-union expansion after 1898 provoked widespread public debate throughout North America on the 'labour question,' as it was euphemistically called in those days. One segment of public opinion, influenced by favourable reports from Australia and New Zealand, called for compulsory arbitration of industrial disputes. Proponents of this method assumed that judges or civil servants could intervene impartially and expose the issues to the light of public opinion in order to secure a fair settlement. Gompers, mindful of the damage that government intervention had inflicted on organized labour during the railway strikes of 1877 and the Pullman struggle in 1894, bitterly opposed compulsion from whatever quarter. He feared that strikes would be compromised by legislation subject to a judge's whim. Then again, the AFL stance coincided with the social Darwinist outlook of its leaders. Big Capital could only be tamed by Big Labour; the remedy to industrial conflict would germinate in the industrial, not governmental, garden.[39]

Organized labour in Canada had experienced no such hostile treatment at the hands of the government, and a plank demanding compulsory arbitration was included in the first Trades Congress platform of principles without much controversy at the convention of 1898. By 1901 Ralph Smith publicly noted the divergence between the AFL and the TLC on arbitration. He admitted that Gompers' opposition to compulsory arbitration was 'worthy of consideration' in the American political arena. But conditions were different in Canada, Smith pointed out, and he was convinced that compulsory arbitration was worth a trial.[40]

The Liberals, in a move to satisfy the political demands of organized labour, brought down a compulsory arbitration bill in May 1902. The measure proposed to introduce compulsory arbitration on railways when the disputants were unable to reach a voluntary agreement. It provoked a mixed reaction among trade unionists. While the Hamilton Trades and Labor Council endorsed it, the Brotherhood of Locomotive Engineers, meeting in convention in Toronto, expressed decided opposition. The Brotherhood, with a membership spread over the United States, Canada, and Mexico, had already negotiated contracts with 90 per cent of the railways on the continent, and feared that the Canadian bill would be taken up by other governments in North America to their disadvantage.[41]

Since Gompers shared the fears of the Engineers, he reacted strongly to the Canadian government's moves. First he asked Draper to forward copies of the *Labour Gazette* which had discussed the bill; then he dispatched fifty pamphlets to Draper setting forth the hostile AFL view to the compulsory idea. 'It would be well to distribute these among your organizations,' Gompers told the Canadian, 'and should your [sic] desire more, I would be glad to send them to you.'[42] The AFL leader clearly desired to secure the defeat of any compulsory arbitration legislation in Canada. Not only would the proposed legislation directly affect Canadian locals of the international unions, but it would bring the 'New Zealand approach' a giant step closer to the United States. It was important to the AFL that the Trades Congress abandon its endorsement of compulsory arbitration and actively oppose the Laurier government's measure.

The growing divergence between the Canadian and American labour movements was publicly acknowledged by the American Federation of Labor at its convention in 1901. A committee regretted the secessionist tendencies among Canadian workers. 'Movements of this character not only vitiate Labor's forces but cause general confusion, friction, and sometimes bitter antagonisms – all resulting in injury to our cause and danger to our integrity.' The committee endorsed Gompers' proposal that the AFL send ambassadors to the Western Federation of Miners and to the Trades and Labor Congress, 'with a view to bringing about the unity so essential to the welfare of the toilers of America.' It was necessary, one unionist said, to show 'our Canadian Brothers [that] we recognize no imaginary boundary line and believe all should be under one grand banner marching on together for the protection and assistance of all wage-workers on this Continent.'[43]

During the spring of 1902, Gompers laid plans to counter the dual-unionist threats that had begun to challenge the Federation's supremacy in North America. Matters said to be of the utmost importance, and 'involving the largest interests of our organization and our movement generally,' were placed on the agenda of the AFL Executive Council.[44] Gompers invited TLC secretary Draper to come to AFL headquarters and participate in the discussions. Draper reached Washington, DC, on 14 April and attended some of the Executive Council sessions. He told AFL leaders that the labour movement in Canada was making splendid progress, and attributed the gains to the work of John Flett and the international union organizers who had been put in the field by the American craft organizations. But the TLC secretary admitted that a 'small element' in Canada was opposed to international unions, and recommended that Gompers or Frank Morrison attend the next Trades Congress convention, which was to be held in Berlin (now called Kitchener), Ontario, in September. Meanwhile, in order to carry the battle against dual unionism into the American west, the Executive Council agreed to hold a summer meeting in San Francisco.[45]

On their journey to the Pacific Coast in July, the Federation leaders conducted a vigorous six-week tour through the heart of the Western Federation of Miners-American Labor Union region. At every stop Gompers stressed the need for unity in the labour movement. He publicly hoped that the AFL leaders would accomplish 'the absolute unity of the labor forces in America.' Such unity was essential, he maintained, because of the growing concentration of capital. Boasting of the AFL's two-million-plus membership figures, he intimated that only the Federation could guarantee labour's future prosperity.[46]

Gompers did not hesitate to criticize the AFL's rivals. 'If a Western labor union is a logical argument,' he reasoned, 'so is a Northern and a Southern and Eastern federation of Labor. Our employers do not divide on sectional lines and stop at state boundaries.'[47] Had Gompers spoken in Canadian cities in mid-1902, he undoubtedly would have used the same argument against the proposed Canadian federation of labour. But events unfolded in such a way as to make a personal appearance in Canada unnecessary. In June Draper corresponded with Flett about dual unionism in Canada, and the AFL's Canadian organizer forwarded the letters to Gompers. Then the AFL affiliates in Montreal enlisted their Toronto brethren in their war against the Knights-dominated Central Labor Council of Montreal. At the same time the president of the Boot and Shoe Workers' International Union wrote the Toronto Trades and Labor Council to protest the affiliation of independent locals of the shoeworkers to the TLC. The Toronto unionists, although they listened to Draper's side of the case, cast their lot with the international unions.[48] The stage was set for the momentous deliberations at Berlin.

7
Berlin victory

About 150 delegates gathered at Saengerbund Hall in Berlin, Ontario, on 15 September 1902 to take part in the opening ceremonies of the Trades and Labor Congress convention. Labour representatives from every province in Canada listened to the greeting extended by the acting mayor of this city in German-speaking Ontario. After president Ralph Smith of the Trades Congress had delivered brief welcoming remarks, the delegates got down to business. Smith directed the credentials committee to make its report.[1]

Much of the controversy related to dual unionism was embedded in the problems faced by this Trades Congress committee. They had to decide which trade-union delegates would be recognized and seated. They possessed the power, subject to convention ratification, to draw the line between legitimate organizations and others which they might outlaw. After a great deal of discussion the committee decided to receive the credentials of both the Knights-dominated Central Trades and Labor Council and the crafts-controlled Federated Trades Council of Montreal. But they recommended that the Congress amend its constitution to eliminate dual central bodies. The committee also agreed to seat delegates from two Montreal independent locals (Federal Labor Union no. 36, and a coopers' local), meanwhile urging them to join the international unions of their trades.[2]

The committee was bombarded with other credentials contests. Apparently the dispute in Montreal between the national and international unions of boot and shoe workers touched off the most clamour. On the floor of the Trades Congress convention, John Tobin sat with twelve delegates from the International Boot and Shoe Workers' locals in Canada, who doubtless came fully mobilized to wage war against the Canadian union in their trade. President Tobin probably made strong representations against the seating of rival delegates from the Montreal shoe trades. Finally the credentials committee concluded that the Trades Congress constitution did not permit them to reject the documents of the Canadian Federation of Boot and Shoe Makers (the dual national union), and they urged the Congress to make changes in its constitution.[3]

After the credentials committee's report was read, J.A. Rodier, the president of the Montreal Federated Council, jumped up to move an amendment calling for the exclusion of Central Trades Council delegates. He had attempted the same manoeuver to unseat these dual unionists at the convention the year before. This time Smith ruled the amendment out of order 'and what promised to be a lively debate was averted.'[4] To resolve all these issues, Smith appointed the credentials committee to sit as a special panel to recommend constitutional amendments. He adjourned the convention until the committee could report its suggestions the next day.[5]

Whether Ralph Smith knew it or not, the credentials committee – now the committee on constitutional revision – was heavily weighted with supporters of international unionism. The chairman, Hugh Stevenson of Toronto, was a member of Local 91 of the International Typographical Union and of the International's executive board, as well as a friend of AFL secretary Frank Morrison.[6] Joseph Marks of London, who represented that city's central council at the Congress, was a printer long known for his reform activities and trade-union sympathies. He was also editor of the *Industrial Banner,* the leading labour newspaper in Ontario.[7] J.A. Rodier was a printer and Typographical Union member as well as the bitter enemy of the Knights-dominated Central Council in his city. William Berry of Hamilton belonged to a craft international union, and William Huddlestone was president of the Toronto local of the Stereotypers and Electrotypers' International. A.M. Gossel, a printer who hailed from Winnipeg, was an active supporter of independent political action who endorsed the international viewpoint on trade-union organization. Only two of the nine-member panel consistently endorsed the dual unionist cause. J.S. Fitzpatrick was a prominent member of the Knights of Labor and of a horseshoers' local affiliated with the Central Council in Montreal. The Quebec city Central Council delegate, F.X. Boileau, backed Fitzpatrick's stand, and was probably a member of a local assembly of the Knights of Labor. Finally, the group's secretary, C.S.O. Boudreault, a bilingual printer in the Ottawa local of the Typographical Union and an AFL volunteer organizer, apparently tried to steer a course between the dual unionists and the internationalists.[8]

On the afternoon of Monday, 15 September, the panel devoted several hours to a careful scrutiny of the Trades Congress constitution. The next morning

Boudreault told the convention that the special committee had altered the constitution 'to obviate, in the future, questionable representation calculated to injure the work which ... should be fostered.' Some of the committee's recommendations provoked no debate and were quickly adopted. For example, the national character of the Congress executive committee was enhanced by the addition of vice-presidents from each province. Another section specifically granted Trades and Labor Congress leaders permission to use funds for organizing purposes. But two other amendments proposed by the panel generated an explosion of debate and controversy, and turned the Berlin convention into the most fateful trade-union session in Canadian labour history.[9]

The first proposal forbade the Congress from organizing and chartering locals in trades already staked out by an international or national union. The committee's amendment specifically burdened the Congress officers with responsibility for funneling the membership of Canadian federal labour unions into the international craft unions. Henceforth such groups as the Montreal waiters would not be eligible for a Trades Congress charter. Groups such as the Montreal coopers were to be ordered to affiliate with the Coopers' International Union. The last sentence of the amendment provided 'that no National Union be recognized, where an International Union exists.' This barred the Trades Congress from recognizing the Canadian Federation of Shoe Makers and the Knights of Labor assemblies, or any other union in Canada trespassing upon international union jurisdictional claims.[10]

The other controversial amendment stated that 'in no case shall there be more than one Central Body in any City or Town, said Central Body to be chartered by the Trades and Labor Congress of Canada.' This proposal seemed to clear up the Montreal disturbance to the advantage of the Congress-chartered Central Council. But the special panel recommended at the conclusion of its report that the AFL-chartered Federated Council 'be recognized as the *bona fide* Trade and Labor Council of the City of Montreal.' It also suggested that the Federated Council change its name to 'The Montreal Trades and Labor Council' and take out a charter from the Trades Congress. 'This change will, we believe, be conducive to the reestablishment of peace and harmony in the Metropolis.' Since the two proposals were not to go into effect until January of 1903, the Congress officers were expected to use conciliatory means to harmonize the conflicts.[11]

The internationalists failed to get the whole report adopted in one motion; the convention decided rather to take it up clause by clause. Immediately two dual unionists moved an amendment to the first suggested change, calling upon the Congress to recognize district assemblies of the Knights of Labor. This proposal triggered the full-scale debate, and the remainder of Tuesday afternoon was given over to arguments on it.[12] 'There was a determined fight,' the *Globe* noted, 'in which many hard things were said by delegates on both sides, especially in connection with the unfortunate situation in the Montreal council by the existence of rival trades councils ... French-Canadian members led in the fight for recognition of national organizations.' Delegate Horan of the Waiters' Federal Labor Union no. 36, Montreal, said that the committee's amendments would 'destroy and wreck the labor movement in Quebec.' The Hotel and Restaurant Employees Union would never gain a foothold there, he insisted. Another Montrealer, T.J. Griffiths, who held a card from a Montreal brass workers' independent local, pointed to the division in the Canadian labour movement that would emerge from exclusion of the Knights of Labor. The avowed object of the Trades Congress, he declared, was to unite all of the country's labour organizations. V.H. Annable, one of the delegates from the Ottawa central body, complained that the proposals 'would shut out some of the ablest representatives in the congress.' He may have been thinking of some of the older leaders of Canadian labour, such as D.J. O'Donoghue, George Beales, and P.J. Jobin, who carried credentials to the Berlin convention from assemblies of the Knights of Labor.[13]

Proponents of the constitutional changes counterattacked. Joseph Marks, one of the members of the credentials committee, suggested that the Knights of Labor amalgamate their membership and apply for a federal labour union charter. Of course it would have meant that any Knights in trades with international unions already established would remain excluded or be forced to join an international. J.S. Fitzpatrick, Marks' colleague on the committee, assured the convention that the Knights would not be coerced into federal labour unions. 'The Knights would go forward as they had in the past, because they held the key to the situation in Montreal and Quebec Province.' They refused to 'come sneaking into the congress under another name.'[14]

The venerable, white-bearded Daniel O'Donoghue, the father of the Canadian labour movement, soon realized that the dual unionists were hopelessly outnumbered. He rose from his chair to declare that decisions by majorities were not always right or just. He told the delegates that he had represented the Knights at Trades Congress conventions from the very beginning. At the same time he had also carried his International Typographical Union card for thirty-seven years without cease. The amendments, he concluded, 'would be disastrous to the interests of labor, and would practically shut Quebec Province out of the congress.'[15]

The internationalists retaliated, speaking about the union label difficulties engendered by dual unionism. Samuel Landers, a Hamilton garment worker, said that the existing situation, which permitted dual labels, confused consumers of union-made goods. J.A. Rodier pointed to the labels controversy in the shoe trade. 'One organization of boot and shoe workers,' he said, 'had passed a resolution fining any of its members who purchased boots bearing the label of the other body.' A Hamilton printer, Henry Obermeyer, declared that the proposed amendments were a defensive measure by internationals to protect their labels and thereby 'secure them the benefits which they had purchased at heavy cost.' He was probably alluding to the cigarmakers' strike in Montreal, which had been hindered by the existence of rival Knights' locals in the cigar trade who used their own label.[16] The Cigarmakers' International Union had a large delegation (eleven members) at the Trades Congress convention in 1902, and their most illustrious card-carrying member, Samuel Gompers, was leading the struggle against dual unionism throughout all of North America.

It is interesting to note that the international unions most desirous of the changes advocated in the proposed amendments, the Boot and Shoe Workers and the Cigarmakers, not only had very large delegations in attendance, but also voted unanimously for the constitutional changes. In fact, no less than fifty-one of the sixty-seven delegates who represented Canadian locals of international unions threw their support to the international cause. In addition twenty-one of the thirty Trades Council representatives stood solidly behind the revision committee's proposals, and a good many of these men also carried international union cards. As the debate dragged on, perhaps the most revealing comment of all was made by E.S. Jackson, one of the delegates from the Toronto local of the International Typographical Union. He told the Congress that his union had instructed him to vote against dual organizations. The dual unionists were defeated by an eighty-seven to thirty-two vote.[17]

The overwhelming unity of the international union vote suggested once again that the confrontation between the dual unionists and the internationalists at Berlin in 1902 was not happenstance, but had been planned by American labour leaders as part of their war against dual unionism on the North American continent. At least two participants in the week's proceedings saw it this way. In their report to the Winnipeg Trades Council, A.M. Gossel and A.B. Cowley observed that the Congress 'was packed with delegates who through their respective internationals are affiliated with the A.F.of L., and further organization and lobbying had been going on for months' to achieve the desired ends.[18]

The dual unionists did not give up their fight, and Daniel O'Donoghue rose again to speak on the constitutional changes. After lunch, a number of delegates protested O'Donoghue's request to speak once more on the issue. Tension filled the hall and tempers rose to a fever pitch. Nearly thirty minutes were consumed in points of order and appeals against the rulings of the chair. When the tumult had subsided, O'Donoghue reminded the delegates that the proposed changes would forbid joining forces with the Maritimes-based Provincial Workmen's

Association, a project that Trades Congress leaders had taken up back in 1898. Then A.L. Gareau, another Knight, strongly supported the claims of the dual unions in Canada. But the debate died away after Sam Landers of Hamilton vigorously defended the international unions against Gareau's assertions. The previous question was put to end debate, and overwhelmingly passed. The first amendment to the constitution was then declared carried by a vote of forty-three to twenty-three. Twenty-three unions with 2287 members, or about one-fifth of the Trades Congress membership, were thereby expelled.[19]

Two members of the committee immediately moved to adopt the other controversial section, which would recognize only one central council in Canadian cities. 'The friends of the Knights of Labor did not, however, give up the contest' after their defeat on the first issue. F.X. Boileau of Quebec City, one of the two dual unionists on the revision panel, offered an amendment allowing the admission of district and local councils of the Knights of Labor to the Trades Congress 'provided they are affiliated with the Trades Councils chartered by the congress.' His motion would have granted a kind of local option by allowing each city central to decide whether or not to seat dual union locals. The special committee's proposal, he warned, would divide organized labour into two councils in his city. He was supported by Daniel O'Donoghue, who 'expressed surprise that men in this congress would vote to exclude from it men with whom they worked in harmony in the local trades council, as for eighteen years had been the case in the city of Toronto.'[20]

At this point in the debate Congress secretary Draper entered the fray. Without openly criticizing the international unions, he revealed his sympathy for the dual-unionist position. He strongly appealed for recognition of the principle that the Trades and Labor Congress should remain the supreme legislative body of the country. He took pains to point out 'the great competition the Trades Congress suffered owing to the organization of local unions under the American Federation of Labor.' Nevertheless the vast majority of delegates lined up once again behind the international stance when the previous question was finally moved. The second amendment was declared carried by a vote of eighty-eight to thirty-five.[21]

Following the vote the Congress entertained the committee's recommendation that the Federated Council be recognized as the only central body in Montreal. A.L. Gareau of the Knights and D. Verdon of the Montreal Central Council moved instead that the Central Council be granted sole recognition; their amendment was lost on division. Then chairman Hugh Stevenson and secretary C.S.O. Boudreault of the committee moved that the Congress adopt the report as a whole. O'Donoghue and Fitzpatrick made a last ditch effort to persuade the convention to strike out the core of the committee's proposal, but they tasted defeat once more.[22]

However, P.M. Draper did succeed in making a minor but very symbolic addition to the recommendations. He had noted that a section of the old constitution declared it to be the object of the Trades Congress 'to unite all the labor organizations of the Dominion ... for legislative purposes.' The new declarations in favour of internationalism, he foresaw, would destroy the unity of the Canadian labour movement. After considerable discussion he persuaded Stevenson to accept a substitute for the old statement. The Trades Congress henceforward would 'consist of such Trade Unions, Federal Unions, Trades and Labor Councils and National Trade Unions, as shall conform to its regulations.' Draper's motion replaced the old declaration of purpose with a new statement of fact; it silently recognized the wedge driven into the Canadian labour movement.[23]

Although by Tuesday evening the Trades Congress had resolved the problem of dual central bodies in Montreal, it had not defined its relationship to the AFL in regard to the chartering of Canadian central bodies and federal labour unions. On the following day the delegates listened to reports of the difficulties between Federal Labor Union no. 10 and the AFL-chartered central body in Charlottetown, Prince Edward Island. They were told that part of the trouble in Montreal had been a result of the presence of two competing trade-union authorities in the country. They heard Draper call for an agreement with the Federation over respective charter jurisdictions of the two national labour centres.[24] Joseph Marks promptly introduced a resolution which stated the viewpoint of the Canadian labour leaders:

Resolved, that as the Trades and Labor Congress of Canada has placed itself squarely in accord with the principles of International trades unionism, and as such action will entail the loss of revenues from former affiliated bodies debarred from membership under the amended Constitution, it is the opinion of this Congress that, being the National Legislative organization of labor in the Dominion of Canada, all Federal Labor Unions and Central Trade and Labor Councils should be under the jurisdiction and control of the Congress; and the incoming Executive is hereby instructed to take immediate steps to make such arrangements with the American Federation of Labor looking to the consummation of this object. It is the opinion of this Congress that the existence of dual federal labor unions, holding charters from the Congress and the American Federation of Labor is not conducive to the solidity and effectiveness of the labor movement in Canada.[25]

Henry Obermeyer challenged Marks' motion. He doubted whether the Trades Congress could offer the same protection the unions obtained under the

American Federation and called for consultations on the question between officers of the two national trade-union centres. Marks, in rebuttal, pointed to the Congress declaration against dual unionism passed the day before. 'They should carry the principle to the logical conclusion, and not have a trades union in one town under the congress and a similar union in the next town chartered by the American Federation of Labor. The congress,' Marks declared, 'should insist upon being supreme within the Dominion.' Marks' resolution was carried after Draper told the delegates that it was 'absolutely necessary to come to some agreement with the AFL in order to prevent injurious competition between the two bodies in the matter of issuing charters.' The resolution clearly stated the Trades Congress position, but there was no guarantee that the AFL would accede to the Canadian claim.[26]

The triumph of the craft internationals at Berlin was sealed on Thursday by the election of John A. Flett, the AFL's salaried organizer, to the presidency of the Trades and Labor Congress. That evening the craft delegates celebrated their actions at a German supper cooked by the Women's Label League. In another part of town the expelled dual unionists, predominantly French-speaking delegates from the Knights of Labor assemblies in Quebec, gathered to set up a rival labour federation – the *National* Trades and Labor Congress. They passed resolutions and made speeches deprecating the tendency toward internationalism at the expense of 'nationalism.' The new Congress did not recognize international organizations, and promised to have its own national union label and to issue charters and supplies to organizations affiliated with it. Thus from the start, Gompers' move to end dual unionism in Canada appeared to stumble at the Quebec border. In French Canada dual-union movements could always draw sustenance from a distinct culture, a siege mentality, and the Catholic clergy.[27]

Four days after the historic convention had adjourned, the *Globe* noted the flurry of excitement in labour circles across the country. It recalled that the Trades Congress had been formed eighteen years before to unite all Canadian labour organizations for legislative purposes. Several of its affiliates had 'firmly resisted the persistent efforts which have been made in recent years to persuade them to throw in their lot with the international organizations or with the American Federation of Labor.' The activities of the AFL in Canada had produced friction, and the *Globe* cited the conflict in Charlottetown, the rival central bodies in Montreal, and the situation in the boot and shoe trade of that city. The new policy had been adopted 'to crush out the Canadian organizations as such or to force them to identify themselves with the international organizations.' The paper noted the disastrous effects of the Berlin decisions on cooperation with the Provincial Workmen's Association, on the miners' unions in British Columbia, and on the Canadian-based Western Freight Handlers' Association. It speculated on the effect of the decisions on central bodies such as the Toronto Trades and Labor Council. 'There unfortunately appears to be a probability, unless wiser counsels prevail, that in Toronto and other places there will shortly be two councils. The labor movement must necessarily be considerably injured by such division, and friends of labor everywhere hope that this may be avoided.' The *Globe* failed to note that future events also depended heavily upon the outcome of talks between leaders of the Trades Congress and the American Federation of Labor.[28]

Although the re-alignment of the Trades and Labor Congress in favour of international trade unionism was the most significant event of the Berlin convention, it was not the only change which reflected the triumph of Gompers' continentalist policies. On the day following the passage of the constitutional amendments, Joseph Marks took the floor to give notice of a motion. Marks had expressed reservations about the compulsory arbitration principle for some time, and had spoken out at a meeting of the London, Ontario, Trades Council the year before. He had said then that 'while compulsory arbitration might be all right in New Zealand where the workers had a great deal to say in the running of the country ... it would be a bad thing for Canada where the party machine had too much swing ... Voluntary arbitration was the safest under existing circumstances.' At Berlin he proposed to strike out the Trades Congress platform declaration which favoured the compulsory principle in settling labour disputes. Subsequently a committee of the Congress concurred, and also asked Canadian labour to use 'their utmost endeavor' to defeat Sir William Mulock's new bill in the House of Commons.[29]

Once again several of the international union delegates led the fight for a change in Congress policy. The heaviest attack was launched by J. Harvey Hall of the Railway Conductors' local in Toronto. He gave Mulock credit for honesty of purpose in introducing the bill, but asserted that it threatened the position of the international unions in Canada. He suspected that it had been promoted by the railway companies for the purpose of attacking railwaymen's unions. Marks agreed with Hall, and held that 'to deprive men of the right to strike was to bring them down to the condition of absolute slavery, worse than black slavery.' Peter Sharkey of Saint John, New Brunswick, raised the possibility of one trade arbitrating another's grievance under Mulock's bill. 'A trackman might be called in,' he argued, 'to arbitrate upon a conductors' or engineers' grievance which would be an impossible situation.' Sharkey played upon the traditional pride of skill among craft unionists and their fear of interference from the unskilled.[30]

The strongest support for both the Mulock bill and the compulsory principle came from Western delegates. Manitoba labour leaders told the convention that the working people of Manitoba, and Winnipeg in particular, were in favour of compulsory arbitration of labour disputes. The Canadian Northern strike had greatly strengthened their conviction. They had been sent, Delegate Thoms of Winnipeg asserted, to demand compulsory arbitration, 'under which in New Zealand and Australia increased wages and shortened hours had been obtained, and the condition of the working classes generally advanced.'[31] Nevertheless, when Draper moved to substitute the word 'voluntary' for 'compulsory' in the Congress platform phrase on arbitration, it was overwhelmingly approved by seventy-eight to twelve. Apparently the AFL pamphlets distributed by Draper had done their job well.[32]

If the attack on the Mulock bill weakened Liberal party efforts to capture the Canadian labour movement, then the retirement of Ralph Smith from the presidency of the Trades Congress was an irretrievable defeat for Grit-dominated trade unionism. Smith's labour leadership had been compromised by the leftward turn of organized labour in Nanaimo and other mining communities. The Nanaimo miners, whom he represented at the convention, had withdrawn from the Congress, and although Smith was re-nominated to the Congress presidency and offered other credentials, he declined the honour. On his return trip to British Columbia, Smith took occasion to criticize the influence of American labour leaders in the affairs of Canadian unions. It appeared to him that the Trades and Labor Congress had placed itself in a subordinate position to the AFL, 'and he could not see that much progress could be made under those conditions.' Smith eventually lost his tie to labour and moved into straight Liberal party politics.[33]

Although Smith abandoned independent political action for the security of a major party, many Canadian trade unionists still endorsed the labour party tactic on the political front. Both the Trades Congress and labour parties pursued legislative aims and their objectives often overlapped; hence, their relations were a matter of some dispute. The AFL constitution forbade representation by political parties on the floor of Federation conventions, but Congress debates and resolutions in favour of independent political action seemed to many Canadians to provide sufficient reason for labour party delegates to be seated at Trades Congress conventions. At the Berlin meeting A.M. Gossel of Winnipeg proposed that the Congress grant all floor privileges to labour men who had been elected to provincial or federal legislatures, provided they held paid up union cards. His motion was strongly supported by Westerners; they said they expected to have twenty labour men elected to the next Manitoba legislature.[34]

The same issue had arisen at the Congress convention the year before, when Draper had seconded a resolution to admit labour parties into the fold.[35] For several years the Winnipeg labour party had paid per-capita fees to the Congress, and Arthur Puttee, the Winnipeg labour MP, had come to the convention of 1901 with credentials from both the labour party and his International Typographical Union local. His labour party credentials had not been recognized by the convention; his subsequent complaint had provoked a lively debate over the wisdom of admitting labour parties to Trades Congress membership.[36] George Beales of Toronto, who had served as president of the Trades Congress in 1892 and 1893, had warned that the admission of labour parties would enable 'every hack and ward politician in the country' to use a labour party for his own purposes. The single taxers and the socialists, he had added, would soon besiege the Congress. Charles March, another veteran Trades Congress leader and its first president in 1886 and 1887, had feared that admission of the Winnipeg labourites would open the Congress to organizations not in strict sympathy with organized labour. John Flett had followed the same tack, but had put it more strongly. The Canadian organizer of the AFL was moving steadily to the political right. In 1895 he had fought for the Socialist Labor party at the Congress convention; now he spoke just as vigorously against seating even the more moderate independent labourites. It would open the 'floodgates to all hack organizations that might seek identification with the congress under the guise of labor.' Subsequently the proposal in 1901 to seat labour parties had received only a handful of votes at the convention.[37]

When Gossel brought the issue up again at the Berlin sessions, the discussion promised to be warm. Peter Sharkey feared a repetition of the debates on the constitutional amendments, during which the delegates had behaved 'like a lot of old women washing linen.' But few had stamina for a protracted fight, and Gossel's motion was quickly voted down. Once again the Trades and Labor Congress took a stand identical to that of the AFL. Although subsequent Congress conventions debated and adopted resolutions on independent political action, the Trades Congress and various labour parties that sprouted up from time to time remained organizationally and financially distinct. With few exceptions, only *bona fide* trade unionists, all card-carrying members of international craft unions or national unions not in conflict with them, were seated at Congress conventions after 1902.[38]

In the Canadian labour world at the end of that fateful week in Berlin, the east-west axis of Canadian nationality was crumbling before the new north-south chains binding Canadian workers to American labour organizations. The Congress, for example, even expressed its sympathy for the striking American anthracite miners, but it had none for the British Columbia labour leaders, whose report 'contains so much of a contentious nature on matters already passed on.' At the conclusion of its sessions, the Congress in a light-hearted if rather malodorous moment presented D.D. Driscoll, the AFL fraternal delegate, with a generous slice of locally made Limburger cheese. Driscoll promised to recommend to his fellow Americans that all the international unions send organizers into Canada as quickly as possible.[39]

Flett reported the good tidings to the American who paid his salary. Samuel Gompers was delighted with the accounts of the Congress convention given in Flett's newspaper clippings. 'They are mighty interesting reading,' he told Flett,

and I want to congratulate you and organized labor of Canada upon the splendid stand taken by the recent Congress of the Trades and Labor Unions of the Dominion. The policy declared for, and the officers elected demonstrate beyond question that the spirit of the labor movement is growing toward the recognition that our interests are identical regarding the arbitrary geographical lines. We are doing our level best to protect and advance the interests of our fellow-workers, and those who would preach the policy of isolation are absolutely inconsistent. The aim of the labor movement is to associate the workers in our trades in the various localities, then national, and the next step is international trade unionism. Let me congratulate you and the Congress upon your election as its president and wish you every success.

In a postscript, Gompers added that the 'declaration for international trade unionism was splendid as well as the unqualified protest against compulsory arbitration.'[40]

The representatives of the 2287 dual unionists expelled at Berlin, whether motivated by personal ambition, by the vision of a Canadian federation of labour exercising full autonomy, or by a French-Canadian fear of drowning in a sea of Anglo-Saxons, failed to defend the TLC's shadowy independence. Instead the Congress was consigned to a rank among the American state federations. The bulk of Canadian unionists probably agreed with the Berlin decisions because they wanted assurance that the full weight of the AFL affiliates would always be available to assist them in their struggles on the economic front. Yet by wedding the Congress so tightly to international unionism and by accepting the supremacy of the AFL in Canada they forfeited influence over the shape and direction of the Canadian labour movement.

In effect, labour unity in Canada was sacrificed in return for a promise of continued economic support by the international craft unions. As a result, after 1902 there would always be a group of Canadian workers who would respond to appeals couched in the sentiments of Canadian nationalism. There would always be a few Canadian labour leaders, often ex-international union leaders, who were willing to march with a national movement against the ramparts of international unionism in Canada. Someone was always prepared to announce, as T.J. Griffiths proclaimed in 1902, that 'the time has ... arrived when Canadian workmen should have their own sovereign congress, co-equal with the ... American Federation of Labor and all other national organizations.'[41] Ironically, Gompers' strenuous efforts to bring continental unity to labour in North America created deep and long-lasting divisions within the trade-union movement of Canada.

8
A 'state' federation

The Trades and Labor Congress of Canada charted a long-range course at Berlin, but it did not settle all of its differences with the American Federation of Labor. In effect the convention went on record in favour of international craft unionism, expelled nearly a fifth of its membership, reversed its policy on arbitration, kept labour parties off the convention floor, and elected the AFL organizer to the Congress's highest office. Having thus declared itself, the Trades Congress dumped the unsettled issues over chartering rights and the per-capita tax payments into the laps of its officers. Since concessions had already been made to the AFL, the Canadian labour leaders were not in the best of bargaining positions. When Flett asked for a meeting with Gompers, the latter was 'too busy for the moment' to see the new Trades Congress president. Gompers probably wanted to give the AFL plenty of time to deliberate over its future relations with the Congress before he made any commitments.[1]

The process of defining this relationship began less than a month after the Berlin sessions had ended. In a report to the AFL Executive Council on 7 October, Flett said that the 'spirit of unity' between organized labour in Canada and the United States had been strengthened by the Berlin events. His words received hearty approval from the Council members, who ordered the AFL officers 'to give every assistance to the end that continental fraternity among all wage earners may be more firmly established.' The Council then requested an investigation into the dispute over chartering authority.[2]

Gompers revealed his thoughts on the meaning of the Berlin actions in the columns of the *American Federationist*. 'We realize,' he wrote in answer to a query, 'that it is essential that organized labor [in Canada] shall have full authority in determining the questions which affect it.' He mentioned Flett's efforts and those of the volunteer organizers whose expenses were paid by the Federation. In tangled prose, Gompers tried to tell Canadians that they received their money's worth from their per-capita payments to the AFL. As for the Trades Congress's relationship to the Federation, he said it was 'substantially the same' as relations between the AFL and state federations of labour.[3]

At the AFL convention in late 1902, Gompers proudly announced the actions of the Trades Congress. They had made a clear-cut declaration in favour of the 'closest bonds of unity and fraternity' with the Federation. He called upon both the AFL and the international unions to continue rendering aid to the Canadians. He promised to keep Flett working in Canada.[4] The Congress fraternal delegate, J.H. Kennedy of Toronto, echoed Gompers' sentiments. He asked the international unions to remember that 'the character of our people being largely agricultural, [it] necessarily will mean that our unions will be sparse and fragmentary. We look to our stronger unions to aid us.' Later delegate Driscoll, true to his pledge at the Berlin convention, asked the international unions to send their organizers on a Canadian tour during 1903.[5]

The Federation leaders appointed a special eleven-man committee on Canadian affairs to deal with the Congress statement on chartering rights. The panel included both J.H. Kennedy, the fraternal delegate from the Trades Congress, and Frank Morrison, the AFL secretary.[6] Their report congratulated the Congress on its declaration in favour of international unionism, and hoped that 'no geographical lines may ever separate the close fraternal feelings that now exist in the North American continent.' They recommended that the AFL keep its Canadian organizer in the field, but left it to Gompers to determine the number of volunteer organizers warranted in the country. The Canadians were highly commended for their new policy on arbitration. But the cheering stopped when the charter issue was raised. The committee recognized that federal labour unions had been a source of income for the Congress. Yet after 'careful consideration,' they decided that the grant of federal labour union charters by the Trades Congress (which the Canadians had been doing since 1898) had a 'tendency to divide the labor movement of the United States and Canada, and possibly retard the formation of national or international organizations.' To make up for any loss of income, the committee urged the AFL to raise its annual grant to $500. No mention was made of the controversy involving the charters issued to central bodies. Perhaps for that reason Driscoll moved that the final decision on chartering jurisdiction be left to the AFL Executive Council. The special panel's report with Driscoll's emendation was adopted by the convention. The AFL delegates, in other words, had staked out a position which granted a clear priority to Federation chartering rights, but had then authorized their leaders to bargain with the Canadians.[7]

Now that the convention had defined a policy, Gompers was prepared to meet Congress leaders. 'I would like very much to have an interview with you and talk over the situation as it exists in Canada,' he told Flett. A conference was held in Buffalo in early January 1903. Gompers agreed to draw up a circular letter which asked international unions and their Canadian affiliates to attach themselves for legislative purposes to the Trades Congress, because the Canadian locals had been slow to respond to earlier appeals.[8] On 5 February Gompers sent the AFL's first $500 check to Draper. Gompers asserted once again that relations between the Trades Congress and the AFL were 'substantially the same' as those between the AFL and state federations. His conversations with Flett and his correspondence with Draper had had no noticeable effect on his interpretation of the new relationship between the two national trade-union centres.[9]

Throughout the winter opponents of international unionism continued to exert an influence on segments of Canadian labour. By the end of 1902 the Nanaimo and Phoenix, British Columbia, Trades and Labor Councils had turned in their charters to Trades Congress headquarters, and several Canadian federal labour unions had folded. On 22 January 1903, the Toronto District Labor Council, in a move which contradicted the spirit of the Berlin declarations, voted to keep the Knights of Labor seated at their meetings.[10] The United Brotherhood of Railway Employees continued to push its organization work along the rail lines leading toward Ontario. To offset this opposition, Gompers decided to hold the AFL's spring Executive Council meeting in Toronto. Both Flett and Draper helped Gompers to prepare an itinerary so that Executive Council members could deliver speeches to organized labour in a number of Ontario towns. Their efforts, Gompers told Draper, 'would undoubtedly be efficacious in more firmly cementing the ties of union and sympathy between wage workers of the Dominion and the United States as well as the movement in general.'[11]

The Trades Congress executive officers met in Ottawa on 6 April and discussed the AFL convention resolution of a few months earlier. According to the Canadians' report to the Congress convention later in 1903, the officers agreed at the Ottawa meeting to abandon their desire to charter all federal labour unions in Canada, and decided 'to confine their efforts to Trades and Labor Councils only.' (The account to be given here will show that Draper had not agreed with this tactic.) Flett and Draper were instructed to wait upon the AFL Executive Council at its session in Toronto later in the month.[12]

Six members of the Federation Council assembled on Monday, 20 April 1903, at the Arlington Hotel in Toronto. In addition to Gompers and Morrison, there were James Duncan, head of the Granite Cutters, Max Morris of the Retail Clerks, John Lennon of the Tailors, and Thomas Kidd of the Woodworkers (who had been the first fraternal delegate to the Congress back in 1898). The first session was overshadowed in the press by the death of Sir Oliver Mowat, the famed Liberal leader of Ontario; the next day, the mayor of Toronto formally welcomed the Council to his city. He expressed pleasure that Canadians took a prominent place in the Federation's councils, Morrison 'being a native Canadian, while President Gompers was born under the British flag.' The mayor invited the Council to a banquet, and amid the festivities at McConkey's Cafe on Wednesday evening, he spoke of the growth of organized labour in recent years. Unions had sprung up all over America, he said, and were now stretching out to Europe. 'They all hoped before long [that] there would be one grand federation, whose object would be to obtain and to sustain those rights which were theirs as citizens and as men.' Gompers responded agreeably that the AFL worked for the interests of wage workers everywhere.[13]

On Thursday both Flett and Draper appeared before the Council and the charter controversy was taken up for the first time. As the official report later put it, 'during the discussion the whole operations of the labor movement in Canada were very fully reviewed, and strong exception was taken, especially by President Gompers, to the A.F. of L. abandoning the field, as they had spent much time, energy and money in organization work in Canada.'[14] Had Draper actually asked the Federation to pull out of Canada? Available evidence does not say, but later that evening Draper spoke out in Gompers' presence. While re-affirming Canadian support for international unionism, he insisted that Canadian unionists be granted 'proper' representation on the executive boards of the international crafts. He demanded that Canadians have 'absolute and complete liberty of action in the conduct of their affairs.'[15] Although he appeared to view the Trades Congress as the political or legislative expression of Canadian labour, he wanted authority to issue charters to federal labour unions, to central bodies, and to dissident elements in Canada which the international unions could not or would not reach. He considered the Congress to be equal to the American Federation of Labor as a national trade-union centre, and presumably had argued that idea before the Executive Council earlier in the day.[16]

During the week the Council deliberated in Toronto, large posters, shop window cards, and newspaper advertisements announced a forthcoming meeting of workers on Friday evening, 25 April. When Gompers rose to speak at Massey Hall, he was given an ovation by a very large and enthusiastic assemblage. He touched on a number of issues, pointing, for example, to the spectre of Oriental labour sweeping across the continent. He dealt at more length with the charge that Canadian strikes were fomented by American labour leaders. He dared anyone to find a clause in the constitution of an international union which granted such a power. 'Such a power rests with the local men,' he averred. He closed his address with a call for close union of American and Canadian labour, and gave several instances of the mutual benefits of such a policy. The meeting ended with cheers and the singing of both 'God Save the King' and 'My Country 'Tis of Thee.' Certainly the audience knew the melody if not the words.[17]

On Saturday the Executive Council met for their final session. Again Flett and Draper appeared on behalf of the Trades Congress. According to Morrison, Draper still wanted authority to issue federal labour union charters, but Flett and the Council members argued that the AFL was in a better position, because of its strike fund, to support the members of a federal labour union.[18] Draper gave in on this point, but Flett and Draper maintained that central bodies needed affiliation with the Trades Congress in order to carry out their legislative functions. Both Canadians also urged the AFL to waive the fifty-cent dues required of federal labour union members by the Federation constitution, since it was 'almost impossible' for Canadians, they said, to pay that much. After it had heard the arguments, the Executive Council embodied its decision in a three-point declaration:

1. That the A.F. of L. will make it a qualification of issuing charters to trades and labor councils in Canada that they will affiliate with the Trades and Labor Congress, and central bodies throughout the Dominion now holding A.F. of L. charters will be instructed to take similar action.
2. That trade affairs in the Central Trades and Labor Councils in question shall be transacted as heretofore along the lines of international trade unionism.
3. That all local unions in the Dominion of Canada affiliated through international unions or holding charters direct from the A.F. of L. be notified to become affiliated with the Trades and Labor Congress of Canada, for the purpose of making it a more potent factor to secure the adoption of favorable legislation for the members by the federal and provincial parliaments.[19]

At the Berlin convention six months before, the Canadians had declared their intention to charter both federal labour unions and city centrals throughout the country. Now the Trades Congress leaders had been forced to grant the primacy of the American Federation of Labor in the issuance of federal labour union charters in Canada and to permit Canadian central bodies to hold two charters. In the latter case the Federation agreed not to grant its charter until the Canadian trades and labour councils had first taken out a Congress charter. Canadian central bodies henceforth were to seat only locals of international craft unions. Finally, the AFL promised to request both its own Canadian federal labour unions and the international union locals to join the Trades Congress in order to make it a more potent organization.[20]

As a result of the Executive Council ruling, Canadian chartering rights were severely restricted, and there was still no guarantee that American-chartered international union locals or federal labour unions would accede to requests that they pay additional dues required to join the Trades Congress. Canadians, on the other hand, were still required to pay per-capita tax to the AFL — either through their international union headquarters, or directly as in the case of Federation-chartered federal labour unions. The AFL now gave $500 a year to the Congress for legislative expenses, and continued to provide the services of a full-time organizer (under AFL command) and some part-time organizing help.

From the Trades and Labor Congress's point of view, there were a number of drawbacks to the Executive Council ruling. Apart from the fact that the chartering authority of the Congress had been constricted, the Canadians had no means to compel locals to affiliate themselves with the Canadian national trade-union centre. Trades Congress leaders could use the 'carrot' and point out the advantages of united action by labour on the Canadian legislative front, but they had no 'stick,' such as the power to isolate a local by withdrawing its charter, to enforce assessments or other decisions. Then again the Trades Congress exercised no control over the expansion of trade unionism in the country. If the international unions or the AFL did not wish to organize a particular industry, or class of workers, or area in Canada, there was little the Congress could do about it. Flett took his orders from Gompers and Morrison — not from Draper. Finally, as the labour movement grew in Canada and poured more dues money into international union and AFL coffers, there was no guarantee that the Trades Congress would share in the prosperity. As a matter of fact, the AFL legislative grant remained at the $500 level throughout the pre-war period. In addition, the AFL convention of 1903 upheld the requirement of fifty-cent dues from Canadian federal labour unions despite the objections of the Canadian labour leaders.[21] The controversy over union revenues was hardly ended by the Executive Council's actions. It seems clear in retrospect that the Trades and Labor Congress of Canada lost most of its influence over the structure and organization of Canadian labour, and became little more than a lobby charged with the defence of the international trade-union movement in the corridors of the Canadian parliament. Yet Canadian labour, by its concessions, laid solid claim to assistance from the international craft unions in future industrial struggles.

For several months during 1903 it looked as though the Canadian labour movement might be forcibly separated from American craft unions despite all that had transpired in recent months. Senator Lougheed's move to bar American labour leaders from Canadian soil, introduced in April, reflected a rising tide of opinion opposed to trade unionism in general and to the American connection in particular.[22] It rode on a wave of strikes which had broken out in the mining districts and on the railways of British Columbia. Actually, the strikes had been fomented by AFL rivals; the United Brotherhood of Railway Employees, the Western Federation of Miners, and other American Labor Union affiliates. Unless something were done, the manager of the Le Roi mines said, it might mean the complete destruction of the mining districts of British Columbia.[23]

The labour conflicts worried the Laurier government in far-away Ottawa. The Liberals were not about to see Lougheed and the Conservatives win political capital on this explosive issue, but it was difficult for Laurier to know which course to chart. The Canadian Manufacturers' Association left no doubt where it stood on nearly all Grit labour policies: 'The Department of Labor has long since lost its prestige with the employers of Canada,' it declared.[24] At the same time Laurier was receiving numerous letters from trade-union locals demanding that the government block passage of the Lougheed measure. Laurier turned to Mulock, who recommended that the troubles in the West be investigated by a royal commission. He told Laurier that the working people of Canada had come under the domination of the AFL, 'whom they appear to regard as their friends.' He thought that an intelligent commission which pointed out the injuries to labour because of American interference might educate Canadian working men in their true interests. The commission's report might accomplish the same result as intended by the Lougheed bill, but to Liberal advantage.[25]

Gompers knew that the Lougheed bill would go a long way to undo the decisions of Berlin and Toronto. He expressed confidence that organized labour and the fair-minded citizenry of Canada would not permit it to become law.[26] After the Toronto Council meeting he decided to throw his own prestige into the struggle. Journeying to Ottawa, he met and conversed with a number of Canadian labour and political leaders. On the grounds of Parliament Hill one evening, Puttee, O'Donoghue, Smith, and Gompers sat and talked, taking in the spring air while O'Donoghue described the extent of the great fire of a few years before. That evening Gompers spoke at St Patrick's Hall before an audience which included Mulock, Robert Borden, Senator Templeman, and other politicians as well as trade unionists. If the Lougheed bill became law, he said, it would make an act unlawful when performed by an alien but legal when engaged in by a citizen. 'This was a breach in the relationship that was maintained between nations.'[27]

Gompers' speech was not reported in Ottawa newspapers; their attention was focused on the labour crisis in Montreal. The city's carpenters had threatened a general strike, the longshoremen had already walked off their jobs, and the electricians talked of throwing the city into darkness. Some thirteen hundred troops stood guard on the docks. The president of the Montreal board of trade linked the waterfront troubles to international unionism. 'The outcome of the present dock struggle,' he told reporters, 'will mean either the freedom of the port of Montreal or its manipulation to the detriment of Canada from Washington.'[28]

On the eve of May Day Gompers and his entourage swept into Montreal. 'What will happen to-night when President Gompers ... and Secretary Morrison arrive in Montreal?' the *Herald* asked. 'What effect will the big union labor demonstration in their honor have upon the longshoremen's strike? Just when the city and the Senate at Ottawa are ringing with denunciations of American labor agitators meddling with Canadian labor concerns, Samuel Gompers, the biggest of all the American labor men, comes quietly to town, puts up at the Queen's Hotel, registers under his own name, and goes about as if he were in the house of his friends, quite unconscious apparently, that his visit involves any discourtesy to the people of Montreal.'[29] That night, the trade unionists of Montreal showed the *Herald* that indeed Gompers was among friends. The greatest labour demonstration in the city's history – upwards of 15,000 men, the *Globe* said – marched to Sohmer Park. Crowds jammed the streets, and the air was grey with swirling dust. Men marched without order behind their union banners and mottoes, flanked by solid ranks of spectators. The bands, rockets, shouts, and wild huzzas for Gompers were deafening. Mounted marshals cantered by in silk hats and glistening lace collars. With apparent ease they performed the difficult feat of smoking cigars on horseback in a gale of wind. 'Huzzu, Monsieur Gompers,' they shouted as the labour leader passed in his carriage. Gompers bowed to the left and right in acknowledgment of the cheers. 'Just like the Prince of Wales,' suggested an enthusiastic admirer.[30]

At the park, Gompers announced the settlement of the carpenters' strike to the union's satisfaction. He cautioned the striking longshoremen: 'If you value your honor, your liberty and your future, keep the peace. Do not allow your enemies to provoke you to breaches of the law.'[31]

The AFL leader spoke at length on the Lougheed bill. The bill meant, he said, 'that so mild a mannered man as my friend, Frank Morrison, or even myself, would be entitled to a punishment of two years' imprisonment to dare to talk to you as I am talking here to-night.' He was confident that the bill would not be permitted to become law, and won a round of applause when he told the assemblage that 'if I read the history of Canada aright ... they will see that this violent attempt upon the rights of humanity and liberty by the Government will be swept beneath their utter contempt.' Gompers noted that American businessmen faced no such hostile legislation and repeated his Toronto statement that international craft unions had no power to order strikes in Canada. Before he had finished his speech, though, a good part of the heavily French-speaking audience had drifted away. He had doubtless blundered when he proclaimed himself a Londoner with the sanctifying virtue of American citizenship.[32]

Gompers left Montreal for Boston, his mind still on the Canadian labour movement when he talked to reporters in the Bay State capital. Canadians, he confidently asserted, would not break away from the American labour movement. Although Canadian politicians aimed to divide continental labour, he said, the working people of Canada were enthusiastically ready and willing to continue the friendly and beneficial affiliation they had enjoyed with the American trade unions. Perhaps a good share of his optimism could be attributed to a clipping from the *Toronto Globe* which Puttee had handed to the AFL leader during the visit to Ottawa. The mouthpiece of Ontario Liberalism had editorially endorsed international trade unionism in most laudatory terms. 'The labor organizations have been first to bridge the gulf of international hostility on this continent. They are preserving democratic traditions threatened with extinction, they are resisting the growing spirit of militarism, and, with the discipline and experience of age, will become a means of averting danger from the power of colossal fortunes and the weakness of widespread poverty and dependence.' The *Globe* heaped praise on Gompers, calling him a man of conservative views, sound judgment, and recognized ability. Gompers may have concluded from this and from his reception in Montreal that the outlook for international unionism in Canada was encouraging. Still, the Lougheed bill remained to be killed and interred.[33]

Draper and Flett kept Gompers fully informed of events connected with the bill. The Canadian Manufacturers' Association had turned its editorial guns on international unionism. Foreign labour agitators were 'drunk with power,' *Industrial Canada* said. Although the CMA had a good word for Gompers, it found that labour leaders in general abused their positions and advised workers to follow unreasonable courses.[34] Gompers called the CMA attack unjustified and complained to Flett about 'the false position which Senator Lougheed's bill aims to place us.' He added: 'I trust that you may be successful in preventing its enactment and to allay prejudice and bitterness aroused.' Flett was ordered to remain in Ottawa, and Gompers suggested that the Trades Congress dispatch a circular letter to Canadian trade-union locals, urging them to write letters, adopt resolutions, and forward their protests to members of parliament. 'More than likely if the members hear from their own home districts how organized labor feels upon the matter in question, it no doubt will have a salutary influence.'[35] The Federation leader offered to underwrite the cost of preparing a pamphlet of articles endorsing international unionism and criticizing the Lougheed bill. He was careful to avoid being accused of meddling, and stressed the need of having the pamphlet printed in Canada under the stamp of the Trades Congress. Ultimately the Canadians went over a thousand dollars in debt in their campaign against the bill.[36]

On 4 June 1903, a Senate committee held public hearings and all sides were given an opportunity to present their views.[37] Accompanied by Flett, Draper, and several other Canadian labour leaders, John G. O'Donoghue, counsel for the Trades Congress (and elder son of Daniel O'Donoghue), read a statement on behalf of the trade unions. The unions reflected the general rise of interest groups in an industrial society, he said, and pointed to the presence of international religious, fraternal, social, manufacturing, and educational associations. He cited the international associations of employers and specifically the United Typothetae of America and the National Metal Trades Association as examples. Turning next to the reasons why Canadian trade unions opposed the Lougheed bill, O'Donoghue said that Canadian workers had a financial stake in the international organizations which would be forfeited if the tie were severed. Contrary to the supposition of the bill's supporters, international union officers could not order strikes in Canada. Besides, the bill was poorly drawn and would affect many categories of immigrants who sought Canadian citizenship. If enacted the measure would invite retaliation from American legislatures. The exclusion encroached on treaty obligations with foreign powers.

What difference is there between exclusion and denying the rights of citizenship? The recent South African war was for the recognition of a principle that this Bill will deny ... Is Canada to be the first to say that, although an employer may import international detectives to tempt Canadian workmen to crime; although foreign agitators of the Kirby stamp may be brought into Canada to insult Canadian citizens; although an employer may safeguard his business by the employment of competent representatives from any country, yet the workman is to be denied the same right? Is not this class legislation of the most pernicious kind?

O'Donoghue asserted the identity of interests between labour and capital. There were those who taught the opposite, he admitted, and some no doubt wandered into the ranks of labour. But, he concluded without actually naming the socialists, 'we declare that they are a menace to the society in which they live.'[38]

Then the bill's supporters presented their statements. One employer cited a letter from Robert McLaughlin, the Oshawa carriage maker; the case turned into a high point in the confrontation between employer and labour interests. 'Up to the time of these foreign agitators,' the employers alleged, '[McLaughlin's] men had been content with their wages and their surroundings.' Later McLaughlin spoke on his own behalf. 'The story is short and simple,' he began. 'A gentleman named A.D. Mulholland came there in 1901, and held a meeting with a considerable number of our men, and said: "If you want a union we will form one in the Oshawa Hotel," and the outcome was the union that was formed in 1903. I do not think the gentleman who formed that union was near Oshawa at the time of the strike. But that doesn't matter. By the influence of an American that union was formed, they got the international by-law, and were acting under it, and they claim they got [strike] pay. I think that is quite clear.' Why could not Canadian labour take care of itself? he asked.

O'Donoghue's response effectively dynamited McLaughlin's whole argument. 'Mr. Chairman, I put in a copy of the Ontario *Reformer*, containing a signed statement by Mr. McLaughlin in which he blames the strike on the interference of politicians, and he thanks the officers of the union *for the part they took in settling it*.' McLaughlin said nothing – in fact, no one had anything more to say about the Oshawa strike. O'Donoghue had trumped the testimony of the bill's supporters.[39] By the end of the hearings most of the employers appeared to oppose international unions because they were against all unions. The labour leaders, on the other hand, had presented a strong case for the conservative nature and democratic structure of international craft unionism.

Draper sent a full report to Gompers after the Senate's hearings had ended; somewhat later, the AFL president dispatched a circular letter to all the international unions warning them about the Lougheed bill. 'The influence of a number of large and unfair employers in Canada is urging the hostile press to create prejudice against the trade unionists of the United States,' Gompers wrote. 'They do this without declaring their opposition to organized labor as such, but more subtly urge a division of the movement. Realizing that if the Canadian workmen were isolated they would be an easier prey to the employers' opposition and greed, they therefore urge division on the grounds of "patriotism" and protection from the "foreign agitator," as they designate the trade unionists on this side of the line.' He urged the international union heads to send representatives throughout Canada and to confer privately with groups of Canadian trade unionists 'in order that they may be fortified in their position of unity of the labor movement and against the effrontery and attacks of their opponents.' Gompers also recognized that the payment of dues to American unions provided a target for the enemies of international unionism. He asked each of the international union heads to send him exact figures on their Canadian income and expenditures, in order to demonstrate the benefits granted Canadian workers through their connection with American labour. 'In the meantime,' the Federation president wrote, 'I propose to do all that I possibly can in order to bring every influence at the command of the A.F. of L. in favor of unity, fraternity and success.' The Lougheed bill passed third reading in the Senate in late July, but Flett told Gompers that it was not likely to pass the Commons.[40] Later in the summer of that year the report of the royal commission appointed to look into the industrial disturbances in British Columbia was made public. It laid bare the connections between the United Brotherhood of Railway Employees, the Western Federation of Miners, and the American Labor Union leadership, who appeared to have directed the strike activity in Canada from their American headquarters. 'Whether the wheels of Canadian industry shall run or shall not,' the commissioners said, 'ought not to depend upon the decrees of a secret council [of the above-named unions] at Denver.'[41] The report concentrated on conditions in Western Canada and on the radical unions there which were, of course, unaffiliated with the American Federation of Labor and bitter enemies of the Eastern crafts. Nevertheless the report made no clear distinction between the American Labor Union and the AFL, although it implied that not all international unions were guilty of unconscionable behaviour in Canada. In other words, hasty readers of the report could find much evidence with which to tar unions in general.

Gompers had a copy of the report in his hands almost before the ink was dry, and set out immediately to separate the AFL in the public mind from the radical unions of the West. He said that the Canadian parliament would be guilty of the 'grossest injustice' if it enacted a law which placed the AFL affiliates in the same category 'with the irresponsibles and those who want to tear down.' Gompers implied that the United Brotherhood of Railway Employees was backed by corporations intent on blackening the name of organized labour. 'It must cause a feeling of indignation and outraged injustice,' he proclaimed, 'to think that despite the straightforward course the honest, legitimate trade unions of the American Continent have pursued, and which is acknowledged in the Royal Commission's Report, that we should be classified and come under the category of such concerns which the Commission has exposed to the contumely of the civilized world.'[42]

In his presidential address to the Trades Congress convention in September, Flett gave prominent place to the AFL's attitude of hostility toward the radical unions. The Congress executive committee expressed confidence that the Lougheed bill would never become law. The public discussion that had arisen over the proposal, they said, had been a source of 'liberal education' for both the government and the people. At the end of the year Draper distributed copies of the Lougheed bill to the delegates at the AFL convention in Boston, and told them of the strong fight waged by Canadian labour against it.[43] Finally, Gompers revealed to the AFL gathering that he had conversed with Mackenzie King, the deputy minister of labour, who had served as secretary of the royal commission during its tour of the West. King had assured Gompers that the report did not question 'the honor, integrity, and faithfulness of any organization affiliated to the American Federation of Labor or upon any of its men.'[44] The Lougheed bill did not become a government measure, and with its burial in the graveyard of the Canadian Senate, the threat to international unionism withered away.

The Lougheed bill had been occasioned by attempts on the part of business and political interests to cleave North American labour at the boundary line. By 1902 there were also dissident Canadian labour groups who opposed the international union tie. But the Berlin decisions and the successful campaign against the Lougheed measure had vanquished much of the opposition. The victory had been accomplished as much through the shared intellectual outlook of workers in the United States and Canada as by the scheming of American and Canadian labour leaders. Probably a majority of Canadian trade unionists believed in the inevitable expansion and internationalization of organized labour. They thought that the laws governing the organization and operation of trade-union institutions in industrial societies transcended 'politics' and 'culture.' They were unlikely to conclude that the goals and policies of the AFL merely reflected the forces underlying American commercial and geo-political expansion during and after 1898. Trade unions, most Canadians thought, followed in the wake of capital across political boundaries in order to match the power and influence of big business combinations. Purely Canadian unions could not be expected to offset the bargaining power of international combinations of capital.

The Darwinism of the age made it easy for Canadian supporters of internationalism to lose sight of the fact that the AFL and its leaders were motivated as much by self-interest as by an altruistic concern for their Canadian brethren. For example, American job market standards were protected by the internationals' Canadian locals, but Canadian workers were only aware that their international union card gave them quick entrance into that market. Since much of Gompers' influence within the labour movement derived from his public role rather than from the powers formally vested in him by the AFL charter, his stature grew in proportion to the spread of the Federation throughout North America. At one time Ralph Smith and Paddy Draper may have dreamed of a comparable place for themselves in the Canadian labour movement, and Draper, it should be remembered, voted solidly against the constitutional amendments at Berlin. But it was Gompers whom the *Montreal Herald* could truthfully call in 1903 'The Napoleon of Labor, with a continent for his kingdom,' and add that his fief was 'not the whole of North America only, but the adjacent islands from Porto Rico to Hawaii.'[45] And, like many newly crowned kings, Gompers was soon preoccupied with the defence of his continental realm against what seemed like hordes of jealous enemies.

9
External enemies

The Berlin decisions represented a tactical victory in the AFL's strategy of self-aggrandizement. Dual-unionist enemies in Canada were thwarted for the moment. But no trumpet blast signalled the final triumph of international unionism in the country. The amendments to the constitution of the Trades and Labor Congress only promised that the Congress would not succor the Federation's enemies; they did not guarantee that international unionism would forever remain unchallenged in Canada. Similarly, the Berlin decisions did not foreshadow a re-ordering of priorities by the AFL and its affiliates. Whatever the Federation did in America was likely to influence its course in Canada. Only those elements in Canadian industrial life which paralleled conditions in the United States caught Gompers' eye. Both economies rode the same roller-coaster up and down the business cycle; Canadian locals seemed to be at the mercy of similar economic forces (and the same corporations) at work in the American economy. Both trade-union movements faced the wrath of a well-organized business community. Both were offered the sympathy and assistance of middle-class reformers. Immigrant labour posed serious organizing problems for trade unionists in Canada as well as in the United States. In each nation organized labour struggled to cope with political uncertainties.

While the problems were often the same, they arose in different circumstances. So far, apart from its appointment of a Canadian organizer, the AFL had failed to recognize most of the variants in Canada which could conceivably require some modification of tactics or policy as applied to that country. Neither the Berlin decisions, nor the successful blocking of the Lougheed bill in Ottawa, enhanced Gompers' or Morrison's awareness of the significant differences between the Canadian and American political and cultural milieus.

Federation leaders continued to stress the similarities between the Canadian and American trade-union environments, and ignored most of the incongruities. Ironically, their attitude tended to blind them to those intangibles – whether they were the political habits of recently arrived British mechanics, the traditions of Nova Scotia miners, or the linguistic preferences of French-Canadian workers – which often spawned the very disruptions or dual unionism that international union leaders abhorred.

At the start of the century, business boomed on both sides of the border. The erection of American branch plants in Canada, Flett reported in 1903, was provoking a demand for labour in the building trades. Yet the North American economy refused to stay on an even keel. A dip in the business cycle in 1904 brought a downward tendency in wages in both nations, and the panic of 1907 had a similar and even stronger effect.[1] Draper told Morrison in March 1909 that the weather had been bad throughout Canada and men were out of work, their union dues in arrears. 'What is true in Canada is true in this country, where the winter has not been severe,' Morrison replied. Still, he added, 'the International organizations seem to be holding their own, some of them even securing an increase in membership.'[2] By the spring of 1909 prosperity had returned, though seasonal variations remained sharper in Canada. Then in mid-1913 another acute depression struck. The AFL's monthly magazine told the Canadian side of the story: Calgary, 'The condition of organized labor here is not good, owing to unsteady employment and depressed financial conditions and the large influx of immigrants'; Moose Jaw, 'Work has been very scarce, with practically fifty per cent of the men in the building trades idle'; Vancouver, 'Thousands of men are out of employment, owing to a so-called money stringency.' Not until late 1914 was a war-stimulated improvement in the Canadian economy noted.[3]

Ignoring fluctuations in the business cycle and labour supply, the Canadian Manufacturers' Association adopted a consistent and adamant anti-labour stand. The CMA concentrated upon legislative lobbying in Ottawa and left bargaining policy to newly organized employers' associations in Canadian industrial centres. 'It is to be regretted that Canadian labour unions are so completely allied with, and so largely under the control of, central organizations having their headquarters in the United States,' the president of the Association intoned in 1903.[4] His words became a constant refrain. 'If only it were possible to get rid of the agitator,' the Association journal said five years later, 'there are a lot of fine features to unionism that would have the hearty support of all employers ... It is the professional labor man who makes all the trouble ...'[5] In 1909 the CMA passed a unanimous resolution asking the Laurier government to enact a Lougheed-type law.

Senator James McMullen, who had unsuccessfully advocated such a measure in 1907, took up the proposal. His bill in 1909 to exclude American labour leaders from Canadian soil was given first reading on a Thursday. Not until it was quietly scheduled for a second reading just five days later did the Trades Congress lobbyist notice it. Even so, O'Donoghue rounded up enough senatorial opposition to get the bill defeated. Later the Congress convention took note of those who had supported McMullen's effort and resolved to 'offer up a sincere prayer that the light of common sense may yet reach the Canadian Manufacturers' Association.'[6]

In 1910 Senator N.A. Belcourt of Ottawa proposed that any trade union whose members were not primarily British subjects be declared an illegal conspiracy in restraint of trade. Though his bill had been endorsed by the president of the national trade-union movement, now called the Canadian Federation of Labor, there were enough opponents on the floor of the red chamber to stymie it. One new friend of international unionism was none other than Lougheed. Noting his own earlier interest in the matter, Lougheed said he had since concluded that most international unions were a public benefit. Businessmen 'had more to gain by appealing to the responsible organizations of an international character than if the strike in question had been instituted simply by a local, limited and largely irresponsible organization.' International unions had a vested interest which they would be disposed to protect through conciliatory tactics.[7] Other senators read letters from trade-union locals criticizing Belcourt's bill. Most agreed with Senator Mitchell, who thought that Canadian and American trade unions had 'as much right to amalgamate as the rubber trust, and the cement trust and all the other trusts.'[8] So overwhelming was the opposition that Belcourt asked permission to drop the bill rather than have it receive a humiliating six months' hoist. Two years later Congress leaders advised Canadian workers to bequeath the Senate to the Mexicans, where they would be 'in their element amidst the making and unmaking of constitutions.'[9] The demise of these measures no doubt impressed many other politicians with the folly of trying to legislate against international unions in Canada without real cause or public clamor.

By the First World War a good many Canadian employers had grown rather fond of using the nationalist 'stick' to beat the labour 'dog.' They 'tell us that it is unpatriotic and un-Canadian for us to send our good Canadian money south of the line,' R.A. Rigg of Winnipeg told AFL delegates. 'They tell us it is a serious breach of this principle of self-respect for us not to have our own Canadian trade unions.' But international trade unions, he declared, represented the common interests of all wage-earners. As Europe teetered on the edge of conflict, Rigg claimed that international unions helped to prevent wars.[10]

Canadian employers pursued one particular anti-trade union tactic with notable success. The Laurier government had lowered immigration barriers to hasten settlement of the prairies. Manufacturers took advantage of this policy (as well as of loopholes in the alien labour law) to import contract labour or to stimulate the flow of specific trades to Canadian employers who wanted workers, sometimes as strike breakers. In mid-1908, *Industrial Canada* pointed to the valley of the Clyde in Scotland as an excellent source of mechanics, and printed its informant's address for the convenience of Canadian employers.[11] The Canadian immigration agent in England lent a helping hand. 'Let me tell you this,' W.T.R. Preston admitted to a reporter, 'if we had not turned English labour into Canada, the American agitators would have had a strike in full swing by now in our country, which would have meant paralysis to every industry, from farming to railroad building.' Montreal manufacturers publicly praised Preston's 'conscientious and energetic' work.[12]

In Western Canada the wave of British immigrants reached tidal proportions. Transportation companies and public and private immigration agencies induced thousands to settle on the prairies. A Vancouverite noted more 'bums' in his city during the recession of 1904 than in all the previous decade. Urban joblessness stemmed partly from the inability of many to adjust to frontier conditions and the harsh climate. 'When those new arrivals experience some of the exhilarating temperature of Manitoba with its 45 below, with a forty-mile wind blowing around the corner of Portage and Main,' one old-timer predicted, 'they are more than likely to inquire for rates to the Old Land.' Though organized labour protested that the Interior Ministry's imported agricultural labour drifted into the cities to compete with industrial workers, the government was not very sympathetic. It was the tendency of the age for people to flock from country to towns, the deputy minister said, and no government or man could stop it.[13]

The Trades and Labor Congress constantly battled CMA efforts to lower immigration barriers. Until exposed by the Congress, Sifton's Glasgow and London agents openly cooperated with the Association. Upon Draper's recommendation the government sent Mackenzie King to England in 1906 to investigate the false representations allegedly made by Canadian agents. The Congress also dispatched one of its officers to give British unions the 'true' picture, but the westward tide across the sea failed to slacken.[14] 'Salvation army announces several thousand more old country job seekers are to be dumped into Western Canada,' a Vancouver unionist reported in 1909. Congress officers declared that 141,841 general labourers and 72,512 mechanics had arrived in Canada during 1912-13, and expressed a 'fearful foreboding as to what the winter of 1914-15 holds in store.'[15]

The Canadians did not hesitate to complain to American labour leaders about the immigration problem confronting them. The Federation convention in 1914 learned that the Canadian government went so far as to offer bonuses in money and land grants to agencies that procured immigrants. Sometimes the AFL aided the Trades Congress, as when Gompers answered European queries with accurate information on labour conditions in Canada. But the only real solution was political in nature, and the AFL did nothing to strengthen the Congress's clout on Parliament Hill. When Draper requested on more than one occasion that the Federation increase its legislative grant to the TLC, the AFL refused, and the immigration problem remained acute until the First World War.[16]

While the waves of immigrant labour hurt some labour groups, others benefited. Many British craftsmen carried their trade-union loyalties across the ocean with them. For example, over 300 of the 850 new members enrolled by Ontario unions in 1904 brought union cards and dues-paying habits from the United Kingdom. 'Unionism is bred right in your blood over there,' one workman recalled. 'I've been a member for thirty-five years. I can't conceive of any circumstances in which I would leave the union ... I'll be a unionist till I die.'[17] The influx of British unionists exerted an important influence on labour politics in Canada. Many sought to defend British institutions on 'British' soil. 'When they appeal to that sentiment,' James Bruce observed, '... there is a spirit that will cause them to fight for British institutions prior to and independent of anything else, whether there is merit in them or not.'[18] Certainly the British influx was partly responsible for the more nationalistic, more politically conscious, more labour party-oriented colouration reflected by Congress conventions by the First World War.

The AFL was much more concerned with the importation of Orientals to the Pacific slope of North America. Because the Laurier government felt bound by the Anglo-Japanese treaty not to bar coolies by edict, mining companies were said to be able to import them at $10 per head. According to one Canadian unionist, over 4000 were landed on the Canadian Pacific coast between January and October of 1907. Some were believed to be crossing the border into the United States. Racist feelings erupted; tempers rose to the boiling point in September of 1907 when a riot broke out in Vancouver. Both Canadian and English newspapers, knowing that American trade unionists had been invited to a rally by the Vancouver branch of the Asiatic Exclusion League, blamed them for the disturbance.[19] The *Toronto Globe* quoted an assertion that the riots had been carefully planned to impress a visiting Japanese official of the need for further restriction. 'It is significant that the leaders of the Seattle organization against Japanese immigration were in Vancouver heading the demonstration,' the

Globe's source declared. Morrison was probably more accurate when he observed that the widespread public hostility to Orientals was the real culprit. 'What is needed,' he went on, 'is careful action which will result in the exclusion of Oriental labor. White labor cannot compete with them. The only remedy is to exclude them.' By emphasizing that Canadians also opposed the influx, Morrison hoped that the Vancouver episode would help the AFL persuade the United States Congress to enact restrictive laws.[20]

Immigrants to Canada from southern and eastern Europe posed another difficult problem for Canadian unions. Labour leaders frequently complained about the competition from Russian Jews and Italians. Some of the Jews were skilled tailors, carpenters, wheelwrights, and blacksmiths; a good many of the Italians swelled the ranks of unskilled labourers. The newcomers were greeted by ethnic prejudices which seemed firmly entrenched in trade-union ranks. 'Of late an inferior class of immigrants are arriving from Continental Europe,' Flett complained at the Congress convention in 1904. 'They do not assimilate, [and] are very slow to adopt our methods of living, herding on the communal plan.'[21] Prejudice made organization work within the building trades doubly difficult. The AFL translated portions of its organizing literature into Italian and Flett attempted to bring labourers in Toronto into the International Hod Carriers and Building Labourers' local. English-speaking labourers in the local refused to have anything to do with the immigrants. They feared that 'if they take the Italians into their union it will draw additional numbers of that particular nationality and eventually [will] drive out those who are born in and around Toronto.' The Federation was continually made aware of the need to organize such groups in Canada, yet the best Morrison could do was to contact the Italian-speaking secretary of a labourers' union in Montreal. He admitted that the AFL had 'no constitutions and other matter in Italian except a few of our organizing leaflets.'[22] Although the high level of immigration was considered a menace to international trade unions, Gompers and his colleagues were unsuccessful in their efforts to obtain legislative relief in either Canada or the United States. Pure-and-simple unionism had failed by 1914 to obtain the political solution to what was admitted to be a serious economic problem, lending weight to the arguments of Canadians who called for greater independent political action by organized labour.[23]

Thanks to the Berlin decisions, the Trades and Labor Congress was perennially challenged after 1902 by a rival, the National Trades and Labor Congress (NTLC), as well as by lesser all-Canadian labour groups. Branching out from its base in Quebec, the NTLC claimed 28 affiliates scattered throughout Eastern Canada by 1907. In the same year restaurant workers from as far as Winnipeg met at a convention in Montreal and made both English *and* French compulsory in locals where both nationalities were represented. A Canadian federation of shoe workers and one of textile operatives flourished in Quebec despite the hostility of the international crafts in those trades. In 1908 A.R. Mosher and M.M. MacLean launched what was to become later the most successful all-Canadian trade union. The Canadian Brotherhood of Railway Employees joined the NTLC (renamed the Canadian Federation of Labor in 1909) and promptly earned the undying enmity of the AFL. Gompers assured one international union official that Canadian national union leaders were working 'ignorantly or knavely' against North American toilers. Unity and solidarity between Canadian and American workers had to be strengthened, not severed or impaired. However, J.W. Watters of the Trades Congress blamed the rise of national unions squarely on the internationals. He said that 'the growth of purely Canadian unionism will be measured by the indifference of the international unions to the necessity of organizing the unorganized Canadian workers.'[24]

As the head of the CFL observed, the degree to which the international crafts feared the Canadian national labour movement could be roughly measured by the level of vituperation and abuse they vented upon the CFL. When the Provincial Workmen's Association of Nova Scotia joined the CFL in 1909, Gompers began a ritual of pronouncing the impending demise of hostile labour groups in Canada. In September 1910 he released a statement to the press from AFL headquarters in Washington roundly denouncing the CFL. There was no question in his mind that the Canadian Federation was financed by the Canadian Manufacturers' Association to keep labour divided at the border. On the other hand, he said, the Trades and Labor Congress realized that 'the industrial interests and the moral and social interests of the workers of Canada and the United States are identical.' Canadian interests were well represented, he claimed, mentioning three international union officials who had been born in the country. He had no doubt that Canadian workers would continue to stand by the 'advantages of mutual cooperation.' But the national movement managed to limp along on periodic infusions from dissatisfied or disgruntled men fleeing from their international craft locals. Contrary to Gompers' almost annual declamations, dual unionism in Canada was neither down nor out by the First World War.[25]

With the shift by the AFL in 1903 from an offensive to a defensive posture, Flett's activities broadened considerably in scope. Expected to rekindle faith and enthusiasm wherever he went, he was frequently called upon to address union meetings. He attended many Trades Congress gatherings, and sometimes appeared at international union conventions as well. He wrote articles for the *American Federationist,* filed weekly reports with Federation headquarters, conducted a voluminous correspondence with Gompers and Morrison, handled problems brought to the AFL's attention by its directly affiliated federal labour unions in Canada, carried out requests by international union heads to service their Canadian locals, investigated crackpot letters, and infrequently greeted foreign labour dignitaries touring the country. On the road for weeks at a time, Flett spent long hours away from his family and took no regular vacations except for a few days during the Christmas season.[26]

After the Berlin decisions, the AFL felt comparatively free to use Flett on both sides of the border. In 1907 Gompers sent the Canadian on an assignment to Bath, New York, a town about a hundred miles from the Niagara frontier. Although Flett had worked before on the American side at Niagara Falls, the Bath assignment was the first drawing the Canadian some distance away from his assigned territory. Apparently Flett welcomed the new opportunity, for he asked and was granted permission to work for two weeks along the southern tier of New York State. Later Morrison found it necessary to discourage Flett's southward movements. 'I believe it will be better for you to continue your work in the Dominion of Canada, except in rare cases, where we have extraordinary work, which requires the most available organizer to do the work.' Despite the Federation's change of mind, the trip to Bath had established two precedents: Flett found that he liked to work on the American side, and AFL leaders decided thereafter to bring the Canadian across the line when the occasion warranted.'[27]

After the great steel strike of 1909 was declared, the Federation sent a number of its organizers to places where there were non-union factories to persuade workers there to join the struggle. Morrison ordered Flett into the fray. For the better part of four months he toiled among the steel operatives of Pennsylvania and Ohio. The needs of the Canadian labour movement took a back seat during this period, and Morrison on at least one occasion instructed Flett to disregard a call for help from a Canadian local.[28]

What at first had been infrequent episodes in Flett's working life became a steady diet by the First World War. In January 1913 Morrison directed Flett to Rochester to assist a United Garment Workers' strike. The union's own organizers had been called to New York City, Morrison explained, and Flett was told to maintain the organizing efforts that had been 'moving the hearts of the Garment Workers in Rochester.' Flett remained on the south shore of Lake Ontario until the strike ended three months later. But less than two weeks after he had returned to his Canadian work, Morrison ordered him to Buffalo where the streetcar workers had struck. Flett stayed in Buffalo for over a year and one-half to help reorganize the huge central body there. The AFL's Canadian organizer spared only one week for the Canadian labour scene during this period.[29]

By the First World War the needs of the Federation craft affiliates in the United States took clear precedence over those of the Trades Congress. Though the AFL debited Flett's expenses to its work in Canada, for all intents and purposes he had worked in the country less than a month during 1913-14. The international crafts used Flett and other Federation organizers as reserves to be thrown into American industrial struggles at critical moments. Requests for Flett's aid from Trades Congress leaders and Canadian locals were honoured when convenient, but they were denied preference over demands from Gompers' colleagues. A regional survey will show that the Federation's chief efforts in Canada reflected the primacy of Gompers' interests and experiences in the United States.

THE MARITIMES

During the summer of 1903, while Flett and Draper worked in Ottawa to defeat the Lougheed bill, Flett laid plans for his second trip to the Maritimes. The AFL's Canadian organizer was anxious to return to the east in order to settle the controversy over Federal Labor Union no. 10 in Charlottetown, to moderate the clamour raised by Maritime unionists for an organizer in their area, and to blunt criticism of the Berlin decisions by workers sympathetic to the Maritimes-based Provincial Workmen's Association. By this time Gompers had full confidence in Flett's abilities and his loyalty to the AFL. Assuming that Flett was thoroughly familiar with industrial conditions in the Maritimes, he let the Canadian draw up his own plan of work.[30]

Although Flett made little headway in organizing new locals, he did settle the dispute in Prince Edward Island. He arrived at the island capital in September with William V. Todd, a Toronto cigarmaker, and persuaded the Charlottetown Council to seat a representative from the Congress-chartered federal union. By June of 1904 Secretary Morrison of the Federation had received word that 'the dove of peace was hovering around that locality,' yet he was still sceptical of the outcome. 'I imagine that that little Federal Labor Union cannot be of much account anyway,' he told Flett. 'If it was, it would take out a charter from the A.F. of L. direct and be in a position to receive strike benefits.' Morrison had little use for any group unanointed by the American Federation of Labor.[31]

Flett returned to the Maritimes in the spring of 1905. Gompers had received word that the American Labor Union had begun to organize some 17,000 lobster fishermen working along the coasts of Maine and the Maritimes. To prevent incursions by its rival, the Federation chartered a lobster fishermen's union and dispatched both Flett and Stuart Reid, the AFL New England organizer, to the scene. Reid hired an old fisherman with a boat and began spreading the union message along the rocky coasts of Maine. Within a short time seven locals had been set up in as many different towns. Morrison sent Reid's enthusiastic reports to Flett, and suggested that he take up the work in Nova Scotia in the same manner.[32] Flett, however, seemed resentful at having been yanked away from his stomping grounds in Ontario, and was even gloomier over his lack of success in Nova Scotia. With each glowing letter from Reid, Morrison received a depressing tale from Flett, who asked finally to be permitted to return to central Canada. 'I do not know what to think about Flett,' Morrison told Reid, 'except that unless he has some better success, it would probably be well to have him return to a district where he can accomplish some material good.'[33]

A few days later Flett sent the AFL secretary some newspaper clippings with discouraging news. They probably recounted moves by the government of Nova Scotia to establish fishermen's unions under a law passed by the provincial assembly on 7 April 1905. The measure set out to create 'unions' under provincial ægis by enabling any fifteen fishermen to incorporate a 'station' in the 'Fishermen's Union of Nova Scotia,' a body apparently designed to keep the farmers of the sea out of the regular trade-union movement. At the first meeting of the new body later that year, the fishermen decided not to accept help from any trade-union organizers. Upon receiving the clippings, Morrison telegraphed Flett to return to Ontario. The Canadian organizer of the AFL reached Hamilton suffering from a severe headcold after having spent six fruitless weeks tramping up and down the soggy, frigid coves of Nova Scotia. His experiences seemed to have soured him on the efficacy of organizing work in the whole region, and he revisited the Maritimes only once during the next decade.[34]

It was not long before an organizer for the Journeymen Tailors brought the deteriorated condition of Maritimes trade unionism to Gompers' attention and pointed to the need for vigorous organizing work there. AFL leaders demurred, citing the distance, the costs, and the improbability of significant gains. When carpenters in Amherst asked Morrison for help, the Federation secretary calculated that Flett would be required to travel a thousand miles and decided it would be too expensive 'for just one little city.' The Amherst men were turned down again eighteen months later.[35] Sydney steel workers, some working a seven-day week for $30 per month, pleaded with Morrison and Draper for help. After consulting with Flett, who expressed considerable doubt about undertaking the trip, Morrison decided to allow Cape Breton 'to rest for the moment.' Trades Congress leaders journeyed east to revive flagging interest, but without much success.[36]

Draper blamed the Provincial Workmen's Association for exerting a disruptive influence. In the PWA Nova Scotia clerks, printers, plumbers, and blacksmiths were all jumbled together with the coal miners. Draper told the Congress in 1905 that he wanted John Mitchell to go to Nova Scotia, destroy the Association, and organize the miners under the United Mine Workers of America. It seems likely that Gompers, Flett, and the international unions decided to mark time until their powerful affiliate, the United Mine Workers, ousted the Provincial Workmen's Association from control of the Nova Scotia minefields.[37]

The Provincial Workmen's Association had sprung up among the Maritimes coal miners in 1879. Conflicts with the Knights of Labor reduced the PWA to less than a thousand members by the late 1890s. In 1899 the union began a campaign to win back the confidence of the miners. It was not without good results; by 1903 the Association had a membership of nearly eight thousand in forty-four lodges. The union's finances similarly improved when steel workers, retail clerks, shoeworkers, railwaymen, garment workers, and other trades were attached in 1903. But in the same year a strike in the steel mills panicked the other trades, who quickly left the union, fearing that a call for a sympathetic strike would throw them all out of work. The company was able to break the strike with the aid of the militia, and thereafter the Provincial Workmen's Association never quite recovered.[38]

After the Trades Congress had pledged its allegiance to the AFL, it sought to establish friendly relations with the Association. The Congress learned from Kempton McKim, an AFL organizer in Halifax, that the PWA was not in sympathy with other labour organizations. In March 1904, a committee of the Halifax Trades and Labor Council conversed with the Association's directorate and suggested that PWA lodges link up with the central bodies of Nova Scotia, a plan directly contravening paragraph 2 of the AFL Executive Council decisions made in Toronto the previous year. Later, the Halifax Council regretfully informed the miners that direct affiliation of the Association with the Trades Congress was impossible under the Berlin amendments. Then a Trades Congress committee called for renewed efforts to get the Provincial Workmen's Association into the international union movement, and the Association's leaders agreed to consider sending a delegate to observe the next Congress gathering.[39]

Gompers learned much about the Provincial Workmen's Association from a volunteer organizer in Halifax. Thomas Sheehan told the Federation president a bit about the background of the miners' union, noted their penetration into nearly every county in Nova Scotia, and quoted their membership at 28,000. 'I might state,' he added, 'that they are against the international movement and will not affiliate with anything outside of Nova Scotia.' Sheehan blamed the Association for the weakness of international unions in the Maritimes, and warned Gompers of the consequences of delay.

Sometime ago I organized a painters' union in Truro, N.S. and after the local was working along nicely, a member of the P.W.A. sought an interview with its officers and secured an invitation to address a meeting, the subject being to cut loose from their international body and join the P.W.A.; but I happened to be in Truro at the time and hearing about this thing going to take place went to the meeting hall, and just arrived as the president was going to put the vote to the members, and of course interfered and addressed the members as the only salvation for the wage workers and the union man was by being affiliated with the international movement. I just mention this and show you what we are up against in this province of Nova Scotia.[40]

If the AFL did not take action, Sheehan said, 'then the International movement in this part of the globe goes out of business.' He offered to represent the Federation on a salaried basis, but his plea for a job put Gompers on guard. The Federation made no move to enhance its strength in the Maritimes, and shortly thereafter Sheehan resigned his volunteer's commission.

In 1907 the United Mine Workers (UMW) began to aid international unionism in the Maritimes, and rapidly won the sympathy and support of a minority within the Provincial Workmen's Association. At a meeting of the Association's Grand Council on 17 September 1907, the dissidents introduced a resolution which asked the Association leaders to invite either John Mitchell or a Mine Workers' organizer to visit the lodges and inform them of the aims, objectives, and workings of the international union of miners. The motion also called for a vote on amalgamation to follow upon the organizer's visit. The resolution, which was seconded by James McLachlan, later the leading spokesman for the Mine Workers in Nova Scotia, was lost. Subsequently, several lodges broke with the Association and switched over to the Mine Workers. In May 1908 the Grand Council, retaliating against agitation by the international union, took action to have the recalcitrant lodges expelled from the Association. The Mine Workers responded with a campaign to dislodge the Association by compelling coal mine operators to recognize the international union.[41]

The Trades and Labor Congress convention of 1908 could not remain aloof from the conflict between the Mine Workers and the Provincial Workmen's Association. One Congress official told the delegates that the secessions from the Association to the international union of miners had reflected a desire to get out of the 'narrow rut of "Provincialism" which has been the prevailing feature for so long a time.' Later the Congress passed a resolution congratulating the miners who had broken away from the Association. By early 1909 about three thousand miners had joined the United Mine Workers, about the same number remained in the Association, and the rest were outside the trade-union movement entirely. The PWA, forced out of its isolation by the inroads of the international union, moved to link up with the Canadian Federation of Labor.[42]

In order to compel recognition of their union by employers, the United Mine Workers called a strike in Dominion Coal Company mines at Glace Bay, Inverness, and Springhill. A board appointed under the Lemieux Act endorsed the company's refusal to recognize the union. 'Foreign officials,' the report declared, 'sitting at Indianapolis [headquarters of the UMW], should not have the power to decree that Nova Scotia miners, even when without a grievance, must stop working, and thereby cripple a great Nova Scotia industry.'[43] Violence broke out in early July when striking UMW supporters tried to prevent PWA men from working, and the militia was called out in Glace Bay and Inverness. Several UMW men were arrested on charges arising out of the riots and their families suffered eviction from company homes. Though the strike dragged on for months, it failed to halt mining activities, and as early as 14 July the company claimed that production levels were steadily improving.[44]

The battle for control of the Nova Scotia coal mines attracted wide notice. On the floor of the Canadian Senate, old warhorses like Sir Mackenzie Bowell denounced international unionism. Some employers charged that the UMW incursion represented a scheme by American coal operators to capture the St Lawrence trade.[45] Meanwhile the Toronto District Labor Council endorsed the UMW's tactics, and the Trades Congress criticized the Provincial Workmen's Association for failing to join the Mine Workers' strike.[46] At UMW request the American Federation adopted a resolution in 1911 which condemned PWA leaders, branding them outlaws, a menace to civilized communities, and traitors who cooperated with employers' thugs, thereby placing themselves lower than 'the meanest scab or strikebreaker.'[47]

The harsh rhetoric reflected the AFL affiliate's declining fortunes. UMW reports showed the expenditure of over $960,000 in strike benefits in Nova Scotia during 1910, but the strikes came to naught. By 1915 there were less than thirty members of the American union in the whole province. It had been defeated by the combined efforts of hostile public officials, an entrenched PWA, and a stubborn employer. The charter of UMW District 26 was withdrawn and the international union of coal miners turned its attention to other fields. Though the Trades Congress president later endeavoured to reconcile the conflicting labour interests, both sides remained embittered. By the First World War Canadian workers had gained nothing from the attempts of this AFL affiliate to extend its tentacles into Nova Scotia. 'But for the outbreak of war in 1914, PWA secretary Moffatt wrote long afterward, 'it is doubtful if any attempt would have been made by the U.M.W. of A. to re-organize for many years later.'[48]

QUEBEC

Nowhere did Gompers' efforts to achieve a continental monopoly falter more significantly than in the citadel of French Canada. Indeed, the Berlin decisions seemed almost 'racial' in their consequences, for seventeen of the twenty-three unions expelled from the Trades and Labor Congress in 1902 were predominantly French Canadian. In Montreal the Central Trades and Labor Council, five assemblies of the Knights of Labor, four locals of the Canadian Boot and Shoe Makers, a barbers' local, and a coopers' local were placed beyond the pale. In Quebec city the central body, two Knights of Labor assemblies, and two Shoe Makers' locals joined their Montreal brethren. Together these seventeen organizations, totalling over 1600 unionists, formed the core of the National Trades and Labor Congress which arose in reaction to the Berlin decisions.[49]

Of course no one in the craft internationals thought dual unionism would survive in Quebec. Equating urbanization with Anglicization, they fully expected to win over French Canadians to international unionism in the near future in Quebec city and other urban centres just as they had done in Montreal in the recent past. Since they were confident that the French-Canadian industrial worker would eventually accommodate himself to North American trade unions, they saw no need to cater to what later generations would call the 'French fact.' The Anglo-Saxonism of the pre-First World War era gave craft-union leaders a very false sense of security.

It is doubtful whether Gompers or the international union leaders at the time were aware of the strength of clerical influence in Quebec, or that the Roman Catholic clergy considered themselves arch defenders of the French-Canadian language and customs as well as of the faith. With the rise of factories in the late nineteenth century, Quebec clergy turned for guidance to the Church social policy laid down in *Rerum novarum* in 1891. By stressing the factors uniting employers and workers, the encyclical contradicted the socialist outlook on society. When it spoke of the need to give social institutions a religious orientation, it challenged a trade-union philosophy dedicated exclusively to secular goals. But church-backed unionism in Quebec was not designed simply to combat secularism or socialism. French-Canadian clerics thought that they were preserving the French language and culture from a new threat by neighbouring Canadian and American Anglo-Saxons. Hence the Quebec clergy readily sympathized with dual unionism, partly because it was more difficult for clerics to influence an international union local than a national one, and also because the international unions were thought to purvey a secular Anglo-Saxon culture (and sometimes an atheistic Marxist philosophy). Dual unions became an important way of shielding French Canadians from *les anglais* – Canadian or American.[50]

Confessional unionism did not immediately appear after the Berlin decisions; the first Catholic syndicates were set up under the guise of national unions. After Mgr Bégin settled the Quebec city shoeworkers' strike in 1901, many locals in the province were persuaded to admit a chaplain into their councils and accept the Church's guidance. Thereafter the clergy led the attack on international unions in Quebec. To strengthen their case, they sometimes accused the Federation of wanting to impose socialism upon workers, and they joined those who criticized the flow of Canadian money into American labour's treasuries.[51]

On the Sunday following the AFL leaders' Toronto meeting in 1903 (where the Trades Congress had been formally incorporated into the AFL structure), Archbishop Bruchési of Montreal denounced international unionism in a letter read from every pulpit in his diocese. '... With the greatest anxiety do we see the labor organizations of our city seeking for affiliation with foreign associations. The majority of the leaders and members of those international unions have nothing in common with our temperament, our customs and our faith.' He admitted that the AFL affiliates were not subverting Christian principles, nor were they allied with secret societies condemned by the Church. His criticism, in other words, actually emerged out of the unique French experience in North America and did not derive its primary impulse from religious doctrine.[52]

By and large the American Federation of Labor failed to understand the French-Canadian worker and his society; Gompers could only express astonishment at Bruchési's pastoral letter. Yet the Federation had made no effort to gallicize itself to the extent of printing union literature in French, though some was available in English, Spanish, German, and Italian.[53] More important, AFL leaders were hesitant to admit the need for a French-speaking organizer in Canada. '... Il foudrait de toute necessité un organisateur parlant les deux langues, l'anglais et le français,' Quebec labour leaders noted in 1905, 'car la masse des ouvriers de Québec ne comprennent pas l'anglais.'[54] Gompers and Frank Morrison were repeatedly given this message, in English as well as in French – to no avail. Rather than adopt a strategy designed to cope with the unique aspects of the Quebec situation, the AFL and the international union heads were content for the most part to sit tight and deal with each dual union as it appeared. Federation leaders seemed more preoccupied with warding off rival unions than with expanding the organized sector of French-Canadian labour.

As we have seen, the dual-unionist threat in the Montreal shoemaking trade was important in bringing about the Berlin amendments to the Trades and Labor Congress constitution in 1902. In the fall of 1903 president Tobin of the Boot and Shoe Workers' International Union reported the defeat of the dual shoe workers' union in Montreal. Flett had been instrumental in the victory, he told

Gompers, and his twin roles as president of the Trades and Labor Congress and AFL organizer had been particularly valuable in bringing about a favourable result. But dual unionism would surface again and again. For example, four years later Flett noted the formation of a Canadian Federation of Textile Workers in the same city, and once again the international movement went into action. In December 1909 the threat diminished when 5000 members of the dual union voted to join the United Textile Workers of America.[55]

Throughout these years Quebec labour leaders annually pleaded for the services of a French-speaking organizer. Their requests were often submitted to Patrick M. Draper, the Congress secretary-treasurer, whose organization was both powerless and penniless to fulfil the need. Morrison told Draper in 1905 that he favoured an appointment, though the Federation could not afford the added expense. Later he admitted placing little importance on the language factor. He had been told frequently that only a bilingual man could effectively organize unions in French Canada, but reports had convinced him 'that the very best work that has even been performed in Montreal and those localities has been accomplished by a one-languaged man.'[56] Although Flett also noted the demands for a French-speaking organizer, and mentioned them to Morrison, he did not press the issue to the point of risking his job, or studying the French language. Consequently, international trade unionism tended to slumber outside of the Montreal area. At the Congress convention in 1908 Quebec labour leaders pronounced the movement dead in Quebec city, and declared that 'the demand [for an organizer] should be definitely and immediately settled.'[57] It was taking some time for the AFL to see the connection between the 'French fact' and the presence of a separate national trade-union movement in Quebec. 'Some day,' Morrison told Flett, 'we will have to put an organizer in Quebec and keep him there until that situation is cleaned up ...' By 1909 the AFL was finally ready to take that first step.[58]

Responding in the spring of 1909 to Draper's perennial request, Morrison finally agreed to hire Joseph Ainey, a bilingual Montreal carpenter. The great steel strike of 1909 in the United States intervened to divert Morrison's attention for a time, but at last he arranged to place Ainey on the payroll for two months starting in September. Ainey was promised $5 a day for a six-day week, and $2.50 a day for expenses. 'While I realize that two months is rather a short period to give the best results, yet I believe that you can be of considerable assistance ...' he told the Montrealer.[59]

The suspicious Ainey had no doubts about the magnitude of his task. He reported to Morrison that the Trades Congress convention at Quebec city was being overshadowed in the local press by a gathering elsewhere in the city of the Roman Catholic hierarchy. It was just a coincidence that the clergymen were meeting at the same time as the Trades Congress, Morrison assured him, though 'coincidences sometimes appear very strange.'[60] Later Ainey procured a thousand organizing circulars from the Federation and began working among textile operatives in Magog. After he had addressed a meeting of three hundred workers, they voted to join the international union. Returning to Montreal, he laboured among shoe workers until sent to Ottawa to assist Congress leaders making their presentation to the Laurier government. Although his progress was slight, the AFL decided to keep Ainey on the payroll through the winter, and early in 1910 Morrison urged Flett to go to Quebec city to assist him.[61]

At that moment Ainey requested a three-week leave of absence in order to run for the office of controller of Montreal. Morrison, obviously displeased with dabbles in politics, doubted whether there would be sufficient money to retain him after the Montreal election. 'You will have to go it alone in Quebec and do the best you can for a short time,' Morrison instructed Flett, and 'then come back to Montreal and then Ottawa.' The move to put a bilingual organizer into French Canada having aborted, Federation leaders resumed their old argument about the AFL shortage of funds.[62]

Assisted by Michael Walsh, a French-speaking volunteer, Flett worked throughout January to secure the affiliation of the Quebec city Trades and Labor Council to the AFL. Morrison made it clear that dual unionism was still the Federation's prime concern: '... We have heard so much about Quebec, and this so-called National Organization, that it is necessary for the American Federation of Labor to thoroughly organize that district, and if possible wipe out this organization ...'[63] After securing an AFL charter for the Quebec Council, Flett remained another month to pursue his organizing work. Locals of blacksmiths, bookbinders, and tailors were set up before he left Walsh in charge and returned to English-speaking Canada. Flett's efforts were not enough, though, to still the clamour for another Ainey.[64]

The Trades and Labor Congress, the Montreal Trades Council, and Ainey himself (who had won his electoral bid) all reminded Morrison of the critical need for a French-speaking organizer.[65] There was no possible chance of filling the post, Morrison responded, 'any more than there is to appoint an organizer for each State.' The Federation had fourteen organizers in the field at that time and Flett was Canada's fair share as far as the AFL was concerned.[66] But Morrison could not easily ignore the persistent requests from north of the border. 'What do you say to going down into Montreal and putting in some time there?' he asked Flett in early 1911. 'We are short of organizers and at the present time have no money to add new ones and there is a great cry coming up from Montreal for a French speaking organizer.'[67]

Flett arrived in Montreal in late February 1911, prepared to spend several weeks stirring up trade-union interest. He reported the near collapse of a dual union of shoemakers in Montreal, and began working among textile workers at once. There were seven or eight thousand workers in the Montreal clothing industry, he said. Several locals of the international union, the United Garment Workers, had folded and had been supplanted by a couple of independent locals. 'I approached these people with the proposition to become affiliates with the U.G.W. of A. They appointed a committee to confer with me, at this meeting they expressed a willingness to take a charter direct from the A.F. of L ...' The workers were fearful of losing their autonomy as well as their money to dishonest business agents if they joined the United Garment Workers. Flett explained that the AFL could not encroach upon international union jurisdictions, and suggested that they organize a district council within the Garment Workers to protect their local interests. The workers rejected Flett's advice; the Federation's Canadian organizer recounted their story to give Morrison 'an idea of what confronts the organizer here.'[68]

Flett again added his voice to the pleas for a francophone associate, making it clear to Morrison that little could be done in Quebec without one. 'I think I thoroughly understand,' Morrison replied. '... I have always felt that an English speaking organizer had more effect in bringing about organization ... but I suppose the sentiment that exists must be catered to to a certain extent, and the Federation, if it has the funds, may arrange to put a man in the field for a short time ...' There was no pressing need, Morrison felt, because two Federation affiliates already had French-speaking men at work in the province.[69]

If the success of international unionism in French Canada was measured in 1911 by the weakness of its enemies, then Federation leaders had no visible cause for alarm. Trades Congress leaders reported that the national labour movement was practically dead in Montreal, and international unions had scored gains recently in Quebec city. Even Henri Bourassa's crowd agreed with the political and social aims of Montreal international union leaders, finding their independence from Grits and Tories especially attractive. Thus, in the first decade of this century, no one goaded American labour leaders into testing the affection of French-Canadian workers by a concerted organizing effort. Despite pleas from the Trades Congress for a bilingual organizer, Flett continued to handle international union affairs in French Canada. Relying upon the litmus of dual unionism to pattern their activities, Federation leaders left the initiative to others. By the First World War both Bourassa and the most powerful institution in Quebec were ready to take up the challenge posed by international unionism.[70]

Church-influenced unionism had made little headway over the decade since Mgr Bégin had settled the strike in the Quebec shoe trade. Until 1907 the clergy rarely participated in the formation of trade unions, but at a meeting of the League of the Sacred Heart in Montreal that year, Mgr Bruchési called for the creation of confessional unions. The Société Saint Jean Baptiste set up the first Catholic unions among women employed in Montreal factories. Pulp and paper workers in Chicoutimi, previously ignored by the Federation, were organized by a priest.[71] Then, in the spring of 1911, the Ecole sociale populaire was founded with clerical support to tell French-Canadian workers about the merits of Catholic unions. The secretary of the Ecole deplored the presence of international union locals in Quebec because, he explained, the AFL affiliates were neutral with regard to the French race and religion. They willingly sympathized with socialists, entertained left-wing ideas, and possessed anti-clerical tendencies. As proof of the latter charge, he cited the international unions' endorsement of compulsory public education and their constitutional bar against the discussion of religious issues at union meetings. By 1914 the secretary had brought many Montreal teamsters, carpenters, and office employees into a city-wide labour federation rivalling the Montreal Trades and Labor Council.[72]

French-Canadian clerics were powerfully aided in 1912 by a new papal encyclical, *Singulari quadam*, which had been prompted by conditions in Europe rather than in North America. Pope Pius X called for the establishment of confessional unions in Catholic countries 'and also in other regions wherever it will appear possible to fill the different needs of the members.'[73] Within weeks Bishop Emile Cloutier of Three Rivers was citing this document to buttress his exortations among the workers of that diocese. A meeting of employers and workers was held at the Hotel de Ville in Three Rivers on Boxing Day 1912, under the mayor's gavel. Bishop Cloutier, the curés, the aldermen, and J.-A. Langlois, an industrialist and member of the provincial legislature, were among the prominent assembled. Both the bishop and the industrialist praised Quebec city unions formed under Mgr Bégin's rules. Cloutier afterwards launched *La Corporation Ouvrière Catholique des Trois-Rivières*, enrolled over two hundred carpenters, moulders, shoemakers, and carters, and placed them under the guidance of his appointed chaplain. When membership spiralled to six hundred by March of 1913, Cloutier gave the new group land to build a Maison des Ouvriers with officers, rooms, a lecture hall, and an employment bureau. On Labour Day of the same year he spoke at Mass of the *Corporation*'s success; in the afternoon a civic festival culminated in ceremonies dedicating the *Maison*. Under the ægis of the clergy, the confessional movement spread rapidly and claimed 6325 members throughout the four dioceses of Quebec by 1914. Such successes won Bourassa to the cause of Catholic unionism.[74]

The United Brotherhood of Carpenters and Joiners probably devoted more attention to pre-World War Quebec than did any other AFL affiliate and was the first to feel the brunt of confessional unionism. Even before Bishop Cloutier had launched his campaign, Frank Duffy of the Carpenters had vigorously complained to Baltimore's Cardinal Gibbons about denunciations of international unionism by Quebec clerics. He argued in Bruce Barton style that Christ had been a carpenter, an organizer of men, and an advocate of trade-union principles. Christ had commanded men to love one another, feed the hungry, clothe the naked, visit the sick, and bury the dead, and 'that is just what our trade unions are doing,' Duffy declared. 'How objections can be raised to them by the clergy anywhere is more than I can understand ...' While the Cardinal acknowledged that unions had generally been a force for good, he disclaimed familiarity with conditions in Canada and said he could only speak with reference to the United States.[75]

The next year Duffy and the union president went to Quebec to see for themselves, were astonished at what they encountered, and conveyed their incredulity to Gompers. Americans had long since abolished chattel slavery, the president reported, and trade unions were struggling against wage slavery, 'but while in Canada I encountered a new proposition in the way of religious slavery. I found the Catholic clergymen utterly arrayed against the Internation[al] Trade [Union] Movement ... The Parish of Three Rivers has erected a large brick building for the headquarters of this Organization and the pulpit is used for the purpose of exhorting people to join.' Although the confessional unions had not yet gained a strong foothold in Montreal, he had found them entrenched at Three Rivers and elsewhere. He promised to fight them because 'we realize that if they are not beaten at home, they will spread.' He hoped that the other trades and the AFL would lend a helping hand.[76]

The Federation dared not ignore a situation threatening one of its most powerful affiliates. In June 1913 Morrison agreed to finance jointly with the Trades and Labor Congress a four-month organizing effort by G.R. Brunet, a francophone. Brunet journeyed from Montreal to St Hyacinthe, Sherbrooke, Quebec City, Rivière-du-Loup, and Three Rivers and returned convinced of the need for a full-time organizer in Quebec. The Federation secretary asked him for more information about confessional unions; Brunet told Morrison that they had just set up a local among girls in the Montreal cotton mills and were 'working hard to extend their system.'[77]

The international union organizers in Quebec faced a new barrage of criticism. Local newspapers called them socialists, freemasons, and desperate characters. Hotel owners refused them halls for mass meetings. One hostile circular read:

If they loved and desired the welfare of the workers they would not make such efforts in trying to abstract from their souls their confidence in their priests and their bishop and also their love for the teachings of the Holy Church.

WORKERS BEWARE.

A dangerous assault is now being waged against you.

In the worst circle where the most hideous plots are being organized against the Catholic Church, they have pledged themselves to capture you.

Let not these agents of the enemies army enter into your christian homes.

Workers beware, do not give your money nor your name to become members of a society whose chiefs you do not know.

The pope, your bishop, and your priests cry to you, beware do not pass to the enemies camp.

And the enemy cries do not listen to your priests they do not know what they say as this question does not interfere with religion.

CATHOLIC WORKERS BEWARE:– If Mr. Arcant is as good a Catholic as he pretends why does he come here and oppose our bishop and our priests? Why does he not obey the pope and his parish priest? What do you call a Catholic who does not attack the priest in his face but insinuates all sorts of injurious suspicions on his conduct.[78]

The promoters of confessional unionism, Quebec labour leaders pointed out, included some of the most influential people in French-Canadian cities. It became increasingly evident to AFL leaders that the international trade-union movement confronted a threat of considerable magnitude. Gompers concluded that any Quebec trade-union faction which challenged the international form of organization posed a distinct menace to workers in both Canada and the United States.[79]

The Quebec situation received considerable attention at the American Federation convention in 1913. The Congress fraternal delegate, Gus Francq, told the Americans something of the history of unions in French Canada and of the unique circumstances encountered there. Whereas Anglo-Saxons were imbued with trade-union principles since youth, he explained, French-Canadian workers, 'owing to a peculiarity of the Latin race,' resisted collective efforts. Isolation had bred a native suspicion of foreigners, and was reinforced by community leaders who denounced international unions as unpatriotic and advised workers not to send their dues out of the country. Francq pointed to the need for constant organizing efforts to keep up with the stream of people moving from country to city, and stressed the importance of French-speaking organizers and literature in French. He related the case of a Quebec local which had been suspended by union headquarters because of a misunderstanding spawned by the linguistic barrier. The local failed to understand why its dues had been raised. 'There had followed an exchange of letters, in French from the local parties, and in English from the general headquarters, with the result that this local having been suspended, returned its charter and started an independent union ...' More than a little effort would be needed to induce them to rejoin the international trade-union movement. The Federation fraternal delegate to Canada seconded Francq's analysis of the situation in Quebec and urged the AFL to comply with the request for an organizer. After the convention the Federation decided to keep Brunet on its payroll for an indefinite period.[80]

Throughout 1914 Brunet laboured to counter the gains made by the cleric-backed unions. He established federal labour unions at Chicoutimi and Jonquière, and worked among the hod carriers, leather workers, and garment makers in Montreal. In the spring Morrison sent him to Quebec city to restore life in the international movement at the provincial capital. Brunet found labour groups there in very poor condition but his efforts received a 'hearty response' and prospects looked good, he said, for locals of plumbers, tobacco workers, and electricians. At Three Rivers, the centre of confessional unionism, Brunet tried but failed to persuade Morrison to halve the fifty-cent dues levied by the AFL on federal labour unions. By the outbreak of the First World War the international union movement claimed eighteen new locals in Quebec and a Trades Council in Three Rivers. Trades Congress leaders attributed the gains largely to Brunet's efforts. Publicly and privately, Canadian and American trade unionists believed that they had stemmed the tide, but dual unions proved to have roots much deeper in the soil along the banks of the St Lawrence than international unions ever realized. After the First World War, confessional unionism burst into full bloom in Quebec.[81]

ONTARIO

During the heyday of organizing activities in 1901 and 1902, dozens of federal labour unions (FLUs) had been set up in Ontario, many in small towns containing insufficient numbers to warrant a craft local. Now, letters began to pour into AFL headquarters detailing their trials and tribulations. A member in Collingwood begged for an organizer to arouse the enthusiasm of his fellow workers. Although Flett did his best, apparently it was not enough. 'I never saw a man who tried harder,' this worker noted, 'and yet, the workers of the town are so apathetic that, even he accomplished little or nothing.' The Collingwood FLU remained completely disorganized.[82] The same condition was repeated in other Ontario towns. 'We are holding our own among a lot of opposition and would very much like you to send Mr. Flett amongst us for a few days,' a Chatham unionist wrote. Two months later, their request ignored, they repeated their pleas for 'someone who can put new life into the cause.' The secretary of the Thorold FLU returned the local's charter to Morrison and informed him that there were not enough members left to maintain the union. A local in Lindsay disbanded and placed its funds under the trusteeship of Senator McHugh.[83] The Niagara Falls district was particularly turbulent. Flett was called there a half-dozen times to help federal labour unions involved in the construction of hydro-electric power installations. In 1904 he amicably settled a strike of the Rock Drillers and Helpers no. 10160 at the Ontario Power Company works. Later other locals in the area got into difficulty, but despite Flett's best efforts the labour movement had declined precipitously along the Niagara frontier by mid-1907.[84]

The Federation's Canadian organizer repeatedly urged the American inter-national unions to hoe the garden already planted. 'Ontario has nearly half as many unions as all of the other provinces in Canada combined,' Flett wrote, 'and with few exceptions these are affiliated with international bodies; but in order to maintain that activity so necessary to success, periodical visits should be paid by their respective international officers or representatives.'[85] Flett continued to carry much of the burden. Morrison sent him back to the Falls in 1907, knowing that it was 'discouraging to an organizer to put him into a locality where he may work for weeks without seeming to accomplish any tangible results.' Flett was called upon to use his 'very best efforts, experiences and knowledge to bring about the desired results,' and he finally succeeded in organizing a new trades council in late August.[86]

At times Flett found a way to preserve a local or bail it out of difficulty. He saved a labourers' protective local in Berlin by arranging to transfer it into the Hod Carriers' International without payment of an initiation fee. He intervened in a strike of porcelain enamellers at Port Hope whose union president had been fired when the firm had learned of the existence of a local. The company was persuaded to back down and the men returned to work.[87] During the winter of 1907-8 Flett's difficulties were enhanced by the presence of 2000 unemployed in Toronto, 1000 or more in Hamilton, 800 in Berlin, and smaller numbers in other Ontario towns. Throughout the country civic authorities were compelled to provide work for unusual numbers of unemployed.[88] Many trade-union leaders concluded that the times were not ripe for new organizing efforts. There-after the bulk of Flett's work in Ontario, the best organized province in the country, involved combating secessions and jurisdictional disputes – the enemies within the craft unions (see chapter 10).

WESTERN CANADA

The tasks facing the AFL throughout those vast stretches of Canadian territory west of the lakehead matched the problems encountered elsewhere in the country. At first glance the biggest difference stemmed from the left-wing politics entertained by so large a segment of Western workers, yet radical politics often manifested itself in the familiar danger of dual unionism. Prairie cities also were very hard hit by immigration after 1903, and workers in Pacific coast cities feared inundation by the boatloads of Orientals regularly putting into port. Organising work was made even more difficult by the great distances between urban centres and the near-total reliance by American unions upon volunteer efforts. Both Gompers and Morrison kept a close watch on the international trade-union movement in Western Canada, and their interest was clearly revealed when they sent Flett into that region on two different occasions. As in the Maritimes, Quebec, and Ontario, the Federation desired above all to prevent interlopers from gaining a foothold in British North America.

The withdrawal of the Vancouver Trades Council from the Trades and Labor Congress in April 1903 underlined the inroads that political radicals had made into international trade-union strength. The AFL organizer on the Vancouver central body, J.H. Watson, came under bitter attack for stating publicly that 'every Socialist must be thrown out of our trade unions if we mean to uphold their integrity.'[89] The Vancouver men asked for Watson's removal, and later endorsed industrial unionism before voting to withdraw from the Congress. At the Trades Congress convention in September Draper reported that the Western Federation of Miners, the American Labor Union, and the United Brotherhood of Railway Employees (all dedicated, he said, to 'international, semi-political, industrial socialism'), were actively combating the Trades Congress and the AFL in British Columbia. Both J.H. Watson and George Bartley, without elaborating, put a large part of the blame for the success of the leftists on the international crafts. They may have been referring to the failure of the Federation and its affiliates to place full-time organizers in the district.[90]

The dissension in Vancouver spread across the water to Victoria, where the American Labor Union (ALU) had set up locals of hack drivers and lumbermen. In contrast to the AFL, the radical American union had kept a special organizer in the city for three months. His activities provoked an uproar when the American Labor Union lumbermen asked to be seated in the crafts-dominated Victoria Trades Council. The crafts denied the eligibility of the lumbermen to a Council seat, and pointed to the Berlin amendments in support of their stand. The Council's secretary decided to write to Draper for advice. In a surprising display of subservience, Draper sent the letter to Gompers and asked the American how it should be answered. Gompers took advantage of the occasion to blast the ALU. The woodworkers' local, he stated in a draft meant for Draper's signature, was ineligible to sit on the Victoria Council because it had not joined the craft union holding jurisdiction in that industry – the

Amalgamated Wood Workers. Gompers branded the American Labor Union's activities as 'inconsistent, unfair, and unfraternal, and should be discount-enanced and discouraged, rather than accorded representation. If these Wood-workers are earnest thorough-going trades unionists,' he declared, 'they will attach themselves to their International Union, and be in full accord with the spirit and purposes of the labor movement of the continent of America.' In other words, the great sin of the American Labor Union was its challenge to AFL monopoly. Presumably the British Columbians received Gompers' letter over Draper's signature.[91]

The Federation used a mixture of threats and enticements with the radical Western unions. While it actively opposed the organization of dual-union locals throughout the continent, it also tried to lure the key dissident group, the Western Federation of Miners, back into the AFL fold. At the Executive Council meetings in Toronto in 1903 (whose decisions regarding the Trades and Labor Congress had culminated one phase of Gompers' war against dual unionism), the Federation issued an invitation to the Miners to re-affiliate with the AFL. The unity of labour was essential, Gompers argued. 'Wealth is concentrating – indus-try is developing as never before. Employers of labor, and the possessors of wealth will not permit geographical lines, mountains, rivers, or even oceans to divide them. Their alliances, associations, companies and corporations are as broad and wide as our continent – even overlapping it.' If businessmen found it advantageous to act in unison, he concluded, certainly workingmen who owned and controlled nothing but their power to labor were compelled to forge a comparable unity.[92]

The Western Federation of Miners spurned Gompers' olive branch, but its dual unionism failed to make much headway in Western Canada after 1902. First of all the United Mine Workers moved into the coal fields of British Columbia and supplanted Western locals. By mid-October of 1903 this AFL affiliate had concluded an agreement with the Crow's Nest Pass Coal Company in Fernie, BC. A month later locals of the Mine Workers spread to Alberta, where nearly 3300 Canadians were enrolled by the end of the year. Secondly, in 1904 the Rossland local of the Western Federation of Miners was hit by a $12,500 damage suit which further weakened the trade-union base of radical politics in that area. At the same time the AFL began to offset the lure of industrial unionism by setting up building trades councils. These groups facilitated the coordination of policy among several crafts in the same industry, and by 1908 both Victoria and Vancouver had organized such bodies. Prosperity also helped to slacken the militancy in trade-union ranks. By the spring of 1904, some forty-five locals in the Vancouver building trades already had won the eight-hour day, and printers worked only seven and one-half hours. Still, employer-labour sentiment in

British Columbia was embittered. 'Nowhere else in Canada is the labor question so prominent,' J.A. Hobson wrote in 1906. While some blamed it on American agitators, Hobson thought the true causes were related to the use of Asian labour.[93]

It was suggested that the AFL send a man to work on the prairies, but the Federation continued to rely upon the efforts of volunteer organizers. Daniel Stamper was placed on the payroll for a month in mid-1904; Gompers refused to extend his tour, however, which had been spent mostly along the rail lines on the American side. 'I realize the good work that might be accomplished in the Western provinces and territories of Canada,' Gompers conceded. After Stamper was dropped, the Federation tried to cover British Columbia with organizers assigned primarily to Oregon and Washington.[94] In 1908 Morrison received a complaint from a Vancouver printer that the Canadian provinces were being ignored by these men. The printer referred to his large family, perhaps in hopes of winning an appointment to the Federation staff. 'I am very much pleased to notice that you have five children,' Morrison replied. 'I realize that a man with five children must be working continuously.' Nevertheless he promised only to dispatch the Washington state organizer to Vancouver at the first opportunity.[95]

Flett first suggested a transcontinental organizing tour in 1904. Morrison was disposed 'to an organizer covering that particular district and lining it up against the socialist movement, which is more or less anti-trade unionist.' Flett drew up an itinerary and submitted it to Federation leaders, but Gompers cancelled the project.[96] When Flett saw Morrison at the end of 1904 he again urged the case for covering Western Canada in order to wipe out any places where the American Labor Union might still be flourishing. Morrison was sympathetic but thought that Flett ought to wait for warmer weather. 'While thirty-six below is a good temperature for skating and curling,' the Canadian-born Federation secretary observed, 'I am inclined to believe it would not be effective for organizing work.' Then in the spring of 1905 Flett fought the American Labor Union in Nova Scotia and was laid low afterwards by a cold. Again the western trip was postponed.[97]

A number of circumstances combined to persuade Gompers to launch the twice-deferred enterprise. The Industrial Workers of the World (IWW) had risen phoenix-like from the ashes of the American Labor Union and had refurbished the threat to the American Federation of Labor's western flank. The Trades and Labor Congress was scheduled to hold its convention in September in the very seat of radical unionist sentiment at Victoria, British Columbia. Gompers asked Flett to plan an itinerary that would place the Canadian in Victoria a few days before the start of the Congress convention.[98] Federation leaders counted upon Flett's efforts to help offset manoeuvers by Canadian socialists intent upon capturing the Trades and Labor Congress leadership (see chapter 11). 'If it is necessary for you to take four months on this trip, well and good,' Morrison said. 'We want this Northwestern part of the country thoroughly covered. If we do not cover it, the Industrial Workers [the IWW] or, the International Laborers [a dual union], or, some of the derelicts will float out there, and secure the confidence and affiliation of the workers of those rapidly growing cities.' Already the Wobblies had established their first Canadian branch in Vancouver, had absorbed the Canadian locals of the American Labor Union, and had captured a federal labor union in Nelson, British Columbia.[99]

By mid-July Flett was working in Winnipeg; a month later he had made his way to Regina. 'Do you see anything of the I.W.W. in your travels?' Morrison asked. Flett spent most of September and October working in the vicinity of Vancouver and Victoria. Morrison told him that it was not probable that the AFL would send another organizer into Western Canada for some time to come, and Flett was instructed to remain there as long as his efforts bore fruit. He did not return to take up the work in Eastern Canada until mid-December.[100]

The prairies were not very conducive to organizational stability. Under pioneer conditions the populace tended to 'float', leadership of locals changed hands repeatedly, and there was a rapid turnover of the rank and file. The situation required constant attention by the craft unions and frequent visits by their organizers, even during normal times. Consequently the products of Flett's organizing efforts in 1906 weakened within a short time, and the deterioration of trade unions was compounded by the panic of 1907. 'Unemployment ... means disorganization and all that goes with it,' a Vancouverite noted.[101] Less than 75 per cent of organized workers in his city could claim steady work in February 1909. Of course, the IWW as well as the international craft unions experienced the same difficulties in spreading their message. The Wobblies remained bottled up in the British Columbia coal fields with less than a half-dozen locals.

The Western Canadians kept pressuring the Federation to appoint an organizer in their district. At that time (1909) the AFL men were assisting the Iron and Steel Workers' strike in the United States and could not be spared. Again Gompers sent the Washington state organizer to cover Canadian territory. 'Organizer Young has been doing good work in this section. His visits to many unions established new life in the membership,' it was reported. But Young was soon diverted to more urgent work among woodsmen in Montana, and Gompers said it was absolutely impossible for the AFL to bear even half the expense of an organizer in the Vancouver area. Yet he, along with eight craft unions, was willing to contribute $100 to cover the expenses of a man organizing metal trades along the rail lines.[102]

'What do you think about taking a trip across the continent for the purpose of taking up work in Winnipeg and the cities out to the coast?' Morrison asked Flett in April 1910. While he conceded that it was a long trip, there had been a considerable cry from that area for organizers. 'Those cities are growing and probably it would be a good field to do some work.'[103] Morrison was also concerned about the disruptive effect on central bodies of a split within the Electrical Workers' Union. He told Flett to organize Winnipeg thoroughly, sign up its central body, and cover all the other important cities in Western Canada. From Sault Ste Marie and the Lakehead Flett moved on to Winnipeg and tried to persuade unionists everywhere to take out an AFL charter. The Winnipeg Trades Council resisted, having no desire to expel the electrical workers' local unrecognized by the Federation.[104] Flett left Winnipeg empty-handed and journeyed to Brandon, Regina, and Saskatoon. 'Perhaps by the time you have returned conditions may have changed,' Morrison said encouragingly. At Calgary Flett reported twenty-eight locals in the central body, and persuaded them to apply for a Federation charter. Reaching Vancouver, Flett organized locals of seamen, hod carriers, upholsterers, and signpainters by the end of October.[105]

At this time Flett proposed that he cross into the United States and work his way southward along the Pacific coast. 'I thought the idea was that you could return the same way you came and take up the work of organizing on your way back,' Morrison retorted. The AFL secretary cited the complaints of neglect from British Columbians and urged Flett to remain in that district. 'It will keep them quiet and still establish the A.F. of L. ideas in and around Vancouver.' There was some talk of going north to Prince Rupert and Stewart, but winter set in and Flett headed back to Ontario in mid-December. 'Well, you had quite a trip through that part of the country,' Morrison said, 'and I feel that it is only just that you should get back and visit with your family for a time at least.'[106] As in 1906, Flett's western trip had originated less in a desire to organize immigrant workers than in a determination to prevent radical unions or secessionists from establishing a toehold in North America.

Flett had left the Vancouver building trades in well-organized shape and fully prepared to resist an attempt in early 1911 by the master builders to institute an open shop. In June 5000 men in the construction trades called a general strike against fifty-four firms. Chinese carpenters, although not unionized, made common cause with the men. The contest lasted nearly two months before the unions' united front was broken and each trade bargained for whatever it could get. '... Although the settlement reached was not all that was desired,' the Federation newsletter conceded, 'a great many of the organizations succeeded in bettering their conditions ...' Vancouver carpenters asked Morrison to sent Flett back to British Columbia, but the AFL relied once again on its man in Seattle. Morrison asked him to file a full report on the Vancouver labor scene.[107]

A month after the strike had ended, Gompers himself arrived in the Coast city to address the labour movement there. Heckled by a handful of Wobblies, the AFL leader found it necessary 'to talk with more than ordinary force.' The IWW centre of strength in Canada was in British Columbia, but it is doubtful whether there were half the ten thousand members claimed by the Wobblies throughout the country.[108] A number of their free speech cases in Calgary attracted attention just before the outbreak of the war. The IWW combination of radical talk and shadowy structure probably made them appear more threatening to craft unionists than they were in actuality. Certainly there was no Canadian equivalent of a Lawrence strike to panic the hearts of craft-union leaders in Eastern Canada. Gompers, satisfied that he had disposed of his hecklers, resumed his American tour.

The Canadian fraternal delegate to the AFL in 1912 urged the international unions to offset the Wobblies by organizing migratory workers. Earlier that year Morrison had anticipated the need and had agreed with the Vancouver Trades Council to sponsor a joint effort among loggers in the province. George Heatherton, a former Western Federation of Miners official, began working in the lumber camps along the Coquitlam River in the spring of 1912. After a time Heatherton's wages were taken over by a new Federation affiliate, the International Shingle Weavers, while the AFL continued to pay his hotel bill and railway fare. Although the new organizer seemed to engage in rather extensive travel throughout British Columbia, charter applications dwindled. Finally the president of the Shingle Weavers visited Vancouver and found that Heatherton had been 'drinking more heavily than can be done by a successful organizer.' Heatherton was fired a few months before the start of the First World War. The Federation did not replace him; by then the RCMP had taken up pursuit of the Wobblies.[109]

A profile of the Canadian trade-union movement in 1914 clearly reveals a number of significant facts. Nearly a quarter of trade unionists in Canada could still be found in railway unions, though the building trades appeared to be gaining ground (Table 4). Union activity during the prewar decade reflected the effects of business downturns in 1905, 1907-10, and in 1914. Table 5 also reveals the flurry of trade-union activity on the prairies during these years. A more striking picture of the same expansion can be seen by comparing the percentages of locals by province in 1914 (Table 6) with the figures for the years 1897 and 1902 as presented in Table 1 (Chapter 4, p. 52); the prairie provinces rose from 7.2 per cent in 1902 to 21.3 per cent in 1914. Ontario still remained, of course, the most heavily organized province in Canada, with 805 of slightly over 2000 locals in the country.

The international union movement commanded 88.3 per cent of Canadian union locals by 1914. Ninety-one of the AFL's 110 affiliates enrolled Canadians.

140 Gompers in Canada

TABLE 4
Distribution of trade unionists in Canada by groups
of industries

Industry	Percentage
Railway employees	24.9
Building trades	18.9
Metal trades	8.6
Mining and quarrying	8.7
Personal service, amusement trades	8.2
Other transport, navigation trades	8.0
Clothing, boot and shoe trades	7.0
Printing trades	4.7
All other trades and general labour	10.7

SOURCE: Canada Department of Labour, *Report on
Labour Organization in Canada* (1914), 10

The Maintenance-of-Way Employees, the Carpenters, and the Bricklayers claimed the largest membership in the country.[110]

At the turn of the century the American Federation of Labor had grown bigger and more rapidly than its enemies in business, labour, or government had expected. Employers unleashed unprecedented hostility upon internationalism in both Canada and the United States, but most of these battles were waged by Federation affiliates through strike action. At first Gompers moved vigorously into the Caribbean as well as Canada, and contemplated organizing the Latin republics around the rim of what had recently become an American lake. But most of his efforts were devoted to the struggle against enemies in the United States.

The individual craft unions dealt with employers; Gompers chose to wrestle with dual unionism because economic conflicts in a certain industry usually involved only the unions organized in a few specific trades, while dual unions often cropped up in a geographical form. The territorially oriented American Federation of Labor showed more sensitivity to the challenges from Western radicalism and confessional unionism than did the heads of many international unions, who were less concerned when only a few scattered locals seceded or collapsed. Gompers and Morrison were particularly attuned to such developments because dual unionism usually spawned a rival trade-union centre such as the American Labor Union or the Canadian Federation of Labor.

The Canadian slice of the AFL pie reflected policies and priorities dictated by the over-all Federation stance. The fight against dual unions took precedence

TABLE 5
Canadian unions formed and dissolved, 1905-14 *

	1905		1906		1907		1908		1909		1910		1911		1912		1913		1914	
	F	D	F	D	F	D	F	D	F	D	F	D	F	D	F	D	F	D	F	D
Nova Scotia	13	5	14	18	11	1	33	15	23	15	14	6	6	14	17	4	17	19	19	16
PEI	0	1	0	3	0	0	2	1	3	1	1	2	0	0	0	1	1	0	1	0
New Brunswick	5	6	1	5	1	1	20	5	3	5	10	3	11	4	13	6	16	3	7	7
Quebec	18	18	37	19	57	11	27	15	17	11	17	11	18	23	27	27	36	17	26	16
Ontario	40	57	44	23	94	33	41	33	49	34	52	44	73	73	98	41	108	63	69	74
Manitoba	9	5	17	3	6	4	12	3	8	5	10	5	17	8	30	2	9	8	7	6
Saskatchewan	5	0	10	1	13	1	12	4	16	2	15	2	19	5	30	5	23	4	8	4
Alberta	9	1	18	5	28	1	21	8	22	5	23	5	22	18	20	8	31	10	10	15
British Columbia	4	8	12	8	22	6	27	6	20	12	27	12	31	19	34	11	30	13	15	38
Yukon							1		1					1						
Total	103	101	153	85	232	58	196	90	162	90	169	90	197	165	269	105	271	109	162	176

SOURCE: Canada Department of Labour, Report on Labour Organization in Canada (1911), 114; (1913), 171; (1914), 221
* Includes both international unions and independent locals

TABLE 6
Distribution of trade-union locals by province, 1914

Province	IU locals	Percentage	All locals	Percentage
British Columbia	216	12.2	235	11.7
Prairies	412	23.2	427	21.3
Maritimes	172	9.7	229	11.4
Quebec	230	13.0	301	15.0
Ontario	739	41.7	805	40.1

SOURCE: Canada Department of Labour, *Report on Labour Organization*
in Canada (1914), 193

over the unorganized masses. Flett was used largely to protect Federation investments in Canadian labour. Gompers sent him to the Maritimes to forestall the
American Labor Union, and later the United Mine Workers attacked the Provincial Workmen's Association in Nova Scotia. Gompers and Morrison consistently ignored or downgraded the unique cultural and linguistic heritage of
Quebec encouraging the formation of confessional unions there; instead, dual
unions were combatted as they appeared. In central Canada the AFL used Flett
primarily to preserve the gains of an earlier period of explosive organization.
They sent him to Western Canada to fight against dual-unionist challenges
offered by Canadian socialists who supported the American Labor Union and
the Industrial Workers of the World. But the external enemies of a continental
trade-union movement in Canada – whether depressions, employers, hostile politicians, waves of immigrants, a national movement, radical unions, or Catholic
syndicates – were often easier for Gompers and Morrison to handle than some
of the bitter jurisdictional disputes and secession movements which periodically
wracked craft unions.

10
Jurisdictional disputes and secessions

The accession of thousands of new members at the turn of the century presented a mixed blessing for international trade-union leaders. The new unionists were anxious to reap the benefits of affiliation. They expected unconditional support from union headquarters in all their grievances against employers, but were less willing to pay the relatively high dues assessed them. Workers in some factories resisted separation into different craft locals and could not understand why the American Federation of Labor refused to mix them all into one federal labour union. Technological changes forced locals to merge or reorganize after the men had grown accustomed to working with one another. Personality conflicts inevitably cropped up. Jurisdictional disputes originating among craft unions in the United States were exported to Canadian locals, where the issues so hotly debated at Federation conventions at times seemed unimportant or irrelevant. Disgruntled men in either country could find a thousand such reasons to secede from the parent trade union. For Canadians in particular, the presence of the boundary and of a different set of politicians and political hopefuls with nationalistic viewpoints, the French-English divisions in many trades, and the alternative shelter offered by the National Trades and Labor Congress coalesced to make secessions even more likely whenever a grievance arose between Canadian locals and their headquarters south of the border.

Draper generally warned AFL leaders and international union heads of schisms and rumors of dual unionism. He reported in 1907 that Canadian locals of the Horseshoer's Union were talking about forming a national union. A year later Calgary musicians and hod carriers threatened to withdraw from their respective internationals. It has already been observed that the Congress secretary was instrumental in prosecuting the war against the Provincial Workmen's Association in the Maritimes. Draper also notified the international unions of the rise of the Canadian Brotherhood of Railway Employees, one of the few Canadian unions that successfully bucked international union jurisdictions. It was in Draper's and the Trades and Labor Congress's interest to do this after 1902, since dissident unions usually sought assistance from the rival National Trades and Labor Congress.[1]

The Federation handled a number of minor jurisdictional problems very carefully in order to prevent frictions which could blow up into a secessionist movement. A few American craft unions, for example, refused to admit Canadian locals. In 1905 the National Association of Machine Printers and Color Mixers denied a charter sought by a local in Toronto organized by Flett. In cases like this the AFL affiliated the men directly to itself. In Kingston a labourers' protective union chartered by the Federation came into conflict with a local of the Hod Carriers and Building Laborers' Union. Flett was able to effect a merger of the two locals.[2]

More indicative of the jurisdictional wonderland which international craft unionism exported to Canada was a dispute between brewery workers in Hamilton and the Glass Bottle Blowers' Union. A non-union brewery in Hamilton whose beer was sold in union-made bottles had captured the taste of the Toronto beer-drinking public. Toronto brewers, knowing that the Hamilton brewery was unorganized, tried to undermine their competitor by asking the Toronto District Labor Council to place a boycott on Hamilton beer. The Glass Bottle Blowers' local, whose product thereby would have suffered an indirect ban, vigorously protested the move.[3] The quarrel went all the way to Gompers in Washington, and bordered upon the ridiculous. The Glass Bottle Blowers' local should have known, the secretary of the Toronto Council wrote, that Toronto workers would refuse non-union beer, even if the bottles were union-made. 'We think that the goods to be consumed is the first considerable and the Package in which it is packed the second consideration ... Scab beer is Scab beer, even if put up in union bottles ... Our Council ... regret that the Glass Bottle Blowers are not more practical.[4] The storm blew over after the Hamilton brewery was organized, and union beer began flowing out of union bottles into the gullets of union men doubtless wearing union suits.

The picture mould workers of Toronto were one of those groups who resisted the imposition of craft jurisdictions. Flett suggested that the AFL keep them together under a federal union charter. The Brotherhood of Carpenters, however, refused to permit this, and sent its own organizer (Tom Moore, later president of the Trades Congress) to investigate. The Carpenters claimed jurisdiction over those who operated woodworking machinery, but they would not accept the guilders, varnishers, and finishers. Flett was obviously discouraged at the unwillingness of the AFL craft affiliate to permit the organization of a picture frame workers' local. 'I sympathize, and in part agree, with your state of mind,' Morrison admitted. The issue was at length resolved when the Carpenters relinquished their jurisdictional claims, and the workers formed a local of the Painters and Decorators' Union. The case, although settled without great difficulty, well illustrated how the desires of a group of Canadian workers might clash with the organizational imperatives of autonomous American craft unions.[5]

Undoubtedly a jurisdictional dispute between two international unions of carpenters presented a far more serious obstacle to a united Canadian labour movement. The Amalgamated Society of Carpenters had been carried from England by emigrating craftsmen and planted in both Canada and the United States. After a temporary merger with the American-based United Brotherhood of Carpenters had failed in 1905, both groups continued to organize workers in the same trade. The Amalgamated Society set up an autonomous Canadian district office to service its membership and retained a strong hold on Canadian carpenters. In the United States, the Brotherhood of Carpenters waxed more powerful than its rival, and persuaded an AFL convention in 1911 to order the Amalgamated to unite with it. In August of 1912 the Federation revoked the Amalgamated's charter.[6]

Across Canada carpenters rose in defence of their British-born trade union. In the west the dispute followed upon the heels of the disastrous 1911 building trades strike and compounded an already widespread feeling of unrest. A United Brotherhood official found 'quite a strong sentiment' in Vancouver favouring a break from the AFL 'and forming an independent organization.'[7] The Coast city's building trades council adopted a resolution to sever its Federation connection and set up a new group that would 'settle all jurisdictional disputes on the basis of awarding work to the craft receiving the highest rate of wages.'[8] In Eastern Canada Flett was dispatched to Hamilton, where there was a large group of carpenters, and told to remain 'until the matter is adjusted or it is so well in hand that you can safely leave it.' The Toronto District Council asked its leaders to hear arguments from both carpenters' locals before recommending a course of action.[9] Although the issue involved a jurisdictional rather than a legislative question, it was impossible to keep the dispute off the floor of the Trades Congress. Indeed, two Vancouverites noted in 1911 that there was a strong disposition in the Congress 'to resent interference by the American Federation of Labor in Canadian affairs where such interference is likely to disturb the autonomy of its affiliated unions.' They referred to a 'well-known' and growing desire by the Congress to control the economic as well as the political activities of its affiliates.[10]

Such rumours had some basis in fact. Some Canadian unionists refused to affiliate with Federation departments because the Americans required their subordinate councils to unseat independent locals. At the Congress meeting in Calgary in 1911, Alberta unionists cited the 'internal warfare forced upon Canadian Unionists' through jurisdictional decisions by the Building Trades Department of the AFL which had upset building trades councils in Edmonton, Lethbridge, and Calgary. The Albertans concluded that it was time for the Trades and Labor Congress to 'declare for absolute supremacy in not merely legislative matters alone, but also all economic questions which concern the welfare of Canadian trades unionists as a whole.' Their remarks, they hastened to add, were not to be interpreted as a blanket condemnation of international unionism.[11]

At the same TLC convention Victor Midgley of the Vancouver Trades and Labour Council came to the traditional left-wing conclusion about jurisdictional frictions. Craft unions, he observed, were heavily absorbed in internal disputes which prevented continuing cooperation among trades in a given industry. Craft unions had demonstrated their inadequacy in combating aggregations of capital. 'Therefore, be it resolved, that this convention endorse the principle of industrial unionism.' Immediately Draper moved to smother the fires of discontent. He offered an innocuous substitute calling upon the Congress to endorse every movement 'tending to greater union and harmony among the organized workers.' Nevertheless Midgley's resolution was adopted by a vote of seventy to fifty-two over Draper's substitute. Later the Congress fraternal delegate to the AFL attempted to explain away the resolution, but no one was fooled into minimizing the danger such motions presented to the craft organizations. The vote in favour of industrial unionism reflected the convergence in Western Canada of left-wing sympathies with a deepening resentment over jurisdictional warfare in the American crafts.[12]

Apparently the Montreal delegation of the United Brotherhood, led by Narcisse Arcand, decided to bring this hostility out into the open at the Trades Congress convention of 1912 in order to defeat it. Arcand moved that the Congress follow the AFL's lead and expel the Amalgamated Society of Carpenters. When the resolutions committee sided with the Amalgamated, a heated debate broke out on the convention floor. The United Brotherhood was entitled to exclusive affiliation with the Trades Congress, Arcand declared, because it was the second largest union in North Amerca and ten times bigger than its rival. The Amalgamated Society had degraded itself by agreeing to do work which the United Brotherhood considered unfair to organized labour. He and his Montreal brethren had had to fight the clergy, the politicians, the capitalists – and now a misguided portion of the labour movement.[13]

'We are not here to adjust jurisdictional squabbles,' Congress president James Watters interjected. 'The Congress confines its efforts to protecting the wage earner. To attempt to fight trouble which originated in the American Federation of Labor would interfere with the usefulness of the Dominion Congress.' Trades Congress leaders took the disingenuous stand that Arcand's motion encroached upon the prerogatives of the AFL. Since the Congress was concerned only with legislative matters, they reasoned, it was under no obligation to conform to the Federation's action, which had been based on purely economic considerations. On a roll call vote, 124 delegates supported this viewpoint, and 76 endorsed the United Brotherhood's stand.[14] The AFL fraternal delegate predicted that the vote would not settle the dispute, 'as the question will come up in the next Congress stronger than ever.'[15]

The Congress's refusal to expel delegates from the Amalgamated Society sharpened the debate being waged in Canadian central bodies. The St Catharines Trades and Labor Council recognized both carpenters' locals despite protests from the United Brotherhood. Flett, who was present at the discussions, secured permission to explain the Federation position, but 'all to no purpose.' The Council already possessed a Congress charter and cared little whether its Federation charter was revoked.[16] In Toronto, the United Brotherhood locals ran into similar obstacles. The Amalgamated Society, Flett reported, was waving the Union Jack and issuing circulars denouncing Gompers. James Simpson was said to have told the Council that they were 'not in any way compelled to obey any mandate' issued by the AFL. The Torontonians were stalling, an informant asserted, 'in order that they may be represented at the convention of the A.F. of L., after which they would relinquish the charter, and headed by the Reds, make a move along National lines.'[17] The Toronto District Council finally voted to set aside the controversy until hearing further from the Federation. Morrison moved cautiously, advising the United Brotherhood local in Toronto to take up the matter with their international union officials in the United States. It would require good judgment on the part of international union leaders, Flett observed, 'to prevent the A.S. of C. from playing the role of martyrs.'[18]

During the ensuing winter the Federation Executive Council took steps to resolve the dispute. United Brotherhood secretary Frank Duffy, advised by Tom Moore, presented his charges, while Draper and Simpson defended the Congress's actions. Gompers, playing a conciliatory role, managed to come up with a statement that was endorsed by all those present 'as being the intent of our movement in Canada.'[19] It was quickly apparent, though, that the United Brotherhood had won the day. In January the Executive Council ordered Gompers to see that Amalgamated Society locals were expelled from the Toronto District Council. Within a month the Toronto group agreed to comply with the Federation's demands. It remained to be seen what action would be taken on the national level by the Trades and Labor Congress.[20]

When the Amalgamated Society forwarded its per-capita tax payment to the Congress in April 1913, Trades Congress leaders were forced to make their decision. They refused the money. Draper assured W.W. Young, the Amalgamated secretary, that the Congress's decision had been reached only 'after viewing the matter from every conceivable point; weighing well every consideration; looking to the probable effect on the organized movement in Canada.' To accept the Amalgamated Society's dues would '*invite a disintegration of the organized Labor forces in Canada.*'[21] Congress leaders saw no obstacle to prevent the Amalgamated Society from merging with the United Brotherhood. When Young asked what clause of the Trades Congress constitution had been invoked, Draper stated evasively that the Congress recognized the supremacy of the AFL 'in trade autonomy and jurisdictional matters.' This admission provoked a bitter outburst from Young, who thought it a sorry spectacle to see Congress leaders truckling to an organization officered by 'men whose allegiance is to another country.' He hoped that some day British institutions would no longer suffer dictation from Americans. 'Mr. Young certainly does not mince matters,' Morrison commented.[22]

Congress leaders redoubled their efforts to direct convention energies away from jurisdictional problems. Canadian and American workers, they asserted, were engaged in the same struggle against a common enemy. The business climate called for worker solidarity and concentrated political effort. Nevertheless Christian Sivertz of the Victoria Trades and Labor Council turned the delegates' attention to the 1911 resolution on industrial unionism, and moved that the Congress seek a 'universal, interchangeable membership card' which would enable workers to join any union regardless of craft specialty, and would thereby convert craft unions eventually into industrial organizations. An amended version of Sivertz's resolution was approved. An attempt later by a Toronto railroad telegrapher to scuttle the action of the Calgary convention was more successful. The delegates agreed to 'clarify' their meaning by stating that the 1911 motion had been only of 'an educative permissive nature.' There was no compulsory principle implied, and no intent 'to attack or malign the policy of craft unions.' Although the railway telegraphers were not satisfied, there was little doubt that the radical anti-craft union resolution of 1911 had been neutralized.[23]

The continuing dispute between the two carpenters' unions kept the issue alive. Finally in 1913 both the president and secretary of the United Brotherhood of Carpenters attended the Trades Congress convention. Their influence was quickly felt. Despite strong support voiced on behalf of the Amalgamated

Society from Western Canada, the delegates amended the Congress constitution to exclude any group from their ranks which had been expelled or rejected by the American Federation of Labor. Early the next year a poll of Amalgamated Society members in the United States showed a lopsided vote in favour of union with the United Brotherhood. In Canada the vote was much closer, with 928 in favour and 849 opposed to merger. During the following months Amalgamated locals across Canada abided by the tally and linked up with their former rival.[24]

The Congress had bowed again to the powerful interests represented by an AFL affiliate. The demise of the Amalgamated Society of Carpenters, one of the oldest trade unions in Canada, solidified the authority of American labour leaders over Canadian trade-union organizations. United Mine Workers' locals in British Columbia tried in 1913 to revive Congress interest in industrial unionism, but Draper successfully kept the delegates on the straight and narrow path, and the Trades and Labor Congress weathered the crisis with its loyalty to the AFL unimpaired.[25] 'Matters that affect the jurisdiction of trade unions or the control of trade unions along industrial lines do not come within the province of our congress,' R.A. Rigg of Winnipeg assured craft union leaders in America in 1914. The Congress claimed only to be the legislative mouthpiece of Canadian workers; of course, that was all that a good state federation of labour was entitled to claim.[26]

The cases involving the Glass Bottle Blowers, the picture mould workers, and the carpenters all represented jurisdictional problems among trade-union locals that endangered the AFL's continental structure. But secession movements within international labour organizations also threatened Federation leaders. Among building laborers, for example, where organization was fraught with difficulties arising from ethnic clashes, the enforced mobility of these workers, the seasonal nature of their work, and their dearth of marketable skills, dual unionism found an easy point of entry.

There were two dominant international unions in this trade at the turn of the century: the Building Laborers' International Protective, and the Hod Carriers and Building Laborers' Union. In 1903 a Canadian, William Burleigh, was elected secretary of the Building Laborers' International. Burleigh, a well-known labour leader in the London, Ontario, area for several years, served on the Trades Council of that city. In 1904 the AFL granted recognition to the Hod Carriers and ordered Burleigh's union to merge with it. Burleigh and several others in the Building Laborers' Union refused and associated themselves instead with a dissident group called the International Laborers' Union. Morrison told Flett to follow Burleigh through Ontario and counteract his influence among AFL affiliates. Despite Flett's efforts Burleigh persuaded locals in Galt and Hespeler to take out International Laborers' Union charters, and his group set up unions in Hamilton and Toronto as well.[27]

Stimulated by the competition between rival trade-union groups among the labourers, secessionist sentiments appeared at the Trades Congress convention in 1906. One motion called upon the Congress to amend its constitution so that it could issue charters for an all-Canadian general labourers' union. It was defeated, but the delegates did tell the AFL 'to use every endeavor' to unite the various unions which claimed jurisdiction over labourers. The next year the Federation began a continent-wide campaign to force locals of building labourers into the officially recognized Hod Carriers. By 1908 Morrison thought that the rival International Labourers' Union faced imminent collapse.[28]

Burleigh was not so easily put down. After the demise of the International Laborers' Union in the United States, he sent a circular to Canadian laborers' locals announcing the formation of an all-Canadian organization in his trade. Draper immediately sent the document to Morrison. 'I want that gentleman taken care of,' Morrison told Flett, 'and I want those organizations to affiliate with their international as soon as possible.' Morrison did not ignore the ethnic factors which complicated Flett's work. 'You and I have discussed that proposition about Italians many times,' he told the Canadian, 'and it will be difficult to have the members [of the Toronto local] take any other view than what they have at the present time relative to foreigners.' By the end of March 1908 the Federation's Canadian organizer was able to report the affiliation of the Galt and London Labourers (the latter was Burleigh's own local) to the Federation-sponsored Hod Carriers. 'It is good news,' Morrison responded. 'It means the passing of the Critchlow [International Laborers' Union] organization in Canada.' Although rumours of secession did not cease, the American Federation of Labor had preserved the reality behind the words of the Berlin amendments, at least in so far as unskilled building labour was concerned. Only one labourers' union remained active in Canada, and it was the international union affiliated with the AFL.[29]

One of the most important secession movements exported to Canada before the First World War occurred among electrical workers. In 1908 the international union claiming 32,000 workers in this trade split into two factions of about equal size as a result of a dispute among its officials over the interpretation of their constitution. The AFL placed its mantle of legitimacy on the McNulty group, whereupon the Reid faction endorsed Gompers' perennial socialist rival for the Federation presidency. The power struggle within the electrical workers' union spread to locals throughout North America. Every central body faced the prospect of expelling the Reid group or losing its own Federation charter. In Canada, where Reid won the support of all the electrical workers' locals save one, the issue appeared first in the councils at Hamilton, Toronto, and Montreal. The Hamilton central body expelled the Reid faction; the Montreal and Toronto District Councils stalled. 'Perhaps it is just as well to temporize with the Electrical Workers,' Morrison suggested, 'until the situation so shapes itself in the United States as to demonstrate beyond a doubt that the Reid secession movement has fallen by the way.' The fact that the AFL was scheduled to hold its first convention in Canada (at Toronto) later in 1909 complicated the issue considerably.[30]

In September Morrison told the Executive Council that the work of compelling central bodies to expel the Reid group was progressing. The charter of the Iowa State Federation of Labor and the Logansport, Indiana, central body had been revoked. Councils in Duluth, St Louis, San Francisco, and Cedar Rapids had been ordered to suspend locals of the Electrical Workers at their next meeting. The Toronto Council faced comparable pressure but could not agree on what action to take. 'Those [Reid] locals must be suspended, or that charter will have to come away,' Morrison warned Flett.[31] Finally, one of the two Toronto locals agreed to withdraw from the Council pending a settlement, and the other was discovered to be in arrears in Council dues. The news delighted Morrison. It would have been embarrassing for Federation leaders to direct a convention in a city whose charter had been revoked. Meanwhile, Ainey laboured to get the Reid faction expelled from the Montreal central body.[32]

The AFL convention appointed an arbitration committee to seek an adjustment between the two disputants. Over the next five years the struggle dragged on in the courts and within the AFL. In 1911 the Toronto District Council re-instated its two dissident locals. The next year, however, seceding members of the Ottawa local voted unanimously to return to the McNulty faction, and by the outbreak of the First World War the Federation-backed segment appeared to have gained the upper hand. Delegates at the Trades Congress convention in 1914 greeted an announcement of the impending amalgamation of the two groups with considerable enthusiasm. Throughout the period of contention, the dispute had hindered organizing work in the electrical trades, had disrupted city centrals across Canada, and had generated much harmful enmity in the Canadian trade-union movement.[33]

A quarrel within Canadian printers' locals revealed the difficulty of preserving an international union monopoly in the country when both the government and the rival national trade-union centre facilitated secessions. The case centered upon C.S.O. Boudreault, the Ottawa printer who had been an AFL volunteer since the late 1890s, and who strongly desired to become a full-time member of the Federation staff. In 1904 Boudreault was appointed a temporary salaried organizer, but his selection was immediately criticized by the Shoe Workers' locals in Montreal. The Montrealers pointed to published articles over Boudreault's signature which, they alleged, cast doubt upon the Canadian's loyalty to international unionism. Perhaps the Shoe Workers also remembered how Boudreault had attempted to straddle the ramifications of the Berlin amendments when they had been put to a vote in 1902.[34] At any rate, Draper came to his defence. Morrison put Boudreault on the payroll while Gompers was away from AFL headquarters, and gave Draper the impression that the difficulty had been resolved. But when Gompers returned he abruptly dropped Boudreault from the Federation's employ in deference to the complaints from the Boot and Shoe Workers' Union.[35]

The AFL leaders tried to placate both Boudreault and Draper. They told the two Canadians that they expected the Montrealers' protests to die down within a few months. They held out the hope of a renewed appointment. The Canadians began to suspect Flett of having opposed Boudreault behind the scenes, and although Morrison denied the charge, Ottawa became a centre of anti-Flett sentiment.[36] 'The Federation might as well have no representative at all,' one Ottawa unionist said, 'as to have a useless official, leisurely existing at a high pay derived from the unionist per capita.' Flett's continued employment, they charged, threatened to provoke the secession of many Ottawa locals from their international unions. Boudreault and his friends found an opportunity to vent their anger in 1906.[37]

Shortly after the International Typographical Union convention of 1905 had agreed to fight for the eight-hour day, a continent-wide strike of several printers' locals was declared. About 200 locals, mostly in the United States, were ultimately involved, and the protracted struggle severely depleted the union's coffers. By May of 1906 the union had invested over $1.5 million and still had not won the battle. A good many locals not on strike, including Local 102 in Ottawa, began to tire of the burden of special dues levied upon them. For eighteen months Canadian printers had been assessed 10 per cent of their wages, and by October 1906 the Ottawa local had paid only half the $24,000 owed to union headquarters. Some sixteen locals in other Canadian cities were in the same predicament; the international threatened to expel them all.[38] At this stage several members of the Ottawa local, including a good many employed at the government printing bureau, proposed to secede from the International Typographical Union and form the nucleus of an all-Canadian union of printers. They calculated that a Canadian national body could be run on dues of fifty cents a month, which was considerably less than the international union fee. 'It was bad enough to have to put up good money to pay benefits to American strikers,' one printer said, 'but when the International convention last August boosted the salaries of the president and secretary $600 each ... we thought it was about time to take some action to free ourselves from such an American-run organization.'[39] Not unexpectedly, C.S.O. Boudreault was prominent among the dissidents. They banded together to form a local of the National Trades and Labor Congress, and the government's open-shop policy in the printing bureau protected them from retaliation by the international union. Though the seceders appealed to printers throughout Canada to join them, they failed to establish a national union, partly because the president of the International Typographical Union actively opposed them. Morrison agreed: 'I am one of those who believes that temporizing with secessionists strengthens instead of weakens their position,' he told Flett. 'No surrender and no quarter should be the position taken by organized labor ...'[40]

Secession threats and rumours persisted, especially in Ontario. In 1912 locals of bakers, sheet metal workers, bookbinders, and pressmen in Toronto, 'the cradle of international trade unionism' in Canada, wrangled with union headquarters in the United States. Boilermakers and blacksmiths' locals in St Thomas threatened to break away, with fully 90 per cent of the members of the former reported ready to secede. They complained of high dues and special assessments, an empty international union treasury, and a lack of courtesy and consideration from union officers. Two years later, iron workers' locals in Toronto, Hamilton, and Niagara Falls were said to have withdrawn from their international union. It was alleged that government officials had encouraged the iron workers to form a Canadian union. Morrison was asked to tell Draper not to grant a Trades Congress charter to them.[41]

When grievances were left unattended, the locals became prime candidates for membership in the Canadian Federation of Labor. In 1909 parts of two locals of the printing pressmen in Toronto, complaining of 'many petty annoyances,' seceded from their international union. They were joined in the CFL by the local of Ottawa printers, the national union of shoemakers in Montreal, and nine lodges of the Provincial Workmen's Association. The national movement's fortunes were brightened in the next few years by accessions of Toronto bookbinders and boilermakers, and the blacksmiths from St Thomas. The CFL secretary admitted that his organization depended heavily upon grievances within the international union locals. Hearing in 1912 of dissatisfaction in London, he dispatched an organizer to take advantage of it. In 1913 he reported that Toronto locals of the Amalgamated Society of Engineers favoured joining his organization; they had been turned out of the Toronto District Labor Council because they had refused to affiliate with the AFL. 'Dissatisfaction is voiced all over the International field,' a CFL official jubilantly proclaimed, 'and we feel that our cause is sure to grow.' By the outbreak of the First World War the centre of national unionism in Canada had moved westward and consisted largely of Ontario locals once allied with the international crafts.[42]

It would be false to conclude from these accounts that all would have been harmonious within the Canadian labour movement in the absence of American unions. Yet the international tie *did* result in the export of acrimonious jurisdictional and secession disputes to Canada. Perhaps, too, the rather narrow craft organizational structure better suited a larger and more 'advanced' American industrial economy. In the relatively agrarian Canada of that era, the international tie squelched efforts on behalf of an industrial union structure which might have better suited Canadian workers and strengthened their political voice as well. But the fear of dual unionism overrode all other considerations. Nothing dissuaded Gompers and his colleagues from battling relentlessly to perfect a continental monopoly over the North American labour world. Morrison succinctly expressed the dilemma this posed for Canadians when he told Flett to temporize until the Electrical Workers' dispute had been resolved in the United States. It did not matter to him that Canadian electricians overwhelmingly supported the ostracized Reid faction. For Canadian trade unionists, it seemed, minority rank was the price of American labour continentalism.

The fact that P.M. Draper, by at least 1905, was eager to prevent secessions and preserve the integrity of international unionism in Canada immensely aided the AFL's work. Had he encouraged the secessionists at any point, he could have undermined the Federation's dominance in Canada. On the other hand, the Congress secretary would have risked his own position within the Trades and Labor Congress if he had followed an ultra-nationalist course, or encouraged dual unionism. He stood for reelection every year at Congress conventions dominated by international union delegates. He must have observed that the Canadian landscape was dotted with former international union members who had taken the nationalist road to oblivion. Still, Draper and his associates chafed under the restrictions growing out of the Berlin decisions. They resented the TLC being caricatured by its enemies as the tail of an AFL kite, and they struggled manfully to escape the political, financial, and chartering limitations which the continental craft-union structure imposed upon state federations of labour.

11
Political action

'What we desire for ourselves – we wish for all,' James Woodsworth was fond of saying.[1] The statement captures an element that sets Canadian labour politics apart from the interest-group lobbying of American craft unions. More often in Canada the object of political activity was to create a just social order as well as to expand labour's slice of the national wealth. Broad political objectives advocated by many Canadian unions were not always coupled with traditional American laissez-faire concepts. In this respect many Canadians differed from Samuel Gompers, who bitterly opposed most forms of governmental intervention in the American economy. Gompers never grasped the fact that Canadian trade unionists operated within a different historical tradition. In Canada governmental initiative had become a mainstay of the economy, because economic growth and development secured continued political independence from the United States. Many Canadian unionists were more willing than their American brethren to seek political solutions to economic problems. Their outlook was reinforced by infusions of immigrants from England attuned to the program and tactics of the Labour party there. Periodic visits to Canadian labour conventions by Keir Hardie, Will Crooks, and Will Thorne stirred up sentiment on behalf of political action.

But several factors tended to undermine effective political action by Canadian unionists. Foremost was the fact that Canada before the First World War remained essentially agricultural; its industrial centres, concentrated in a few scattered urban areas, employed a relatively small proportion of the labour force. Under such conditions political action required extensive collaboration and the pooling of scarce resources by trade unions if it was to generate results.

Yet the decentralization of political power in the Canadian federal system and the regional disparities in the rate of industrialization eroded efforts by trade unionists to establish a national labour party. Nor did Canadian unions seem strong enough to sustain a provincial party during the arid months between elections.

These political weaknesses, in turn, arose partly from a continuing debate within Canadian trade-union ranks over the best route to political salvation. Some advocated an independent labour party standing apart from both the trade unions and the Marxists; others called upon trade unions to endorse the socialist party or even affiliate with it. The American Federation of Labor accentuated the split over tactics and contributed to the failure of labour political action in Canada through its unrelenting hostility to Canadian socialists.

The failure of labour politics in Canada before the First World War can also be attributed in part to the ability of both the Grits and Tories to woo a considerable segment of the labour vote. The parliamentary discipline that allowed room for minor party politics also permitted major parties to orchestrate a carefully balanced dispensation of favours designed to win over various segments of the electorate. In this connection it is worth noting that the Liberals set up a department of labour in Canada (in 1900) years before the Democrats in the United States responded to much more powerful trade-union pressures (in 1913).

The fluctuations in the Liberal party's labour policies kept Trades Congress leaders off balance. In the beginning, Congress leaders persuaded the Laurier administration to end collaboration between Canadian immigration agents in England and officials of the Canadian Manufacturers' Association. It had taken a great deal of pressure, including criticism in the labour press, resolutions of censure by labour parties, an appeal from the head of the national labour movement, petitions sent directly to Laurier, and the election of a labor MP in 1906, before the government was persuaded to act. Draper later praised Mackenzie King's efforts to prevent the fraudulent encouragement of immigration to Canada.[2] Yet the government's uneven enforcement of the alien labour act revealed the uncertainty of Liberal help. At the start a man from trade-union ranks was appointed to report violations, and deportations followed without the formality of a court order. Then the government decided to require a legal prosecution. Somewhat later it reverted to its original policy after coming under the fire of a prominent Toronto MP. By 1909 the government once again demanded court orders, and judges often made a mockery of the statute's intent. For example, when an employer in British Columbia advertised in the United States: 'Machinists wanted in Vancouver. Apply at —,' and gave the name of the factory, Judge Duff held that the advertisement was merely an invitation to come to the city and was not to be considered an offer of employment.[3]

The Liberals relied upon Ralph Smith to keep them informed of labour political strategy.[4] Trades Congress leaders similarly depended upon him to gain the government's ear, though he was treated abruptly by some of Laurier's own ministers. 'I am a strong supporter of *you, personally* ...' Smith told Laurier, 'but if my position is to be maintained in the interests of the party, I will have to continue to feel, as I have done in the past, that the Government is favorable to reasonable legislation for the [working] classes ...' Scarcely three weeks later, Laurier revealed the frailty of labour's voice in Liberal circles. 'Matters have arisen which makes it imperative that I should try to close the session at the earliest possible moment,' he told Smith. 'I hope therefore that you will be kind enough not to insist upon trying to get your [union label] bill through this session ...' The Trades Congress had been working to get the bill through Parliament for several years. The next year it passed the Commons but ran into the solid limestone walls of the Canadian Senate. The Congress's solicitor 'amended the Bill in every shape and form to suit the wishes, suggestions, and even the whims of the Senate, but without avail.' It would be useless to reintroduce the measure, he thought, because the Senate stood adamantly opposed as long as they were permitted a free vote, and Laurier was unwilling to make it a government bill.[5]

Failure to win concessions from the reigning Liberals goaded trade unions to change their political tactics. Flett complained in 1903 that annual presentations to cabinet ministers were a waste of time, energy, and money, and early the next year Congress leaders decided to hire a solicitor (John G. O'Donoghue) to give full-time attention to labour interests during the parliamentary session. Six months later, O'Donoghue's report to the Trades Congress convention candidly outlined Canadian labour's political difficulties when it relied upon traditional lobbying tactics.

The manufacturers ... have, by the nature of things, special representatives at all times on the floor of the House of Commons, and, more particularly, in the Senate. Their financial resources enable them to rush representatives to Ottawa on a hour's notice, as was shown in connection with the Alien Labor Act ... Were your body in a position to duplicate these efforts, there is no gainsaying the fact that much better results would accrue to organized labor.

As a stopgap measure O'Donoghue asked central bodies to appoint small committees to assist him in mobilizing immediate labour response to legislative measures. He called upon trade unions to find the wherewithal to rush labour groups to Ottawa on short notice. O'Donoghue and other Congress leaders considered these measures as only temporary expedients 'until such time as there is a Labor Party at Ottawa.'[6]

Although a number of Tory and Grit MPs harboured kindly feelings toward the interests of organized labour, they could do little without government backing for their proposals. O'Donoghue urged the nomination of trade-union candidates in promising ridings, exempting constituencies already taken by Grit or Tory friends of labour. In effect, O'Donoghue was encouraging Canadian unionists to follow a three-fold political strategy: to elect straight labour men in a few likely districts; to work for the nomination of Grit or Tory labour men; and to vote for the friends of labour regardless of party. The last was the traditional Gompers policy, and the second was adopted by the American Federation of Labor in 1906. However, the first reflected a combination of factors distinguishing the Canadian from the American political environment; the strict party discipline which reduced labour's ability to influence either the Grits or Tories, the willingness of labour leaders to seek economic goals through political action, the appeal of the example of labour in the Mother Country, the need to counter the entrenched political power of the Canadian Manufacturers' Association, and the sometimes vague desire on the part of many workers to seek a new social order.[7]

The political warfare between the Manufacturers' Association and the Trades Congress ruled out a corporatist movement along the lines of the National Civic Federation in the United States. The manufacturers were not interested, perhaps because, as André Siegfried wrote, the rich were 'at the stage where they declare themselves to have at heart the welfare of the workers, while preferring that these should not go too thoroughly into the question for themselves. In this respect,' he added, 'the Liberal employers do not seem to differ appreciably from the Conservative.'[8] There appeared little that Canadian labour leaders could do on the legislative front except to work for independent labour representation in Canadian legislative chambers and hope that the government would back one or two labour measures in the interim. A few labour MP watchdogs, they thought, could alert the labour movement to hostile governmental actions, and might also provide the nucleus for a great working-class political movement destined to attain power at some time in the future.

The clamour for independent political action burst forth at the annual sessions of the Trades Congress. In 1903 the Congress sanctioned the nomination and election of straight independent labour candidates for parliamentary and municipal offices. A year later John Flett cited the success of unionists in New Zealand, Australia, Great Britain, and Ireland in labour politics and called upon his Canadian brethren to renew their own efforts. Flett repeated part of this speech at the AFL convention in San Francisco, and it brought no visible censure from either the delegates or the AFL leadership. Nor can any criticism of Flett's views be found in the letters of Gompers and Morrison.[9]

In response to the sentiment in favour of independent political action, labour parties sprang up in several places in Canada in 1904. Most were similar to the Toronto District Labor Council's Labor League, which advocated public ownership of all 'natural opportunities' and public utilities, abolition of child labour, the franchise for women, abolition of the Senate, and adoption of the initiative, referendum, and recall devices so popular at that time with American reformers. With one exception these efforts met defeat. Even Arthur Puttee, the Winnipeg labor MP, was crushed between the Grit and Tory candidates in 1904, although his program 'was a very reasonable one, amounting only to state socialism, and making no reference to the social revolution or the war between the classes.'[10] Toronto workers elected James Simpson, a printer, to the Board of Education. Elsewhere only Ralph Smith achieved victory, but he was scarcely independent of the Liberal party. At the Trades Congress convention in 1905, labour leaders were reduced to claiming credit for the election of prominent Grits known to be sympathetic to some labour demands.[11]

Lack of sufficient money was a serious obstacle for independent labour politics in Canada. The Toronto District Labor Council decided that a grant to the Winnipeg labour committee would be 'illegal.' When the Toronto body's secretary polled locals on a proposition to back labour candidates for municipal elections in 1905, only twenty locals responded, and just four of these promised financial aid. Several offered 'moral support' and four suggested backing any Grit or Tory nominee favourable to labour. The Council voted to file the results of the secretary's survey without taking further action. As a result of the widespread failure of independent political action in 1904, the Trades Congress officers, while continuing to endorse labour politics, recommended 'that where no trade union candidates are in the field, support either, or neither, party candidates, whichever is at the time, considered in the best interests of labor, but let the interests of labor be predominant at all times.' It was the classic Gompers approach, of course, and it is clear that the tactic was stressed as a result of the prior failure of independent political action. The one point of departure by the Canadians from traditional Federation policy was spelled out in a denunciation of trade unionists who appeared on the Grit or Tory platforms. Trades Congress delegates probably hoped to prevent further penetration into trade-union ranks by the two major parties, so that independent political action would continue to be a viable option.[12]

Canadian socialists within the labour movement were equally interested in halting the inroads made by the Liberals. In 1906 James Simpson won nomination by the socialists in Toronto to contest the north Toronto seat in the Ontario legislature. He counted upon the endorsement of trade unionists, and a fellow socialist, Fred Bancroft, asked the Toronto central body to back

Simpson's candidacy. Bancroft's motion would have forbidden the Toronto Council from supporting any Grit or Tory politician, but an amended version did not make this distinction. The Toronto District Labor Council thereby preserved its option to endorse Grit or Tory candidates as well as the independent labour or socialist standard-bearers. But the debate within the Council revealed a cleavage between right-wing and left-wing politics in Çanadian labour circles.[13]

The split between socialists and labourites over trade-union politics in Canada grew wider and deeper. The Socialist party of Canada enrolled scores of working-men, many of whom were members of trade unions; yet there was no connection between Congress-sponsored independent political action and the socialist party. 'On the contrary the Socialists condemn the Trade Unionists' political movement and will not vote for the nominee of the Trade Unions, being bound by a pledge not to vote for anyone else than a Socialist nominee.'[14] The ideological split between the two factions revealed a geographical dimension as well. Socialists still wielded predominant influence in many trade-union circles in British Columbia, although the grip of dual-unionist labour organizations such as the United Brotherhood of Railway Employees, the American Labor Union, and the Western Federation of Miners had weakened significantly after the Berlin decisions. In the provincial elections of 1903, two socialists won the balance of power again in the British Columbia assembly. 'In Newcastle and Nanaimo we have a bad state of affairs with Socialism,' Ralph Smith reported. 'The ever changing electorate of these mining camps with so many discontented men it [sic] make matters risky ...' Smith pointed to the heavy criticism he was receiving from western socialists, and said that he expected 'to be reasonably renumerated by the [Liberal] party.' Smith's career suggested that an independent labour politician of necessity operated on the fringes of one of the major parties in order to find sufficient financial support.[15]

Gompers voiced few qualms about independent labour politics in Canada, but *socialist* labour politics was another matter. The distinction was vitally important because he identified socialism with dual unionism. 'It is not Socialism that we have been called on to combat,' he said, 'but the pernicious activity of Socialists who seem to have made it their particular mission in life to either dominate or destroy the trade unions. They defame and assassinate the character of men who dare to defend their convictions and who stand for the organization of trades unions.' Gompers waged war against socialists on both sides of the Canadian-American boundary. He called one of his British Columbia critics a 'political socialist,' and revealed his definition of that malady. They denounced all the good accomplished by trade unions, they perverted the facts in every case affecting trade unions or trade unionists, and they charged active unionists with dishonesty, unfaithfulness, and self-seeking. Neither the head of the National Association of Manufacturers, nor George Baer, the leader of the coal operators in the anthracite strike of 1902, was half so malignant or malicious an enemy of trade unions as were the 'political socialists.' Gompers' tirade exposed his priorities among the enemies of labour. Apparently he feared his trade-union opponents on the left more than the most arbitrary employers.[16] Federation leaders lost no opportunity to denounce or smear socialists within the ranks of labour. 'Socialism is un-American, unpatriotic, and it ought to have no footing in this or any other Convention,' the Federation convention of 1904 was told.[17] Of course Flett could not help but sense the bitter hostility of both Gompers and Morrison to anything smacking of left-wing ideology. He kept AFL leaders fully informed of the political activities and leanings of Canadian labour leaders.

One of the first Canadian socialists to be brought to Gompers' attention was the aforementioned James Simpson. Born in Lancashire in 1874, Simpson emigrated to Canada at age fourteen, and worked for three years in a factory before becoming a typesetter's apprentice. He joined the composing staff of the Toronto *Star* and Local 91 of the International Typographical Union at the turn of the century, and apparently enrolled in the socialist party at the same time. His youth and vigour, along with his obvious intelligence and speaking talents, rocketed him to prominence in Toronto labour circles. A leader in the trade-union movement and a popular worker in the Methodist church and in temperance circles, he was favourably known among other groups as well. Simpson's Methodism was to win him the vice-presidency of the Moral and Social Reform Council; his prohibitionism burst forth at the Trades Congress convention in 1905 after some delegates had moved to adjourn a few minutes early in order to tour a brewery. 'I would rather do fifteen minutes' business than spend two hours in a brewery,' Simpson exclaimed. A prairie newspaper called Simpson 'a sort of eloquential locomotive, and ... a modern type of the fighting circuit rider of the pioneer days of the old Methodist local preachers.' Obviously Simpson was no bearded Marxist who spoke in a thick accent and sat in the shadows of dank Toronto cellars plotting revolution; he was a thoroughly domesticated reformer with many ties within the community. A dedicated craft unionist for thirty-seven years, he worked to harmonize international unionism with a left-wing political ideology. His socialist principles were definitely evolutionary.[18]

Flett told Gompers about Simpson's political views when the Trades Congress convention of 1903 chose to send Simpson to the AFL convention as its fraternal delegate. Simpson may have participated in the political debates which consumed much of one day's session at the convention in Boston; at any rate, the socialists were handily defeated. When Simpson returned to Toronto, the District Council re-elected him to its presidency. This mystified Gompers, who believed that no one could be both a socialist *and* a trade unionist. Flett began reporting Simpson's words and movements to AFL leaders. A few weeks later Gompers expressed pleasure upon learning that Simpson had been 'curbed' in a speech by the presence of a number of trade unionists in the audience. 'Perhaps, too, the trouncing which the Socialists received at the Boston Convention may have helped to moderate either his views or his language. Be it as it may, I am not astonished at his course,' Gompers added. Simpson became a marked man in Gompers' eyes – a trade unionist who could not be trusted because he compromised his loyalty to his union by endorsing political views irrevocably associated in Gompers' mind with dual unionism.[19]

Gompers feared that Canadian socialists would gain control of the Trades and Labor Congress and repudiate the Berlin amendments linking most Canadian unionists to international crafts. While Flett was president of the Congress, the danger seemed remote. But after his narrow re-election victory, Flett decided not to risk running again. Shortly after the Trade Congress convention of 1904 opened, James Simpson presented the socialist challenge in a motion calling upon the Congress to dedicate itself to the principle of common ownership of the means of production. James Wilson of the Toronto printers and J.A. Rodier of the Montreal printers threw their support behind Simpson's measure. Several unionists spoke against it; then Flett offered a scathing denunciation of both the resolution and its framer, blasting the Toronto socialist in good AFL fashion. Simpson was one of a group of men who wished to destroy trade unionism, and proposed nothing but pipedreams in its place. His party had already declared its opposition to independent labour candidates in Toronto. His resolution threatened the Trades and Labor Congress with danger. 'It is the work of Socialist fakirs in this country, who worm their way into the congress in order that they may scuttle the old ship.' Thanks partly to Flett's energetic opposition, Simpson's motion lost by a lopsided sixty-one to seventeen vote. Alphonse Verville succeeded Flett in the Trades Congress leadership while Simpson was chosen vice-president. Despite Simpson's election, the Congress had been preserved, in Gompers' opinion, from the scourge of socialism.[20]

At the Trades Congress convention in 1905, Simpson and Flett clashed once again – this time on the tariff issue. When the debate turned to labour politics, a Congress committee took cognizance of the failure of most independent labour candidates in the elections of the previous year, and stressed the Gompers alternative of supporting Grit or Tory candidates who endorsed Trades Congress goals. Several delegates condemned this suggestion. Toronto socialists argued that their party deserved Congress support; they pointed to Simpson's victorious election upon a socialist platform to a seat on the Board of Education. Delegate Armstrong inquired whether the socialist party was a labour party. 'Most certainly,' Simpson replied. Nevertheless the AFL political strategy was adopted by forty-nine to fifteen, and several socialists (including Simpson) asked that their negative votes be officially recorded. Once again Simpson won the Congress's vice-presidency.[21]

As long as Canadian and American socialists controlled no important trade-union vehicle, AFL leaders remained reasonably confident of their ability to contain socialist penetrations into craft unionism. But when the Industrial Workers of the World (IWW) was launched in 1905, Morrison alerted his organizers to the new danger. 'The American Labor Union was practically down and out, and its promoters had to take the one desperate chance left to keep a rival organization in the field ...' Morrison said. A few months after the IWW's birth, the Federation secretary assured Flett 'that the trade unions are holding their own, that the new industrial organization that was inaugurated at Chicago, Ill., has been unable to secure recruits, and its efforts will be confined within the ranks of the Western Federation of Miners and the DeLeonite socialists.'[22]

Like many American reform movements, the Industrial Workers of the World generated a wave of fervour which swept across the Canadian-American boundary. Doubtless aware of the political activities of many Canadian unionists, Eugene Debs toured Ontario in February 1906. He told the Toronto *World* that Canadian labour was in 'a more healthy condition' than American labour. Crude phonograph records distributed as gifts by *Wilshire's Magazine* spread Debs' voice throughout the Ontario countryside. In the wake of these efforts, a few locals of the Wobblies sprang up in Canada in early 1906. Flett discovered one among Hebrew garment workers in Montreal. 'The "Wonder Workers" are making a desperate effort to reach Hebrews throughout the country, and in some places they are in a measure successful,' Morrison admitted. He told Flett of a rumour that the Wobblies were trying to secure a foothold in Toronto. At his request, Flett persuaded the Toronto District Labor Council to deny its rooms to the Wobblies for organizational meetings, and a Council committee publicly denounced the rival union. Highly pleased, Morrison congratulated Flett and added that the Wobblies 'should be given no consideration whatsoever. They live on abuse.' If the allegation was true, certainly Morrison and Gompers could not be charged with denying the Wobblies sustenance.[23]

The threat loomed even larger when the Western Federation of Miners established its first local in eastern North America at Cobalt, Ontario, in 1906 and brought the Wobblies with them. Federation leaders feared a linkup between the Cobalt Wobblies and the Toronto socialists. 'Our friend James Simpson is a socialist, and is probably wrapped up in the Industrial Workers' organization,' Morrison said. 'All the socialists are, or nearly all of them. Brother Simpson is fully aware of the position he occupies. He is a member of the I.T.U.

[International Typographical Union] but a Socialist first and like all other men of that ilk, stands for that which is nearest to his heart.' Morrison decided to ask Flett 'to get hold of one of the other good boys in Toronto, and call on Brother Simpson and endeavor to have him modify his support of this dual organization.' A few days later Morrison told Flett that president Boyle of the Maintenance-of-Way Employees International Union was in Toronto and would see what he could do with Simpson.[24]

Boyle relayed his conversations with Simpson to Morrison. The Toronto socialist had 'informed Brother Boyle that he was misrepresented as to his actions there; that he is in favor of the American Federation of Labor, first, last and always.' Morrison, however, clearly distrusted Simpson's protestations of loyalty.[25]

Less than a week later, when Flett informed him of the possibility of Simpson's election to the presidency of the Trades Congress at its fourthcoming convention in British Columbia – the centre of Canadian socialism – Morrison became alarmed. He had just received word that the Industrial Workers were trying to gain a foothold in British North America. 'Wherever there are any socialists, there you have advocates of Industrial Workers ... and, to make any success, they have to disintegrate the Internationals ...' Morrison feared that the heads of the international craft unions would react too slowly to the Wobbly threat. He and Gompers took it upon themselves to prosecute the craft union war against dual unionism.[26]

In early August 1906 Draper and other Canadian unionists warned Gompers that the forthcoming Trades and Labor Congress convention being held in British Columbia might well fall under the domination of socialist delegates from that province. A worried Gompers notified the heads of twenty-three international craft unions, asking that they make sure that their Canadian locals sent loyal and trustworthy delegates to the Trades Congress convention 'so that the continuity and safety of the Canadian trade union movement and particularly in its international aspect may be guaranteed beyond peradventure.' He told the international union leaders to keep him informed of the actions they took in response to his request. Flett had already been sent on his organizing trip into the Canadian West the month before, and was in a good position to help assure the election of non-socialist delegates during his travels. Consequently, while many had anticipated that locals in central Canada would not send delegates to distant Victoria in 1906, 'the liberal aid and affiliation of many international unions ... resulted in about the usual attendance of delegates.' No one flatly admitted, of course, that Gompers and the international unions manipulated attendance at the Trades Congress convention of 1906 to guarantee international craft unionism's Canadian investment, or that AFL leaders worked through Flett and Draper to prevent the capture of the Congress by socialists who in Gompers' mind had been perpetually guilty of the sin of dual unionism.[27]

Sentiment among Canadian trade unionists on behalf of labour politics reached new heights prior to the Congress convention of 1906. The AFL had drawn up a 'bill of grievances' in March of that year and had presented it to American legislators and the public. 'The first concern of all should be the positive defeat of those [legislators] who have been hostile or indifferent to the just demands of labor.' Then, shifting from its traditional political policy, the AFL urged that 'wherever both parties ignore legislative demands a straight labor candidate should be nominated, so that honest men may have the opportunity in exercising their franchise to vote according to their conscience.' The AFL warned against such endeavours deteriorating into a scramble for office. 'It should be a determined effort, free, absolutely, from partisanship of every name and character, to secure the legislation we deem necessary.' Wherever it was apparent that independent labour candidates could not be elected, 'efforts should be made to secure such support by endorsement of candidates by the minority party ... and by such other progressive elements as will insure the election of labor representatives.'[28]

While the AFL sanctioned the nomination of independent labour candidates after 1906, it made no move to establish a labour party. Whenever labour had tried to organize a party, Gompers cautioned, 'control has been wheedled out of their hands by a lot faddists, theorists or self-seekers, and thus perverted from its true labor interests and working-class characteristics.'[29] Federation leaders obviously feared that their new policy might give birth to a political monster which would compromise the loyalty of workers. But they really had no choice; the judicial onslaught upon American trade unions and the failure of the AFL to win exemption from anti-trust laws had forced them into independent labour politics. 'The American Federation has put its hand to the plough,' the fraternal delegate told Canadians in 1906, 'and is determined to show its enemies that the wage-earner will stand no longer idly by and see Labor Bills pigeon-holed in Committee, while those of the capitalist interests carry by large majorities.' After 1906 several AFL organizers shouldered unaccustomed duties as political campaign managers.[30]

Neither the Canadian nor the American labour movements existed in a vacuum, and events overseas and particularly in England often produced shock waves in North America. Some fifty-four trade unionists had been sent to the British parliament in the elections of late 1905, impressing Federation leaders with the success of labour politics in the face of working-class voting restrictions in England. 'If the British workmen, with their limited franchise, accomplish so much by their united action, what may we in the United States not do with universal suffrage?' In the minds of contemporary observers, American trade-union leaders seemed to have taken another step down the road traveled by their British and Australian brethren. It seemed that labour was asserting its political power and presenting proposals that tended toward state control and a re-distribution of the wealth in all the industrial nations.[31]

The course of events in both British and American trade-union circles gave Canadian labour politics a double impetus in 1906. Even before the American Federation of Labor had issued its bill of grievances, the Trades Congress president, Alphonse Verville, had won election from a Montreal constituency to the House of Commons on an independent labour ticket. 'Hope that the triumph of Viverville [sic] will be of benefit to the trade union movement of Canada,' Morrison said. With the announcement of the new AFL political policy, the tactics of both Canadian and American labour leaders began to converge. Gompers did not oppose independent political action by Canadian locals of international craft unions. In the minds of both Gompers and Draper at this time, the prime purpose of independent labour politics was to exercise leverage upon the two major parties, and not to create a permanent trade-union political movement with its own party and political ideology.[32]

Thus by September of 1906 when delegates gathered at the Trades Congress convention in Victoria, labour politics charged the atmosphere. In British Columbia, of course, unionists had traditionally generated a lot of political electricity, much of it of a revolutionary nature which more conservative Eastern trade unionists found distasteful. Even the more conservative unionists in British Columbia had long supported independent labour politics. Political trends elsewhere in the labour world seemed to reaffirm British Columbia labour's predilections. Labour politics coloured nearly every report and debate after the Trades Congress delegates had assembled at Victoria.

Congress officials told the delegates that they hoped to see a dozen labour representatives at the next parliament. Quebec labour leaders announced another labour candidacy in Montreal and expected to repeat Verville's victory. Delegate W.R. Trotter, a Congress volunteer organizer, reported on the enthusiastic reception in western towns of the decision by Congress leaders to inaugurate a program of independent political action throughout the country. The Congress lobbyist on Parliament Hill emphasized his belief in the absolute importance of increasing the representation of labour in the House. 'That is Labor's first and best remedy for its many grievances.'[33]

American labour leaders attending the Congress sessions joined the refrain. The AFL organizer in nearby Washington state had been ordered to Victoria to assist Flett. The only way the working class could get justice, C.O. Young said, was to elect men who carried union cards. The Federation fraternal delegate, T.A. Rickert of the United Garment Workers, was delighted to see that the Trades and Labor Congress had a president who represented a labour constituency in the House of Commons. 'I trust your movement will develop along these lines until you will be such a power in your local and Federal Legislatures that both Parties will fear you.' Responding to Rickert's speech, James Simpson paid high tribute to the 'worth' and 'stability' of Gompers, and praised international unionism. He said it would be ridiculous if Canadians ever cut their trade-union ties with Americans.[34]

The surface harmony at Victoria belied the political struggles going on behind the scenes. Canadian socialists worked to persuade the delegates to endorse the principles and program of the Socialist party of Canada; Flett, Young, and other international unionists lobbied to prevent the socialists from capturing the Congress and thereby threatening international unionism in Canada. Although the political debates were not scheduled until the fourth day's session, tension filled the hall and broke out much earlier.

Delegate Stevenson [Ed J. Stephenson], of Moose Jaw, pointed out that the Socialistic platform handed to the delegates did not bear the union label. (Loud Applause)

Delegate Rollo moved that all literature not bearing the union label be gathered up and destroyed.

Again Delegate Pettipiece [the Vancouver printer and socialist] rose to his feet and asked to be appointed a committee of one to inspect all the clothing of members and see if it bore the union label. If not that should be thrown out, too. (Loud Applause)

Delegate Anderson [Montreal carpenter and socialist] suggested all non-union cigars in the room be destroyed.

Delegate McNiven — 'How can you tell they are non-union cigars?'

Delegate Anderson — 'I could smell them anywhere.' (Laughter)

It was apparent that the socialists could outwit their opponents; it remained to be seen whether they could outvote them.[35]

On the third day of the convention, the Congress entertained a resolution interpreted by a few of the British Columbia delegates as an implied condemnation of the Industrial Workers of the World. The Wobblies, delegate Surgess countered, were not an unfair society. Robert Hungerford rose to a point of order and said that it was improper for Surgess to advocate the Wobblies because it was an organization opposed to the Congress. Vice-president James Simpson, who happened to be in the chair, ruled Surgess in order. Then the president of the Victoria Trades and Labor Council, a staunch trade unionist, appealed Simpson's ruling. He wanted an immediate debate in the expectation that the Congress would decisively condemn the Wobblies. At this juncture most delegates were in no mood to declare war upon the 'Wonder Workers,' and Simpson's ruling was upheld by a forty-three to twenty-five vote. The socialists had chalked up another victory of sorts.[36]

Throughout the week several motions concerning labour politics were introduced and referred to committee; finally, Thursday, 21 September, was given over to debates on the Trades and Labor Congress's future political platform. The clash of sentiments which had broken through at times earlier in the week now erupted into a wide-open debate. Draper, fully sensitive to the desire among delegates for some kind of political stand, wrestled the initiative from the socialists. He introduced a resolution designed to tie together many of the political motions already submitted. Draper called for the establishment of a Canadian labour party 'independent of either of the old line political parties, and equally independent of socialistic tenets and control.' The party, to be organized into provincial wings, would maintain a separate existence from the Trades Congress and would nominate only union-card carrying candidates.[37]

The socialists, put on the defensive by Draper's motion, immediately sought to amend it to their satisfaction. Delegate Dutton moved that the Congress endorse the principles and program of the Socialist party of Canada. 'The hottest kind of debate followed, with the prospect at one time of socialistic triumph.' But Dutton's amendment was ultimately defeated, and the decision for a independent labour party was affirmed by the delegates. Sixty-eight unionists endorsed Draper's proposal; only seven, including Simpson, Pettipiece, Surgess, and Anderson, were recorded in the negative. Many socialists had voted for Draper's motion; the seven dissidents were said to represent the 'impossibilist' faction. Both Draper and the *Winnipeg Tribune* thought that the decision to organize a labour party overshadowed the other Congress actions. 'Five or six men,' the newspaper editorialized, 'holding firmly to their convictions ... can accomplish more at Ottawa than can a flock of two score sheep merely following their leader in opposition to everything proposed by the other side.' The *Western Clarion* detected a personal vendetta against Simpson. Delegates had come from Eastern Canada to take his scalp, and the vote did not accurately reflect convention sentiment. 'The question under discussion was not so much political action as how to queer Simpson.' Yet the young Torontonian, although admitting that he would be bound by socialist party loyalty not to vote for any candidates of the forthcoming labour party, won re-election to the Congress vice-presidency.[38]

For the American Federation of Labor and the international crafts, the Congress vote was assessed in a way more immediately related to their own concerns. 'I have noticed that the Socialists did not win out,' Morrison told Flett. 'In other words, that the Trade Unionist[s] dominated the convention ...' Morrison was highly critical of the re-election of Simpson by the Canadian unionists. 'What process of reasoning caused the delegates to the Convention to vote for a man who declared that ... he could not vote for a single one [sic] trade unionist for office? ... I say [Simpson] forfeits the right to hold office in a trade union.' Once again the Federation secretary asserted the AFL maxim that a man could not be consistently loyal to both his trade union and a political party. It was particularly true when loyalty was pledged to a left-wing party which had backed dual unions since the 1890s. Morrison thought Simpson's re-election 'mostly a matter of sentiment.'[39]

At the AFL convention later that year, Trades Congress fraternal delegate Sam Landers gave American unionists a full report on the Congress's decision to venture into labour politics. He pointed to the clear defeat of the socialists at Victoria, and spelled out the 'immediatist' nature of the Trades Congress political platform. In the context of the AFL's own entry into politics that year, the Congress's actions were hardly out of step. But in case anyone concluded that the Canadians were embarking upon a divergent path, Landers assured the Americans that 'the loyalty of the Canadian trade unionist is unwavering and evidenced by the fact that the mention of President Gompers' name, or the name American Federation, brings spontaneous applause.'[40]

Landers' words symbolized what Gompers and Flett, with frequent assists from Draper, had worked hard to preserve. It had required special efforts on their part – including assurance through international union heads of the selection of loyal trade-union delegates to the Victoria convention, the dispatch of Flett on an expensive, six-month organizing effort throughout the Canadian West, and the timely presentation by Draper of a comprehensive political policy, broad and radical enough to capture the enthusiasm of the delegates, but carefully drawn to keep labour politics out of socialist clutches and at arm's length from the trade unions themselves. The AFL's preparations had paid off. The Trades and Labor Congress had succeeded in holding a convention in one of the centres of left-wing dual unionism in North America and had come away from Victoria with its commitment to both international craft unionism and a pragmatic political policy still intact.

The Victoria convention revealed the failure, once again, of Canadian labour leaders to forge a unity among socialists, supporters of independent labour politics, and pure-and-simple trade unionists. Lack of cooperation between these elements was evident to Ramsay Macdonald during his 'flying visit' to Canada in mid-1906. Macdonald doubted whether a successful Canadian labour political movement would ever emerge. Well aware of the effects of the international tie, he said that Canadian trade unions had first to go through a nationalizing fire. Secondly, he criticized Canadian socialists for grinding away 'at their cold aggressive academic formulae about the "class war",' and calling their opponents 'a failure or a scoundrel of some degree or other.' He concluded that British Columbia was 'the first Canadian province to develop the economic and political state from which labour and socialist movements like ours grow up.'[41]

While Macdonald's remarks about Canadian labour's international tie drew heavy fire from Sam Landers at the AFL convention in 1906, events partially confirmed the British labour leader's analysis of labour politics in British Columbia. Shortly after the Congress convention at Victoria ended, the Trades Congress vice-president in the coast province, G.F. Gray, called a meeting to organize a provincial labour party. The district council of the Western Federation of Miners managed to wrest control of the meeting from Gray, with immediate political consequences. Contrary to the desires of both the AFL and most Trades Congress leaders, the socialists became 'the political expression of discontent among the British Columbia workers.'[42]

The labour political situation some three thousand miles to the east stood out in bold contrast to the radicalism of British Columbia labour. Trades Congress affiliates in Quebec selected Joseph Ainey to contest a Commons seat on a labour platform in Montreal. Not only was he opposed by the Grits and Tories, but even the leader of the National Trades and Labor Congress was nominated for the seat. The latter threw his support to the incumbent who rather easily won re-election. After their overwhelming success in electing Verville, this defeat came as a surprise to Quebec labour leaders, who attributed Ainey's loss to a lack of working-class support at the polls.[43]

In the Maritimes as in Montreal, the divisions within the Canadian labour movement hampered ventures into independent political action. Considerable sympathy for a new political course was voiced at meetings of the Provincial Workmen's Association in 1906. 'I am in favour of labor politics,' D. McDougall told the Council. 'I have thrown party politics overboard long ago. If we cannot succeed like our British Bros. across the waters [sic]. By dint of hard work they have succeeded and now hold the balance of power. I believe that the lodges ought to discuss this matter ...' A year later, though, the Association shied away from setting up a separate committee to mobilize support for an independent labour political campaign. The international union locals in Halifax found the political soil insufficiently fertile even to nominate labour candidates.[44]

If the labour political picture on either coast presented a study in contrasts, the movement in the remaining provinces seemed to follow a course somewhere between the two political and geographical extremes. Winnipeg trade unionists had been first to call a meeting to carry out Draper's resolution. Many Old Countrymen attended and displayed their determination to support independent political action as they had done in Britain. As in British Columbia, Manitoba socialists questioned the wisdom of creating an independent labour party. But in this case it was the socialists who withdrew after being outvoted, and organizational efforts proceeded along independent labour party lines under the chairmanship of Arthur Puttee, the ex-labour MP. Trade-union organization was still weak in Saskatchewan and Alberta; labour political efforts emerged more slowly and were heavily influenced by developments in adjoining provinces. 'Little has been done in this Province looking towards the formation of an Independent Labor Party,' Saskatchewan leaders reported in 1907. A few weeks later, however, a party was founded in Regina. At first Alberta leaders reported a lack of interest in Draper's resolution in their province. Later that year a convention was called to set up a labour party. It was captured by socialists with an assist from their brethren in neighbouring British Columbia.[45]

The most important developments took place in Ontario, the province with the heaviest concentration of trade unionists closely tied to the American Federation of Labor. Before 1906 was out, workers in Hamilton adopted a political platform and nominated Allan Studholme, a stove mounter, to contest a seat in the provincial legislature. Running on a straight labour ticket, Studholme defeated the leader of the Hamilton Tories by a majority of 853 votes.[46]

The news reverberated throughout Ontario and whetted the desire of unionists to proceed immediately to the formation of a provincial labour party. In the wake of the Hamilton victory, Trades Congress secretary Draper issued the call for a convention to assemble in Toronto on 29 March 1907. While Gompers and Morrison showed mild interest in the labour political picture elsewhere in Canada, they were deeply concerned about events in Ontario. 'You should by all means be present,' Morrison told Flett. 'It will be unfortunate if the effort to commit the convention to a declaration in favor of socialism succeeds.'[47]

Six hundred delegates from all over the province gathered at Broadway Hall in Toronto and chose Walter R. Rollo, a broom-maker from Hamilton, to preside over the meeting. 'It was a singularly interesting gathering,' the *Globe* said. 'Old men, their backs bent with hard toil, the middle-aged who prided themselves upon their brawn and sinew, and young men, exuberant and eager for debate, were contrasting figures that held the eye. Excitement marked the entire discussions,' and Rollo relied upon a heavy pine slab to gavel the men into a semblance of order.[48]

Just as Flett and the business unionists expected, the fireworks came after Draper had submitted his motion calling for the creation of an Ontario Labour party. They were ignited by James Simpson, who moved that instead of forming a labour party the delegates give their endorsement to the Socialist party. His action provoked 'a prolonged and most ungovernable controversy,' causing 'uproars that drowned out the speaker and ignored the chair absolutely.' Simpson's amendment was received

with about the same courtesy that a hornet would be by ladies at an afternoon sewing circle. The mover, being widely known amongst unions, and being capable of making himself easily heard, was given a good hearing when he first rose, but when he came to the clauses which dwelt on the ethics of the Socialist party, into the fray went the six hundred.

'Sit down,' shouted one dissatisfied person.

'Mr. Chairman —' but the old gentleman with the feeble voice who said this got no farther. A short man with a heavy beard and glasses, who shook his head with indignation because others tried to drown his voice, persisted in saying that he had an amendment to the amendment. Four or five other delegates sprang up and shouted that Socialism was not in order. Two hours later the short man with the beard and glasses succeeded in getting his amendment before the meeting. In the meantime all the excitement and outbursts of a political campaign characterized the proceedings.

'I say, sit down, sit down,' yelled the Chairman as he gave the table a pounding that threatened to break the slab where it had a big knot, but the pandemonium went on.

'I rise to a point of order.' 'I want a hearing, Mr. Chairman.' 'Question' and 'Who's got a right to talk here, anyway?' were some of the numerous cries that filled the hall. When the noise was finally subdued, Mr. Simpson continued. What he asked was that the principles of the Socialist party be endorsed because he believed they were sound and in the interests of the laboring classes. At the conclusion of his remarks Delegate Drake of Hamilton held up his hand to catch the eye of the Chairman.

'I see there's going to be a split here,' he shouted. 'I say that if this meeting was called by the Congress then we have no right to listen to a Socialist.'

Mr. Rollo tried to explain away the grounds on which Mr. Simpson was privileged to speak.

Delegate Flett of Hamilton followed, and stated that he could not understand how any man could get up and try to square the principles of trades unions with those of Socialists.

'We object to being maligned,' he said, 'by these men who call themselves Socialists and who shout their doctrines at us from every soap-box on the street corner. These men are like the proverbial bay tree, they spring up and flourish for a time and then —' But he did not finish either.

'I rise to a point of order,' said Mr. Simpson, coming out on the platform. A dozen delegates were on their feet in a second. The chair pounded some more and then the shouts of 'sit down' were so loud and many that Mr. Simpson retired ...

... A sturdy tradesman who had kept the floor through all the uproar expressed his views. 'If I were to move a resolution that we endorse the platform of the Conservative party, would that be in order?'

With promptness the Chairman shouted: 'No, because they have no platform.' Cheers and prolonged laughter followed.

Delegate Todd's remarks were similarly broken off a few minutes later. When speaking he said: 'That reminds me of a story I once —' 'No, no. Sit down,' 'No stories go here,' 'Cut it short' and 'Time's up' were the words used to express strong disapproval of any stories.

... Uncontrollable excitement prevailed till nearly half-past five. Delegates from various parts of the Province spoke, some in favor of Socialism, some denouncing it in the most vigorous way, and others admonishing their fellows for taking up so much time. Both the Liberal and Conservative parties were opposed, and the methods of the politicians were called bunco games, trickery, and several other names that are known to everyday parlance. The result of it all was a vote which recorded thirty-four for the amendment of Mr. Simpson, and the remainder of the convention as in favor of the main resolution.[49]

One Torontonian was troubled by the passions which the debate had stirred up. 'If we may judge from the temper shown here by Labour and its champions,' Goldwin Smith wrote shortly after the shouts at Broadway Hall had died away, 'there is ample need for every sedative that can possibly be applied. Nothing can exceed the virulence of the appeals to antagonism of class.' The more sympathetic *Globe* concluded that 'the experience gained through trade unions in organizing and unity of effort may in time be made to serve in organizing a political force.' But neither the heated rhetoric nor the breaking of new political ground excited Flett's superiors in Washington. 'I note the defeat of the Socialist proposition by a vote of 34 out of 600,' Morrison gloated.[50]

Perhaps partly because their own political efforts had fallen short of expectations, AFL leaders kept themselves fully abreast of Canadian labour's political ventures. Morrison took pains to inform the Executive Council of the Broadway Hall meeting at which the Ontario Labor party had been launched, and listed the sixteen planks in the new party's platform. All were moderate statements, and he offered no criticism of either the launching of the labour party or the items on the platform. Yet he made a point of mentioning the defeat of the socialists after their 'tremendous effort' at the 29 March meeting. While Gompers and Morrison may have had theoretical objections to some of the political tactics adopted by the Canadians, they made no effort to oppose the launching of provincial labour parties. Apparently the demise of the socialists was all that really concerned them.[51]

The nascent Ontario Labor party failed to win a commitment from the rank-and-file. Three months after the 29 March convention, the Toronto District Council instructed its secretary to communicate with the new party with a view to organizing Queen City unions for the forthcoming elections. First the Council decided not to limit its political endorsement to independent labour party candidates; later they finally agreed that 'the nomination and endorsation of all candiates [sic] for municipal Provincial or Federal Honors be relegated to the Independent Labor Party.' But the Council refused to bar its officers from appearing on the platform of Tory or Grit candidates. More important, it denied financial aid to independent labour nominees in either Toronto or other cities.[52]

While the ideological nature of the split over labour politics was readily apparent in such forums as the Toronto District Labor Council, the geographical aspect continued to appear at Trades Congress gatherings. At the Winnipeg convention in 1907, for example, R. Parm Pettipiece submitted a resolution that would have placed a stamp of approval on the socialist capture of the labour political movement in British Columbia. The debate quickly blossomed into a struggle between the East and the West. Pettipiece argued that the Socialist party of Canada embodied the advanced thought of the Canadian labour movement; his motion, he maintained, would permit each province to 'frame its policy to suit its needs or limitations.' He was opposed by several delegates including Draper. It was unfair, Draper said, to introduce the resolution in advance of Eastern opinion. Pettipiece's motion was defeated by fifty-one to thirty-nine. Thereby the Congress refused to recognize the socialists in British Columbia, and later in Alberta, as legitimate representatives of the political movement sanctioned by the Trades and Labor Congress. There was enough radicalism present, however, to redound to the advantage of James Simpson. 'I notice that, notwithstanding the sweeping threat, the Socialist Wing of the Trades Congress met defeat [but] that my fellow craftsman, Mr. James Simpson, has been re-elected with loud acclaim,' Morrison wrote.[53]

Simpson, by now the leading trade-union socialist in Canada, remained an object of suspicion, and his loyalty to international craft unionism was still doubted. Gompers used the opportunity afforded by Simpson's visit to the AFL's Norfolk convention in 1907 to call the Canadian to account. 'You will remember,' he wrote some months later to Flett, 'that when riding in the car in Norfolk the gentleman [Simpson] was present and a remark which I made rather jolted him because of his vascillating policy ... I think he never got over the effect of it and more than likely has some little personal spleen because I had the temerity to suddenly call him to account for the course pursued. He always seems friendly, however ...' Gompers criticized the Canadian's 'ambiguous methods.' '... It requires something more than simple honesty of purpose to guide a man aright in his course, understanding is no less a requirement.' Later in 1908 Simpson earned more AFL enmity when he voted against the Toronto District Labor Council's decision to take out an AFL charter.[54]

By 1909 it was clear that independent labour political tactics still faced many obstacles. The Canadian Labor party failed to elect four candidates in Toronto, partly because all four seats had been contested by the socialists. The Congress's vice-president in Quebec, Gustave Francq, met defeat in a provincial contest. Studholme won re-election to his provincial seat, but the bleakness of the outlook elsewhere forced Congress leaders to admit that Canadian unionists were only 'feeling their way to the light.' The *Voice* thought that workers were standing aloof until trade unionists agreed upon their political tactics. Quebec leaders concluded that past failures had resulted from the Congress's lack of control over the working-class vote, and urged that the Congress turn itself into a political party in the same manner as workers in Belgium. Others disagreed, and thought it undesirable and unwise to commit their organization in such a way, because the Congress also needed to obtain legislative favours from the parties in power. 'The political organization of the workers,' they asserted, 'must be carried on independent of the work of the Congress.' This view was identical to that of the AFL and the international unions, who feared the dissolution of their organizations if they were permitted to become political bodies as well.[55]

After the Congress leaders had enunciated this position at the Congress convention in late 1908, Sam Landers of Hamilton offered an alternative proposal. He recommended that the Congress endorse all independent labour candidates 'who when elected will form a separate party in the Dominion Parliament on the lines which have proved so successful and productive of beneficial results to the wage-earning classes of Great Britain, Australia, New Zealand and other countries.' Landers also called upon Canadian socialists to vote for independent labour candidates. The discussion which followed turned into an attack upon the socialists for their doctrinaire ways.[56]

A distinguished visitor to the convention, J. Keir Hardie, joined in the debate. He told his listeners that he had been a socialist for the last quarter of a century as well as one of the pioneers of the Labor party in the Old Country. In England the term socialism had no such restricted meaning as in Canada and the United States. Although Canada had all the materials for a great socialist movement, the conflict between doctrinaire socialists and pure-and-simple trade unionists had harmed both their causes. Hardie criticized the socialists for autocratic attempts to force their ideas upon people, but he also said that it was vital that trade unions finance the political movement of organized labour.[57] Hardie may not have known that Canadian trade unionists lacked complete control of events. As long as Gompers, Morrison, and Flett countered Simpson's efforts to bridge the gap between trade unionism and socialism, the ideological divisions were likely to continue. As long as trade-union funds remained under the control of international craft unions, there was little likelihood that the labour political movement in Canada would be adequately financed. After Hardie sat down, Landers was persuaded to withdraw his motion, and Simpson attempted to restore some harmony. But it proved impossible again to forge a political policy which everyone would support; the *Globe* concluded that Canadian trade unionists were 'not yet prepared for a Third party movement.'[58]

During the next five years, internal schisms and internecine warfare undermined the socialist movement in North America. In the United States, a fight broke out between left-wing radicals and the Hillquit faction, which advocated 'boring from within' the AFL. The party, according to one historian, began to break up at the moment it was scoring some spectacular electoral successes. Canadian socialists, wracked by the same chiliastic tendencies, splintered into several tiny revolutionary sects and a moderate Social Democratic party (SDP) numbering James Simpson and some of his trade-union colleagues among its adherents. The divisive effect of these disputes was compounded by the uneven pattern of Canadian industrialization as well as by ethnic and political differences, all of which made the continentalizing tasks of the American trade-union leaders somewhat easier.[59]

James Simpson and his associates struggled to find a common political denominator. They recognized that 'gas and water' socialism was more palatable to many, though they did not abandon their Marxist view of society and history. Marx, Simpson wrote, had envisioned an emancipated working class freed from its exploiters in order to enjoy the fruits of its labour. 'This was no idle dream,' he declared. 'It was a well-reasoned deduction from a clear interpretation of past history and prophetic vision of the conditions of the future.' The state only protected the property interests of the ruling class, 'and if the working class is ever to become the only class in society, it must capture the state and all that is comprehended in the state and use it in the interests of that class alone.' Simpson urged trade unionists to begin their efforts at the municipal level. What still differentiated the Simpsonites from other Canadian socialists was their desire to harness the bulk of Canadian trade unionists — which were enrolled in the international crafts — to a common political platform.[60]

The failures on the provincial level led Canadian unionists to devote some effort to municipal contests, where they were a bit more successful. Joe Ainey won election to the Montreal Board of Control in 1910, two unionists contested municipal offices in St Catharines, a member of the Piano and Organ Workers' Union became the mayor of Guelph, and organized labour in Vancouver elected a union supporter as mayor. In 1912 three union men were chosen for the Brantford city council and one placed on the school board. By the outbreak of the First World War Canadian cities listed scores of trade-union aldermen. Meanwhile, other costly political campaigns proved fruitless. John Joy lost a bid for the Nova Scotia legislature in 1910. Fred Dixon of Manitoba came within seventy-four votes of capturing a provincial seat; the labour vote was split between labour and socialist candidates. In the 1911 federal election R.A. Rigg unsuccessfully challenged a Winnipeg riding, and the next year three socialists put up by British Columbia miners lost because 'the intelligence of the electorate was not high enough.'[61]

In order to coordinate their political efforts, as well as to assert their independence from American influence, the British Columbians set up a provincial federation of labour in the spring of 1910. Chartered by the Trades and Labor Congress, this body replaced the provincial executives formerly appointed by Trades Congress leaders, and confirmed the decentralized approach to TLC political action. The British Columbia and Alberta federations criticized international union rules forbidding the discussion of political questions at trade-union gatherings. A Vancouver printer advised locals to change their constitutions or ignore them – most doubtless pursued the latter alternative. By 1914 New Brunswick labour leaders had set up a labour federation in their province and Ontario unionists were moving to follow suit.[62]

The Toronto District Council remained one of the few municipal labour centres where labour and socialist groups successfully cooperated. In 1910 the city's socialist party instructed its members to join the unions of their respective crafts 'wherever possible.' Little came of these efforts at first. Then, in mid-1912, Fred Bancroft moved that the Council appoint a committee to secure the cooperation of the SDP, ILP, and other bodies 'with a view to entering the forthcoming Municipal Contests.' The resolution was carried by a 'substantial majority' and later that year the Council and the socialists laid down a manifesto outlining the necessity for working-class control of political machinery. James Simpson won Council endorsement and financial help and polled over 10,000 votes in a losing bid for a Board of Control seat. In 1914, with the same program and backing, Simpson triumphed with over 20,000 ballots. The results, he said, 'indicate that the trade unionists and socialists cooperated as they never did before, and give an emphatic denial to the statement that the workers will not unite for political action.' Simpson's victory showed that it really was possible to find sufficient common ground between trade unionists and socialists to erect a political platform and wage a successful contest for office. But there were only a handful of Simpsons, and they laboured under the shadow of AFL proscription.[63]

The Congress renewed its endorsement of independent political action, and still left it to the provinces to organize labour parties. In 1911 motions calling for collective ownership and asking the Congress to take 'an active part in political labor representation' failed, but the TLC called upon AFL affiliates to rescind constitutional provisions barring discussion of political issues. It refused to intervene in provincial labour political disputes or to endorse socialist candidates. Congress leaders, citing gains made by the Australian and British labour parties, wondered how long Canada would remain 'in the rut of the old Parties,' and praised efforts of workers to elect their own representatives. They called for unity and endorsed motions reaffirming independent political action. Some Congress leaders took a more controversial position; William Glockling called for state ownership of all public utilities in 1910. In 1911 James Watters, a British Columbia left-winger, was elected to the Congress presidency. Watters told the Congress delegates that 'it is just about time that the political field was invaded in earnest by the workers with their own candidates.'[64]

Keir Hardie reinforced the new call for political action again in 1912. 'While the strike may secure small reforms for the worker, it can never solve the industrial problem,' he told the Canadians.

The conquest of political power alone can do that ... In six years we have accomplished what would have taken six hundred years if we had depended entirely upon the old parties. Go thou and do likewise. (Laughter) Don't be ashamed of being called a Socialist. The capitalist class will make you proud of being called a Socialist. The railways and land of Canada should be owned by the people of Canada instead of by the people who even don't live among you. See to it that you hand over to your children a nobler life than you yourselves have entered into. (Prolonged applause.)[65]

Such talk in 1912 by Hardie and the next year by Will Thorne, coupled with worsening economic conditions, gave a powerful impetus to demands that the Congress set up a national labour party. The clamour was reinforced by the gains made by the AFL in the years since 1906 when its bill of grievances had been issued. Canadians were told in 1913 that the Federation could identify seventeen trade unionists in the House of Representatives, one in the Senate, and two in Woodrow Wilson's cabinet (Franklin Lane, Secretary of the Interior; W.B. Wilson, the first Secretary of Labor). Later a delegate called upon the Trades

Congress to organize a labour party and lend its financial and moral support to labour candidates. This motion failed, as did one asking the Congress to endorse the socialist platform. Congress leaders were not prepared to commit their organization directly. 'Provincial autonomy is giving the movement time and opportunity to develop toward a National Political movement of the working class in Canada.' They saw no reason to interfere with provincial autonomy in political matters. All signs pointed to the political awakening of the Canadian working class, they said.[66]

As long as the Congress limited its own political efforts to the realm of exhortation, it did not stray far from AFL policy. Men like Studholme were considered politically 'sound' by AFL leaders. Morrison even dispatched Flett on two separate occasions to assist Studholme's election campaigns. '... I think that every effort should be made to elect our labor men. If you can be of assistance do so by all means,' he told Flett. The AFL newspaper was careful to note that the Independent Labor Party of Ontario was opposed to socialism.[67]

In Gompers' view, the links forged at Berlin between Canadian and American labour were secure as long as Canadian socialists did not gain full sway over the Congress. Consequently Flett continued to keep AFL leaders informed of the activities and political views of Simpson, Bancroft, R.P. Pettipiece, W.R. Trotter, and James Watters. Morrison was pleased that 'our good friend Glockling was elected over Simpson, Socialist' at the Congress convention in 1909, 'though Simpson is a fellow Printer, or newspaper writer.' When Bancroft was chosen fraternal delegate to the AFL, Flett informed Morrison of his socialist views. Sometimes Flett relied upon scanty evidence; he labelled Watters a socialist largely because the Congress leader had received a 'Dear Comrade' letter from a socialist party official.[68]

Gompers insisted that the experience of organized labour in Europe did not apply to the New World arena. A labour party might be a necessity in a nation such as England where the state did not pay a salary to legislators, where many workers were excluded from voting, and where hereditary lords were the enemies of democracy. And Gompers was careful to note the exaggerated hopes of British and American socialists. 'What has come from Keir Hardie's prophecies that there would surely be one hundred labor Members of Parliament elected this year [1910] to the House of Commons?' he asked. Gompers drew the apparent lesson: 'Fellow-workingmen of all countries, the American Federation of Labor is on the right political road, at least for America.'[69]

In the United States, AFL leaders kept socialists within the Federation at bay. Ironically, it was a task made easier by the virulence of the attacks on Gompers by the business community. In Canada, Flett performed a similar chore. In 1910, Morrison heard rumours that 'the Socialists are going to make a determined effort to capture the Canadian Trades and Labor Congress at its next session.' Flett provided information and advice on the matter. Two years later, Frank Duffy, the secretary of the United Brotherhood of Carpenters, unleashed a tirade against the Canadians. He had always believed the Canadian labour movement to have been chiefly a political affair. Now he was sorry to see it become 'so strongly Socialistic.' He had heard the usual rumour that socialists would attempt to capture the Trades Congress at its next session. 'As the Socialists have no use for the trades unions and their milk and water politics they should be given to understand that the sooner they get out of the labor movement the better it will be ...' He asked Gompers to use his influence to 'preserve the trade union movement of that Dominion.'[70]

Congress fraternal delegates struggled to explain to sceptical Americans why Canadian labour exhibited so strong a propensity for political action. In 1912 John Bruce told the Federation delegates that workers the world over were clamouring for an organization giving political expression to wage workers. He denied that political activity by unionists was harmful. They merely demanded 'a political system that will bring some recognition of the efforts of wage workers, and at least try to make a better and brighter life for the wage workers of this civilized world and of this continent in particular.' The next year, however, Gustave Francq admitted that organized labour in Canada had not been able to agree on a political program 'sufficiently advanced to rally the extreme radicals and at the same time sufficiently moderate to win over the strictly trade-unionists.' Certainly the policies of the international craft unions bore some responsibility for that fact.[71]

By 1914 the AFL and Trades Congress political programs virtually coincided, which was not surprising given the dominant role played by the international unions in both organizations. The Federation identified nearly a score of trade unionists seated in the halls of government at Washington. According to Gompers the labour group in Congress acted in unison regardless of their party 'and with advantageous results' to American labour. The Federation, Morrison declared, had secured more beneficial legislation than during the preceding twenty years. But the Trades and Labor Congress had achieved less success. Only Alphonse Verville represented labour in the Commons. There were a few other MPs whose ear could be turned, 'but only when they deem it in their own particular political interest.' The only political alternative seemed to be the election of more labour MPs to the Commons.[72]

Draper's remedy in 1914 hardly differed from John O'Donoghue's recommendations nearly a decade before. First, he wrote, trade unions must select and put forward their own candidates. 'A number of them will be defeated, but by dint of putting men in the field, one or two, now and again, may carry the day, and this would add that one or two to our representation.' Eventually Draper thought there would be enough in the Commons to exert leverage between the two major parties. Until that day arrived, he urged trade unions to vote for Grit or Tory candidates who had proven friendly to labour's cause. Trades Congress leaders had learned from experience that it was 'more important to have a man in Parliament who will devote his attention to all the details of legislation affecting the Labor cause than it is to have one supporting the party in power for the time being.'[73]

Profound differences in the culture, industrial developments, and political behaviour of the provinces accounted for many of the obstacles confronting political action by the Trades and Labor Congress. 'In British Columbia the sentiment of the trade union movement is thoroughly socialistic. And so it is in a great measure right down to Port Arthur. Toronto has made tremendous strides in socialist sentiment too of late years. But when you reach Quebec it is a different proposition. The rank and file there can hardly be called as socialistic as British Columbia.' Recognizing the diversity of political opinions, the Congress had adopted a policy of provincial autonomy at the Victoria convention in 1906. Provincial labour groups generally took on the political colour of trade unions in their province; some socialist, some ILP, and others working within the two major parties. In nearly all federal and provincial electoral contests, however, the labour element did not appear sufficiently strong or united to elect its own candidate. Labour candidates invariably fell between Liberal and Conservative stools. 'And after having been opposed by a Labor candidate, the new member is not very prone to assume the duties of a representative of the Labor interests.'[74]

The Trades Congress political program suffered because the structure of international trade unionism in Canada left control of most of the money and machinery in the hands of international union heads who resided in the United States, and who did not wish to devote their resources to Canadian labour politics. Dozens of small craft locals could be brought together for limited objectives in a central body such as the Toronto District Labor Council. But there was no way that Council officers or Congress leaders could force international union locals in Canada to devote money and manpower to a labour party. Everything depended upon voluntary efforts, and this usually shifted the burden onto a few.

AFL leaders could not be blamed entirely for the weakness of independent labour politics in Canada. The Grits and Tories had penetrated into the ranks of labour long before the great expansion of trade unions at the turn of the century, and were not easily dislodged by the new working-class political movement. Gompers and Morrison may have had doubts in 1906 and 1907 about the wisdom of launching a provincial labour parties in Canada, but they kept their doubts to themselves, and made no visible move to prevent Flett and other Federation workers from participating in efforts along independent political lines. Perhaps the employers sensed the major reason for the failure of labour politics. 'The truth is, there is no such thing as a labor vote at all,' the Canadian Manufacturers' Association asserted. '... The labor vote which the leaders refer to is the union labor vote, and even that, if it were united, which it is not, is only a mere fraction of the total vote cast by labor.'[75]

On the other hand, the American Federation of Labor and its affiliates bore considerable responsibility for the lack of labour unity noticed by the employers. The failure of Canadian labour politics before the First World War was due partly to the fighting between supporters of independent political action and advocates of socialism. In large measure this division had been aggravated by the AFL leaders. Their conviction that socialism in trade-union ranks inevitably mushroomed into dual unionism led Gompers and Morrison to exert every effort to secure the defeat or isolation of those Canadian socialists who were attempting a reconciliation of trade unionism and socialism. The words and actions used by John Flett, Canadian organizer for the AFL, to carry out Federation campaigns against socialist resolutions, against left-wing dual unions, and especially against the 'Simpsonians' within trade-union ranks, clearly indicated that the failure of the socialists to win adherents in Canada was not explained merely by the 'Phariseeism,' as Keir Hardie had called it, of their doctrines.

12
Master and servant

At Berlin and Toronto in 1902-3, the Trades and Labor Congress had been reduced to something akin to a state federation. But it was difficult for Gompers and Morrison to keep the Congress confined to that rank; contrary to the Americans' annual declarations, the forty-ninth parallel kept getting in the way. Canadian labour leaders still aspired to lead a truly national trade-union centre some day. They toiled to preserve the last vestiges of chartering rights assumed back in the 1890s when there had been talk of creating a Canadian federation of labour, and struggled with Gompers for control over Canadian city central bodies. The Canadian constantly pressured international union leaders to divert funds to their own country. They sought a seat alongside the AFL at meetings of the secretaries of European trade unions. More importantly, they endorsed a pioneer labour relations law, the Canadian Industrial Disputes Investigation (Lemieux) Act, only to succumb to Gompers' fear of governmental involvement in labour matters. It seemed clear by 1914 that Gompers and American international union leaders never really trusted Trades Congress leaders, and would always oppose Canadian attempts to escape the confines of 'statehood.'

By the time that the Trades and Labor Congress had gathered again in convention a year after the historic Berlin meeting, some Canadians were having second thoughts about the wisdom of the amendments of 1902 to the Congress constitution. Strong sympathy for the Knights of Labor had already erupted in the Toronto District Labor Council. Two Toronto delegates, both of whom had supported the Berlin resolutions a year earlier, introduced a motion to re-admit the Knights. Delegate Henderson pointed to 'a feeling all over the country now of "Canada for the Canadians." ' Peter Sharkey, of Saint John, 'warned the

Congress that the people of Canada were strongly in favor of the free government of themselves, and that all the labour organizations in this country would
in a few years become nationalized.' Although his prediction was met with cries
of 'no, no' from different parts of the hall, the debate revealed how much
nationalist sentiment reinforced the dual unionist cause of the Knights of Labor.
Then the president of the Montreal central body, claiming to speak for fifty-
three delegates from his city, threatened to walk out of the Congress if the
Knights were seated. The motion to re-admit the Knights was ultimately
defeated by the majority who favoured international craft unionism.[1]

With the Canadian commitment to the American Federation of Labor guaranteed for another year, discontent shifted and gathered force on a related issue.
Even some convinced internationalists had winced at the election of the AFL's
paid organizer to the presidency of the Congress at Berlin. They thought that
Flett's leadership blurred the 'political' separation of the Congress from
American labour. Some of these delegates expected that Canadian locals would
sever their connection with international unions as soon as they were able
financially to stand alone. These delegates backed the candidacy of Arthur
Puttee, the Winnipeg labor MP, against Flett's campaign in 1903 for a second
term in the Congress presidential chair. The contest was so close that there were
several recounts; Flett emerged the victor by only one vote. 'Certainly the combination in order to defeat you was not very creditable,' Gompers wrote. He
thought the Congress should have taken more kindly to the idea of a leader who
could devote full-time efforts to the labour movement, even if he was in the pay
of the American Federation of Labor. As usual Gompers blended the interests of
Canadian labour with the AFL cause.[2]

In 1904 Federation leaders still feared the repeal of the Berlin amendments.
Morrison heard rumours of a plan to re-admit the Knights at the Congress
convention. 'We will certainly depend upon the International organizations to
prevent any such action,' the AFL secretary responded. Despite the scare (which
proved to be without foundation), Flett decided even before the convention to
remove himself from contention. He was succeeded by Alphonse Verville, a
Montreal plumber. The convention selected Flett to represent the Congress at
the AFL gathering in San Francisco. On the train to California later in 1904 Flett
conferred with Federation leaders about Canadian labour affairs. At the
convention he told the Americans that the 'labor movement in Canada may be
generally regarded as conservative in character.' There was a 'radical' national
element here and there, he admitted, but the bulk of locals were affiliated with
the AFL crafts.[3]

P.M. Draper still endorsed international craft unionism, but he was determined to expand the power and prestige of the Trades and Labor Congress. He

told the delegates in 1904 that their organization could not mark time; it must either advance or stagnate. He called again for the appointment of a Trades Congress organizer, and bombarded the AFL with requests for more organizing assistance. Far more than did the Federation, Congress leaders focused on the need to organize immigrants on the prairies. 'It becomes our duty,' the Canadian labour leaders explained, 'to see to it that the principles of our movement and the aims and objects of our Congress, for which we in the East have been striving and fighting, shall be transplanted to our fellow-workers in the West, thus forming a link that will tighten the bonds which bind the wage earners of the East and West together in a united and federated movement ...' Finally, in June 1905 the Congress entered into an agreement with the Leather Workers on Horse Goods to share the organizing expenses of William Berry for a few months. Berry, however, got no farther west than Sarnia, and most of the international union locals even in Ontario still remained unaffiliated with the Trades and Labor Congress.[4]

The strength of the Trades and Labor Congress, Draper well knew, depended upon the number of its dues-paying affiliates, and labour organizations chartered by the Congress were the most likely to become loyal members. Draper also wanted Canadian trades councils affiliated to the Congress for political purposes, and set out to establish one in every town. Under terms of the agreements made in Toronto in 1903, Canadian central bodies could hold charters from both the Trades and Labor Congress and the American Federation of Labor. Draper hoped to 'evolve a scheme whereby this Congress could select and finance the election of trade unionists to the Federal Parliament and Provincial Legislatures in industrial centres ... the same as is now done by the British Trades Union Congress in Great Britain.' Labour politics was very much a part of the atmosphere when Draper embarked on this plan. The British Labour party had just scored its first stunning victory at the polls, and the AFL had begun its own campaign to elect men sympathetic to labour.[5]

Draper steadily expanded the number of central bodies holding Trades Congress charters. In 1904 only twenty-seven of the forty-eight councils had taken out Congress charters; by 1908 nearly all of them had followed suit. It was vitally important to forge a legislative link across Canada, he argued, because it established the Congress 'in its rightful position as the supreme head and parent institution in the Dominion, for legislative purposes, of the legitimate international trade union movement.' Draper believed that the Congress's tie with Canadian central bodies refuted assertions of those who put the TLC in the same category with American state federations. It gave a 'crushing rebuke' to the critics of the Congress in Canada who maintained that its policies were dictated from Washington.[6]

At the same time, only a handful of these Canadian central bodies bothered to take out AFL charters. At the end of 1904 councils in Victoria, Fort William, Galt and Preston, Sarnia, Charlottetown, and Montreal paid Federation dues. Then Morrison asked Flett to enlarge the list. 'It is our desire,' he said, 'to keep the unions we now have in good standing intact by getting as many Central Bodies affiliated with the A.F. of L. as possible ...' A year later Gompers explained the concept behind Federation policy. Both the international unions and the AFL were dependent upon central bodies to carry out policies decreed by American Labour leaders. Central bodies enforced jurisdictional decisions 'of the highest court in the realm of labor' – the AFL. 'No Central Body,' Gompers said, 'should under any circumstances give representation or encouragement to any local organization which for any reason has seceded, or has been suspended from, or has demonstrated its hostility to, a bona fide international union, and especially when such an international union is affiliated with the American Federation of Labor.' In other words, Gompers looked upon central bodies as the first line of defence in the perennial war against dual unionism, and it has already been shown how important they became during the troubles with the electrical workers' and carpenters' unions. By 1908, though, only five of nearly fifty Canadian central bodies had been persuaded to affiliate with the Federation. Of these, the most important by far was the Toronto District Labor Council, which took out an AFL charter in December of 1908.[7]

When several jurisdictional disputes and secession movements began to cloud the Federation's horizon, AFL leaders decided to bring central bodies throughout North America into line. Morrison obtained a list of Congress-chartered councils and directed each of them to apply for an AFL charter. Letters were also dispatched to locals in cities without a Federation-chartered central body, urging them to set up a trades and labour council in their city under AFL ægis. Only a Federation charter, Morrison said, would enable central bodies to keep in touch with organized labour 'throughout the country.' The charter fee was $5, the seal an additional $2.50, and dues $10 per year.[8]

Vancouver printers were astonished to receive a request from Morrison to set up a central body in their city; their trades and labour council had been thriving for two decades, and for part of that period under a Trades Congress charter. Morrison assured the British Columbians that 'we are all working for the same cause, and should not let geographical boundaries isolate or divide us.' The Canadians were not being asked to shoulder an unequal financial burden, and were obligated to the Trades Congress in the same way that American central bodies supported state federations of labour. But Gompers revealed another side of the coin when he informed Vancouverites that independent locals of the engineers and bricklayers now on their council would have to be expelled for being dual unions under an AFL charter. Both the Vancouver and Winnipeg councils informed Draper of the Federation's request to charter them.[9]

Congress leaders fumed; they considered Canadian central bodies a major instrument for carrying out the Congress's policies. Draper believed that the Federation was encroaching upon the 1903 Toronto agreements. Morrison countered: '... We have the right under Clause 1 [see chapter 8, p. 102] to issue charters to Trades and Labor Councils in Canada.' The AFL still promised not to grant its charters to Canadian central bodies unless the latter also affiliated with the Trades and Labor Congress.[10]

Draper took even stronger issue with Morrison's characterization of the Trades Congress as a state federation. He may have feared that the Federation's move to establish ties with Canadian central bodies, coming at a time when provincial federations of labour were being set up in Canada, might undermine the TLC. After all, the provincial federations conformed much more closely to American state federations. Where would that leave the Congress in the American Federation of Labor's continental hierarchy? Morrison admitted to Flett that such fears might be justified in the long run. 'What may result in years to come when the population is ten times what it is now is hard to say ...' But Morrison refused to back down, repeating his views to unionists in Victoria.[11]

These issues greatly agitated labour groups in Canada during the summer of 1910. Some of the members of the Toronto District Labor Council thought that Canadian central bodies had no need for AFL charters. Congress leaders protested to their convention about being classified as a state federation. 'So long as Canada is one country and the United States another,' they declared, 'just so long will the Congress speak as the supreme mouthpiece of the workers of this country.' While they pledged unwavering loyalty to international unionism, they believed that Canadian central bodies should not be requested to take out AFL charters. The convention endorsed and reinforced their leaders' views, and authorized a request to the Federation that Morrison's efforts be discontinued. The Trades Congress, they asserted, 'is as supreme in economic and legislative matters in Canada as the American Federation of Labor in the United States, or the British Trades Union Congress in Great Britain, or similar bodies in France, Germany or elsewhere.' It remained to be seen how this assertion, clearly challenging the AFL's supremacy in Canada, would be harmonized with the Berlin and Toronto decisions of 1902-3.[12]

'It would look to me as if the Executive Council of the Dominion Trades Congress desires to violate the agreement they entered into some years ago at Toronto,' Morrison said, after Flett had sent him a clipping of the Congress deliberations. In Morrison's opinion the whole dispute was a 'tempest in a teapot.' The Federation, so far as he knew, had complied with the understandings reached in 1903. He understood that a few federal unions still held charters from the TLC but admitted that the Congress had ceased issuing new charters to such groups.[13]

As it became clearer to Draper that Federation leaders had forever relegated the Congress to a dependent status, the Canadian took an increasingly belligerent stance. The Congress had chartered nearly two score federal labour unions at the turn of the century and a few, such as a building labourers' local in Vancouver, were still paying hard coin into the Congress treasury. When Flett, during his western Canadian trip in 1910, moved to transfer this local to an AFL craft affiliate, Draper told the Vancouverites to resist. Their Congress charter 'would stand the investigation of Mr Flett or anyone else,' he wrote, adding that the Trades and Labor Congress had not yet relinquished the right to issue charters.[14]

Thus the whole chartering issue had been reopened by late 1910. Canadians asserted the parity of their national trade-union centre with the American Federation of Labor and still claimed the prerogative to charter locals, including the exclusive right to license Canadian central bodies. Morrison considered the Trades Congress to be nothing more than a state federation of labour, with no exclusive chartering powers, and no constitutional right to demand revenue from the international unions. Both sides prepared to fight it out at the AFL convention in St Louis in November 1910.

A large contingent of veteran Canadian labour leaders attended the Federation proceedings, including Draper, R.P. Pettipiece and V.L. Midgley from Vancouver, I.H. Sanderson, J.H. Kennedy, Hugh Stevenson, James Lindola, W.W. Young, and D.A. Carey from Toronto, and S.L. Landers of Hamilton. Stevenson had served on the Congress committee in 1902 which had brought about the Berlin decisions; Kennedy had represented the TLC at the AFL convention in 1902 which had confirmed them. Young was Canadian secretary of the Amalgamated Society of Carpenters, and Midgley, Pettipiece, and Lindola were well-known socialists. The battle opened when the AFL fraternal delegate to the Trades Congress convention of a few weeks before presented his report. In it he quoted Draper's charge that Morrison had equated the TLC with state federations. Thereupon Morrison suffered a lapse of memory: 'The secretary is not aware of ever having made such a statement,' he announced to the assembled delegates. He had only noted the similarity between payment by international unions of per-capita taxes to the Congress and contributions to state federations. There was no doubt in his mind that the Federation had lived up to its agreements. He was not accusing Congress leaders of putting his views in a false light, 'yet in reading the report it appears to me such is the case.' He hoped that a committee would clear up the dispute. President Mahon of the Streetcar Conductors immediately jumped up to move that a special panel be created to define the 'proper relations' between Canadian and American trade unions. The thirteen-member panel, oddly enough, included no one from the Canadian delegation. Even Robert Glockling, Toronto-born president of the Bookbinders, now resided in the United States.[15]

After both sides had presumably argued their positions, the committee submitted to the convention a four-point interpretation of the relationship between labour in the two countries:

1 That the Trades and Labor Congress of the Dominion of Canada have the sole right to speak and act for organized labor in all economic, political and legislative matters in the Dominion and all of its provinces.
2 That the autonomy of International Unions in Trade matters be maintained as heretofore.
3 That the Canadian Trades and Labor Congress shall have the sole right to issue charters (certificates of affiliation) to provincial or local central bodies in Canada.
4 That Canadian provincial or central bodies holding charters from the Canadian Trades and Labor Congress may at their discretion also hold charters from the American Federation of Labor.[16]

Since the first paragraph granted the Congress supremacy on *economic* as well as political and legislative issues in Canada, TLC leaders implicitly retained a chartering prerogative. The second paragraph implied that they could not encroach upon jurisdictional limits defined by the international crafts. The third and fourth paragraphs made it clear that Congress charters to provincial and central labour bodies took precedence over AFL charters. In all the report seemed to vindicate the position of Congress leaders and to guarantee a larger measure of autonomy for their organization. But the committee's report received a critical modification on the convention floor. On a motion by Andrew Furuseth of the Seafarers' Union, the convention struck out the word 'economic' from the first paragraph. At one stroke the Congress's implicit authority to charter unions was removed. The Congress once again remained something much closer to a state federation, weak and dependent upon the AFL and its affiliates.[17]

'So far as I see there has been no change ...' Morrison informed Flett. True, the TLC could charter provincial labour bodies, but thanks to Furuseth's timely amendment (which Morrison did not mention), the agreement forbade the Congress to charter federal labour unions or other locals. Morrison admitted that the Congress had been given priority over the AFL in chartering Canadian central bodies, but he insisted that 'conditions are just the same as they were.'[18]

If Congress leaders were disappointed at the results of the St Louis meeting, they disguised their feelings. Pettipiece thought that the arrangement would free the Congress from 'pernicious trade and jurisdictional disputes,' although the controversy between warring carpenters' unions would soon prove him wrong. Trades Congress executives spoke publicly of a 'perfect understanding' between the TLC and AFL. In 1912 they announced that the notion of their organization being something akin to a state federation had been almost completely obliterated. Within a few hours, though, the AFL fraternal delegate exposed such wishful thinking: 'This Congress is very much like our State Federations of Labor ...' he blundered.[19]

Congress leaders, whether smarting under this verbal dart or not, assiduously protected their newly recognized supremacy over Canadian central bodies during succeeding years. Draper had to remind Morrison of the St Louis decision more than once when AFL directives routinely sent to North American cities strayed across the border. Apart from this small gain, the Trades and Labor Congress remained for all intents and purposes in the category that Gompers and Morrison had placed it back in 1903. As long as Canadian trade-union leaders remained committed above all to international trade unions, the centres of real authority and decision-making on the most important questions would be found only in the United States. The Congress had preserved power only to charter provincial and city labour councils. It was obligated to enforce craft-union jurisdictions regardless of local sentiment. It could not accept dues from organizations seceded from or dual to the AFL affiliates, and it was still dependent upon the largess of the international unions for its own survival.[20]

According to Gompers' statistics, American unions were literally flooding the country with gold. His survey of the international unions' Canadian balance sheet, taken in 1903, showed that American unions expended nearly $317,000 in benefit payments to Canadians, but collected only about $87,000 in dues. Another $12,000 was spent by American unions for organizing purposes in Canada. Although Gompers' figures were based on returns from less than one-half of the international unions with locals in Canada, he still concluded that 'it speaks for itself, of the vast benefit that unity in the labor movement has been to the wage-workers' of Canada.[21] From Draper's point of view, little benefit had accrued to the Trades and Labor Congress. Only 238 locals of some 1500 in the country paid dues to the Congress in 1903. Its receipts had risen from $828.45 in 1900 to $3858.34 in 1903, but its income was insufficient to maintain full-time organizers or officers. Its growth depended upon bringing about the affiliation of all those international union locals in Canada which had so far avoided Draper's proddings.[22]

At the Trades Congress convention in 1903, the secretary submitted a three-point program designed to lift the organization to new heights. He called for an organizer to be placed at work under Canadian labour leaders, and asked the Congress to cover part of the costs incurred by the provincial committees of the Congress. The key proposal involved requesting international unions to affiliate their Canadian membership directly from their headquarters. If carried into effect, this plan promised to end the almost hopeless task of annually persuading hundreds of widely scattered groups to pay Congress dues. It would establish a kind of 'check-off' system whereby international union headquarters automatically deducted Trades Congress dues from payments by its Canadian members and forwarded a lump sum to Trades Congress offices. The advantage of this scheme to the Congress was immediately apparent, but it depended entirely upon the international union heads who were the real guardians of wealth and power within the American labour movement.[23]

At the AFL convention in Boston in late 1903, Draper directed a team of six Canadians who campaigned for the Congress proposal. Draper himself appeared before the resolutions committee and won that panel's blessing. After an eloquent appeal on the floor by D.A. Carey of Toronto, the resolution passed with only one delegate speaking against it.[24]

A year later Draper lauded the International Brotherhood of Maintenance-of-Way Employees for becoming the first to affiliate all its Canadian members through payment of per-capita tax directly to the Congress. 'If the same energy were shown by other International officers,' Draper noted, 'one half the burden of office would be removed and who can prophecy [sic] what results would accrue in a legislative sense[?]'[25] The 'energy' was not forthcoming. Although Gompers, at Trades Congress request, sent out circulars urging Canadian locals to affiliate with the Congress, the efforts bore little fruit. Draper tried a little arm-twisting, but to no avail.[26] By 1905 only the Journeymen Tailors, the Coopers, and the Paving Cutters had acceded to his request and their Canadian membership was only a fraction of the total strength of international unionism in Canada. Without more affiliates, the Congress's coffers remained low, and in 1905 Draper was forced to ask for a $300 advance from the American Federation. Though the Canadian promised to refund the loan when Congress per-capita taxes were paid, the AFL Executive Council turned him down.[27]

Draper attempted to obtain the AFL Executive Council's endorsement of his scheme. The Council refused, merely telling Gompers to 'inform' the international unions of Draper's proposal and of the resolution passed by the AFL convention in 1903. In a letter to several international union officials, Gompers asked labour leaders to give Draper's plan their 'earnest and careful consideration.' But Morrison noted that Draper's request was the equivalent of the 'state of Illinois making an application to the officers of the International unions to pay the per-capita tax required by the State Federation to entitle their local unions to be represented in the state convention.' A good many craft-union leaders, it appeared, were fearful that acquiescence to the Canadian scheme would open the floodgates to demands from state federations of labour across the United States for similar consideration. A shift of power from the international unions to the state federations would have had profound political and economic ramifications within the North American labour movement. International union leaders, of course, were dead set against such an outcome.[28]

In 1905 Trades Congress leaders added a refinement to their campaign to lure international union officers into active support of the Congress. They changed the constitution to permit international unions who affiliated their Canadian locals to send extra representatives to the Congress. This bait provoked no great pounding upon the Congress's door, and a year later Draper decided to ask the AFL to double its legislative grant to $1000. In justification he pointed to the expenses involved in holding the convention in distant British Columbia. The Executive Council did not feel that it could appropriate the money, and Draper was forced to return to his first tactic – badgering the international union heads.[29] He asked Morrison to help him present the Canadian case to the Mine Workers and Machinists. Both the leaders of those unions had been present when the Executive Council had dismissed Draper's proposal, 'but I will write to them, in accordance with your request.' Despite all Draper's hard work, only six international unions had complied by September of 1906. 'While the efforts of the Congress enure to all,' he complained, 'it is hardly fair that a few should be left to bear the expense attaching to the maintenance of the Congress.'[30]

Draper kept up his drumfire on the international union heads, and several of them finally decided to write to Morrison for information and advice. For one thing, they wondered whether they had to continue paying per-capita dues to the AFL on their Canadian membership if and when they agreed to pay a per-capita tax to the Trades Congress on their Canadian membership. The United Brotherhood of Carpenters, for example, decided to pay on their membership in Canada to the Trades and Labor Congress, and to pay to the American Federation of Labor on their membership in the United States. Morrison pointed to an AFL constitutional provision which required international unions to pay the Federation a sum based upon *all* their members. 'I am fully aware of the provisions of the Constitution,' Carpenters' secretary Frank Duffy retorted, 'but when that law was made it was never thought that the Canadian Trades and Labor Congress would demand that the ... International Labor organizations of this country should pay direct to that body tax on their Canadian membership.'[31] In letters to other International union leaders, Morrison emphasized his opinion that AFL per-capita dues were required on the Canadian membership. 'In Canada they have Local Unions, City Central Bodies, the Trades and Labor Congress, and the AFL,' he declared. 'In the United States they have Local Union, City Central Bodies, State Bodies and the American Federation of Labor.' The Federation stood at the apex of both labour movements; the implication, of course, was that the Trades and Labor Congress was no more than a state federation of labour.[32]

At the AFL convention in late 1907, the Carpenters' Union introduced a motion asking to be exempted from AFL dues on its Canadian members. They did not object to paying per-capita tax on their Canadian members to the Canadian Trades Congress, but they opposed 'double taxation.' On the floor of the convention the issue was discussed by several Canadians present, including D.A. Carey, S.L. Landers, and James Simpson. The convention concluded that the Carpenters were not to be excused from paying per-capita dues to the AFL on their Canadian members. Meanwhile, Draper's persistence had finally begun to bear fruit when eleven international unions agreed to pay $1639 in dues directly to the Trades Congress in 1907. The income was still insufficient to permit Draper to devote full-time efforts to his tasks, and Congress leaders continued to point to the pressing need throughout the whole country for organizers appointed and directed by the Congress executive committee. Although they were able to underwrite piecemeal efforts by W.R. Trotter in Western Canada, by Allan Studholme in Ontario, and by Alphonse Verville in Quebec and the Maritimes, they were not satisfied. On a motion by R. Parm Pettipiece, the TLC convention of 1907 instructed its leaders to urge an arrangement with the AFL 'whereby the moneys devoted by that body for organization and legislative purposes in Canada shall be paid over to the Executive Committee of this Congress and expended under their supervision.' It was unanimously carried. The measure, in effect, proposed to transfer Flett's job to Congress control. Such a move promised to enhance significantly the Trades Congress's power and authority throughout the country.[33]

Flett had no desire to see the Congress's wishes carried out. He warned Morrison and Gompers that James Simpson was being sent to the Norfolk convention of the AFL to press for Flett's transfer to TLC control. He told both men that he wished to be on hand in Norfolk if the AFL Executive Council planned 'to entertain so impudent a proposition.'[34] Morrison did not think there was any particular danger of the Congress gaining jurisdiction over Flett. He told the Canadian that he could not imagine the Executive Council receiving Simpson, a man known for his socialist views, with any special favour. But events confirmed Flett's warning about Simpson's intentions, and on 14 November Morrison ordered Flett to come to Norfolk 'at once.'[35]

In a highly revealing report published at the Trades Congress convention months afterward, Simpson described his efforts at Norfolk. The document told a great deal about the attitudes of the international unions toward the Trades and Labour Congress.

I decided to go to Norfolk by way of Washington, with a view to meeting the Delegates as they assembled at A.F. of L. headquarters in Washington ... In taking this route I was enabled to do considerable work among representatives of International Unions. I found that the real work of the Congress was not clearly understood, and I was afforded a splendid opportunity to dissipate many erroneous impressions that were entertained with reference to its status as the legislative mouthpiece of the wage workers of Canada. Without reciting individual cases ... I wish to refer to an impression that the Congress should be classified with the State Federations of Labor in the United States, and for that reason should receive no special recognition from International Organizations that are now paying per capita tax to the American Federation of Labor for legislative purposes. It was only necessary, however, to point to the special field of opportunity open to the Congress because of geographical boundaries that are entirely closed to the A.F. of L. in their efforts to secure legislation for the benefit of those in affiliation with the International Trades Union Movement. It was also pointed out that while the American Federation of Labor only asked half-a-cent per member per month as per capita tax from the International organizations the Congress asked a cent and a-half per member per month. This objection had to be met by fully explaining the limited population of Canada and the limited number of trades unionists from which to draw support for the Congress. I assured the International officers, however, that the Congress could seriously consider the advisability of reducing the per capita tax if the movement to secure the affiliation of trades unionists in Canada from International headquarters was successful. In one specific case I was met with the objection that the Congress was fostering a national sentiment in the trade union movement in opposition to the International sentiment. I endeavored to trace the source of the information ... but was unsuccessful ... These objections and others of minor importance had to be met before the way could be opened to bring some of the International officers into full sympathy with the work of the Congress ...

Simpson concluded his report with a brief account of his conversations with leaders of twenty-seven different international unions. A few promised to affiliate their Canadians; some expressed sympathy for the Congress but made no promises; others agreed to bring the matter up at their unions' next convention. Many were openly sceptical. For example, President Tobin of the Boot and Shoe Workers 'classified the Congress as similar to a State Federation, and therefore he did not think it advisable that the International Executive Committee should take any action. He thought the Canadian Locals could deal with the proposition as separate organizations.'[36]

Gompers and Morrison told Simpson that the Executive Council would be 'too busy' until after the convention to entertain the proposal about organizing work. When he finally appeared before the Council, Simpson, according to his own account, made no mention of transferring Flett to Trades Congress command, but asked only that the AFL 'either place an additional organizer in the field or re-organize the districts of organizers who were engaged near the frontier, so that they could make more frequent visits to Canadian Territory.' Not too suprisingly, the forewarned Council members were unmoved by Simpson's plea, and argued that Canada had been thoroughly covered by international union organizers. No decision was made, however, and Gompers assured Simpson that the Congress's request would receive careful attention. Two months later, when Trades Congress leaders had received no further word from the Federation, Simpson asked Gompers for an answer. 'We have not as yet been able to make any arrangement for an additional organizer,' the Federation leader responded, and he referred as in the past to a shortage of funds. 'I am sure you appreciate the fact that the demand made upon the Federation for special organization work is far beyond our financial ability to meet,' Gompers added. 'We simply endeavor to do our best with the limited means at our command and to place the Federation organizers where they will accomplish the greatest good for the greatest number.'[37]

Once again Congress leaders had failed to enlarge the power and influence of their organization. Once again their plans had been held in check by the AFL and its international union affiliates. One reason why the Federation had acted as it did was revealed on the floor of the Trades Congress convention immediately after Simpson had delivered his report. Draper charged that many American labour leaders had had their minds 'poisoned' against Congress leaders; they believed Draper to be a nationalist and Simpson to be a socialist. Simpson took the floor and blamed delegate William V. Todd, a Toronto cigarmaker and friend of Gompers, for the 'poisoning.' Todd demanded proof, and Simpson pointed to Fred Bancroft, another Toronto socialist, as his authority. After several delegates had joined in, Todd rose to defend himself. He maintained that the Congress fraternal delegate to Norfolk, W.R. Trotter, could have done all that Simpson had been sent to do at the AFL meeting. He had meant to criticize the cost of sending Simpson to Norfolk. 'If Mr. Bancroft or anyone else accused him of caballing in secret against anybody, he had told an untruth.'[38] The discussion ended at this; nevertheless, it had shown that the Congress leaders felt they were not fully trusted by AFL and international union leaders in the United States. Gompers had apparently told Simpson to his face at Norfolk that it was impossible to be a loyal trades unionist and a socialist at one and the same time.[39] Draper's politics were known to be 'safe,'[40] but his driving energy and well-known desire to build up the Trades Congress into a powerful national trade-union centre led American unionists to eye the Canadian with suspicion. The Americans had no desire to watch the Canadian equivalent of a state federation grow into a rival centre of power within the North American labour movement.

By 1908 relations between the Trades Congress and the AFL seemed to have come full circle. The Canadians had failed to increase significantly the financial resources obtained from the AFL and the international unions. Once more, as they had begun to do some nine years before, Canadian unionists reiterated the complaint about payment of dues to the American Federation of Labor without any return, they alleged, of equivalent benefits. Early in 1908 the Victoria Trades and Labor Council notified Morrison of its decision to withdraw from the American Federation for just this reason. Morrison denounced their assertions. About 45,000 Canadians, he estimated, had paid $2700 in dues to the AFL in 1907. The Federation had granted not only the customary $500 for legislative work in the country, but it had paid Flett's expenses, amounting to $1950. '... You will see therefore,' Morrison told the British Columbians, 'that the $2450 went directly back for work in [the Congress's] special interests, and this sum does not take into account the small amounts paid the district [that is, volunteer] organizers throughout the Dominion. This allows nothing for the pro rata expense which should be borne by Canadian members for conducting work at Headquarters of the A.F. of L.' Hence, the Federation secretary concluded, the AFL had not only aided the Trades and Labor Congress, but was giving 'a fair share of attention to the general interest of the movement of Canada.'[41]

Morrison's calculations conflict with other evidence available. In 1907 the *Toronto Globe* cited a Congress report which counted 765 AFL-affiliated locals in Canada, with 51,779 members.[42] These men must have paid $3106.74 in dues to the Federation; adding $40 in fees from central bodies holding AFL charters, the Federation's Canadian income totals $3146.74. Subtracting the $500 legislative grant and $2150 paid out in organizing expenses (from which Flett's New York work costs have been subtracted), the AFL still collected $496.74 *more* from Canadians in 1907 than was spent by the Federation in Canada. The Canadians appear to have been paying rather large overhead for the paperwork performed by the AFL in Washington.

After the Federation refused once more to appropriate more money for organizing work in Canada, Trades Congress leaders renewed their efforts to secure the cooperation of individual international union leaders. Morrison doubted whether the Canadians would make much headway. '... It is just possible that [direct affiliation] can be brought about without trouble,' he conceded to Flett, 'but I am fearful that some of the internationals, when they have a very large membership, will object. Not now perhaps, but when the different State Federations come in to make the same request; then, comes the hour of discontent, and it is possible it might result in a reaction all along the line.'[43]

Despite the Federation secretary's dire prediction, Draper's efforts finally began to succeed. His report to the Trades Congress convention in 1908 listed twenty-two international unions who paid $3578.45 directly to the Congress in per-capita dues on their Canadian membership. Draper was still rankled that several American labour leaders compared the Trades and Labor Congress with state federations. He construed a quotation from a Gompers speech to demonstrate the inaccuracy of such comparisons, at least to his own satisfaction. 'The Trades and Labor Congress of Canada,' he stated, 'is co-equal with the British Trades Union Congress and the American Federation of Labor. It is to the Canadian organized wage-earners what the British Trades Union Congress and the American Federation of Labor is to the organized workers of the British Isles and the United States, a sovereign and supreme body within the confines of its own territory, the Dominion of Canada, for legislative purposes.' Yet Draper and the AFL leaders had different conceptions of the breadth of the Congress's 'legislative purposes.' Many Canadians thought that the phrase encompassed organizing work, some chartering rights, and independent labour or socialist politics. For the Americans, the meaning was confined largely to the button-holing of public officials in legislative corridors. Above all the AFL leaders were determined to protect their vested interests.[44]

By 1909 there was enough unrest within the Canadian labour movement to concern AFL leaders. They decided to publicize their cause and overwhelm their critics by holding an AFL convention on Canadian soil. Gompers journeyed to Toronto in May 1909 to assist in the preparations. He acknowledged the presence of 'some little dissention within the ranks' of Canadian unions. It was merely the product of differences of opinion among 'sane, full-blooded men,' he averred.[45] Later in the year a distinguished group of Canadian labour leaders attended the Federation deliberations at Toronto. From that city came D.A. Carey of the Musicians, Hugh Stevenson of the Typos, N. Quesnel of the Boiler-makers, William Noyes of the Maintenance-of-Way Employees, and John Bruce representing the Toronto Trades and Labor Council. Hamilton locals sent Sam Landers of the Garment Workers, Hugh Robinson of the Tailors, and C.I. Aitcheson from the Trades Council. Joseph Gervais, Stonecutters, James Somerville, Machinists' Helpers, and G.R. Brunet of the Trades Council presented credentials from Montreal locals. The Amalgamated Society of Carpenters dispatched James

Reid from Vancouver, and Paddy Draper arrived from Ottawa on behalf of the Trades Council in the Canadian capital. Fred Bancroft of Toronto was present, having been selected earlier by the Trades Congress as Canadian fraternal delegate to the AFL.

A parade from the Prince George Hotel to Massey Hall inaugurated the festivities. Two delegates carrying the Union Jack and the Stars and Stripes led mounted police and a massed band of 120 musicians, followed by the convention delegates, through the streets of Toronto. As the crowd filed into Massey Hall to the strains of 'The Maple Leaf,' they passed under an arch formed by the two flags. The stage was decorated by a group of national flags in the shape of a crown, resting upon a base formed by large Canadian and American flags. Apparently, internationalism was supposed to reign triumphant at this Federation gathering.[46]

In his welcoming address to the assemblage, president William Glockling of the Trades and Labor Congress of Canada ignored the flags and stuck closely to the issues dividing the Canadian and American national labour centres. He cited the 'misconceptions' held by many international union officers concerning the Congress's purpose. He stressed its need for money: 'All we ask you to pay on is the membership in the Dominion of Canada.' The Congress, of course, had no power to command payment from individual locals who were 'not as keen as they ought to be' when asked to contribute voluntarily. The Congress was a constituent part of the continental labour movement. 'You want, as well as we do, to make this a big movement in Canada. We are part of you, and for that reason we think you ought to give us all the assistance you possibly can.' Though he denied it, Glockling was literally begging for money to enlarge the Congress's functions.[47]

In contrast to Glockling's plea, Gompers' speech echoed the convention decorations. In lofty phrases he asserted that international trade unions did not contradict legitimate expressions of Canadian patriotism. 'I would not if I could, our movement would not if it could, and it could not if it would, take away the loyalty of Canada's workers to Canada.' He spoke of the destiny of the English-speaking people to fight 'for civilization and right.' Then, moving without pause from these sentiments to more mundane considerations, Gompers asserted his belief that there were more Canadians than Americans in leadership positions among international unions. Trade-union officers had made innumerable visits to Canada; it was only the customs posts on the border that reminded them of which country they were in. There was no imbalance between international union dues collections and their expenditures in Canada. The Canadian-American boundary ('the imaginary line that designates in the mind or on the map that this side is Canada and the other is the United States') did not disrupt the unity of American workers — 'and I use the term American in its broadest sense, including every man, woman, and child on the North American continent.'[48]

Some of the Canadian delegates decided apparently to flatter their way into the AFL treasury. Hugh Robinson sponsored a resolution praising the contributions already made by the AFL and international unions to the Canadian labour movement. His motion commended the AFL Executive Council in particular and recommended only that 'as far as possible, the good work begun be continued.' The measure was routinely adopted, but there was little indication in the following months that it had succeeded. A year later Draper reported that only seven more international unions (making thirty in all) had affiliated their Canadian locals to the Congress and paid dues directly from union headquarters in the United States.[49]

While the AFL convention may have been a propaganda success, it had not given the Trades and Labor Congress any financial security. The depression of 1909-10 brought about a dip in Canadian membership and income. In 1910 Draper persuaded the Federation to conduct another survey of international union membership in Canada. According to Gompers, the returns showed the presence of 923 locals in the country with 68,309 members, who claimed to have paid almost $366,000 into unions and obtained over $645,000 in benefits. Gompers concluded that the Canadians were receiving enough money; his proof was contained in his observation of 1911 that 'the last year has witnessed the practical disappearance of any manifestations of dissatisfaction or endeavors to undermine the international movement' in Canada. In other words, dual unions, secessionists, and hostile politicians had been kept at bay. A year later the Federation Executive Council rejected a request from Draper for $200 to assist in organizing workers in the Ottawa area.[50]

In a move to entice more affiliates, Congress leaders in 1911 offered to award one delegate will full voice and vote at TLC conventions to each international union paying Congress dues from headquarters in the United States. The United Brotherhood of Carpenters, pointing to its large membership in Canada, asked unsuccessfully to send five representatives. The next year the Telegraphers dispatched two delegates to the Congress. James Simpson led the opposition, noting that 'strong and wealthy international organizations could unduly influence a deliberation of the Congress by sending more than a reasonable number of delegates to represent them.' Again, only one delegate was seated.[51] By 1914 the Congress seemed to have lured about 80 per cent of the international unions with a significant Canadian component into its ranks. Its income jumped from $7900 in 1909 to over $23,700 in 1914, and its membership shot up from 36,000 to 80,000 during the same period. The Congress had come a long way since 1899 (just before Draper had taken over the reins) when there was only $63.76 in the treasury. The ambitious young secretary-treasurer was proud of the Trades and Labor Congress, and thought that it merited international recognition. Gompers thought otherwise.[52]

The issue surfaced after Gompers attended a meeting of the secretaries of various European trade unions (called the International Secretariat) during a visit to Paris in 1909. He obtained permission to speak on behalf of a proposed international federation of labour 'for the protection and advancement of all the rights, interests, and justice of the wage workers of all countries.' The AFL leader recalled his own scheme of many years before to bring about international cooperation through an exchange of fraternal delegates. Then as now there were two divergent tendencies in the labour movement – 'toward Parliamentary Socialism and toward independent trade-unionism' – and Gompers still dreaded the left-wing political slant common to trade unionism on the Continent. He carefully noted that he had not been authorized to attend the secretaries' meetings as an official delegate from the AFL. The Europeans listened politely to Gompers' scheme.[53]

His proposed international federation of trade unions was still under consideration when the secretaries laid plans to meet once again in the summer of 1911. The AFL leader picked a trusted colleague, James Duncan of the Granite Cutters, to represent North American workers. Shortly thereafter Carl Legien, the German trade unionist in charge of arrangements, routinely invited the Trades and Labor Congress to send a delegate. Congress leaders promptly chose one of their vice-presidents, Gustave Francq of Montreal, to represent Canadian workers.[54]

Gompers adamantly opposed the invitation to the Canadians. He told Draper that each national trade-union centre was entitled to only one delegate. 'The Trades and Labor Congress being part of the American Federation of Labor[,] for it to be represented by a delegate at Budapest would be equivalent to the American Federation of Labor being represented by two delegates.' Francq was welcome to attend, but only in an unofficial capacity as far as Gompers was concerned. The Federation leader was more candid about his reasons with Legien. Francq was not an intimate of AFL leaders; he might very well differ with Duncan on various issues coming before the secretaries. Then 'we would have the duly accredited delegate's vote neutralized by a possible opposing vote of our Canadian brother, and thus possibly nullify the vote and influences from the American trade unions upon important subjects of laws, policy, or principle.' Furthermore, the Industrial Workers of the World planned to seek recognition as a representative of the American labour movement. If the Canadians were also seated, it would weaken Duncan's ability to protest the recognition 'of any other delegate to represent the American labor movement.' As a result, the Secretariat ruled that the Trades and Labor Congress was not entitled to a seat at the Budapest meeting.[55]

Canadian labour leaders did not give up. In 1912 Legien visited North America on a speaking tour which included a stopover at Toronto. Draper talked with him and later told the Congress convention that 'Canada should have a representative at this important gathering.' They should send a Canadian, either as part of a two-man AFL delegation or separately. The delegates told Draper to make an arrangement suitable to the AFL, and the same issue was brought up at the Federation convention in late 1913.[56]

Not surprisingly, a Federation committee opposed Canadian membership, using the old argument that Canadian trade unions were part of a larger movement. Besides, they were 'just as eligible' as Americans to fill the AFL delegate post. The Federation paid a per-capita tax to the Secretariat based upon its membership in both countries; separate Trades Congress seating would duplicate both representation and taxation. The whole idea was 'impracticable and unwise,' they concluded, and the delegates on the floor sustained their view. Legien told Draper that the AFL decision settled the issue at least until the next congress of the Secretariat, scheduled for San Francisco in 1915.[57]

Given the adamant opposition of Gompers, there was little that Draper could do. Gus Francq, who had been present at the AFL convention in 1913, disagreed with the Federation stance. The Secretariat was an international body of working men gathered together to discuss legislative matters in particular. Since Canada was 'entirely distinct and separate from the United States' juridically, the Congress ought to be seated. But Francq and the other Congress leaders could only regret that the AFL 'opposed our right to be represented,' and promise to continue their efforts to rectify the situation. The advent of the First World War forced cancellation of the next meeting of the Secretariat, and led to its demise. But Draper had learned a lesson. After the war he accompanied Borden to the Paris Conference and played a part in the formation of the International Labor Organization, a group which recognized and granted separate Canadian membership.[58]

Draper learned another lesson from Gompers when the American's fight against compulsion in industrial relations reached into Canada. Many Canadian unionists, unlike Gompers, thought government fully capable of acting impartially, or even in the interests of labour. They were attracted to Australian and New Zealand precedents enacted by their sisters within the Empire. Moreover, a good many Canadians equated their survival as a nation with the smooth flow of grain-laden boxcars to eastern ports. Wheat exports underwrote the Canadian economy, they reasoned, and a prolonged railway strike might grow into a national calamity. Their desire to devise ways to bring governmental power to bear upon industrial strikes brought them into conflict with the AFL's traditional aversion to any form of intervention by the state. Despite the Berlin amendments, Congress leaders followed a course at some variance from that of the American Federation of Labor after 1907. Yet North American labour unity, to Gompers' way of thinking, required a uniform stand by all labour groups against the principle of compulsion, and the Congress finally agreed to this in 1916.

A bill introduced into the House of Commons by Sir William Mulock in 1902 first aroused Gompers' fears that compulsory arbitration might flourish in Canada. After the Trades and Labor Congress (at the Berlin convention) had adopted a new constitutional provision endorsing voluntary arbitration, which had delighted Gompers, the Commons greatly modified Mulock's bill and retained coercion only in regard to the investigation and publication (in the *Labour Gazette*) of government findings. The reports were not binding upon the parties to the dispute.[59]

A strike of coal miners in Alberta in 1906 brought renewed public demand, especially after the onset of winter, for government intervention into industrial disputes in Canada. The premier of Saskatchewan reported that 54 localities in his province counted only a thousand tons of coal on hand, but would need a hundred thousand tons for the coming winter. Laurier dispatched the deputy minister of labour, W.L. Mackenzie King, to effect a settlement. King shared with many American progressive reformers an explicit faith in the ability of 'experts' like himself to draw up impartial agreements. He believed that mere exposure of the 'facts' to the public would guarantee enforcement of an investigating board's findings. King's mediation, which included a visit to United Mine Workers' Union headquarters in the United States, ended the strike. Upon his return to Ottawa, he called for the referral of future disputes to an impartial board and urged that strikes or lockouts be restrained until the experts had published their findings. On 6 December 1907, the subject was discussed in the Commons; a week later, the minister of labour, Mr Lemieux, gave notice of a bill embodying King's recommendations.[60]

Gompers and Morrison carried too many scars from past wars to retain faith in either an impartial panel or in the efficacy of public opinion. When Flett told Morrison about the government bill, the Federation secretary asked to be kept informed. 'We do not want anything that savors of compulsory arbitration, whether in coal fields or transportation, or in any other industry,' he added. Later Morrison told the AFL Canadian organizer that he hoped 'you will be able to prevent passage of this Bill.'[61]

Reaction to the government's proposal seemed much less hostile within the ranks of Canadian trade unions. At a meeting of the Toronto District Labor Council in February of 1907, for example, only three votes were cast against a motion in favour of the bill. On the floor of the Commons, Alphonse Verville, president of the TLC and labour MP from Montreal, joined with the Grits in endorsing the bill and opposing a Conservative manoeuvre to postpone action until a special investigation could take place. '... What I want is legislation,' Verville told the House. 'Give me bad legislation if you will, but give me legislation, for I would rather have bad legislation than no legislation at all; bad legislation we can amend, but if we have no legislation we cannot improve it. I prefer legislation to inquiry by committee.' Verville not only revealed his dependence as a labour MP upon the government's initiative, but he also spelled out an attitude in direct opposition to Gompers' view. In March 1907 the Lemieux bill passed both the Commons and Senate and became law.[62]

Six months later Canadian trade-union leaders heartily endorsed the act. Unions did not want to strike, they declared, and the act assured labour a fair hearing before the public, but still gave them the right to strike if they so desired. At the Congress convention in Winnipeg, Premier Roblin expressed faith in the feasibility of replacing strikes with boards of arbitration, and his words were greeted with loud applause. The solicitor for the Congress considered the Lemieux act a step on the road to a fair deal for labour without the need for strikes. Nevertheless, the motion providing for Congress endorsement of the act provoked a three-hour 'battle royal' on the convention floor. Robert Hungerford of the Toronto District Labor Council 'seemed to insinuate' that political reasons had induced Congress leaders to support the government bill. He charged that they had not given due consideration to the interests and wishes of labour. Railway men added their voice to the criticism and alleged that the act had been aimed especially at the railway trades. Despite these objections an amendment calling for exclusion of railways from the act was rejected, and the main motion endorsing the government statute was adopted by an eighty-one to nineteen vote.[63]

Flett sent newspaper clippings and a copy of the Lemieux act to Gompers. He told the American of the diversity of opinion in the ranks of Canadian labour, and offered to go into the details of the law more fully. A few months later Flett told Morrison of a rumour that a representative of the United States government had been sent to Ottawa to consult on the workings of the act. Morrison, completely unaware of this latest news, anxiously sought Flett's opinion on the workings of the Canadian law. Flett sent newspaper columns to his superiors in Washington, but delayed outlining his own views until he had arranged to serve on a conciliation board formed under the act to investigate a dispute involving Kingston seamen and their employers. Morrison told Flett that the Federation would pay his expenses if the government did not cover them. 'I hope your experience with the "Industrial Disputes Investigation Act" will be so favorable that you can recommend it. If it does not[,] do not hesitate to say so.'[64]

The next month Flett dispatched his evaluation of the act to Washington. His comments were moderate in tone but included some detailed criticism. Labour had to be well organized in order for the law to work in its behalf. Employers could take advantage of the law's delay features to employ strike-breakers. Unions were forced to declare war on employers before the law could be invoked, and the law could be made to punish the labourer. A little later, when Morrison learned that a Michigan congressman had introduced a bill patterned after the Lemieux act in the House of Representatives, he sent copies of Flett's report to members of the AFL legislative committee at the Capitol. He also sent the Canadian's observations to the Federation Executive Council for their information and consideration. Thus the battle over the Lemieux act grew to continental proportions.[65]

At first a variety of interested parties in North America took different stands on the much-publicized Canadian law. A committee of the Canadian Manufacturers' Association, after discussing the principles involved in the bill, cautiously recommended that their members refrain from going on record in respect to the measure. No doubt they wished to see how their interests fared before committing themselves to its defence. Both Canadian trade-union and general public sentiment, however, appeared fairly sympathetic to the act's purposes, if not to some of its details. While the Grand Council of the Provincial Workmen's Association decided to call for outright repeal of the act, leaders of the Canadian Federation of Labor asked that the law be made applicable to *all* industrial disputes. Adam Shortt, the noted professor of economics at Queen's University in Kingston, became a strong supporter following service on several conciliation boards set up under the act's auspices. After Wallace K. Nesbitt, KC, had represented several employers on the act's boards, the well-known Ontario barrister concluded that there were 'two sides to a story, and the people are interested in knowing, when a quarrel springs up, as to what the other side has to say. The Act accomplishes this by bringing the parties together and an adjustment then becomes easy. Popular opinion will do the rest.' In a speech at the National Civic Federation in New York, Sam Landers, the Hamilton, Ontario, labour leader, called the Lemieux act 'the best measure yet enacted in the interests of capital and labour.' At the same gathering President Charles W. Eliot of Harvard University spoke for many who hoped to see permanent peace brought to the industrial battlefields of North America. He expressed his faith in the new Canadian law, labeling it 'the best piece of industrial and social legislation produced in the last two decades.' In subsequent years he became one of the most prominent of the law's American proponents.[66]

The degree of public favour won by the new law tempered suspicions of parliamentary intentions in the minds of many Canadian trade unionists. W.R. Trotter, the fraternal delegate of the Trades Congress to the AFL convention, told the Americans that organized labour had nothing to lose from an investigation. However, he added that some of the clauses of the Lemieux act revealed the cloven hoof of the Canadian Manufacturers' Association, and the Trades and Labor Congress hoped to remedy this at the coming parliamentary session. At the Congress convention in 1908 differences of opinion over the act provoked several hours of debate. The Congress leadership clearly favoured the law and headed off a motion (sponsored by Canadian locals of the United Mine Workers' Union) calling for its repeal. Draper, Simpson, and Verville asked instead that trade unions submit revisions to the act. This proposal was backed by a majority of the delegates.[67]

A year later the Congress executive committee complained that only one Canadian trade-union official had bothered to submit any proposals designed to modify that act. Although the United Mine Workers' locals had been loudest in their condemnation, they had failed to suggest revisions to the act and had allowed their affiliation to the Congress to lapse. Then the Congress's solicitor drafted some proposals and presented them to the House of Commons, but the Congress-backed amendments never left the Order Paper. Finally in 1910 the government moved to satisfy a few of the Congress demands, enacting some minor changes urged by the railway unions. Congress leaders concluded that the adoption of the principle of compulsory investigation had been a step forward, but it was still too early to pass final judgment upon the act. 'It would be madness to make the final jump to compulsory arbitration before compulsory investigation has been thoroughly tested,' they said. If labour sounded hesitant, it was because of their fear of arbitrary officialdom. And these fears were to come to life not on Parliament Hill, but in the courtroom of a Nova Scotia judge.[68]

The campaign of the United Mine Workers against their bitter rival, the PWA, had escalated industrial conflict in that province. Late in 1909 a court convicted David Neilson, a Mine Workers official, of aiding an employee of a coal company 'to continue on strike by gratuitously providing him with means to procure groceries and other goods contrary to the provisions of the Industrial Disputes Investigation Act.'[69] This was all that Gompers needed to vent his deep suspicion of the act. 'That decision plainly determines that giving food to a hungry striker is an offense under the Act,' he wrote. 'It means that if men go on strike contrary to the provisions of the Act that an ordinary benefit concert could not be held to provide funds ... If a hungry striker asked you for a quarter to buy a breakfast and you gave it to him you could be punished under the Act ... Nothing more startling has occurred in Canada anytime in so far as the effects upon Trade Unionists are concerned ...'[70] The Neilson decision turned many Trades Congress delegates against the act. At the Calgary convention in 1911 a special committee recommended that the Congress press for its repeal. Draper and other Canadian labour leaders opposed going so far, and through their efforts the panel's recommendation was rejected by a narrow seventy to sixty-five vote. A substitute motion approved by Congress leaders reaffirmed Canadian labour's belief in the principles of investigation and conciliation, but said that in view of rulings by the Department of Labour, and in consequence of judicial decisions, the Congress would ask for repeal of the act if amendments to it were not forthcoming. This motion was carried unanimously. The Congress thereby endorsed the compulsory investigation idea in principle but denounced some current applications of the Industrial Disputes Investigation Act of 1907.[71]

While Gompers collected additional information on the workings of the Canadian law, Flett publicly voiced the Federation's hostility to it. At a meeting of the Allied Trades and Labor Association in Ottawa in 1912, he lambasted the Department of Labour's administration of the act. 'The department of agriculture helps the farmer, and the department of trade and commerce, the merchant; but the department of labor seems to have considered it its duty to act as the restraining influence upon the labor organization in this country. Under the Lemieux Act we find that we are the sufferers to the last extent, for it makes criminal the humane acts of men to feed and clothe strikers.' Despite Flett's criticism, the Trades Congress reaffirmed its stand at conventions in 1912 and 1913, partly as a result of continuing efforts by Draper to prevent passage of a motion for outright repeal of the law. Meanwhile Draper kept Federation leaders fully informed of developments in relation to the law. 'We get constant inquiries concerning the workings of the Act in Canada,' Morrison told him, 'and the attitude of organizations of labor toward it.'[72]

By early 1913 publicity surrounding the Lemieux act had stirred up considerable interest in such legislation in the United States. On the international scene, the campaign to substitute arbitration for warfare had approached a climax with the election of Woodrow Wilson and the elevation of William Jennings Bryan to secretary of state. It was an easy matter for large segments of American opinion to equate Bryan's 'cooling off' treaties abroad with the need for similar legislation to end industrial strife at home. The American Academy of Political and Social Science took up the cause in a spate of articles. In one of them an official of the National Civic Federation issued the call for an American law patterned after the Canadian act. 'Why should not our states profit by the experience of Canada?' he asked. He noted some trade-union opposition, but dismissed it as 'theoretical.' At least one international union, the Maintenance-of-Way Employees, defied Gompers and endorsed the act at its convention, forwarding their motion to the Canadian prime minister.[73]

Gompers leveled his editorial guns and fired a broadside at the notion of government intervention into industrial disputes. 'Would a compulsory arbitration law, with its provisions enforced by the Government, prove a deterrent to strikes?' he asked in January 1913. 'We think not. But even if it did, such a law would only repress the feeling of anger and resentment at unjust decisions ...' In an article entitled 'Tying Workers to Their Tasks Through Compulsory Government "Investigation," ' Gompers bombarded the Lemieux act. He branded it as another if milder form of compulsory arbitration. Whereas the latter promoted industrial peace by depriving workers of their right to strike, the Canadian statute, while not so harsh, had the effect of grinding the edge off of labour's most important weapon. For example, the imposition of a delay made quick and effective strikes impossible. The loose wording of the law permitted employers to evade it, and, finally, public opinion was not the disinterested, immutable judge and champion of the downtrodden that the theory presumed. Gompers noted that the law had worked to the disadvantage of the United Mine Workers in their fight with the PWA in Nova Scotia. Yet the favourable publicity surrounding the act had enabled the idea to gain currency across the border in the United States, and had prompted the states of Vermont, New York, and Wisconsin, among others, to consider or adopt a similar law. The Vermont bill, Gompers warned, while 'purporting to be in the interests of general welfare and industrial peace, is charged with innocent looking clauses that can be dexterously turned against the toilers and in the interests of employers.'[74]

Despite the fact that the Trades and Labor Congress had been unable by 1914 to persuade the Borden government to amend the Lemieux act, Congress officers still blocked outright condemnation of it. Shortly after the Congress convention had adjourned in that year, John Tobin, the president of the Boot and Shoe Workers' International Union, learned that Congress leaders planned to consult the railway unions on a new set of amendments to be submitted to Ottawa for consideration. Tobin told Gompers that the proposed changes would affect other kinds of labour, and suggested that the TLC should consult with all interested unions and not just the railway running trades. 'We have a decided antipathy to anything that approaches compulsory arbitration, and [the Boot and Shoe Workers' Union would oppose] any legislation that would require organizations to file notice of their intention to strike at a given date.' When Draper was informed of Tobin's views, he proposed that the international unions offer amendments for the consideration of the Trades Congress. But then the AFL Executive Council intervened and decided to hold a conference of all interested parties, including the Canadians, during the Federation convention in Philadelphia in November 1914. Gompers agreed that any changes approved by the international unions at Philadelphia 'should be presented by and through the officers of the Dominion Trades and Labor Congress.' At the meeting the international union leaders concluded that the Canadian law required important revisions if organized labour was to derive benefit from it.[75]

The Philadelphia meetings had been prompted in large part by fears that a number of states were about to follow in the wake of Vermont and enact laws patterned after the pioneer Canadian statute. While Gompers may not have persuaded Draper that the Lemieux act was a total failure, he made his own objections very clear in a letter to an officer of an American state federation of labour.

I find, (1) After a careful inquiry and observation, that the Canadian Industrial Disputes Act has not been helpful in increasing the wages or improving the conditions generally of the workers; (2) The administration of the Act has not resulted in the extension of the trade union movement in Canada; (3) It has not assisted in the better organization of industry; (4) It has not made the relations between employer and employed more cordial. It has not retarded or restrained employers from using the lockout, but it has restrained employes at times from using the strike at opportune moments; (5) There is no large body of citizens in the Dominion demanding an extension of the principle of compulsory investigation to the extent of making compulsory awards, or an adoption of a further approach towards compulsory arbitration.

Upon hearing of a move to enact a similar measure in England, Gompers warned a British unionist of the dangers inherent in the Canadian law.[76]

Finally in 1916 the rank and file at the Trades and Labor Congress, possibly under instructions from international union headquarters in the United States, overrode their leaders' advice and thoroughly denounced the Lemieux act. 'It is indeed good news,' Gompers told Flett. The action of the Canadian Congress helped the labour movement in the United States because the Colorado State Federation of Labor was at that moment working to secure the repeal of a state law modeled upon the Lemieux act. According to Gompers, the Canadian rank and file had provided 'an unanswerable argument' in support of labour's demands for repeal of the Colorado law. True, there was still considerable clamour in the United States for a federal law with similar purpose, but Gompers could henceforth point to the 'failure' of the Lemieux act in Canada now that the Congress had condemned it. Of course, the Congress's action did not wipe the law off the statute books in Canada, but it served Gompers' most important purpose. It united organized labour in North America against that spread of 'compulsion.' Gompers' stand against the Lemieux act illustrated his overriding desire for unity among trade-union groups throughout the continent, his belief in the universality of his own trade-union principles, and the ability of the American Federation of Labor to bring the Trades and Labor Congress of Canada over to its point of view despite the opposition of that body's leadership.[77]

The decisions made at Berlin and at Toronto early in the century dictated the relationship between the Canadian and American national trade-union centres in the years afterward. While Gompers and Morrison worked hard to preserve their empire throughout North America, Trades and Labor Congress leaders struggled to carve a niche within the limits set by the Canadian commitment to international unionism. The AFL wanted to maintain its chartering powers in Canada in order to enforce a continent-wide unity under its direction. The power to charter conveyed the authority to tax; Gompers and the AFL leadership feared that chartering prerogatives diverted to Canada would cause the Federation's income to shrink. American union leaders hesitated to guarantee the financial security of the Trades Congress, but always denied the perennial Canadian charge that more money flowed southward into union coffers than was spent in Canada in the form of union benefits and strike support. Gompers' successful resistance to Canadian demands for greater power and autonomy was confirmed by the recognition accorded to the AFL's continental boundaries by European trade unions. And Canadian trade-union leaders also discovered during this period that American continentalism overrode the desire of many Canadians to experiment with positive state action in industrial disputes.

13
Labour continentalism

American craft unions first invaded British North America during the middle of the nineteenth century. Older, larger, and richer than their Canadian counterparts, they were welcomed by Canadian workers who sought strike support and insurance benefits of a kind unavailable to them elsewhere. American unions willingly lent such help in order to organize the Canadian segment of a new continental product and labour market which developed at mid-century. The unions wanted to protect generally superior American wage levels and working conditions from the deteriorating effects of cheaper labour. Their penetration into Canada was facilitated by the widely held conviction that politics and economics occupied totally separate spheres. Nineteenth-century Darwinian and Marxist determinists pointed to identical economic forces and institutions at work in all nations undergoing industrialization and stripped political boundaries of any cultural or economic significance.

The international craft unions brought to Canada structural characteristics and policy predilections that were products of the American environment. Craft-union organization, short-term economic goals, apolitical unionism, and the pursuit of monopoly developed within the AFL over years of struggle in the United States. Gompers and his colleagues had witnessed the collapse of many labour political and reform movements in America. The Knights of Labor, the Federation's bitter rival, had not only associated skilled with unskilled in violation of craft-union pride, but also had admitted white-collar workers into its ranks. Even worse, from the craft-union viewpoint, the Knights had competed with the crafts by chartering dual bodies of skilled labour. Under the mantle of Samuel Gompers the crafts organized the AFL in 1886; the AFL developed a different philosophy, superseded the Knights of Labor, and gradually achieved ascendancy over other American trade-union movements.

The coincidental formation of a Canadian national trade-union centre in the same year revealed important variations in the labour movement of that country. The Trades and Labor Congress linked a wider variety of labour groups. Canadians were less concerned with jurisdictional issues and structural conformity and more interested in political action along the lines of labour groups in Great Britain. The relative smallness of the Canadian labour movement, combined with the various struggles which focused the attention of Federation leaders on matters at home, postponed formal contact between the two national trade-union centres until the end of the century. By then the Trades and Labor Congress appeared to be on the verge of claiming full status as a national centre. The Congress decided to respect international union jurisdictional lines for the most part, but it also began to charter unions and central labour bodies on its own.

At this moment Gompers set out to build a multinational association of trade unions. His decision, which had been occasioned partly by conflicts with American socialists, led to the first interchanges between the Canadian and American national trade-union centres. Gompers pressed the Canadians to exchange fraternal delegates; they in turn complained about the American alien labour law and about per-capita dues paid by them to the Federation. Finally in 1898 the AFL agreed to pay an annual sum to the Congress for legislative lobbying purposes, and Canadian labour leaders acquiesced to yearly exchanges of fraternal delegates. The roots of Gompers' continental thrust had sprung from his vision of worldwide labour solidarity.

But a new impulse soon changed the rationale if not the direction of AFL policy. A wave of business consolidations and technological innovations in America presaged a new round of economic competition with European industrial nations. American businessmen, seeking new markets and raw materials, turned their attention to Canada. American capital and technology began to flow northward on an unprecedented scale, attracted in part by the economic boom arising in Canada out of the settlement of the prairies and the growth of the economy to national proportions. American branch plants flourished, American machinery equipped them, American trusts extended their operations into Canada, and continental associations of employers were formed. More Americans advocated the continental point of view and openly predicted the economic unification of Canada with the United States. All these new developments seemed to demand a comparable expansion by the American labour movement into Canada. Gompers and his colleagues decided that it had become absolutely essential for them to organize Canadian workers in order to protect the North American labour and product market. While some Canadians debated whether to create their own autonomous federation of labour, others, caught up in the deterministic values of that age and conscious of the weakness of their own groups, accepted the growth of American organizations to a continental scope as inevitable and even desirable.

The Americans began to devote considerable time, attention, and money to the organization of Canadian labour on a scale impossible for the Trades and Labor Congress to match. A network of volunteer workers, led by John A. Flett, set up scores of locals and central bodies in Canadian towns, funneling information on labour conditions and personalities to AFL headquarters in Washington, DC. Soon Gompers' battles with his rivals in the United States spilled over the border. The American Labor Union set out to capture large segments of Canadian labour newly organized by the AFL. This dual-unionist challenge from the West was matched by the efforts of the Liberal party to break the international union tie on behalf of its own electoral interests. At the time these threats arose the AFL and its affiliates had not yet secured the loyalty of their new Canadian members, and feared losing them to a rival trade-union centre which might provide a haven for every new local carrying a grievance against American trade-union officialdom. And by 1902 the operations of the AFL in Canada had raised issues with the Trades and Labor Congress concerning chartering rights and the policy of organized labour toward compulsory arbitration.

Surrounded by hostile employers and jealous trade-union rivals by 1902, the AFL counterattacked. Gompers moved to rationalize the structure of North American trade unionism. The momentous decisions engineered by the crafts at the convention of the Trades and Labor Congress at Berlin, Ontario, tied the Canadian labour movement to the AFL and shaped the future course of Canadian labour history. Unions dual to the Federation were expelled from the Congress, labour party representatives were denied seats, the Congress stand on arbitration was changed to reflect the viewpoint of Gompers, and the Canadian organizer of the Federation became president of the TLC. When chartering privileges were adjusted the next year to guarantee the primacy of the American Federation of Labor in Canada, the Trades and Labor Congress became one of scores of American 'state' federations. The Canadian labour movement never again achieved the unity exhibited before the Berlin convention. Gompers' war against dual unions, waged in the name of unity, resulted in the permanent division of the movement in Canada.

After the great organizing boom had tapered off, the American Federation of Labor adopted a defensive outlook and pressed its war against rival unions. Usually it seemed more interested in protecting its past gains than in organizing new groups of workers. In the Maritimes the Federation moved to prevent incursions by the American Labor Union, and paused until the United Mine Workers attacked a provincial union of coal miners in that region. In Ontario the Federation struggled to preserve various locals against erosive pressures from hostile employers, waves of immigrants, jurisdictional disputes, and secession movements. The Federation confidently expected to force dissident French-Canadian unionists in Quebec, many of whom had been members of unions expelled from the Congress at Berlin, into locals of international craft unions. But AFL leaders failed to take into account the special history and culture of French Canada, and though they fought dual unions there as the occasion demanded they did not deal with the circumstances which nourished them and failed therefore to bring all of Quebec labour within their domain. Finally, Gompers noticed Western Canada only when the Industrial Workers of the World offered a challenge to the AFL; he sent John Flett to protect the Federation's interests against socialist-inspired dual unionism.

The AFL preserved and clarified the policies first spelled out at Berlin and a year later at Toronto. Dual unions were kept out of the Congress, and 'unsafe' leaders out of Congress office. The TLC remained dependent upon American unions for revenue, and the Americans kept control over both the structure and direction of the Canadian trade-union movement. The Congress possessed no power to enforce collection of dues or to impose a comprehensive policy on economic and political matters. The Federation refused to expand its efforts in Canada beyond the levels reached in 1902, denied loans to the Congress, declined to appoint a bilingual organizer until confessional unions had already arisen, and refrained from giving the Congress control over Flett's organizing work. It is true, of course, that the Federation's resources were limited, and Gompers admittedly faced enormous pressures from hostile employers and politicians in the United States. But it is also true that Gompers and his colleagues feared that a strong and independent Congress would encourage the transfer of wealth and power from the craft unions to state federations of labour in the United States. And some of them distrusted Draper and condemned the moderate socialist ideas of Congress vice-president James Simpson.

The structure and policies of the American Federation of Labor exerted a powerful influence upon the Canadian labour movement in the early twentieth century. As a result of decisions prompted by American conditions, scores of Canadian carpenters were forced to abandon the British-born Amalgamated Carpenters for the American-born United Brotherhood. The crafts exported their jurisdictional wars to Canada, and effectively sidetracked strong sentiment on behalf of industrial unionism. AFL leaders denied Canadian unionists separate and equal standing within international labour councils. Gompers and Morrison failed to appreciate how much more power Canadian employers wielded within

214 Gompers in Canada

many legislative halls, and rarely understood why Canadian parliamentary institutions might sometimes require different political tactics, as on the immigration issue.

Canadian trade unionists, failing to win many concessions from the Liberals and inspired by the political success of labour unions in Great Britain, turned to independent political action. All sorts of difficulties were encountered; for one, both the Grits and Tories had captured a large share of the blue-collar vote. While Gompers and Morrison did not directly oppose efforts to establish independent labour parties in Canada, many of the AFL affiliates barred Canadian members from participating in politics. More important, the American trade-union structure concentrated both wealth and decision-making power in the international craft unions with headquarters in the United States and left little money available to Canadian trade-union candidates.

It was the Canadian trade-union socialists who bore the brunt of AFL meddling. Gompers and Morrison denounced James Simpson, directed Flett to work against him and other socialists in Canada, and successfully prevented Simpson's election to the presidency of the Congress. They conspired to thwart the socialists at the TLC convention at Victoria in 1906. The crafts refused to recognize the pre-eminence of socialists within the trade-union movement of British Columbia. Gompers and Morrison, through Flett, widened the split between the independent labour parties and the socialists in Ontario. As a result of the continuing divisions within the Canadian labour movement, aggravated by the AFL, both the Grits and Tories penetrated deeper into the working-class vote and siphoned off discontent which might otherwise have found expression and brought success to Canadian trade-union politics.

In his search for continental unity, power, and authority, Gompers constructed an organizational empire. Most of the traditional elements in the American continentalist ideology could be seen lurking behind his windy prose. A geographical determinist, Gompers believed that the AFL rested upon immutable economic principles valid for all North Americans. And it is not surprising that a poor immigrant Jewish boy, a cigarmaker who had risen to the pinnacle of success, should believe fervently in the myth of American exceptionalism. In Gompers' eyes the Federation's ascension to power and prestige proved the correctness of his own ideas and the fallacy of trying to apply European political prescriptions to the North American labour world. The extension of the AFL into Canada was made easier by the fact that a good many Canadians agreed with Goldwin Smith that the physical and not the political map of North America was answering the Canadian 'question.' Some like Smith had once believed in an independent Canada, but like him had given it up as a 'dream.'[1] Many Americans, of course, never shared such a vision but were enthralled instead by another which took for granted the eventual annexation of Canada to the United States.

Gompers exhibited a messianic desire to extend the fruits of his organization to others. The 'mission' of craft unions helped them to convert strangers into brothers and opponents into enemies among men uprooted from the traditional small-town social structure and newly exposed to all the alienating currents of urban, industrial life. Senator Cloran had understood and endorsed this notion when he denounced the Lougheed bill as an attack on the brotherhood of man. Like missionaries everywhere, American labour leaders were immensely aided by the widespread belief that they bestowed truths of universal validity.

Although Gompers always denied it, there is also evidence to indicate that the AFL reaped a financial profit from its work in Canada. The enemies of the international unions in Canada always claimed this to be so; one story circulated in Quebec compared the Federation to a giant cow whose head reached into Canada and grazed on the fertile land there, but who stood in a position to be milked only in the United States. Gompers repeatedly denounced the charge, and assembled information from his AFL affiliates which would be difficult to verify today. But it is possible to calculate the revenue and expenditures of the American Federation of Labor alone in Canada, and the figures cited in Appendix 2 suggest that the Federation prospered over the years through the affiliation of Canadian workers.

Finally, the expansion of the American Federation of Labor into Canada reflected the vitality of men who laboured unceasingly to further the interests of their organizations. Gompers completely dedicated himself to a task which claimed his whole life's energies. He waged war on rival unions and sought continental unity in the hope of reaching a plateau of permanent stability, success, and recognition for the AFL. But such a goal always seemed a long way off; meanwhile, he reveled in the public recognition that the struggle brought him. Rising from the cigarmakers' local, to the national union, and ultimately to presidency of a continental Federation, this boundlessly ambitious man dreamed even bigger dreams of a world organization of labour. After the First World War had shattered this vision, his ego seemed satisfied with dabbles in Mexican politics and with the public recognition bestowed upon him by the Wilson and Harding administrations. It was revealing that a bystander witnessing the parade in Montreal in 1903 should compare Gompers' acknowledgment of cheers to the mannerisms of a Prince of Wales. In the eyes of the public Gompers was king of a labour empire. Gompers for his part did not hesitate to think and act in the manner expected of him.

It is idle to speculate upon the course of events if the American Federation of Labor had not reached into Canada at the turn of the century and stamped its impression so thoroughly upon the Canadian labour movement. But it seems clear that the AFL operated as a divisive force when the Trades and Labor Congress was transformed from a body unifying Canadian unionists into an arm of the international crafts. In a country wracked if not yet wrecked by regionalism, the loss of a truly national labour institution was doubtless unfortunate. The evidence suggests that Gompers and Morrison retarded the growth of a movement linking trade unions with moderate socialist policies, and perhaps delayed the appearance of labour politics as expressed today in the New Democratic party. Still, wages and working conditions might well be less satisfactory in Canada had not the international unions exerted a constant pressure upon Canadian industry to match American standards.

Since the Second World War there has been a pronounced 'Canadianization' of many international craft unions in Canada. In 1956, shortly after the AFL had merged with the CIO in the United States, George Meany came north to renounce all of his previously exercised powers in relation to Canada. Nevertheless, Canadian newspapers today periodically reveal lingering doubts and conflicts among Canadian trade unionists about the international tie. Many are torn between the desirable economic features obtained through their membership in AFL-CIO unions and the often less attractive American-made policies and values which these organizations impose upon their Canadian branches.

APPENDIXES

Appendix 1

American international unions operating in Canada in 1914

International organizations	No. branches		Membership	
	Canada	Elsewhere	Canada	Elsewhere
American Federation of Labor†	5	565	118	27,076
Asbestos Workers, Int'l Assn of Heat	3	37	125	2,875
Bakery and Confectionery Workers' Int'l‡	6	217	–	15,700
Barbers' Int'l Union	45	688	962	33,572
Bricklayers, Masons, and Plasterers' Int'l*	63	903	7,294	75,222
Bill Posters and Billers of America	3	57	100	1,900
Blacksmiths, Int'l Brotherhood of	11	271	400	8,100
Boilermakers and Iron Shipbuilders of Am.	19	331	996	16,310
Bookbinders, Int'l Brotherhood of	11	120	566	9,189
Boot and Shoe Workers' Union	16	151	1,752	38,248
Brewery Workmen, Int'l Union of United	24	504	1,519	51,749
Bridge and Structural Iron Workers, Int'l Assn	15	96	2,618	11,067
Broom and Whist Makers' Union, Int'l	4	44	47	653
Brushmakers' Int'l Union	1	11	16	584
Building Laborers' Int'l Protective Union*	4	128	412	10,636
Carvers' Assn of North Am, Int'l Wood	1	20	35	1,025
Carpenters and Joiners, United Brotherhood	143	1,845	7,720	204,540
Carriage, Wagon, and Automobile Workers, Int'l‡	3	–	–	3,500
Cement Workers, Am Brot of	1	92	50	2,000
Cigarmakers' Int'l Union of America	23	465	2,523	46,977
Clerks' Int'l Protective Assn, Retail‡	1	–	–	15,000
Cloth Hat and Cap Makers of NA, United	2	26	55	4,425
Commercial Telegraphers' Union of America, The	4	38	–	–
Electrical Workers and Operators, Int'l Brot	40	500	2,800	35,200
Engineers, Amalgamated Society of*	18	897	955	174,392
Engineers, Int'l Union of Steam and Operating	17	281	2,000	18,300
Elevator Constructors, Int'l Union of	1	42	28	2,660
Firemen, Int'l Brot of Stationary	3	321	145	16,355
Freight Handlers, Brot of Railroad‡	5	–	–	2,900
Fur Workers' Union, Int'l	2	13	115	4,385
Garment Workers of America, United	22	242	3,000	47,000
Garment Workers' Union, Int'l Ladies	10	72	4,100	109,900
Glass Workers' Union, American Flint	3	123	189	9,342
Glass Bottle Blowers' Assn of US and Can	3	96	300	9,700
Glass Workers' Int'l Assn, Amalgamated	3	24	50	1,174
Glove Workers' Union of America, Int'l	2	21	90	1,010
Granite Cutters' Int'l Assn of America, The	7	184	179	16,361
Halibut Fishermen's Union of the Pacific	–	–	800	1,000
Hatters of North America, United	1	21	15	8,985
Hod Carriers, Building and Common Laborers' Union	9	220	212	34,788
Horseshoers of the US and Canada, Int'l Union of	7	142	218	5,482
Hotel and Restaurant Employees' Int'l Alliance	27	542	2,315	57,814
Industrial Workers of the World*	3	150	465	30,071

American international unions operating in Canada in 1914 (continued)

International organizations	No. branches		Membership	
	Canada	Elsewhere	Canada	Elsewhere
Iron, Steel, and Tin Workers, Amal Assn of	1	90	96	9,904
Lathers' Int'l Union, Wood, Wire, and Metal	10	225	242	6,458
Leather Workers on Horse Goods, Int'l Union	3	54	74	2,126
Lithographers' Int'l Prot and Beneficial Assn	3	30	185	2,843
Longshoremen's Assn, Int'l	26	394	2,478	22,522
Locomotive Engineers, Brot of*	86	759	5,800	69,200
Locomotive Firemen and Enginemen, Brot of*	88	754	6,421	80,326
Machinists, Int'l Assn of	64	764	4,654	69,346
Maintenance-of-Way Employees, Int'l Brot of	150	230	9,400	8,873
Maintenance-of-Way Employees, Brot of*	–	116	73	3,538
Marble Workers, Int'l Assn of	7	58	375	4,350
Mechanical Trackmen, Int'l Brot of*	–	4	76	316
Metal Polishers, Buffers, Platers, Int'l Union	8	113	315	9,685
Metal Workers' Int'l Alliance, Amal Sheet	18	400	1,000	17,000
Mine Workers of America, United	33	2,541	4,483	323,990
Miners, Western Federation of	20	250	4,015	61,385
Moulders' Union of North America, Int'l	33	378	2,560	47,440
Musicians, American Federation of	42	648	6,000	63,000
Painters, Decorators, and Paperhangers of Am	45	952	2,320	77,726
Paper Makers, Int'l Brot of	10	87	600	3,800
Pattern Makers' League of NA	9	64	486	8,074
Pavers, Rammermen, Flaggers, Bridge and Stone Curb Setters, Int'l Union of	1	58	53	1,600
Paving Cutters' Union of the US and Canada	7	75	200	3,600
Photo Engravers' Union of NA Int'l	4	62	146	5,254
Piano, Organ and Musical Instrument Wkrs	2	13	225	2,975
Plasterers and Cement Finishers' Int'l Assn	21	300	1,922	19,078
Plumbers and Steamfitters of Am, United Assn	44	665	3,000	37,000
Potters, National Brot of Operative	1	67	92	6,858
Print Cutters' Assn of America, National	–	5	6	431
Printing Pressmen and Assistants' Union, Int'l	22	319	1,054	28,946
Pulp, Sulfite, and Paper Mill Workers of US and Can	4	38	700	4,913
Quarry Workers' Int'l Union of NA	6	64	500	5,500
Railway Clerks, Brotherhood of‡	1	151	–	5,000
Railway Conductors, Order of*	56	565	2,826	46,786
Railway Carmen, Brotherhood of‡	68	514	–	31,551
Railway Employees of Am, Amal Assn of Street	15	197	6,000	51,000
Railroad Trainmen, Brotherhood of*	81	800	10,000	123,200
Railroad Signalmen of America, Brot of*	1	16	52	688
Railroad Telegraphers, Order of‡	17	103	–	25,000
Seamen's Union of America, Int'l	2	60	1,000	15,000
Slate and Tile Roofers' Union of America, Int'l	1	27	27	573
Spinners International Union	1	20	25	2,475
Steam Shovel and Dredgemen, Int'l Brot of	9	45	600	5,400
Stage Employees' Int'l Alliance, Theatrical	22	424	316	17,700
Steel and Copper Plate Printers' Union of NA	1	8	47	1,372

American international unions operating in Canada in 1914 (continued)

International organizations	No. branches		Membership	
	Canada	Elsewhere	Canada	Elsewhere
Steel Plate Transferrers' Assn of America	1	2	6	65
Stereotypers and Electrotypers' Union, Int'l	8	112	197	4,571
Stonecutters' Association of NA Journeymen	31	200	1,200	5,550
Stove Mounters' Int'l Union	2	51	50	1,602
Switchmen's Union of North America	3	196	87	9,177
Tailors' Union, Journeymen (Dept of Amal Clothing Workers of America)	21	309	800	11,200
Teamsters, Chauffeurs, Stablemen, and Helpers	6	507	323	51,100
Textile Workers, United	2	200	50	19,950
Tile Layers and Helpers' Int'l Union, Ceramic, Mosaic, and Encaustic	7	55	250	2,850
Timberworkers, Int'l Union of	2	52	30	2,470
Tobacco Workers' Int'l Union	3	31	200	3,600
Travellers' Goods and Leather Novelty Workers', Int'l	2	21	85	1,040
Typographical Union, Int'l	47	686	4,807	53,730
Upholsterers' Int'l Union of NA	5	59	535	3,500
Totals	1,774	26,488	134,348	2,671,594

SOURCE: Department of Labour, *Report on Labour Organization in Canada* (1914), 191-2
* Indicates that union is not affiliated with American Federation of Labor
† Indicates Federal Labor Unions only
‡ Includes members in Canada

Appendix 2

The financial relationship of the AFL to organized labour in Canada, 1897-1914
(see footnotes for explanation of columns)

	1 AFL membership (approx.)	2 Est. of Can. unionists paying AFL dues*	3 TLC membership	4 TLC membership as % AFL membership
1897	265,000			
1898	278,000			
1899	349,000			
1900	548,000			
1901	788,000	10,476	8,381	1.0
1902	1,024,000	16,831	13,465	1.3
1903	1,466,000	20,135	16,108	1.1
1904	1,676,000	27,512	22,010	1.2
1905	1,474,000	27,505	22,004	1.4
1906	1,454,000	34,595	27,676	1.9
1907	1,539,000	40,369	32,295	2.1
1908	1,587,000	50,910	40,728	2.5
1909	1,483,000	45,089	36,071	2.4
1910	1,562,000	63,750	51,000	3.2
1911	1,762,000	71,574 (86,542)†	57,259	3.2
1912	1,770,000	82,660 (92,355)	66,128	3.7
1913	1,996,000	101,001 (104,828)	80,801	4.0
1914	2,021,000	100,117 (99,969)	80,094	4.0

* Assuming 75 per cent of AFL members in Canada paid TLC dues.
† Canada Department of Labour statistics.

INTERPRETATION OF STATISTICAL TABLE BY COLUMN
1 Total AFL membership to the nearest thousand, from AFL *Proceedings* (1914), 44
2 The approximate number of Canadians who were members of international unions paying dues to the AFL. These figures were obtained by assuming that Trades and Labor Congress membership represented 75 per cent of the total number of AFL international union members in Canada. The estimates, judging by the actual statistics obtainable only for the years 1911-14 from the Department of Labour's *Report on Labour Organization in Canada* (in parentheses), prove to be conservative. It is doubtful whether Congress membership approached even 50 per cent of AFL international union members in Canada, before 1907. For example, the report cited in the *Toronto Globe,* 21 September 1907, 5, counted 51,779 international union members in Canada. My estimate for that year is 40, 369. There is a strong likelihood that more Canadians than here estimated paid dues to the AFL.
3 Total membership of the Trades and Labor Congress, compiled from the annual *Proceedings*
4 Congress membership gained at a slightly higher rate than the Federation's, due probably to the increase in the direct affiliation of Canadian locals by international union headquarters. Yet even by 1914 about 20 per cent of international union members in Canada did not pay dues to the Congress.

The financial relationship of the AFL to organized labour in Canada (continued)

	5 TLC receipts	6 AFL receipts	7 TLC receipts as % of AFL receipts	8 Est. AFL revenue from Canada
1897	$ 409.32	$ 18,639.92	2.2	
1898	450.27	18,894.15	2.3	
1899	611.71	36,757.13	1.6	
1900	828.45	71,125.82	1.1	
1901	1,009.88	115,220.89	0.9	$ 658.56
1902	2,342.41	144,498.21	1.6	1,069.86
1903	3,858.34	247,802.96	1.5	1,268.10
1904	3,747.96	220,995.97	1.7	1,720.72
1905	4,700.29	207,417.62	2.2	1,710.30
1906	5,747.40	217,815.18	2.6	2,125.70
1907	7,474.79	174,330.26	4.3	2,462.14
1908	8,906.44	207,655.23	4.3	3,094.60
1909	7,899.47	232,377.64	3.4	2,765.34
1910	9,482.34	193,470.84	4.9	3,925.00
1911	12,454.33	182,188.68	6.8	5,835.92 (7,033.36)
1912	15,699.79	207,373.60	7.5	6,732.80 (7,508.44)
1913	19,871.49	244,292.04	8.1	8,200.08 (8,506.24)
1914	23,713.14	263,166.97	9.1	8,129.36 (8,117.52)

INTERPRETATION OF STATISTICAL TABLE BY COLUMN (continued)
5 Congress receipts, compiled from the annual *Proceedings*
6 AFL receipts, reported in *Proceedings* (1914), 19
7 Congress income gained more rapidly than Federation income, and by 1914 it took in
   9.1 per cent of the AFL's receipts. Again, the accelerating increase was due most likely
   to the increase in the number of international unions directly affiliating their Canadian
   members after 1907 and paying lump sum dues on them to the Congress.
8 The number of Canadians estimated to be in international unions (col. 2) was multiplied
   by the Federation per-capita tax (6¢ per head per annum until 1911, 8¢ thereafter).
   The figures include the $10 per annum paid by Canadian central bodies holding
   Federation charters, as recorded in the *List of Affiliated Organizations, 1902-1917,* I
   AFL-CIO Archives.

The financial relationship of the AFL to organized labour in Canada (continued)

	9 Can. AFL revenue as % of total AFL rev.	10 AFL organizing exp.	11 AFL org. exp. in Can.	12 AFL. Can. org. exp. as % total AFL org. exp.
1897				
1898				
1899		$ 6,363.66		
1900		16,399.69	$1,497.40	9.1
1901	0.57	32,328.74	2,092.51	6.4
1902	0.74	28,186.11	2,077.16	7.3
1903	0.51	60,000.00	2,377.98	4.2
1904	0.77	83,242.23	2,324.10	2.7
1905	0.82	61,694.69	1,750.00	2.8
1906	0.98	59,194.06	2,239.78	3.7
1907	1.4	56,737.11	2,150.00	3.8
1908	1.5	59,820.81	2,409.00	4.0
1909	1.2	48,359.63	1,826.68	3.7
1910	2.0	53,250.80	3,173.93	5.9
1911	3.2	46,962.05	2,481.78	5.3
1912	3.2	71,060.95	2,746.72	3.8
1913	3.3	86,698.94	878.61	1.0
1914	3.1	79,713.76	3,334.65	4.2

INTERPRETATION OF STATISTICAL TABLE BY COLUMN (continued)
  9 AFL income from Canadian affiliates accelerated in proportion to its total income, particularly after dues were raised in 1911.
10 Federation organizing expenses, obtained from the annual *Proceedings* of the AFL
11 Federation organizing expenses in Canada, as compiled from monthly reports in the back of each issue of the *American Federationist*. While these figures do not coincide with those published annually by Frank Morrison in the AFL *Proceedings,* they are probably more accurate. Morrison did not list the small amounts paid to volunteer organizers in Canada. More important, he did not differentiate between those monies paid to Flett for his work in Canada and for expenses connected with efforts on the American side. Using Morrison's Letterbooks, it has been possible to find Flett's location for virtually every week during the period from 1900 to 1914, and therefore to calculate what proportion of his expenses was spent on each side of the border. The amounts in this column are adjusted to take into account Flett's work on the American side, and they reflect in particular the fact that he spent most of 1913 and 1914 in the Buffalo area.
12 The Federation's organizing expenses in Canada are compared with total AFL monies spent on organizing. The percentage fluctuated considerably, being highest during the boom period of 1900-2, declining sharply during business downturns, picking up again, but dropping off precipitously in 1913 when Flett went to Buffalo to help reorganize the central body there.

The financial relationship of the AFL to organized labour in Canada (continued)

	13 AFL legis. grant to TLC	14 Can. legis. grant as % total AFL legis. exp.	15 Total AFL Can. exp.	16 Est. total AFL Can. rev.
1897				
1898	$100			
1899	100			
1900	100			
1901	200	7	$2,292.68	
1902	300	6	2,377.16	$1,537.86
1903	500	35	3,077.98	1,796.10
1904	500	21	2,824.10	1,984.72
1905	500	50	2,250.00	1,900.30
1906	500	35	2,739.78	2,221.00
1907	500	33	2,650.00	2,534.14
1908	500	16	2,909.00	3,178.60
1909	500	21	2,326.68	2,837.34
1910	500	14	3,673.93	4,005.00
1911	500	14	2,981.78	6,087.92
1912	500	6	3,246.72	6,984.80
1913	500	7	1,378.61	8,584.08
1914	500	6	3,834.65	8,393.36

INTERPRETATION OF STATISTICAL TABLE BY COLUMN (continued)

13 The Federation's legislative grant, as printed in the AFL *Proceedings*

14 Until 1906 the Canadian legislative grant represented a high proportion of Federation lobbying expenses, but after the Americans mounted a new political campaign in 1906, the Canadian proportion rapidly declined.

15 Adds col. 11 (the AFL organizing expenses in Canada) with col. 13 (the Federation legislative grant)

16 This figure is based upon the number of Canadian members estimated to belong to international unions (col. 2), and includes the amount of money paid to the Federation by Canadian federal labour unions directly attached to it. The latter was calculated by counting the number of Canadian federal labour unions attached to the AFL each year (obtained from the *List of Affiliated Organizations, 1902-1917*, I, AFL-CIO Archives). It was assumed that each federal labour union averaged twenty members per year; the number of federal unions multiplied by twenty, multiplied by the per-capita tax (actually, half the per capita, because the other half remained in a defence fund maintained by the AFL) gave the financial contribution made by this group of Canadians. By comparing col. 8 with col. 16, it can be seen that federal labour union dues contributed a significant part to AFL revenue during the early years.

The financial relationship of the AFL to organized labour in Canada (continued)

	17 AFL Can. exp. as % of total AFL exp.	18 AFL Can. rev. as % of total AFL rev.	19 Est. AFL income over exp. in Can.	20 Est. net loss or gain by AFL on Can. investment
1897				
1898				
1899				
1900				
1901	1.93			
1902	2.00	1.0	$ −840	
1903	1.57	0.73	−1,281	
1904	0.97	0.90	−840	−$ 3,945
1905	0.97	0.91	−350	
1906	1.02	1.0	−518	
1907	1.66	1.4	−116	
1908	1.48	1.5	+269	
1909	1.15	1.2	+511	
1910	2.06	2.0	+332	
1911	1.70	3.3	+3,106 (+4,304)	+$19,721 (+$21,993)
1912	1.17	3.3	+3,738 (+4,518)	
1913	0.53	3.6	+7,206 (+7,512)	
1914	1.44	3.2	+4,559 (+4,547)	
			Total	+$15,776 (+$18,048)

INTERPRETATION OF STATISTICAL TABLE BY COLUMN (continued)
17 Only twice did Canadian expenses rise above 2 per cent of total Federation expenses.
18 In contrast to col. 17, Federation revenue from Canada appeared to become increasingly important to the AFL.
19, 20 These figures were obtained by subtracting col. 15 from col. 16. It must be remembered that the figures are based on the estimate made in col. 2 concerning AFL membership in Canada. (The amounts in brackets are based upon hard membership data given in the Department of Labour's annual *Report*). Since the estimates are conservative, it is likely that the negative amounts in col. 19, representing the excess spent by the Federation in Canada over what it derived from the country, are actually smaller than the estimates given here. Similarly, the figures given for the surplus collected by the Federation over what it spent in Canada were probably larger, as the parenthetical amounts for 1911-13 confirm. Hence the Federation probably collected more from its Canadian 'investment' than is suggested here. If for example we use the *Globe* report of 51,779 Canadian members of AFL-connected unions in 1907, the Federation Canadian deficit of $116 shown in col. 19 would become a surplus of $568.

Someone once said that there are lies, damned lies, and – statistics. Be that as it may, this set of figures suggests that the AFL conducted its Canadian operations in a manner strikingly similar to the American manufacturers who built branch plants in Canada at this time. Both made a heavy initial investment and waited several years for it to begin paying a return. But costs were kept low enough to insure that the return would be forthcoming relatively quickly and in good volume. In more ways than might have been supposed, these figures suggest that the American Federation of Labor conducted its activities in Canada upon the principles of 'business unionism.'

Notes

PREFACE

1 Taft, *The A.F. of L. in the Time of Gompers* (New York 1957); Mandel, *Samuel Gompers: A Biography* (Yellow Springs, Ohio 1963); Gompers, *Seventy Years of Life and Labor* (New York 1925)
2 Vevier, 'American Continentalism: An Idea of Expansion, 1845-1910,' *American Historical Review* (January 1960), 323-5; Warner, *The Idea of Continental Union* (Lexington, Ky. 1960); LaFeber, ed., *John Quincy Adams and American Continental Empire* (Chicago 1965), 13-26

CHAPTER 1

1 The amendment to the Criminal Code is quoted in *American Federationist* X (June 1903), 469
2 Parliament of Canada, Senate, *Debates,* 29 April 1903, 143-4
3 Ibid.
4 Ibid, 147
5 Ibid., 149
6 Ibid., 22 July 1903, 677
7 Ibid.
8 Ibid., 679-80
9 One who organizes workers into trade unions
10 Ibid., 686-8, 690-1

11 Ibid., 692

12 Ibid., 696

13 The following paragraphs drew upon Gompers' autobiography, *Seventy Years of Life and Labor* (New York 1925), I, Book I, and Bernard Mandel, *Samuel Gompers: A Biography* (Yellow Springs, Ohio, 1963), Part I.

14 Gompers, *Seventy Years*, I, 75

15 The product-labour market theory, first enunciated by John R. Commons, is applied specifically to Canadian trade unions by C. Brian Williams in his unpublished dissertation, 'Canadian-American Trade Union Relations' (Cornell University, 1964), 14-15. See also Steven Langdon, 'The Emergence of the Canadian Working-Class Movement, 1845-75,' *Journal of Canadian Studies* VIII (May 1973), 8-10.

16 J.G. Rayback, *A History of American Labor* (New York 1966), 129-30; Mandel, *Samuel Gompers*, 20-8

17 Mandel, *Samuel Gompers*, 37-42

18 Gompers, *Seventy Years*, I, 207-40; Mandel, *Samuel Gompers*, 43-6

19 Philip Taft, *The A.F. of L. in the Time of Gompers* (New York 1957), chap. 2; N.J. Ware, *The Labor Movement in the United States, 1860-1890* (New York 1964 ed.), chap. 10

20 Ware, *The Labor Movement*, chap. 17; Taft, *The A. F. of L.*, chaps. 5, 7

21 Taft, *The A.F. of L.*, 39-56

22 'The trade unions are the natural growth of natural laws and from the very nature of their being have stood the test of time and experience,' Gompers told Bill Haywood in a letter of 23 January 1908, in Gompers Letterbooks, Library of Congress, Washington, hereafter abbreviated as GL; see also *American Federationist* 8 (May 1901), 198; H.A. Innis, *Essays in Canadian Economic History*, ed. Mary Q. Innis (Toronto 1956), 156-63; W.A. Mackintosh, *The Economic Background of Dominion-Provincial Relations* (Toronto 1964 ed.), 20-37

23 *Fincher's Trades' Review*, 31 October 1863, 87, quoted in Williams, 'Canadian-American Trade Unions,' 17

24 Jonathan Grossman, *William Sylvis, Pioneer of American Labor* (New York 1945), 40-50, 56-61, 82, 145, 148, 200

25 Canada, *Royal Commission on the Relations of Capital and Labor in Canada, Report* (Ottawa 1889), II, 819; M.L. Hansen, *The Mingling of the Canadian and American Peoples* (New Haven 1940), 166-8; R.T. Berthoff, *British Immigrants in Industrial America* (Cambridge 1963), 119; Richard E. Caves and R.H. Holton, *The Canadian Economy* (Cambridge 1959), 56

26 When the AFL secretary sent his Canadian organizer to Windsor, Ontario, in 1911, he asked him to put some new life into the labour movement there

'on account of the proximity to Detroit.' Frank Morrison to John Flett, 26 September 1911 in Morrison Letterbooks, AFL-CIO Archives, Washington, DC, hereafter abbreviated as ML. For an explanation of the reasons for international unionism, see the testimony of Milford Spohn in United States Industrial Commission, *Hearings* (1900), VII, 146-51

27 The figures are from a letter to the author by Eugene Forsey, 1 May 1968.

28 As quoted in Greg Kealey, *Working Class Toronto At the Turn of the Century* (Toronto 1973), 11. This paragraph is based upon data taken from Kealey's pioneering essay on Canadian working-class life.

29 *Labour Gazette* II (August 1901), 90-7; R.H. Coats, 'The Labour Movement in Canada,' *Canada and Its Provinces*, vol. 9, ed. Adam Shortt and A.F. Doughty (Toronto 1914), 297-300

30 This paragraph draws from a reading of the *Proceedings* of the Congress during its first decade and from a letter to the author by Eugene Forsey, 18 April 1969. From 1886 to 1896 Knights outnumbered delegates from the American crafts in every year except 1892.

31 *Trade Union Advocate* (Toronto), no. 21, 21 September 1882, 1. I am indebted to Eugene Forsey for this item.

32 Minutes of the Toronto Trades and Labor Council, 6 January, 15 September, 1882; 16 February, 1 June, 20 July, 4 August, 7 December 1883; 18 July, 1 August, 19 September 1884, Public Archives of Canada, Ottawa (hereafter abbreviated as PAC)

33 AFL *Proceedings* (1886-92), passim; (1893), 17-21; Gompers to Alfred Jury, 24 April 1891; Gompers to P.J. Ryan, 15 April 1892, GL

34 Both William Dick, *Labour and Socialism in America: The Gompers Years* (Port Washington, NY, 1972) and S.B. Kaufman, *Samuel Gompers and the Origins of the American Federation of Labor* (Westport, Conn. 1973) argue that Gompers never relinquished his Marxist goals.

35 Though he calls it by a different name (pure-and-simple unionism), H.M. Gitelman defines it as 'that variety of trade unionism which limits its activities to servicing the *immediate* needs of its members through bargaining and political action, and without more than an indirect regard for the following: the structure of, or distribution of power within, the society in which such unionism exists; the long-range interests of union members, regardless of how these interests are defined; and the welfare of workers who do not belong to the organization, except for those who readily fall within the recognized jurisdiction of a union but have not yet been organized.' *Labor History* VI (Winter 1965), 72

36 In his ms history of Canadian labour in the nineteenth century, Eugene Forsey tells of a conflict between the Knights and a Hamilton local of the Cigarmakers in 1886, but there seem to have been few such disputes.

CHAPTER 2

1 Lewis L. Lorwin, *Labor and Internationalism* (New York 1929), 117-20
2 Ibid., 120
3 Gompers to AFL Executive Council, 8 September 1896 GL
4 Gompers to Dower, 26 August 1896 GL. The letter also appears in the
   Toronto Globe, 16 September 1896, 2, and in the TLC *Proceedings* (1896),
   16.
5 Ibid.
6 Gompers to Dower, 3 September, 12 November 1896 GL; AFL *Proceedings*
   (1896), 24, 53, 81-2
7 *Toronto Globe,* 17 September 1896, 6; TLC *Proceedings* (1896), 16, 29;
   (1897), 10
8 The episode is recounted in a letter from Frank Morrison, AFL secretary, to
   Ralph V. Brandt, 11 June 1907 ML
9 TLC *Proceedings* (1897), 10. By 1897 the AFL's lobbying expenses, while
   only about $420, had risen about seven times above the year before. See
   Morrison to Brandt, 11 June 1907 ML
10 TLC *Proceedings* (1894), 20
11 TLC *Proceedings* (1895), 5
12 Ibid., 6, 10
13 Ibid., 12, 19-20
14 Ibid., 19-20; (1896), 25; *Toronto Globe,* 16 September 1896, 2
15 TLC *Proceedings* (1897), 16
16 This paragraph and the next two are based upon the account given in the
   Toronto Globe, 16 September 1897, 1.
17 Just how infrequently these visits from international union heads were
   undertaken was indicated by a printer after president James Lynch of the
   International Typographical Union visited Quebec. 'This is the first time in
   thirty years that an International officer has visited Quebec. If future visits
   will be as big with results as in the present instance, we hope that they will
   be more frequent.' *Typographical Journal* XVIII (15 February 1901), 166
18 See the statement made by the committee on the president's address and
   executive committee reports, in TLC *Proceedings* (1897), 21-2.
19 Gompers to Loughrin, 21 September, 2 November 1896, 16 February 1897 GL.
   AFL commissions generally restricted organizers to a more specific area.
20 AFL *Proceedings* (1896), 30; Gompers to Loughrin, 19 November 1896, 29
   January 1897 GL
21 Gompers to Loughrin, 18 February, 1, 17 March, 8, 12, 13 April
   1897 GL
22 *Toronto Globe,* 13 April 1897, 4

23 Gompers to Loughrin, 1 May 1897 GL
24 TLC *Proceedings* (1897), 9; *Toronto Globe,* 14 September 1897, 2
25 TLC *Proceedings* (1897), 9, 21-2
26 AFL *Proceedings* (1897), 17, 64, 95, 106.
27 Gompers to Executive Council, 29 April 1898 GL
28 Eugene Forsey, 'The International Unions, 1881-1902,' (ms). The local returned to the Journeymen Tailors' Union of America in May 1899.
29 Gompers to Dower, 24 May 1898 GL. The Executive Council unanimously supported the grant, according to Philip Taft, who has examined its minutes. See 'Differences in the Executive Council of the American Federation of Labor,' *Labor History* V (Winter 1964), 44.
30 *Manitoba Free Press,* 19 September 1898, 2
31 TLC *Proceedings* (1898), 17, 30-1; *Manitoba Free Press,* 21 September 1898, 3. The Congress platform, amended to include fifteen planks, called for (1) free public education, (2) an eight-hour day, six day week, (3) government inspection of industries, (4) an end to contract labour on public works, (5) a minimum 'living' wage, (6) public ownership of railways, telegraphs, waterworks, lighting, etc., (7) tax reform, (8) abolition of the Canadian Senate, (9) exclusion of the Chinese, (10) the union label, (11) abolition of child labour and 'female labor in all branches of industrial life', (12) abolition of property qualifications for public office, (13) compulsory arbitration of labour disputes, (14) proportional representation, (15) a ban on prison labour competing with free labour. Some of the planks were nearly identical to a platform adopted by the AFL in 1894; only the compulsory arbitration measure might have aroused Gompers' ire, and that plank was revised in accordance with his wishes at the Berlin session of the Trades Congress in 1902.
32 AFL *Proceedings* (1898), 60-1
33 Ibid., 62, 94

1 Mira Wilkins, *The Emergence of Multinational Enterprise* (Cambridge 1970), 141; Hugh G.J. Aitken, *American Capital and Canadian Resources* (Cambridge 1961), 77. Wilkins' study, based upon corporate records, provides the most complete analysis of the American business expansion into Canada; see particularly chap. 7, 'The "Spillover" to Canada (1870-1914),' 135-8. For a survey in the 1930s, see Herbert Marshall, F.A. Soward, and K.W. Taylor, *Canadian-American Industry* (New Haven 1936).

2 Quoted in William A. Williams, *The Contours of American History* (Chicago 1966), 368. See also Walter LaFeber, *The New Empire* (Ithaca 1963), 176-96 and passim.
3 Cited by R. Abrams and L. Levine (eds.) in *The Shaping of Twentieth Century America* (Boston 1965), 62
4 Quoted in W.J. Ghent, *Our Benevolent Feudalism* (New York 1902), 29
5 Roosevelt, First Annual Message to Congress (1901), in *Documents of American History,* ed. H.S. Commager (New York, 3rd ed., 1943), 201; Wilkins, *Multinational Enterprise,* 72
6 Donald Warner, *The Idea of Continental Union* (Lexington, Ky. 1960), 233-5; *New York Times,* 19 June 1900, 7; 18 September 1904, 7, where Carnegie's views and the background to the League are discussed in a letter from F.W. Glen; A.K. Weinberg, *Manifest Destiny* (Chicago 1963 ed.), 366; J.W. Pratt, 'The "Large Policy" of 1898,' *Mississippi Valley Historical Review* XIX (September 1932), 231
7 Quoted in Weinberg, *Manifest Destiny,* 368, 370, 374
8 *New York Times,* 5 August 1898, 12
9 Osborne Howes, Secretary of Boston Board of Fire Underwriters, to United States Industrial Commission, in *Hearings* (1901), IX, 718
10 *Toronto Globe,* 4 May 1900, 7
11 Quoted in Weinberg, *Manifest Destiny,* 374
12 *Labour Gazette* V (July 1904), 28, 43-4; R.E. Caves and R.H. Holton, *The Canadian Economy* (Cambridge 1959), 44, 95
13 *Montreal Herald,* 2 May 1903, 23. See also Ronald Radosh, 'American Manufacturers, Canadian Reciprocity, and the Origins of the Branch Factory System,' Canadian Association for American Studies *Bulletin* III (Spring/ Summer 1967), 19-54
14 Wilkins, *Multinational Enterprise,* 141
15 H.A. Innis, in his introduction to E.S. Moore, *American Influence in Canadian Mining* (Toronto 1941), xii. See also Fred W. Field, *Capital Investments in Canada* (Toronto 1911), 23.
16 Quoted by J.A. Hobson in *Canada To-Day* (London 1906), 25
17 'As they [Montreal and Toronto] developed they proved a magnet for the lighter manufacturing industries in the location of which the pull of the market was the chief influence.' W.A. Mackintosh, *The Economic Background of Dominion-Provincial Relations* (Toronto 1964 ed.), 55. Correspondents for the *Labour Gazette* often noted the influx of American enterprise: see III (September 1902), 131, 135; III (October 1902), 213; IV (November 1903), 390; IV (February 1904), 729, 753, 765; IV (April 1904), 988; IV (June 1904), 1208; IV (May 1904), 1093, 1105; V (December 1904), 580.

See also Marshall, Soward, and Taylor, *Canadian-American Industry,* 32, 63, 83.

18 Field, *Capital Investments,* 24-5; *Toronto Globe,* 25 September 1902, 6; Wilkins, *Multinational Enterprise,* 141

19 Hobson, *Canada To-Day,* 53; *Labour Gazette* II (June 1902), 705; III (October 1902), 246ff, 377ff; V (October 1904), 315; *American Federationist* IX (November 1904), 999

20 Caves and Holton, *Canadian Economy,* 37; Field, *Capital Investment,* 21, 29

21 F.W. Howay, W.N. Sage, and H.F. Angus, *British Columbia and the United States* (Toronto 1942), 255, 256-96; also Margaret Ormsby, *British Columbia: A History* (Vancouver 1958), 316-17

22 *Labour Gazette* IV (February 1904), 768. One postmaster in the Kootenay kept his office open on Dominion Day but closed it on the Fourth of July. Howay, Sage, and Angus, *BC and the US,* 296

23 Aitken, *American Capital,* 66-7, 104; Caves and Holton, *Canadian Economy,* 35; J.W. Oliver, *History of American Technology* (New York 1956), 468; *Labour Gazette* V (December 1904), 635; Eugene Forsey, 'The International Unions, 1881-1902,' (ms). Accounts of the introduction of new American machines litter the pages of the *Labour Gazette* for these years.

24 *Labour Gazette* III (October 1902), 198; also III (November 1902), 324, 352-62; IV (January 1904), 647

25 Aitken, *American Capital,* 35-7. 'The most fundamental single characteristic of the period was a high rate of investment induced by improved expectations of profit from the exploitation of natural resources.' Mackintosh, *Economic Background,* 41

26 Canada, Parliament, Senate, *Debates,* 19 February 1902, 61-2

27 *Industrial Canada* III (April 1903), 402

28 See A.D. Chandler Jr, 'The Beginnings of "Big Business" in American Industry,' *Business History Review* XXXIII (Spring 1959), 1-31; R.H. Wiebe, *Businessmen and Reform* (Cambridge 1962), chap. 2.

29 C.E. Bonnett, *Employers' Associations in the United States* (New York 1922), 63ff; *Labour Gazette* III (October 1902), 216

30 Bonnett, *Employers' Associations,* 98-104. For a detailed study of the agreement see W.F. Willoughby, 'Employers' Associations in the United States,' *Quarterly Journal of Economics* XX (November 1905), 110-150

31 *American Federationist* VII (December 1900), 387

32 *Labour Gazette* I (June 1901), 540; F.W. Hilbert, 'Employers' Associations in the United States,' *Studies in American Trade Unionism,* eds., J.H. Hollander and G.E. Barnett (New York 1907), 201-2; *Labour Gazette* IV (August 1903), 151-3; M.V. Sears, 'The American Businessman at the Turn

of the Century,' *Business History Review* XXX (December 1956),
429-30

33 Hilbert, 'Employers' Associations,' 189-90, 208-10, 216; also Wiebe, *Businessmen*, 161-3, 193

34 Editorial, I (July 1901), 310

35 S.D. Clark, *The Canadian Manufacturers' Association* (Toronto 1939), 7, 29;
Canadian Annual Review, 1902, 499-500; *Labour Gazette* III (November
1902), 374

36 *Industrial Canada* II (May 1902), 314

37 *Labour Gazette* II (December 1901), 342; IV (January 1904), 633, 651; IV
(March 1904), 884

38 TLC *Proceedings* (1904), 11; *Industrial Canada* IV (May 1904), 489

39 Quoted in Bonnett, *Employers' Associations*, 436-7; see also his chap. 2,
passim; TLC *Proceedings* (1904), 11

40 AFL *Proceedings* (1904), 15

41 AFL *Proceedings* (1899), 148

42 Henry White, 'Trades Unions and Trusts,' *American Federationist* VI
(December 1899), 245-7

43 *American Federationist* VI (October 1899), 195; see also AFL *Proceedings*
(1899), 15

44 R.S. Maloney, AFL fraternal delegate to Canada, in TLC *Proceedings*
(1907), 39; see also John C. Appel, 'The Relationship of American Labor to
United States Imperialism 1895-1905,' (PHD dissertation, University of
Wisconsin, 1950), 361-3; *American Federationist* XII (November 1905),
865; XIII (August 1906), 558; XXI (July 1914), 588; XXI (March 1914),
252

45 Frank Feeney, AFL fraternal delegate to Canada, in TLC *Proceedings*
(1905), 54

46 *Toronto Globe*, 4 May 1900, 8

47 AFL *Proceedings* (1905), 17

48 To Lord Mount Stephen, 22 May 1901, in *A Selection From Goldwin
Smith's Correspondence, 1846-1910*, ed. Arnold Haultain (London 1913),
372-3

CHAPTER 4

1 The figures are from Eugene Forsey, 'The International Unions, 1881-1902,'
(ms), revised in a letter to the author on 19 April 1969. There were four
international union locals in the territories.

2 Ibid.
3 TLC *Proceedings* (1898), 10; (1899), 10
4 TLC *Proceedings* (1895), 8
5 *Manitoba Free Press*, 21 September 1898, 3
6 TLC *Proceedings* (1898), 10
7 Gompers to P.J. Ryan, 19 April 1897 GL. See also Gompers to A. Gariepy, 4, 27 May 1897, and Gompers to Joseph Ainey, 27 May 1897 GL.
8 Gompers to John Cantwell, 31 July 1897 GL
9 TLC *Proceedings* (1899), 10-11
10 Philip Taft, *The A. F. of L. in the Time of Gompers* (New York 1957), 99-100; editorial by Gompers in *American Federationist* VI (October 1899), 195. By February 1901 organizing expenses averaged about $1300 per month. *American Federationist* VIII (March 1901), 94
11 *American Federationist* VI (May 1899), 62. A map of the organizing districts appears in VI (October 1899), 191.
12 Gompers to George Warren, 29 March 1899; Gompers to George Bartley, 3 May 1897; Gompers to C.S.O. Boudreault, Ottawa, 2 October 1899 GL
13 TLC *Proceedings* (1900), 19; AFL *Proceedings* (1899), 7
14 *Montreal Star*, quoted in *The Canadian Men and Women of the Time*, ed. H.J. Morgan (Toronto, 2nd ed. 1912), 406. See also TLC *Album of Labor Leaders* (Ottawa 1909), NP, and TLC *Convention Souvenir* (Ottawa 1901), NP
15 *American Federationist* VII (April 1900), 107
16 *American Federationist* VII (June 1900), 175
17 *American Federationist* VII (December 1900), 393
18 *Toronto Globe*, 2 May 1900, 4; 3 May 1900, 10; 4 May 1900, 8; Gompers to Flett, 14 May 1900 GL. See also *American Federationist* VII (June 1900), 170.
19 Gompers to Flett, 28 November 1900 GL
20 Gompers to Flett, 18 February, 2 April 1901 GL
21 Gompers to James Scruton, 2, 10, 21 May 1902; Gompers to Flett, 21 May, 5 June 1902 GL
22 Gompers to Flett, 12 March, telegram 13 March 1903 GL
23 Gompers to Flett, 6 March 1903; Gompers to Morley Washburne, 6 March 1903 GL
24 Gompers to Flett, 19 March 1902 GL
25 Gompers to Flett, 2 April 1901 GL
26 *American Federationist* VIII (October 1901), 443
27 *American Federationist* IX (January 1902), 43-4; VIII (November 1901), 462; TLC *Proceedings* (1902), 41

28 TLC *Proceedings* (1901), 48-50
29 AFL *Charter Book,* 1902, in AFL-CIO Archives, Washington, DC
30 Quoted in Gompers to Flett, 23 January 1901 GL. See also letter of 18 January.
31 Provincial Workmen's Association, 'Minutes of the Proceedings of the Grand Council,' 17 September 1901, 375
32 The AFL Canadian volunteer organizers in mid-1901 were: Thomas Keilty, Brockville; William Kelly, Kingston; William Burleigh, London; P.J. Ryan, George Warren and Joseph Ainey, Montreal; Daniel Stamper, Moose Jaw; C.P. Lynch, Norwich; J.W. Patterson and C.S.O. Boudreault, Ottawa; James Carty, St Catharines; C.F. Swartz, Saulte Ste Marie; J. Laughton, Stratford; J.H. Kennedy and George Sangster, Toronto; W.M. Jones, Nanaimo; George Bartley and J.H. Watson, Vancouver; T.H. Twigg, Victoria. *American Federationist* VIII (August 1901), NP
33 Gompers to Flett, 10 May 1901 GL
34 Gompers to Stamper, 23 January 1902, 15 May 1903, 22 January, 2, 13 June, 8 August 1904, 19 January, 23 June 1905; Gompers to J.H. Watson, 23 April, 29 May 1901 GL
35 *American Federationist* VII (April 1900), 106; VII (June 1900), 173
36 Quoted in Michel Tétu, 'Les premiers syndicats catholiques canadiens 1900-1921' (PHD dissertation, University of Montreal, 1961), 34n
37 *Labour Gazette* I (February 1901), 294; also I (November 1900), 153ff; Joseph Levitt, *Henri Bourassa and the Golden Calf* (Ottawa 1972), 100; Allan B. Latham, *The Catholic and National Trade Unions of Canada* (Toronto 1930), 37-40
38 *American Federationist* VIII (February 1901), 57; VIII (March 1901), 85; American Federation of Labor *Proceedings* (1900), 77
39 Gompers to Flett, 29 December 1900 GL; *Labour Gazette* I (February 1901), 265; I (March 1901), 323
40 *American Federationist* VIII (March 1901), 85. See also Gompers to Flett, 2 April 1901 GL; C. Brian Williams, 'Canadian-American Trade Union Relations' (PHD dissertation, Cornell University, 1964), 401
41 *American Federationist* VIII (February 1901), 57, 85; *Labour Gazette* I (March 1901), 323
42 *Labour Gazette* I (March 1901), 323; II (February 1902), 438
43 *American Federationist* VII (November 1900), 347
44 Gompers to Victor Phaneuf, 28 May 1901 GL
45 Gompers to Flett, 27 August 1902; L.A. Gavin (an AFL clerk) to Flett, 12 September 1902 GL; George Perkins to Gompers, 4 September 1902, National Union Files, Reel 2, AFL-CIO Archives

46 Gompers to Warren, 15 May 1902 GL
47 The number of locals is from Forsey, 'The International Unions.'
48 Gompers to Flett, 10 May 1901 GL. See also the letters to Stamper and Watson cited in note 34. 'Organizers are badly wanted,' Stamper said, 'to cover this northwestern country from Ft. William, Ont. to Cariboo, B.C., to look after Labor and affiliated international organizations.' *American Federationist* VII (October 1900), 329
49 *American Federationist* VI (August 1899), 134; VII (February 1900), 45
50 *Labour Gazette* II (December 1901), 343; *Industrial Banner* X (March 1902), no. 6.
51 Compiled from issues of the *American Federationist,* 1899-1902, and from Forsey, 'The International Unions;' *Industrial Banner* X (17 January 1902), no. 4
52 Forsey 'The International Unions,' revised in a letter to the author on 19 April 1969
53 O.R. Wallace, Guelph, in *American Federationist* X (January 1903), 13
54 AFL *Proceedings* (1901), 21

CHAPTER 5

1 The history of Canadian trade-union politics is well summarized in Martin Robin's *Radical Politics and Canadian Labour, 1880-1930* (Kingston 1968), based upon the labour press of that period. I have relied upon Robin and also T.R. Loosmore's 'The British Columbia Labor Movement and Political Action, 1879-1906' (MA thesis, University of British Columbia, 1954), in order to explain how Canadian labour politics related to AFL policies through 1902. For background on 'Conservatives, Liberals, and Labour' in the 1870s and 1880s, see Bernard Ostry's articles in the *Canadian Historical Review* 41 (1960), and the *Canadian Journal of Economics and Political Science* 27 (1961).
2 Daniel O'Donoghue to W.L.M. King, 7 December 1897, in *King Papers,* Correspondence, Primary Series, vol. 1, 639, PAC
3 Ontario Bureau of Industries, 'Report,' in *Sessional Papers* 70, no. 84 (1885); Loosmore, 'BC Labor Movement,' 52, 72; TLC *Proceedings* (1893), 15; (1894), 17; (1895), 27.
4 *Toronto Globe,* 7 September 1895, 15; TLC *Proceedings* (1897), 28
5 Melvyn Dubofsky, 'The Origins of Western Working Class Radicalism, 1890-1905,' *Labor History* VII (Spring 1966), 139-42; John T. Saywell, 'Labor and Socialism in British Columbia: A Survey of Historical

Developments Before 1903,' *British Columbia Historical Quarterly* XV (July-October, 1951), 137-8

6 This paragraph is based upon Vernon H. Jensen's *Heritage of Conflict: Labor Relations in the Nonferrous Metals Industry Up to 1930* (Ithaca 1950), 54-62; the quotation is on p. 61; see also Melvyn Dubofsky, *We Shall Be All* (Chicago 1969), 65-6.

7 Eugene Forsey, 'The International Unions, 1881-1902' (ms); TLC *Proceedings* (1898), 14; Robin, *Radical Politics,* 47. A brief history of the WFM in Canada appears in Canada Department of Labour, *Report of Labour Organization* (1914), 83-97.

8 Dubofsky, 'Western Working Class,' 133

9 See Joseph Rayback, *A History of American Labor* (New York 1966), 227-8 for a summary of these events.

10 G. Weston Wrigley, 'Socialism in Canada,' *International Socialist Review* I (Mary 1901), 686

11 The Socialists also forced through a resolution instructing Congress leaders to send a letter of sympathy to Eugene Debs, then in jail for his part in the Pullman strike. *Toronto Globe,* 7 September 1895, 15

12 *Toronto Globe,* 21 September 1896, 6

13 AFL *Proceedings* (1897), 3; David A. Shannon, *The Socialist Party of America: A History* (Chicago 1967 ed.), 17

14 Shannon, *Socialist Party,* 4

15 Ibid., 17-24; also Wrigley, 'Socialism in Canada,' passim

16 Wrigley, 'Socialism in Canada,' 686-8

17 Jacqueline F. Cahan, 'A Survey of the Political Activities of the Ontario Labour Movement, 1850-1935,' (MA thesis, University of Toronto, 1945), 21-2

18 *Industrial Banner* X, no. 10 (July, 1902)

19 Robin, *Radical Politics,* 40

20 William Bennett, *Builders of British Columbia* (Vancouver 1937), 135; *American Federationist* VI (December 1899), 259

21 Robin, *Radical Politics,* 49-50; Loosmore, 'BC Labor Movements,' 92-4

22 Gompers to George Bartley, 2 June 1899 GL

23 Quoted in Margaret Norell and Jeanette Grosney, 'Labor in Winnipeg: The Rise of Trade Unionism,' paper presented at United College, Winnipeg, 1945, 11, Department of Labour Library, Ottawa. 'Had it not been for the split in the Liberal party [in Winnipeg],' A.R. McCormack suggests, 'Puttee would never have been elected.' See 'Arthur Puttee and the Liberal Party: 1899-1904' *Canadian Historical Review* LI (June 1970), 163

24 Loosmore, 'BC Labor Movement,' 102-3, 117-18

25 Ibid., 137-40; 147-8

26 Forsey, 'The International Unions;' Saywell, 'Labor and Socialism,' 138-9; William Hard, 'The Western Federation of Miners,' *The Outlook* LXXXIII (9 May 1906), 125-33; Jensen, *Heritage,* 68-70; *American Federationist* VII (February 1900), 45

27 Loosmore, 'BC Labor Movement,' 153-60

28 Quoted in Jensen, *Heritage,* 69-70

29 Quoted in Loosmore, 'BC Labor Movement,' 162

30 Quoted in Robin, *Radical Politics,* 60

31 Quoted in *Canadian Annual Review,* 1903, 557

32 Quoted in AFL *Proceedings* (1899), 41-2

33 *Toronto Globe,* 22 September 1899, 4; 23 September 1899, 20

34 *Toronto Globe,* 23 September 1899, 20; TLC *Proceedings* (1899), 23-4

35 AFL *Proceedings* (1899), 41, 80

36 Ibid., 107

37 TLC *Proceedings* (1900), 12

38 Ibid., 18, 19, 21-2; *Industrial Banner* VIII no. 8, 11 May 1900; *Toronto Globe,* 21 September 1900, 7, 24 September 1900, 5

39 TLC *Proceedings* (1900), 5, 20, 26; *Labour Gazette* I (October 1900), 63

40 See R.M. Dawson, *William Lyon Mackenzie King: A Political Biography, 1874-1923* (Toronto 1958), 97-103. The three were Ed Williams of Hamilton, to investigate violations of the alien labor law; Alfred Jury, Montreal, immigration commissioner; and Robert Glockling, Toronto, to head the newly created Ontario Labor Bureau. *Toronto Globe,* 19 September 1900, 7

41 *Toronto Globe,* 24 September 1900, 5

42 *Reminiscences: Political and Personal* (Toronto 1919), 307; Horace Evans to Laurier, 10 December 1900, in Laurier Papers, Correspondence, PAC; *Toronto Globe,* 24 September 1900, 5. R.M. Dawson, *King,* quoting from Mackenzie King's diary, says that 'The Government's labour policy seems to have been of moderate interest during the campaign, but King wrote that "with the exception of Mr. Mulock, most of the Cabinet seem to be afraid of touching it." The election returns were a disappointment to Mulock ... "He said of the labour business that it had had a steadying influence & had worked well in certain places" ' (105).

43 *Industrial Banner* X, no. 6 (March 1902); for manufacturers' opinions see *Industrial Canada* II (November 1901), 137; II (April 1902), 285-6

44 TLC *Proceedings* (1901), 57

45 Dower to Laurier, 27 March 1897, Laurier Papers, Correspondence, PAC; TLC Proceedings (1901), 11. See also Gompers to P.M. Draper, 11 February, 4 March 1902; Gompers to Flett, 11 February 1901 GL

46 TLC *Proceedings* (1902), 25, 33

47 TLC *Proceedings* (1901), 36-7
48 Smith to Laurier, 30 June 1900; Laurier to Smith, 7 July, 4 December 1900, in Laurier Papers, Correspondence, PAC
49 Loosmore, 'BC Labor Movement,' 172-6, 178, 181

CHAPTER 6

1 TLC *Proceedings* (1900), 27, 37
2 *Encyclopedia Canadiana* (Ottawa 1966), III, 302-3; *The Canadian Who's Who* (Toronto 1937), 313
3 R.O. Spreckley, 'Labor Chieftain,' *Saturday Night,* 2 October 1937. The author is grateful to P.M. Draper, Jr, for this item.
4 TLC *Proceedings* (1902), 14, 18, 64
5 Gompers to Draper, 13 November 1900 GL; AFL *Proceedings* (1900), 28
6 AFL *Proceedings* (1900), 77
7 *American Federationist* VII (November 1900), 347
8 TLC *Convention Souvenir* (Ottawa 1901), NP. By 1902 the Trades Congress had issued some 40 charters to federal labour unions and city centrals. TLC *Proceedings* (1902), 64
9 *American Federationist* VIII (July 1901), 258 (quotation); Gompers to Draper, 5 June, 11 June, 12 October 1901 GL; Gompers to Flett, 3 June 1901 GL. The AFL reimbursed Draper by $29.60, which was charged to 'organizing expenses.' *American Federationist* VIII (August 1901), 328
10 TLC *Proceedings* (1901), 4-6
11 Both Laurier and Mulock condemned the international trade-union tie. 'If we must have Labor Associations in this country,' Laurier wrote, '– and [I] think they are producive [*sic*] of some good in some respects – we must endeavour to organize them on National lines.' Laurier to Mulock, 5 February 1902, in Laurier Papers, Correspondence, PAC. Mulock expressed even stronger sentiments in a letter to Laurier, 4 April 1903, ibid.
12 TLC *Proceedings* (1901), 8-9
13 Ibid.
14 See for example the statement given by the president of the Toronto street railway company to the press on 13 June 1902, in *Canadian Annual Review,* 1902, 496
15 TLC *Proceedings* (1901), 77. Some workmen endorsed the employers' point of view. One federal MP received a letter of complaint from a workman who objected to the high initiation fees of international unions. 'I have a large family to support, am a Canadian and cannot get work on a Canadian

contract let by your government. What am I going to do? A foreigner can come here from the U.S. if he is a member of the union, then can go to work while I may sit and starve.' He called for government-controlled national unions in Canada. Canada, House of Commons, *Debates*, 10 May 1901, col. 4871-2

16 Gompers to Draper, 12 October 1901, 24 January 1902 GL; AFL *Proceedings* (1901), 116

17 AFL *Proceedings* (1901), 92

18 John Frey, editor of the Moulder's journal, as quoted in James O. Morris, *Conflict Within the A. F. of L.* (Ithaca 1958), 4

19 Quoted in ibid., 240

20 See the interpretation of the declaration given in *American Federationist* XXI (January 1914) 20

21 AFL circular letter on the American Labor Union, 8 October 1901 GL

22 John Tobin to Frank Morrison, 27 June 1902, National Union Files, Reel 2, AFL-CIO Archives

23 'The Western Labor Movement,' *International Socialist Review* III (November 1902), 262

24 Quoted in Martin Robin, *Radical Politics and Canadian Labour, 1880-1930* (Kingston 1968), 41n

25 *Labour Gazette* III (August 1902), 110ff.; TLC *Proceedings* (1902), 47

26 TLC *Proceedings* (1903), 32

27 Quoted in Canada, Parliament, Report of the Royal Commission on Industrial Disputes in the Province of British Columbia, *Sessional Papers*, no. 36a (1903), 8

28 TLC *Proceedings* (1902), 39

29 R. Robinson, Chairman, Geo. Flemmin, and A. Lackey of Nelson, British Columbia, to W.J. Frid, Hamilton, Ontario, 6 April 1901, National Union Files, Reel 2, AFL-CIO Archives

30 TLC *Proceedings* (1902), 38

31 Ibid., 36

32 John F. Tobin to Gompers, 22 October 1901, National Union Files, Reel 2, AFL-CIO Archives.

33 Ibid.

34 TLC *Proceedings* (1902), 64

35 Ibid., 18

36 Report of the PEI executive committee, in TLC *Proceedings* (1902), 18-19, 44; American Federation of Labor, *Charter Book* (1902), AFL-CIO Archives

37 TLC *Proceedings* (1902), 18

38 Ibid., 38-9

39 For Gompers' opinions on arbitration, see his autobiography, *Seventy Years of Life and Labor,* II (New York, 1925), chap. 30; his article in the *Annals of the American Academy of Political and Social Science* XX (July 1902), 29-34; numerous editorials in the *American Federationist* during the period; and a letter to Miss Mary Roberson, Mound City, Illinois, 19 March 1914, GL

40 TLC *Proceedings* (1901), 8

41 *Labour Gazette* II (June 1902), 738-41; III (August 1902), 69, 80, 81, 214

42 Gompers to Draper, 28 August 1902; R.L. Guard (Gompers' secretary) to Draper, 6 September 1902 GL

43 AFL *Proceedings* (1901), 184, 217

44 Gompers to Executive Council, 8 March 1902 GL

45 Gompers to Draper, 7 April 1902, GL; *American Federationist* IX (June 1902), 331, 336, 338-9. The AFL paid Draper $97 for expenses connected with his attendance at the session. Ibid., 350

46 *Denver Times,* 9 July 1902, reprinted in *American Federationist* IX (September 1902), 509

47 *Denver Post,* 11 July 1902, reprinted in ibid.

48 R.L. Guard to Flett, 28 June 1902 GL; Minutes of the Toronto Trades and Labor Council 24 July, August 28 1902 CLCLibrary, Ottawa

CHAPTER 7

1 *Toronto Globe,* 16 September 1902, 9

2 Ibid.; TLC *Proceedings* (1902), 6-7. When it had chartered the Local 36 of waiters, the Trades and Labor Congress had indirectly sanctioned the union's refusal to affiliate with the Hotel and Restaurant Employees International Union.

3 TLC *Proceedings* (1902), 5-7

4 *Toronto Globe,* 16 September 1902, 9

5 TLC *Proceedings* (1902), 7

6 Morrison's letterbooks contain considerable correspondence of an unofficial nature between the two printers.

7 Flett had approached Marks in 1900 and had suggested the affiliation of Marks' Industrial Brotherhood with the AFL. See *American Federationist* VII (December 1900), 393.

8 The position of the committee members was determined from their vote and statements during the debates which followed presentation of the committee's recommendations. All voted in favour of the constitutional

changes except Boudreault, who split his vote on the two roll calls, and Fitz-patrick and Boileau, who voted against them.

9 TLC *Proceedings* (1902), 8-9
10 Ibid.
11 Ibid., 9
12 Ibid., 10
13 *Toronto Globe,* 17 September 1902, 9
14 Ibid.
15 Ibid.
16 Ibid.
17 Ibid.
18 *Winnipeg Voice,* 3 October 1902, 1
19 *Toronto Globe,* 17 September 1902, 9; TLC *Proceedings* (1903), 47
20 TLC *Proceedings* (1903), 47
21 Ibid. The division is printed in the Congress *Proceedings* (1902), 12.
22 *Toronto Globe,* 17 September 1902, 9
23 TLC *Proceedings* (1901), 84; (1902), 13
24 TLC *Proceedings* (1902), 18, 44
25 Ibid., 55-6
26 *Toronto Globe,* 19 September 1902, 1
27 Ibid., 2; 20 September 1902, 11
28 24 September 1902, 2
29 *Industrial Banner* IX, no. 11 (October, 1901); *Toronto Globe,* 18 September 1902, 8; 19 September 1902, 1
30 *Toronto Globe,* 19 September 1902, 1
31 Ibid. Gompers later asserted that Canadian government officials had pressured the Congress in an attempt to win support for the bill. Gompers to D.J. O'Donoghue, 1 April 1903 GL
32 TLC *Proceedings* (1902), 47
33 *Winnipeg Voice,* 26 September 1902, 1
34 *Toronto Globe,* 19 September 1902, 1
35 TLC *Proceedings* (1901), 73
36 Some of the opposition appeared to have been provoked by the action of the Winnipeg labour party at a meeting on 12 September, when a resolution expressing sympathy over the McKinley assassination was objected to by the president, and finally dropped. *Manitoba Free Press,* 14 September 1901, 2. During debate on the labour party issue at the Congress convention, Gossel claimed that 'the meeting of the party last Thursday night, when a resolution regretting the assassination of President McKinley was laid upon the table, was not representative of the laboring class of Winnipeg.' *Toronto Globe,* 20 September 1901, 7

37 *Toronto Globe,* 20 September 1901, 7
38 *Toronto Globe,* 19 September 1902, 1
39 *Toronto Globe,* 20 September 1902, 11
40 Gompers to Flett, 29 September 1902 GL
41 *Toronto Globe,* 20 September 1902, 11

CHAPTER 8

 1 Gompers to Flett, 29 September 1902 GL
 2 Gompers to Flett, 11 October 1902 GL; extracts from Executive Council
    Meeting, *American Federationist* IX (November 1902), 843
 3 *American Federationist* IX (November 1902), 818
 4 AFL *Proceedings* (1902), 14-15
 5 Ibid., 138, 232-3
 6 Others were: L.K. Marr, chairman (Street Railway Employees), Ricardo
    Vazquez (Ponce, P.R. central body), T.H. Flynn (Boilermakers), Harry
    Skeffington (Boot and Shoe Workers), Edward McKay (United Mine
    Workers), Charles Dold (president of the Piano and Organ Workers), M.J.
    Noonan (Tailors), A.J. Engel (Upholsterers), G.F. Hedrick (New York State
    Federation of Labor). AFL *Proceedings* (1902), 183
 7 AFL *Proceedings* (1902), 225
 8 Gompers to Flett, 12 December, 18 December 1902 GL. See Toronto Dis-
    trict Labor Council, Minutes, 13 November 1902, for an appeal by Draper.
 9 Gompers to Draper, 19 January, 5 February 1903 GL; *American Federa-
    tionist* X (March 1903), 270
10 *Labour Gazette* III (February 1903), 588
11 Gompers to Flett, 31 March 1903; Gompers to Draper, 24 March 1903 GL
12 TLC *Proceedings* (1903), 18-19
13 *Toronto Globe,* 21 April, 14; 22 April, 7; 23 April 1903, 9
14 TLC *Proceedings* (1903), 19
15 *Toronto Globe,* 24 April 1903, 7
16 Since the papers of Draper and the Congress have not survived, the secretary-
    treasurer's views have been inferred from other evidence. One of the most
    important is a letter from John Tobin to Gompers in 1910, in which the
    Boot and Shoe Workers' Union leader said in passing: '... while at one time
    Draper's loyalty to the American Federation of Labor was of a very doubt-
    ful character, I believe that of recent years he has been developing and has
    seen the error of his former ways. The last time I saw him [in late 1909]
    ... he told me how much he had learned during recent years and that
    he had gotten entirely over his idea that Canada should have a Federation

co-equal with the American Federation ...' Tobin to Gompers, 14 September 1910, National Union Files, Reel 2, AFL-CIO Archives

17 *Toronto Globe,* 25 April 1903, 31. The preparations for the meeting were outlined to the Executive Council by Gompers in a letter dated 14 April 1903 GL

18 Morrison gave his version in a letter written to an international union president in 1907. '... When the Executive Council of the Federation met at Toronto ... a discussion was brought about through an objection lodged by myself against the officers [of the Congress] issuing charters to Federal Labor Unions and Trade Unions. This controversy arose through a Federal Labor Union in Prince Edwards [*sic*] Island, which, upon investigation, proved to be nothing more or less than a political organization, and which was refused representation [in the Charlottetown Trades and Labor Council]. I contended that the Canadian Trades and Labor Congress stands in the same relation to the American Federation as do the states of Illinois, Ohio, and New York, etc., and had no right to issue charters, the issuance of charters being the special province of the American Federation of Labor and International Unions. Secretary-Treasurer Draper persisted in his determination to issue charters to Federal Labor Unions and City Centrals without their first being chartered by the A.F. of L. I called his attention to the fact that the Congress was not in a financial condition to protect the members of the local Trade and Federal Labor Unions in the case of strike and lockout, that the A.F. of L. had a substantial defense fund and was able to furnish financial protection. This contention on my part appealed in particular to President Flett, of the Canadian Trades and Labor Congress, and, after a great deal of discussion, president Flett and secretary Draper conceded ...' Morrison to Ralph Brandt, 11 June 1907 ML

19 Extract of Executive Council Meeting, *American Federationist* X (June 1903), 506-7; also *Toronto Globe,* 28 April 1903, 5

20 Gompers informed Draper of the carrying out of this provision in a letter on 9 May 1903 GL.

21 AFL Proceedings (1903), 252

22 See chap. 1, 3-6.

23 Mulock to Laurier, 4 April 1903, Laurier Papers, Correspondence, PAC

24 R.J. Younge, Secretary, Canadian Manufacturers' Association, to Laurier, 29 May 1903, in Laurier Papers, Correspondence, PAC

25 Mulock to Laurier, 4 April 1903, in Laurier Papers, Correspondence, PAC. See also the form letter protesting the Lougheed bill which was submitted by several Montreal locals in May 1903; Local 1 of Building Laborers' Union, Montreal, to Laurier, 14 May 1903; United Garment Workers' Local 209, Montreal, to Laurier, 9 May 1903, in ibid.

26 See Editorial in *American Federationist* X (May 1903), 470.

27 Gompers to A.W. Puttee, 14 May 1903 GL *Winnipeg Voice,* 8 May 1903, 1

28 Toronto Globe, 29 April 1903, 1; 30 April 1903, 14; 1 May 1903, 12

29 *Montreal Herald,* 30 April 1903, 7

30 *Toronto Globe,* 1 May 1903, 12; *Montreal Herald,* 1 May 1903, 1

31 *Toronto Globe,* 1 May 1903, 12

32 *Montreal Herald,* 1 May 1903, 1

33 *Toronto Globe,* 23 April 1903, 6

34 See, for example, the editorial in *Industrial Canada* IV (August 1903), 13. The attacks began during hearings on the union label bill earlier in the year.

35 Gompers to Flett, 2 June 1903 GL

36 Gompers to S.L. Landers, 11 June 1903 GL; AFL *Proceedings* (1903), 64-5

37 Canada, Parliament, Senate Committee on Banking and Commerce, 'Report of the Proceedings at the Meeting ... dealing w/Hon. Mr. Lougheed's Bill ...' (Toronto 1903), in Borden Papers, File Folder no. 167, PAC

38 Ibid., 1-4

39 Ibid., 8, 20; emphasis added

40 Gompers to International Unions, 13 July 1903; Gompers to Flett, 28 July 1903 GL

41 Canada, Parliament, Royal Commission on Industrial Disputes in the Province of British Columbia, 'Report,' *Sessional Papers,* 1903, no. 36a, 68

42 Gompers to Flett, 12 September 1903 GL

43 TLC *Proceedings* (1903), 10; (1904), 29

44 AFL *Proceedings* (1903), 22

45 *Montreal Herald,* 1 May 1903, 1

CHAPTER 9

1 *American Federationist* X (February 1903), 117; *Labour Gazette* IV (February 1904), 753. See the correlations between American and Canadian business cycles made by Keith A.J. Hay in 'Early Twentieth Century Business Cycles in Canada,' *Canadian Journal of Economics and Political Science* XXXII (August 1966), 363

2 Morrison to Draper, 8 March 1909 ML

3 *American Federationist* XX (August 1913), 632; *Labour Gazette* XV (December 1914), 640

4 Quoted in S.D. Clark, *The Canadian Manufacturers' Association* (Toronto 1939), 44n

5 *Industrial Canada* IX (October 1908), 182

6 Canada, Parliament, Senate, *Debates*, 16 March 1909, 161-7; *Toronto Globe*
25 September 1909, 7; TLC *Proceedings* (1909), 11-12, 58
7 Canada, Parliament, Senate, *Debates*, 20 April 1910, 617; 26 April 1910,
676-7
8 Ibid., 3 May 1910, 917
9 AFL *Proceedings* (1910), 54; *Toronto Globe*, 11 September 1912, 1
10 AFL *Proceedings* (1914), 247-8
11 *Industrial Canada* IV (August 1908), 13
12 *Canadian Annual Review*, 1903, 556-7; *Industrial Canada* IV (September
1903), 59. Preston embarrassed the government enough for Mulock to ask
Sifton: 'Would it not be possible for you to prevent Mr. Preston appearing in
evidence before the public in this manner?' Mulock to Sifton, 11 August
1904, Sifton Papers, PAC
13 *American Federationist* XI (July 1904), 611; *Labour Gazette* IV (June
1904), 1225; International Typographical Union, *Typographical Journal*
XXVII (January 1906), 113; Memorandum to Sifton from the deputy
Minister, 6 May 1902, in Sifton Papers, PAC
14 Mulock to Sifton, 24 October 1902, Sifton Papers, PAC; *Labour Gazette* VII
(April 1907), 1115
15 *American Federationist* XVI (March 1909), 261; TLC *Proceedings* (1914),
20
16 AFL *Proceedings* (1914), 244; Gompers to Draper, 8 February 1914;
Gompers to P. Nowack, 16 February 1914; Draper to Gompers, 12 February
1914 GL
17 Quoted in Lloyd G. Reynolds, *The British Immigrant: His Social and
Economic Adjustment in Canada* (Toronto 1936), 163; see also *Labour
Gazette* V (November 1904), 503
18 AFL *Proceedings* (1912), 216
19 AFL *Proceedings* (1907), 139; W.T. Dunlap to Morrison, 31 January 1914
ML; *American Federationist* XIV (October 1907), 793; XVII (April 1910),
309; *Toronto Globe*, 12 September 1907, 3
20 Portland *Oregonian*, 10 September 1907, as quoted in the *Globe* of 11
September 1907; Morrison to C.O. Young, 16 September 1907 ML. Young
had been present at the riots. See also Robert E. Wynne, 'American Labour
Leaders and the Vancouver Anti-Oriental Riot,' *Pacific Northwest Quarterly*
LVII (October 1966), 172-9, which exonerates the labour leaders; for an
account written by one of the AFL observers, see Grant Hamilton,
'Canadian Anti-Asiatic Demonstration,' *American Federationist* XIV
(November 1907) 866-9
21 TLC *Proceedings* (1904), 12

22 Morrison to Flett, 2 December 1908 ML; Morrison to Louis La Porta, Montreal, 25 April 1911 ML. See also Morrison to Flett, 29 May 1906, 8 July 1907 ML

23 'Just at the moment that we think that we have covered the ground and built a wall around ourselves by organizing our workers,' John Bruce told the AFL, 'we find that there is another influx of workers due to the changing seasons and the immigration policy.' AFL *Proceedings* (1912), 216

24 *Labour Gazette* VII (February 1907), 887, 922; IX (December 1908), 606; VII (May 1907), 1184; VIII (July 1907), 65; VII (February 1908), 981; Gompers to G.W. Gibson, 18 July 1911 GL; TLC *Proceedings* (1912), 55

25 J.W. Patterson, in CFL *Proceedings* (1909), 3; statement to the press, 14 September 1910, in Gompers Files, Reel 4, AFL-CIO Archives. The next year the Department of Labour still counted 232 Canadian locals unaffiliated with international unions, and the number remained virtually the same in 1914 (234 locals). *Labour Gazette* XI (April 1911), 1090; Dept. of Labour, *Report on Labour Organization in Canada* (1914), 193

26 Indirect evidence suggests that Flett exchanged a significant amount of confidential correspondence with Gompers and Morrison in which personalities and politics were discussed. Some of the talk spilled over into 'official' letters and was preserved in the Letterbooks, but only two confidential letters were discovered in the microfilmed records of the AFL-CIO. Both are in Flett's handwriting.

27 Gompers to Flett, 27 April, 8 May 1907 GL; Morrison to Flett, 8 January 1908 ML

28 Morrison to Flett, 17 August 1909 ML. For the strike activities of Flett, see Morrison to Flett, 7, 13, 27, 30 July, 10, 17, 24, 25 August, 13 September, 25 October 1909 ML. See also Morrison to Gompers 9 July 1909; Morrison to Executive Council, 17 July 1909 ML

29 Morrison to Flett, 14 January 1913 ML. Flett's locale was revealed in his weekly correspondence with Morrison during the period.

30 Gompers to Flett, 24 July 1903 GL

31 Gompers to Flett, 24 July 1903; Harry Corcoran to Gompers, quoted in Gompers to Flett, 13 January 1904 GL; Morrison to Flett, 20 June 1904 ML

32 Morrison to Flett, 21, 23, 30, 31 March, 12, 15 April, 10 May 1905; Morrison to Reid, 12 April 1905 ML

33 Morrison to Reid, 22 April 1905 ML; also R.L. Guard to Flett, 18 April 1905 GL; Morrison to Flett, 19 April 1905 ML

34 Morrison to Flett, 3, 8 (telegram) May 1905 ML; Morrison to Reid, 10 May 1905, in Gompers Files, Reel 6, AFL-CIO Archives; *Labour Gazette* VI (October 1905), 415

35 Gompers to Hugh Robinson, 3 January 1906 GL; Morrison to Flett, 20 October 1905, 28 May 1907 ML

36 Morrison to H. Gregory, Sydney, 15 December 1909; Morrison to Flett, 15 December 1909, 31 January, 7 February 1911 ML: Morrison to P.J. McArdle, 15 December 1909 ML: *American Federationist* XVII (January 1910), 72; Morrison to Draper, 17 June 1910 ML; Gompers to J.R. Martin, Sydney, 7 July, 29 August 1911 GL

37 TLC *Proceedings* (1905), 27; *Toronto Globe*, 23 September 1905, 20

38 John Moffatt, 'History of the Provincial Workmen's Association,' type-written manuscript, ND, in Department of Labour Library, Ottawa; Eugene Forsey, *Economic and Social Aspects of the Nova Scotia Coal Industry* (Toronto 1926), 19

39 TLC *Proceedings* (1903), 20; (1904), 25, 55; (1905), 11; *Labour Gazette* IV (November 1903), 378; Provincial Workmen's Association, Minutes of the Proceedings of the Grand Council, 12 September 1905, 497

40 Sheehan to Gompers, 30 June 1905, in a letter from Gompers to Flett, 12 July 1906 GL

41 Provincial Workmen's Association, Minutes of the Proceedings of the Grand Council, 17 September 1907, 642; 21 May 1908, NP

42 TLC *Proceedings* (1908), 78; *Toronto Globe*, 26 September 1908, 23; J.B. McLachlan to Eugene Forsey, 4 March 1926, cited in Forsey's *Economic and Social Aspects of the Nova Scotia Coal Industry*, 22

43 *Labour Gazette* IX (May 1909), 1226

44 Department of Labour, *Report on Labour Organization in Canada* (1914), 81-2; G.H. Duggan, Gen. Mgr., Dominion Coal Company, to Laurier, 14 July 1909, in Laurier Papers Correspondence, PAC

45 Canada, Parliament, Senate, *Debates*, 3 May 1910, 916; *Canadian Annual Review*, 1909, 300

46 Toronto District Labor Council, Minutes, 15 July 1909; *Toronto Globe*, 25 September 1909, 7

47 AFL *Proceedings* (1911), 212, 352

48 Moffatt, 'History of the Provincial Workmen's Association,' 5-6; also Forsey, *Economic and Social Aspects of the Nova Scotia Coal Industry*, 28; TLC *Proceedings* (1914), 80. The UMW successfully absorbed the Nova Scotia coal miners after World War I.

49 TLC *Proceedings* (1903), 47

50 For background on the rise of confessional unionism, see Arthur Saint-Pierre, *L'Organisation Ouvrière dans la Province de Québec* (Montreal 1913); Omer Heroux, *Le Mouvement ouvrier catholique au Canada: lettre de Sa Grandeur Mgr. Cloutier, Évêque des Trois-Rivières* [Montreal (1919?)];

M.-Ludovic Maltais, *Les syndicats catholiques canadiens* (Washington 1925); Allan Latham, *The Catholic and National Trade Unions of Canada* (Toronto 1930); André Roy, 'Histoire du syndicalisme au Canada,' *Relations Industrielles* XII (January-April 1957), 11-21; Jean Hulliger, *L'Enseignement social des Évêques canadiens de 1891 à 1950* (Montreal 1958); Michel Tétu, 'Les premiers syndicats catholiques canadiens, 1900-1921' (PHD dissertation, University of Montreal, 1961); Joseph Levitt, *Henri Bourassa and the Golden Calf* (Ottawa 1972), chap. 9; P.E. Trudeau, 'La Province de Québec au moment de la grève,' in Trudeau, ed., *La Grève de l'amiante* (Montreal 1956), 10-84

51 Hulliger, *L'Enseignement social*, 115; Levitt, *Henri Bourassa*, 99-100
52 *Toronto Globe*, 27 April 1903, 9
53 *Ottawa Citizen*, 29 April 1903, 3; Morrison to Flett, 13 February 1906; Morrison to Paul Dumont, 10 December 1907 ML
54 Report of the Quebec executive committee in TLC *Proceedings* (1905), 25-6
55 Copy of Tobin's letter in Gompers to Flett, 4 September 1903; Gompers to Flett, 17 July 1907 GL; *Canadian Annual Review*, 1909, 305; Morrison to Draper, 3 March 1905 ML. The Canadian union still claimed 1006 members in 3 branches in 1914; see Department of Labour, *Report on Labour Organization in Canada* (1914), 193
56 Morrison to Hugh Robinson, 11 June 1907 ML. By 'one-languaged' he obviously meant English-speaking.
57 TLC *Proceedings* (1908), 24
58 Morrison to Flett, 23 September 1908 ML
59 Morrison to Ainey, 18 August 1909 ML. See also Morrison to R.P. Pettipiece, 3 May 1909; Morrison to Draper, 6 May, 20 July, 18 August 1909; Morrison to Ainey, 20 July 1909; Morrison to Executive Council, September 3 1909 ML
60 Morrison to Ainey, 28 September 1909 ML
61 Morrison to Ainey, 18 September, 5, 26, 27 (telegram) October, 15 December 1909; Morrison to John Golden, 5 October 1909; Morrison to Flett, 3 January 1910 ML; Gompers to Hugh Robinson, 18 October 1909 GL; Morrison to M. Walsh, 30 December 1909 ML
62 Morrison to Flett, 12 January 1910 ML. Also Morrison to Flett, 10 January 1910; Morrison to Draper, 10 January 1910; Morrison to Ainey, 10 January 1910 ML
63 Morrison to Flett, 28 January 1910 ML. Also Morrison to Flett, 21, 25 January 1910 ML
64 Morrison to Flett, 1, 3, 8 February, 1, 2 March 1910 ML; Morrison to Napoleon Labreche, 13 April 1910 ML

65 TLC *Proceedings* (1910), 84; Morrison to David Giroux, 7 February 1910; Morrison to Ainey, 9 February 1910 ML
66 Morrison to Flett, 18 April 1911 ML. On the other hand, it appears that 4 per cent of the Federation's members lived in Canada in 1911 but received only 1.7 per cent of the AFL's total disbursements. The Federation collected at least $3000 *more* that year from Canadians than it paid out in the form of services. See Appendix 2.
67 Morrison to Flett, 2 February 1911 ML
68 Quoted in a letter by Morrison to B.A. Larger, 21 March 1911 ML. See also Morrison to Flett, 28 February, 21 March 1911 ML
69 Morrison to Flett, 13 May 1911 ML
70 TLC *Proceedings* (1911), 36, 76; (1912), 37; CFL *Proceedings* (1912), 7, 11; Joseph Levitt, *Henri Bourassa and the Golden Calf* (Ottawa 1972), 101-3, 106-7; see also Morrison to Flett, 4 October 1911, 30 March, 2 April, 13 June 1912 ML
71 Arthur Saint-Pierre, *L'Organisation Ouvrière*, 33-4; M.-L. Maltais, *Les Syndicats*, chap. 1; C. Brian Williams, 'Canadian-American Trade Union Relations' (PHD dissertation, Cornell University, 1964), 334
72 Latham, *Catholic and National Trade Unions*, 46; Saint-Pierre, *L'Organisation Ouvrière*, 14-17
73 Quoted in Latham, *Catholic and National Trade Unions*, 8-9
74 Saint-Pierre, *L'Organisation Ouvrière*, 38; Hulliger, *L'Enseignement Social*, 121-2; Maltais, *les Syndicats*, chap. 3; Latham, *Catholic and National Trade Unions*, 43-4. The Department of Labour listed only 900 members in the Corporation, and 1948 in the *Federation Ouvrière Mutuelle du Nord* in 1914 [*Report on Labour Organization in Canada* (1914), 193], but there may have been other independent locals in the ranks of confessional unions.
75 Frank Duffy to Cardinal Gibbons, 9 April 1912; Cardinal Gibbons to Duffy, 11 April 1912, in Gompers Files, Reel 6, AFL-CIO Archives
76 James Kirby to Gompers, 14 October 1913, in National Union Files, Reel 2
77 Morrison to Brunet, 17 September 1913 ML. See also G. Francq to Morrison, 4 April, 5 May 1913; Morrison to Francq, 25 June 1913; Morrison to P. Leduc, 22 April 1913; Morrison to Draper, 14 May, 20 June 1913; Morrison to Brunet, 10 September 1913 ML; TLC *Proceedings* (1913), 104. Latham, *Catholic and National Trade Unions* (pp. 84-5) appears to have interviewed Brunet, probably in the late 1920s.
78 The circular, translated by Gustave Francq, was forwarded by Morrison to the Executive Council on 7 January 1914 ML (spelling and punctuation as in the original). 'Mr Arcant' was Narcisse Arcand, an organizer for the United Brotherhood of Carpenters.

79 TLC Proceedings (1913), 42-3; Gompers to C.H. Baine, 31 July 1916, Gompers Files, Reel 6, AFL-CIO Archives

80 AFL *Proceedings* (1913), 155, 197-9; Morrison to Draper, 24 December 1913; Morrison to G. Francq, 29 December 1913, 7 January 1914; Morrison to Brunet, 29 January, 6 February 1914 ML

81 Morrison to Brunet, 7, 17 March, 3, 29 April, 15 May, 3 June, 22 July, 23 October, 23 December 1914 ML; TLC *Proceedings* (1914), 24, 27

82 Morrison to Flett, 6 April 1904 ML; Gompers to Flett, 27 May 1904; William Digby to Gompers, copy in Gompers to Flett, 27 May 1904 GL

83 (Chatham) Morrison to Flett, 3 May, 8 July 1904; (Thorold) Morrison to Flett, 28 October 1905, 7 February 1907, 5 April 1909 ML; (Lindsay) Morrison to Senator George McHugh, 3 April 1909 ML; Gompers to Flett, 29 February 1904 GL

84 Gompers to Flett, 30 November, 3, 10 December 1903, 9 February 1904, 4 May 1908; R.L. Guard to Flett, 5 September 1905, Gompers to Edward Glockling, 4 January 1904 GL; Morrison to Flett, 31 May, 6, 28 August 1904 ML

85 *American Federationist* X (April 1903), 293. See also *American Federationist* X (January 1903), 35; X (February 1903), 117

86 Morrison to Flett, 6, 28 August 1907 ML

87 Morrison to Flett, 9 November 1905, 3 April (telegram), 12 April 1911; Morrison to Fred Dickinson, 25 March, 4, 15 April 1911 ML

88 *Canadian Annual Review*, 1908, 112; *American Federationist* XV (March 1908), 293

89 Quoted in T.R. Loosmore, 'The British Columbia Labor Movement and Political Action' (MA thesis, University of British Columbia, 1954), 192

90 TLC *Proceedings* (1903), 32, 50-1. See also George Bartley to Gompers, 13 March 1903 GL.

91 Gompers to Draper, 27 July 1903 GL. See also TLC *Proceedings* (1903), 30

92 Gompers to officers and members, Western Federation of Miners, 19 May 1903; AFL Executive Council to Denver Trades and Labor Assembly, 27 April 1903 GL. Gompers' letter was carried to the Miners' convention by John Lennon.

93 Department of Labour, *Report on Labour Organization in Canada* (1914), 94-5; C.B. Williams, 'Canadian-American Trade Union Relations,' 185-7; *Labour Gazette* V (February 1905), 878; V (September 1904), 306; IV (January 1904), 645; *American Federationist* XV (August 1908), 628; XI (May 1904), 430; J.A. Hobson, *Canada To-Day* (London 1906), 32-3

94 Gompers to Stamper, 8 August 1904; also Gompers to Stamper, 22 January, 2, 13, 15, 17, 21, 25, 27, 29 June, 1 July 1904 GL

95 Morrison to R.P. Pettipiece, 28 January, 28 February 1908 ML
96 Morrison to Flett, 16 July 1904; also Morrison to Flett, 8, 27 July 1904 ML; Gompers to Flett, 22 September 1904 GL
97 Morrison to Flett, 13 January 1905 ML
98 Gompers to Flett, 2 July 1906 GL; *American Federationist* XIII (August 1906), 563
99 Morrison to Flett, 12 July 1906; also Morrison to Flett, 6 July 1906 ML; TLC *Proceedings* (1907), 62; P.W. Fox, 'Early Socialism in Canada,' in *The Political Process in Canada* ed. J.H. Aitchison (Toronto 1963), 85
100 Morrison to Flett, 16 August 1906; also 15 October, 13 December 1906 ML
101 *American Federationist* XVII (January 1910), 72. See also *American Federationist* XVI (February 1909), 179; TLC *Proceedings* (1912), 53
102 *American Federationist* XVI (November 1909), 990; Morrison to R.P. Pettipiece, 7 March 1910; Morrison to James Somerville, 19 February 1910 ML. Somerville amused Morrison with a comment that 'if we survive the year 1910 the future can hold no terrors worth mentioning.' First Gompers' 'jail sentence hanging overhead, then the Comet in May, followed by the home coming of Teddy the Strenuous in the month of June.' Morrison to Somerville, 24 February 1910 ML
103 Morrison to Flett, 19 April 1910 ML
104 Morrison to Flett, 17 May, 8, 24 June, 7, 27 July, 3, 4, 10 August 1910 ML
105 Morrison to Flett, 11 August 1910; also Morrison to Flett, 23, 25 August, 10, 15 September, 8, 29 October 1910 ML
106 Morrison to Flett, 12, 14 October, 5, 16 December 1910 ML
107 *Labour Gazette* XII (July 1911), 78; American Federation of Labor, *Weekly News Letter,* I no. 17 (1911); Morrison to L.H. Burnham, 23 August 1912; Morrison to C.O. Young, 12 September 1912 ML
108 Gompers, *Seventy Years of Life and Labor* (New York 1925), I, 426. The date of Gompers' visit is established in Morrison to Pettipiece, 27 July 1911 ML. The Department of Labour's *Report on Labour Organization in Canada* for the years 1911-14 shows IWW strength in Canada as follows: 1911-9 locals with 3995 members; 1912, 12 locals with 5000; 1913, 13 locals with 1000; 1914, 3 locals with 465 members.
109 AFL *Proceedings* (1912), 218; Morrison to Pettipiece, 19 February, 29 April, 14 October, 5 December 1912; Morrison to George Heatherton, 16, 27 February, 19 June 1914, 4 February, 9, 16 March, 17, 21, 27 April 1914 ML. For RCMP activities, see Albert Fernet, W.H. Douglas, and Harry La Branch to R.L. Borden, 4 January 1914; Borden to W.D. Scott, ND;

Scott to A.E. Bount, 17 January 1914, in Borden Papers, RLC Series 244, PAC

110 Appendix 1 lists international union membership in Canada in 1914.

CHAPTER 10

1 Morrison to Draper, 20 June 1907, 18 May, 8 July 1908; Morrison to McHugh, 18 May 1908 ML; Gompers to Draper, 11 July 1911 GL

2 Morrison to Flett, 13 July, 10 October 1905; Morrison to R.G. Forsey, 22 July 1905 ML; *American Federationist* XII (November 1905), 862-3; Gompers to Walter Shufflebotham, 23 December 1903, 1 February, 3 November 1904, 10 January, 19 October, 9 November 1905; Gompers to Flett, 15 December 1904, 19 October, 9 November 1905; Gompers to E. Villard, 10 January 1905 GL

3 Secretary, Toronto District Labor Council, to George Haines, 16 October 1905, Toronto Council Letterbook; Toronto District Labor Council, Minutes, 2 November 1905, 18 January 1906; Gompers to Flett, 26 January 1906 GL

4 Secretary, Toronto District Labor Council, to Flett, 2 February 1906, Toronto Council Letterbook. See also Gompers to Flett, 14 February 1906 GL, and Toronto District Labor Council, Minutes, 15 March 1906

5 Morrison to Flett, 4 September 1912 ML. See also Morrison to Flett, 1, 16 July, 1, 9, 21, 29 August, 13 September, 10 October 1912; Morrison to Frank Duffy, 25 June, 16, 26 July 1912 ML; Duffy to Morrison, 27 June 1912, National Union Files, Reel 2

6 Thomas Atkinson to Gompers, 8 December 1905, National Union Files, Reel 3; *Labour Gazette* V (April 1905), 1045; V (January 1905), 734; AFL *Proceedings* (1911), 119; Department of Labour, *Report on Labour Organization in Canada* (1913), 18-20

7 W.A. Cole to Gompers, 23 August 1912, National Union Files, Reel 3

8 L.H. Burnham to Gompers, 17 August 1912, National Union Files, Reel 3

9 Morrison to Flett (telegram), 17 May 1911 ML; Toronto District Labor Council, Minutes, 5 September 1912

10 Resolution introduced by J.W. Wilkinson and W.F. Gilmore at AFL Building Trades Department *Proceedings* (1911), 97. The motion was defeated, 110-11

11 TLC *Proceedings* (1911), 24

12 Ibid., 73-4; AFL *Proceedings* (1911), 176

13 TLC *Proceedings* (1912), 68; *Toronto Globe*, 12 September 1912, 7

14 Ibid.
15 AFL *Proceedings* (1912), 200
16 Flett to Morrison, 6 October 1912, National Union Files, Reel 3
17 Morley Clark to Morrison, 4 October 1912, National Union Files, Reel 3
18 Flett to Morrison, 6 October 1912, National Union Files, Reel 3; Toronto District Labor Council, Minutes, 19 September, 3, 31 October 1912; Morrison to Flett, 8 October 1912; Morrison to Clark, 16 October 1912 ML. See also J.H.H. Ballantyne to Morrison, 12 October 1912, National Union Files, Reel 3
19 TLC *Proceedings* (1913), 46
20 Extract from Minutes of Executive Council meeting, January 20-5, 1913, National Union Files, Reel 3; Morrison to Ballantyne, 13 February 1913, Ibid.; Toronto District Labor Council, Minutes, 20 February 1913. See also *American Federationist* XX (March 1913), 241
21 TLC Executive Council to W.W. Young, 4 April 1913, in TLC *Proceedings* (1913), 27-8, emphasis in original
22 Young to Draper, 11 April 1913; Draper to Young, 19 April 1913; Young to Draper, 25 April 1913, in TLC *Proceedings* (1913), 27-31; Morrison to Draper, 17 May 1913 ML
23 TLC *Proceedings* (1912), 18, 82-3, 110
24 Ibid. (1913), 15, 107, 127, 130; Gompers to officers of all locals, 8 January 1914 National Union Files, Reel 2
25 TLC *Proceedings* (1913), 140, 147; (1914), 9-10
26 AFL *Proceedings* (1914), 246
27 *Labour Gazette* IV (November 1903), 517; Gompers to Burleigh, 29 January 1904 GL; Morrison to Flett, 10 February, 6 July, 8, 28 August, 6 September, 6 October 1905 ML
28 TLC *Proceedings* (1906), 54-5, 79; Morrison to George Warren, 2 May 1907; Morrison to Executive Council, 7 January 1908 ML
29 Morrison to Draper, 31 January 1908; Morrison to Flett, 31 January, 14 February, 30 March, 29 April 1908 ML; Gompers to Flett, 26 August 1908 GL
30 Morrison to Flett, 9 March 1909 ML. See also Morrison to Flett, 23 February, 2 March, 2 June 1909 ML; Toronto District Labor Council, Minutes, 4 March, 1 April 1909; Department of Labour, *Report on Labour Organization in Canada* (1914), 41-3
31 Morrison to Flett, 25 September 1909; Morrison to Executive Council, 3 September 1909 ML
32 Toronto District Labor Council, Minutes, 2, 16 September, 6 October 1909; Morrison to Flett, 20, 29 September, 13 October 1909 ML; Morrison to Ainey, 27 August, 8, 15, 28 September 1909; Morrison to G.R. Brunet, 15 October 1909 ML

33 AFL *Proceedings* (1909), 78-82; Morrison to W.R. Rollo, 27 April 1910; Morrison to Executive Council, 18 May 1910; Morrison to Flett, 16 September 1910, 22 March 1912, 7, 11 September, 24 October, 16 December 1912, 8 December 1913; Morrison to R.A. Stoney, 29 April 1911; Morrison to Charles P. Ford, 11 September 1912; Morrison to V.R. Midgley, 12 February 1913; Morrison to P.J. McNulty, 11, 21 August 1913 ML; TLC *Proceedings* (1911), 42; (1914), 83, 120; Toronto District Labor Council, Minutes, 19 October 1911, 16 July, 7 August, 3 September 1914; Gompers to Flett, 4 January 1913 GL

34 Gompers to J.M. Lynch, 16 February 1904; Gompers to C.S.O. Boudreault, 17 February 1904 GL; Morrison to Draper, 30 March 1904 ML. Boudreault's activities at Berlin are discussed in chapter 7.

35 Morrison to C.S.O. Boudreault, 7 April 1904; Morrison to Draper, 12 April 1904 ML; Gompers to Todd, 5 May 1904; Gompers to Ed. A. O'Dell, 5 May 1904 GL. O'Dell was Canadian organizer for the Boot and Shoe Workers' Union.

36 Morrison to Boudreault, 18, 23 June, 19 July 1904; Morrison to Draper, 30 July 1904 ML; Gompers to Draper, 24 June 1904 GL

37 E. Empey to Gompers, quoted in Gompers to Flett, 10 April 1905 GL

38 AFL *Proceedings* (1906), 57; *Canadian Annual Review,* 1906, 302

39 *Ottawa Citizen,* 2 October 1906, 10. See also 3 October 1906, 6.

40 Morrison to Flett, 22 July 1908 ML. See also Morrison to Flett, 26 October 1906 ML; TLC *Proceedings* (1907), 70; *Ottawa Citizen,* 17 July 1908, 2

41 (Toronto) Morrison to Flett, 19, 29 January, 12, 19, 20 February 1912; Morrison to Draper, 19, 29, January 1912 ML; (St Thomas) TLC *Proceedings* (1912), 65-6; Morrison to Flett, 23 April 1914; Morrison to Draper, 9 May 1914 ML

42 CFL *Proceedings* (1913), 14. See also *Toronto Globe,* 5 November 1909, 16; Toronto District Labor Council, Minutes, 18 March 1909; CFL *Proceedings* (1910-1914), passim.

CHAPTER 11

1 Quoted in Canadian Congress of Labour, *Labour's Program for Political Action* (Toronto ND), 4

2 *Canadian Annual Review,* 1906, 294-5; Draper to King, 17 December 1906, in King Papers, Correspondence, Primary Series, vol. 5, 4616

3 *Labour Gazette* V (July 1904), 112-13; also TLC *Report of John G. O'Donoghue* (Ottawa 1904), 13, in Borden Papers, File Folder no. 167, PAC; TLC *Proceedings* (1909), 53

4 President Verville of the Trades Congress showed Smith two affidavits taken from Lethbridge miners who complained that the RCMP had drawn their guns without provocation. Smith wrote to Laurier: 'Mr. Verville intends to read them in the House today, when taking up the orders of the day, and I wanted you to be fully aware of this before his doing so.' Smith to Laurier, 25 March 1906, Laurier Papers, Correspondence, PAC

5 Smith to Laurier, 13 July 1904; Laurier to Smith, 1 August 1904, ibid.; TLC *Report of John G. O'Donoghue* (Ottawa 1905), 7

6 TLC Proceedings (1903), 3; (1904), 18; *Report of John G. O'Donoghue* (Ottawa 1904), 18-19

7 TLC *Report of John G. O'Donoghue*, (Ottawa 1905), 10

8 *The Race Question in Canada* (Toronto 1966 ed.), 167

9 TLC *Proceedings* (1903), 23, 56, 59, (1904), 9; AFL *Proceedings* (1904), 91. Although Gad Horowitz claims that 'Gompers' rejection of socialism and independent political action (that is, a labour party) was complete and unequivocal,' the evidence in AFL-CIO archives clearly indicates only his rejection of socialism, at least in regard to Canadian labour politics. See Horowitz, *Canadian Labour in Politics* (Toronto 1968), 58.

10 Siegfried, *Race Question,* 170-1

11 TLC Proceedings (1905), 15; *Toronto Globe,* 19 September 1905, 9

12 Toronto District Labor Council, Minutes, 6 July, 17 November 1905; TLC *Proceedings* (1905), 48; *Toronto Globe,* 22 September 1905, 6; 25 September 1905, 8

13 Toronto District Labor Council, Minutes, 15 February, 1, 15 March, 11, 19 April 1906. See also chapter 6 in Martin Robin's *Radical Politics and Canadian Labour* (Kingston 1968).

14 [John G. O'Donoghue], Memorandum, in Borden Papers, File Folder no. 167, PAC

15 Margaret Ormsby, *British Columbia: A History* (Vancouver 1958), 336; Smith to Senator Templeman, 9 October 1903, in Laurier Papers, Correspondence, PAC

16 *New York Times,* 7 May 1905, 22; Gompers to George Bartley, 8 April 1903 GL

17 T.J. Mahoney, in AFL *Proceedings* (1904), 198

18 *Toronto Globe,* 21 September 1905, 11; *Winnipeg Tribune,* 23 September 1907, 3; obituary in *Labour Gazette* XXXVIII (October 1938), 1075-6; Henry Morgan, *The Canadian Men and Women of the Time* (Toronto 1912 ed.), 1025; *Western Clarion,* 20 May 1905, cited in Jacqueline F. Cahan, 'A Survey of Political Activities of the Ontario Labour Movement, 1850-1935,' MA thesis, University of Toronto, 1945, 26-7

19 Gompers to Flett, 29 October, 9 December 1903 GL
20 Gompers to Flett, 22 September 1904 GL; *Toronto Globe,* 22 September 1904, 2; 23 September 1904, 8; TLC *Proceedings* (1904), 52
21 *Toronto Globe,* 20 September 1905, 8; 22 September 1905, 6; TLC *Proceedings* (1905), 45-6
22 Morrison to Flett, 3 May, 31 August 1905 ML
23 *Canadian Annual Review,* 1906, 301; P.W. Fox, 'Early Socialism in Canada,' 83; Morrison to Flett, 1 February, 27, 28 March, 6 April, 1 May 1906 ML; Flett to Gompers, 14 January 1906 GL; Toronto District Labor Council, Minutes, 5 April 1906
24 *Canadian Annual Review,* 1907, 281-2; Morrison to C. Boyle, 12 April 1906; Morrison to Flett, 12, 19 April 1906 ML
25 Morrison to Flett, 25 May 1906 ML
26 Morrison to Flett, 25 May, 1 June 1906; Morrison to Thomas H. Flynn, 5 July 1906 ML
27 Gompers to Draper, 8 August 1906; Gompers to W.D. Huber, president, United Brotherhood of Carpenters and Joiners, 8 August 1906 GL (identical letters were sent to officers of the Amalgamated Society of Carpenters and Joiners, Cigarmakers, Machinists, Maintenance-of-Way Employees, Mine Workers, Iron Molders, Musicians, Painters and Decorators, Piano and Organ Workers, Plumbers, Street Railwaymen, Tailors, Printers, Woodworkers, Longshoremen, Sheet Metal Workers, Electrical Workers, Garment Workers, Printing Pressmen, Hotel and Restaurant Employees, Barbers, Boilermakers, and Boot and Shoe Workers); AFL *Proceedings* (1906), 108
28 AFL *Text Book of Labor's Political Demands* (Washington 1906), 36; see also *American Federationist* XIII (May 1906), 293ff
29 AFL *Text Book of Labor's Political Demands* (Washington 1906), 9
30 TLC *Proceedings* (1906), 65
31 AFL *Text Book of Labor's Political Demands,* 36; see also 'The Politics of American and British Labor,' *Chautauquan* XLIV (November 1906), 281
32 Morrison to Flett, 27 February 1906 ML; see Draper's statement in Allied Trades and Labor Association, *Labor Day Souvenir* (Ottawa 1907), NP.
33 TLC *Proceedings* (1906), 7-8, 15, 49, 73
34 Ibid., 29, 65-6
35 *Victoria Times,* 18 September 1906, in Borden Papers, File Folder no. 167, PAC
36 *Winnipeg Free Press,* 21 September 1906, 1
37 Ibid., 22 September 1906, 5
38 Ibid.; *Winnipeg Tribune,* 26 September 1906, 6; *Western Clarion,* 6 October 1906, 1
39 Morrison to Flett, 28 September, 1 October 1906 ML

40 AFL *Proceedings* (1906), 110
41 *Canadian Annual Review,* 1906, 303-4; *Winnipeg Voice,* 19 October 1906
42 AFL *Proceedings* (1906), 127; T.R. Loosmore, 'The British Columbia Labor Movement and Political Action, 1879-1906,' MA thesis, University of British Columbia, 1954), 196-7, 199; *Canadian Annual Review,* 1906, 297
43 National Trades and Labor Congress *Proceedings* (1906), 27, (1907), 13; TLC *Proceedings* (1907), 17
44 Provincial Workmen's Association, Minutes of the Proceedings of the Grand Council, 18 September 1906, 542; 17 September 1907, 619; TLC *Proceedings* (1908), 26; C.A. Scotton, *Canadian Labour and Politics* (Ottawa 1967), 20
45 *The News* [*Winnipeg?*], 27 October 1906, segment in Borden Papers, File Folder no. 167; TLC *Proceedings* (1907), 23-4; (1908), 17; *Canadian Annual Review,* 1907, 287; Robin, *Radical Politics,* 87-90
46 TLC *Proceedings* (1907), 16; the platform of the Hamilton workers is given in *Canadian Annual Review,* 1906, 300.
47 Morrison to Flett, 28 March 1907 ML
48 *Toronto Globe,* 30 March 1907, 1
49 Ibid., 1-2
50 Smith to Mrs Winkworth, 10 April 1907, in Goldwin Smith, *A Selection From Goldwin Smith's Correspondence,* ed. Arnold Haultain (London 1913), 484; *Toronto Globe,* 1 April 1907, 4; Morrison to Flett, 10 April 1907 ML
51 Morrison to Executive Council, 10 April 1907 ML
52 Toronto District Labor Council, Minutes, 20 June, 5, 26 December 1907, 2, 16 January, 20 February, 16 April, [undecipherable date, May], 21 May, 1 October 1908
53 *Toronto Globe,* 23 September 1907, 2; TLC *Proceedings* (1907), 77-8; Morrison to Flett, 28 September 1907 ML
54 Gompers to Flett, 29 May 1908 GL; Morrison to Flett, 28 December 1908 ML
55 TLC *Proceedings* (1908), 2, 12, 24; *Winnipeg Voice,* 12 June 1908, 1
56 TLC *Proceedings* (1908), 80-1
57 *Toronto Globe,* 22 September 1908, 3; AFL *Proceedings* (1908), 132
58 24 September 1908, 9; Robin, *Radical Politics,* 91
59 David Shannon, *The Socialist Party of America* (Chicago 1967 ed.), 62-7, 76; Robin, *Radical Politics,* chap. 8, 104-18
60 TLC *Convention Souvenir* (Ottawa 1914), 23-5
61 Alfred Charpentier, 'Le mouvement politique ouvrier de Montréal,' *Relations Industrielles* X (March 1955), 85; TLC *Proceedings* (1910), 4, 22, 24, 30, 48, 53; *American Federationist* XVII (February 1910), 162; (March 1910), 259, 322; XIX (March 1912), 242

62 TLC *Proceedings* (1910), 12, 71, 78; BC Federation of Labor *Proceedings* (1912), 66; TLC *Proceedings* (1912), 19; See also Morrison to Flett, 24 May 1910; Morrison to Draper, 26 January, 24, 31 May 1910; Morrison to Executive Council, 31 May 1910 ML; TLC *Proceedings* (1914), 6

63 Toronto District Labor Council, Minutes, 14 December 1910; 1 August, 5 December 1912; Cahan, 'Political Activities,' 36; *Industrial Banner,* 9 January 1914, as quoted in Cahan; Toronto District Labor Council Minutes, 20 August 1913; 2, 16 April, 25 November 1914

64 TLC *Proceedings* (1910), 14, 44-5; (1911), 14, 70, 71, 91; (1913), 27

65 TLC *Proceedings* (1912), 7, 25; *Toronto Globe*, 10 September 1912, 4

66 TLC *Proceedings* (1913), 17, 107, 112, 118, 128; *Toronto Globe*, 26 September 1913, 2

67 Morrison to Flett, 7, 22 November, 14 December 1911 ML; AFL *Weekly News Letter* I (no. 35); (no. 39); Morrison to Flett, 16 June, 7 July 1914 ML

68 Morrison to Flett, 29 September 1909 ML; Flett to Gompers ('Personal') 3 October 1916, Gompers Files, Reel 8; see also Morrison to Flett, 1 October 1909, 18 August 1910, 10, 16 December 1912 ML; Morrison to C.O. Young, 7 October 1909 ML

69 AFL *Proceedings* (1909), 38; *American Federationist* XVII (March 1910), 225

70 *Toronto Globe,* 16 November 1909, 1; Morrison to Flett, 27 April, 20, 29 July 1910 ML; Duffy to Gompers, 29 August 1912, National Union Files, Reel 2

71 AFL *Proceedings* (1912), 220; (1913), 199

72 Morrison to Draper, 5 March 1913 ML; AFL *Proceedings* (1911), 58; TLC *Convention Souvenir* (Ottawa, 1914), 20

73 TLC *Convention Souvenir* (Ottawa 1914), 20-1

74 Report of fraternal delegates to the Congress convention, in Toronto District Labor Council, Minutes, 16 October 1913; TLC *Convention Souvenir* (Ottawa 1914), 21 (Draper)

75 *Industrial Canada* IX (December 1908), 428

CHAPTER 12

1 TLC *Proceedings* (1903), 42-3; *Toronto Globe,* 25 September 1903, 7

2 *Toronto Globe,* 25 September 1903, 7; Gompers to Flett, 6 October 1903 GL

3 Morrison to Flett, 26 August, 8 September, 5 October 1904 ML; AFL *Proceedings* (1904), 128

4 TLC *Proceedings* (1904), 47; (1905), 17, 34
5 TLC *Proceedings* (1906), 69
6 TLC *Proceedings* (1903), 49-50; (1908), 54
7 Morrison to Flett, 25 February 1905 ML; AFL *Proceedings* (1906), 14-15; *Toronto Globe,* 18 December 1908, 3
8 Morrison to Draper, 19 March, 3 April 1909 ML. See also Morrison to Ainey, 9 June 1909; Morrison to H.B. Archer, 2 September 1909; Morrison to E. Cadieux, 30 June 1909; Morrison to Geo. W. Zimmerman, 12 October 1910 ML
9 Morrison to R.H. Neelands, 19 April 1910 ML; Gompers to A. Letroadec, 29 April 1910 GL
10 Morrison to Draper, 14 June, 11 July 1910 ML
11 Morrison to Flett, 2 August 1910; Morrison to Christian Sivertz, 21 June 1910 ML
12 Toronto District Labor Council, Minutes, 4 August 1910; TLC *Proceedings* (1910), 12, 80
13 Morrison to Flett, 30 September, 15 October 1910; Morrison to Executive Council, 30 September 1910 ML
14 Flett to Morrison, undated, as quoted in Morrison to D. D'Alessandro, 22 October 1910; Morrison to Flett, 22 October, 4 November 1910 ML
15 AFL *Proceedings* (1910), 162-4; 168
16 Ibid., 270-1
17 Ibid., 271
18 Morrison to Flett, 13 December 1910 ML
19 TLC *Proceedings* (1911), 42-3, 14; (1912), 17, 71
20 Morrison to J.M. Ritchie, 2 April 1913; Morrison to Draper, 2 April 1913; Morrison to J.W. Burgess, 29 April 1913; Morrison to Draper, 15 May 1913 ML
21 AFL *Proceedings* (1903), 21; Gompers to Draper, 6 July 1903 GL
22 TLC *Proceedings* (1903), 52
23 Ibid.
24 AFL *Proceedings* (1903), 159; TLC *Proceedings* (1904), 28-9
25 TLC *Proceedings* (1904), 48
26 *American Federationist* XI (February 1904), 152; Gompers to Draper, 6 January 1904 GL; Morrison to Draper, 7 July 1905 ML
27 Morrison to Draper, 3, 31 March 1905 ML
28 Gompers to International Unions, 23 May 1905 GL; Morrison to Ralph V. Brandt, 11 June 1907 ML
29 TLC *Proceedings* (1905), 60; Morrison to Draper, 22 January, 30 March 1906 ML

30 Morrison to Draper, 9 July 1906 ML; TLC *Proceedings* (1906), 8
31 Morrison to Executive Council, 15 June 1907 ML; Frank Duffy to Morrison, 28 September 1907, National Union Files, Reel 2
32 Morrison to Ralph V. Brandt, 11 June 1907. The same letter was sent to other international union heads.
33 AFL *Proceedings* (1907), 213; TLC *Proceedings* (1907), 11, 55, 64
34 Quoted in Morrison to Gompers, 25 October 1907 ML
35 Morrison to Flett, 28 September, 25, 29 October 1907; (telegram) 14 November 1907 ML
36 TLC *Proceedings* (1908), 59-61
37 TLC *Proceedings* (1908), 62; Gompers to Simpson, 11 January 1908 GL
38 *Toronto Globe,* 23 September 1908, 2
39 Gompers to Flett, 29 May 1908 GL
40 See Flett to Gompers, (marked 'Personal'), 3 October 1916, Gompers Files, Reel 5, in which Draper is called a 'straight line, "pure and simple" unionist'
41 Morrison to Christian Sivertz, 8 February 1908 ML
42 *Toronto Globe,* 21 September 1907, 5
43 Morrison to Flett, 16 September 1908 ML
44 TLC *Proceedings* (1908), 55-7
45 *Toronto Globe,* 7 May 1909, 5; see also Gompers to Flett, 14 April 1909; Morrison to Flett, 4, 13 May 1909 ML
46 *Toronto Globe,* 9 November 1909, 1
47 AFL *Proceedings* (1909), 6
48 *Toronto Globe,* 9 November 1909, 4; AFL *Proceedings* (1909), 7
49 AFL *Proceedings* (1909), 223, 256; TLC *Proceedings* (1910), 56
50 'Situation in Canada' (miscellaneous), National Union Files, Reel 1; AFL *Proceedings* (1911), 28; Morrison to Draper, 8 May, 3 June 1912 ML
51 TLC *Proceedings* (1911), 52, 70; AFL *Proceedings* (1911), 145
52 TLC *Proceedings* (1914), 103-4
53 Gompers, *Labor in Europe and America* (New York 1910), 138
54 Gompers to Draper, 27 April 1911 GL
55 Ibid.; Gompers to Carl Legien, 28 April 1911; Gompers to James Duncan, 22 June 1911 GL
56 TLC *Proceedings* (1913), 17-18; see also Gompers to W.V. Todd, 28 March 1912 GL; Toronto District Labor Council, Minutes, 18 April 1912
57 AFL *Proceedings* (1913), 370
58 TLC *Proceedings* (1914), 47. See also Draper to Legien, 14 November 1913; Legien to Draper, 7 January 1914; Legien to Gompers, 21 January 1914; Gompers to Legien, 26 February 1914; Gompers to Executive Council, 9 March 1914 GL; Morrison to Executive Council, 19 March 1914 ML

59 See chapter 7, 93-4.

60 These events are conveniently summarized in the *Canadian Annual Review,* 1906, 287-8

61 Morrison to Flett, 26 December 1906, 9 January 1907 ML

62 Toronto District Labor Council, Minutes, 14 February 1907; Canada, Parliament, House of Commons, *Debates,* 9 January 1907, 1173

63 TLC *Proceedings* (1907), 10, 32, 39, 55-6; *Toronto Globe,* 20 September 1907, 2

64 Flett to Gompers, 10 October 1907; Gompers Files, Reel 5; Morrison to Flett, 31 March 1908; see also letters of 27 February, 5, 14 March 1908 ML. The US government dispatched a Bureau of Labor official, Dr Victor S. Clark, to look into the Lemieux act. Clark, one of those early economists who had witnessed the Bismarckian state in operation while a graduate student in Germany, warmly praised the new Canadian law, concluding that it was 'the logical first step toward government intervention in labor disputes.' 'The Canadian Industrial Disputes Act of 1907,' *U.S. Bureau of Labor Bulletin* no. 76 (May 1908), 657. See also his article in no. 86 (January 1910), 1-29.

65 Flett, 'Industrial Disputes Act of Canada,' *American Federationist* XV (June 1908), 447-8; Morrison to Flett, 16 April 1908; Morrison to Executive Council, 16 April 1908 ML

66 *Industrial Canada* VII (April 1907), 564; VIII (April 1908), 696 (Shortt); Morrison to Flett, 20 July 1908 ML; Provincial Workmen's Association, Minutes of the Proceedings of the Grand Council, 17 September 1907, 638-9; CFL *Proceedings* (1909), 7; *Canadian Annual Review,* 1907, 271-2 (Nesbitt and Landers); Eliot called upon American states to enact similar legislation in 'Best Way to Prevent Industrial Warfare,' *McClure's* 33 (September 1909), 518. See also his 'Canadian Act to Aid in the Prevention and Settlement of Strikes and Lockouts,' *McClure's* 30 (December 1907), 149-56

67 AFL *Proceedings* (1907), 140; *Toronto Globe,* 25 September 1908, 3; 26 September 1908, 23; TLC *Proceedings* (1908), 79-81

68 TLC *Proceedings* (1909), 12-13, 55-6; (1910), 13, 15

69 A copy of the decision is in the Gompers Files, Reel 5, AFL-CIO Archives

70 Memorandum on the Industrial Disputes Investigation Act, undated, in Gompers Files, Reel 5. The Act was also criticized in the AFL *Weekly News Letter* I, no. 32, 1911, AFL-CIO Archives

71 TLC *Proceedings* (1911), 88-9

72 *Ottawa Citizen,* 4 May 1912, 2; TLC *Proceedings* (1912), 16; (1913), 153-4; Morrison to Draper, 10 February 1914 ML

73 Marcus M. Marks, 'The Canadian Industrial Disputes Act,' *Annals of the American Academy of Political and Social Science* XLIV (November 1912), 5-6; The entire issue of the *U.S. Bureau of Labor Bulletin* no. 98 (January 1912), is devoted to conciliation and arbitration laws enacted in several nations; A.B. Lowe, President of the Int. Brot. of Maintenance-of-Way Employes, to Borden, 25 November 1912, in Borden Papers, Correspondence, PAC

74 *American Federationist* XX (January 1913), 27; (February 1913), 115-25

75 TLC *Proceedings* (1914), 52, 130; Tobin to Gompers, 3 October 1914, National Union Files, Reel 2; Gompers to Draper, 21 October 1914 GL; see also letters of 5, 13, 27 October 1914 GL

76 Gompers to H.P. Corcoran, 5 December 1914 GL; Gompers to W.S. Appleton, 24 September 1915, Gompers Files, Reel 8

77 Flett to Gompers, 25 August, 30 September, 8 October 1916, Gompers Files, Reel 5; Gompers to Flett, 3 October 1916, Gompers Files, Reel 5; Gompers to E. Anderson, 3 October 1916, Gompers Files, Reel 5. See also A.B. Garretson (President of the Order of Railway Telegraphers), 'The Attitude of Organized Labor Toward the Canadian Industrial Disputes Investigation Act,' *Annals of the American Academy of Political and Social Science* LXIX (January 1917), 170-2.

CHAPTER 13

1 Goldwin Smith to Mrs Hertz, 29 October 1900, in *A Selection From Goldwin Smith's Correspondence, 1846-1910,* ed. Arnold Haultain (London 1913) 364

Bibliography

The bulk of this work rests upon letter-press copies of the outgoing correspondence of Samuel Gompers and Frank Morrison, as indicated in the Preface. A
small proportion of the incoming correspondence of the American Federation of
Labor has been preserved in the National Union Files on twenty-one double-
track 8 MM microfilm reels of generally poor reproduction quality. The material
is not indexed, and is arranged according to the various international union
affiliates, including the Amalgamated Carpenters, United Brotherhood of Carpenters, Boot and Shoe Workers, Broom Makers, Cigarmakers, Electrical
Workers, Leather Workers (both unions), Mineral Mine Workers, International
Ladies' Garment Workers, International Association of Machinists, International
Moulders, Printing Pressmen, Street Railway Employees, International Typographical Union, United Garment Workers, and United Mine Workers. Other
incoming letters, along with press releases, speeches, reports, conference proceedings, and summaries of a few Executive Council meetings, were found in the
Samuel Gompers Files, eight microfilm reels, at AFL-CIO Archives. There is a
helpful card index for this material.

   At the Public Archives in Ottawa, file folder no. 167 in the *Borden Papers*
presented a potpourri of items unavailable elsewhere. Most valuable for this
study were the printed copies of legislative reports presented by John G.
O'Donoghue, Trades Congress solicitor, to the Congress conventions in 1904
and 1905; the Canadian Senate hearings on the Lougheed Bill in 1903; a copy
of the constitution and platform of the Montreal Labor party used as a model
by the Congress at its convention in 1906; a memorandum on Canadian trade

unionism drawn up by O'Donoghue for Borden's use; a few newspaper clippings. The *Laurier Papers* delineated the Canadian government's efforts to promote national unionism in 1902 and 1903. The *King Papers* revealed the strong ties to organized labour cultivated in the early years of the century by the future prime minister. The Borden, Laurier, and King correspondence files were checked for letters exchanged with both AFL and Trades Congress officials, but little of consequence was found.

The Minutes of the Toronto District Labor Council are both complete and invaluable. They provide a fascinating account of the political and trade-union issues, as well as the personal conflicts which arose in Canada's most important city central body.

The *Proceedings* of the American Federation of Labor and the Trades and Labor Congress were vital to this study; of lesser value were the *Proceedings* of the National Trades and Labor Congress and of the Provincial Workmen's Association. Much was found at random in the *Toronto Globe,* the *Ottawa Citizen,* and the *Montreal Herald,* and there is doubtless much more that was not discovered and is still buried in the labour columns of Canadian newspapers. Flett, for example, flooded Gompers and Morrison with clippings from a variety of Canadian newspapers (not preserved at AFL headquarters), especially the *Hamilton Herald.* Future studies of the Canadian working class will find such materials invaluable.

A number of periodicals deserve special mention. The Canada Department of Labour's *Labour Gazette,* a monthly report on labour organizations and working conditions throughout Canada, commenced publication in 1900 and offers historians a mine of information in social and economic history. The Department's *Report on Labour Organization in Canada,* published annually since 1911, provided valuable statistical data for the appendixes. The AFL's organizing activities in Canada were followed in the *American Federationist,* edited by Gompers and published monthly from headquarters in Washington. *Industrial Canada,* the voice of the Canadian Manufacturers' Association, revealed the views of business leaders on a number of related topics. Finally, J. Castell Hopkins' *Canadian Annual Review* supplied a number of useful press summaries of events in the labour world.

This study did not draw upon the bulk of the Canadian labour newspaper collection on microfilm at the Department of Labour Library in Ottawa. The writer is indebted to the use made of this material by Martin Robin in his *Radical Politics and Canadian Labour, 1880-1930,* and to a parallel work by Thomas Loosmore, 'The British Columbia Labor Movement and Political Action, 1879-1906.'

MANUSCRIPT MATERIALS

AMERICAN FEDERATION OF LABOR. 'Charter Book.' AFL-CIO Archives, Washington, DC
- National Union Files. AFL-CIO Archives, 21 microfilm reels
BORDEN, ROBERT L. Correspondence, and File Folder no. 167, 'Trades and Labor Congress,' Public Archives of Canada, Ottawa (PAC)
FORSEY, EUGENE A. 'The International Unions, 1881-1902.' Manuscript, 1968
FREY, JOHN P. Papers. Library of Congress, Washington
GOMPERS, SAMUEL. Files. AFL-CIO Archives, eight microfilm reels
- Letterbooks (GL). Library of Congress, Volumes 1-200, 1883-1914
KIMMEL, E. LOGAN. 'History of Organizations.' AFL-CIO Archives
KING, WILLIAM LYON MACKENZIE. Correspondence, Primary Series, 1897-1914, PAC
LAURIER, SIR WILFRID. Correspondence, 1896-1914, PAC
MOFFATT, JOHN. 'History of the Provincial Workmen's Association.' Manuscript, undated. Department of Labour Library, Ottawa
MORRISON, FRANK. Letterbooks (ML). AFL-CIO Archives. Volumes 91-398, 1903-14 (the letters are now preserved in the Manuscripts Section, Perkins Library, Duke University, Durham, North Carolina).
NORELL, MARGARET, and JEANETTE GROSNEY. 'Labor in Winnipeg: The Rise of Trade Unionism.' Paper presented at United College, Winnipeg, 1945. Department of Labour Library, Ottawa
SIFTON, SIR CLIFFORD. Papers, PAC
TORONTO DISTRICT LABOR COUNCIL. 'Letterbook, 1905-08.' Canadian Labour Congress Library, Ottawa
- 'Minutes,' 1880-1914. Canadian Labour Congress Library, Ottawa

PROCEEDINGS

AMERICAN FEDERATION OF LABOR. *Proceedings,* 1881-1914
CANADIAN FEDERATION OF LABOUR. *Proceedings,* 1909-14
NATIONAL TRADES AND LABOR CONGRESS. *Proceedings,* 1903-8
PROVINCIAL WORKMEN'S ASSOCIATION. 'Minutes of the Proceedings of the Grand Council,' 1897-1908 (typewritten)
TRADES AND LABOR CONGRESS OF CANADA. *Proceedings,* 1883-1914

GOVERNMENT DOCUMENTS

CANADA DEPARTMENT OF LABOUR. *Labour Gazette,* 1900-14
- *Report on Labour Organization in Canada,* 1911-14

CANADA. PARLIAMENT. COMMITTEE OF THE SENATE ON BANKING AND COMMERCE. 'Report of the Proceedings at the Meeting of the Committee ... dealing with Hon. Mr. Lougheed's Bill Respecting the Operations of Officers of International Unions in Canada, Ottawa, June 4, 1903'
CANADA. PARLIAMENT. SENATE. *Debates.* 19 April, 22 July 1903
CANADA. ROYAL COMMISSION ON INDUSTRIAL DISPUTES IN THE PROVINCE OF BRITISH COLUMBIA. 'Report.' *Sessional Papers,* 1903, no. 36a
CANADA. ROYAL COMMISSION ON THE RELATIONS OF CAPITAL AND LABOR IN CANADA. *Report.* Three volumes, 1889
UNITED STATES INDUSTRIAL COMMISSION. *Hearings,* 1900-02

BUSINESS AND LABOUR PRESS

AMERICAN FEDERATION OF LABOR. *American Federationist,* 1894-1914
- *Weekly News Letter,* 1911-12
CANADIAN MANUFACTURERS' ASSOCIATION. *Industrial Canada,* 1900-14
Industrial Banner. London, Ontario, 1899-1902
The Lance. Toronto, 1908-9
The Voice. Winnipeg, 1898-1905

NEWSPAPERS

HOPKINS, J. CASTELL, editor. *Canadian Annual Review,* 1901-14
Montreal Herald, 1903
Ottawa Citizen, 1906-12
The News (Winnipeg?), 27 October 1906. In Borden Papers, File Folder no. 167
Toronto Globe, 1896-1914
Victoria Times. 18, 21 September 1906. In Borden Papers, File Folder no. 167
Winnipeg Free Press, 1898-1914

PAMPHLETS

ALLIED TRADES AND LABOR ASSOCIATION. *Progressive Ottawa, 1902.* Ottawa, Labor Day Souvenir, 1902. Canada Department of Labour Library
- *Official Souvenir, Labor Day Demonstration, September 7, 1903.* Ottawa, 1903. Canada Department of Labour Library
- *Labor Day Souvenir, 1907.* Ottawa, 1907. Canada Department of Labour Library
AMERICAN FEDERATION OF LABOR. *Text Book of Labor's Political Demands.* Washington: American Federation of Labor, 1906

ANDRAS, A. *Labor Unions in Canada: How They Work and What They Seek.*
Ottawa: Woodsworth House Publishers, 1948

BARTLEY, GEORGE. *An Outline History of Typographical Union No. 226,
Vancouver, B.C., 1887-1938.* Vancouver: Typographical Union no. 226, ND

CANADIAN CONGRESS OF LABOUR. *Labour's Program for Political Action: A
Handbook for P.A.C. Members and Union Officers.* Toronto: Canadian
Congress of Labour, ND. Canada Department of Labour Library

KEALEY, GREG. *Working Class Toronto at the Turn of the Century.* Toronto:
New Hogtown Press, 1973

LAFORTUNE, L.A., and GÉRARD TREMBLAY. *L'Union ouvrière.* Montreal:
L'Ecole Sociale Populaire, no. 165, ND

MOFFATT, JOHN. *P.W.A.: Grand Secretary Moffatt's Valedictory Report.*
NP, ND

MONTREAL LABOR PARTY. *Constitution.* Montreal: Ed. Pinchette, printer,
ND (1906?)

SAINT-PIERRE, ARTHUR. *L'Organisation Ouvrière dans la Province de Quebec.*
Second Edition. Montreal: L'Ecole Sociale Populaire, 1913, no. 2

TRADES AND LABOR CONGRESS. *Album of Labor Leaders.* Ottawa: Allied
Trades and Labor Association, 1909

- *Convention Souvenir.* Ottawa, 1901

- *An Historical Review [of] the Trades and Labor Congress of Canada,
1873-1950.* Ottawa, 1950

- *Official Book.* Ottawa, 1902

- *Report of John G. O'Donoghue and Return of Vote on Proposition to Establish a National Law Bureau and Defense Fund.* Ottawa, 1904

- *Report of John G. O'Donoghue, Parliamentary Solicitor, to the 21st Annual
Convention.* Ottawa, 1905

- *Souvenir Book.* Halifax, 1908

- *Souvenir.* Montreal, 1913

ARTICLES

BANCROFT, FRED. 'The International Trade Union Movement.' *Canadian Congress Journal* XIII (December 1934), 22-4

BARNES, SAMUEL H. 'The Evolution of Christian Trade Unionism in Quebec.'
Industrial and Labor Relations Review XII (July 1959), 568-81

BRUCE, JOHN W. 'The International Trade Union Movement.' *Canadian Congress
Journal* XIII (December 1934), 19-21

CHANDLER, ALFRED D. JR. 'The Beginnings of "Big Business" in American
Industry.' *Business History Review* 33 (Spring 1959), 1-31

CHARPENTIER, ALFRED. 'Le mouvement politique ouvrier de Montréal.' *Relations Industrielles* X (March 1955), 74-93

CLARK, VICTOR S. 'The Canadian Industrial Disputes Act of 1907.' *U.S. Bureau of Labor Bulletin* no. 77 (May 1908), 657-740

DEBS, EUGENE V. 'The Western Labor Movement.' *International Socialist Review* III (November 1902), 257-65

DRAPER, PATRICK M. 'Organized Labor in the Dominion of Canada.' *American Federationist* VIII (January 1901), 15-17

DUBOFSKY, MELVYN. 'The Origins of Western Working-Class Radicalism, 1890-1905.' *Labor History* VII (Spring 1966), 131-55

FLETT, JOHN A. 'Industrial Disputes Act of Canada.' *American Federationist* XV (June 1908), 447-8

FORSEY, EUGENE A. 'Insights into Labour History in Canada.' *Relations Industrielles* XX (July 1965), 445-77

– 'Toronto Trades Assembly, 1871-1878.' *Canadian Labour* X (June 1965), 17-19; (July-August), 21-2; (September), 32-5; (October), 23-4

– 'U.S. Labor Organizations and Canadian Labour.' *The American Economic Impact on Canada*. Edited by H.J.G. Aitken and H. Easterbrook. Durham, NC: Duke University Press, 1959

FOX, PAUL W. 'Early Socialism in Canada.' *The Political Process in Canada: Essays in Honour of R. MacGregor Dawson*. Edited by J.H. Aitchison. Toronto: University of Toronto Press, 1963

GARRETSON, A.B. 'The Attitude of Organized Labor Toward the Canadian Industrial Disputes Investigation Act.' *Annals of the American Academy of Political and Social Science* LXIX (January 1917), 170-2

GITELMAN, H.M. 'Adolph Strasser and the Origins of Pure and Simple Unionism.' *Labor History* VI (Winter 1965), 71-83

GOMPERS, SAMUEL. 'The American Labor Movement is Continental, Not Local.' *American Federationist* X (June 1903), 469-70

HARD, WILLIAM. 'The Western Federation of Miners.' *The Outlook* LXXXIII (9 May 1906), 125-33

INNIS, HAROLD A., and BETTY RATZ. 'Labour.' *Encyclopedia of Canada* 1936 Edition, III, 353-64

'The I.W.W. in Canada.' *Canadian Annual Review* (1919), 447-95

LANGDON, STEVEN. 'The Emergence of the Canadian Working-Class Movement, 1845-75.' *Journal of Canadian Studies* VIII (May 1973), 3-13; (August 1973), 8-26

MACEWEN, PAUL W. 'Stephen B. MacNeil: The Aftermath.' *Cape Breton Highlander*, 2 February 1966

MCLACHLAN, J.B. 'Still Fighting at Glace Bay.' *International Socialist Review* X (June 1910), 1102-4

272 Bibliography

MARKS, MARCUS M. 'The Canadian Industrial Disputes Act.' *Annals of the American Academy of Political and Social Science* XLIV (November 1912), 1-9

MOORE, TOM. 'Historical Review of the Trades and Labor Congress' *Canadian Congress Journal* IV (August 1925), 9-13

- 'Labor's Half Century of Progress.' *Canadian Congress Journal* XIII (September 1934), 17-18

O'DONOGHUE, DANIEL J. 'Canadian Labour Interests and Movements.' *Encyclopedia of Canada.* 1900 Edition (photostat copy in Department of Labour Library, Ottawa)

OSTRY, BERNARD. 'Conservatives, Liberals, and Labour in the 1870's.' *Canadian Historical Review* XLI (June 1960), 93-127

- 'Conservatives, Liberals, and Labour in the 1880's.' *Canadian Journal of Economics and Political Science* XXVII (May 1961), 141-61

PRATT, JULIUS W. 'The "Large Policy" of 1898.' *Mississippi Valley Historical Review* XIX (September 1932), 219-42

SAYWELL, JOHN T. 'Labour and Socialism in British Columbia: A Survey of Historical Developments Before 1903.' *British Columbia Historical Quarterly* XIV (July-October 1951), 129-50

SEARS, MARIAN V. 'The American Businessman at the Turn of the Century.' *Business History Review* XXX (December 1956), 382-443

SIMPSON, JAMES. 'The International Trade Union Movement.' *Canadian Congress Journal* XIII (October 1934), 21-2

- 'International Trade Unionism Toronto, Canada, in 1912, the Example' *American Federationist* XIX (September 1912), 699-701

- 'International vs. Purely Canadian Trade Unionism.' *American Federationist* XIX (June 1912), 447-8

TIMLIN, MABEL F. 'Canada's Immigration Policy, 1896-1910.' *Canadian Journal of Economics and Political Science* XXVI (November 1960), 517-32

TROTTER, W.R. 'The International Typographical Union and its Canadian Membership.' *Canadian Congress Journal* XIII (March 1934), 25-6

WHITE, HENRY. 'Trades Unions and Trusts.' *American Federationist* VI (December 1901), 245-7

WILLIAMS, C. BRIAN. 'The Development of Canadian-American Trade Union Relations: Some Conclusions.' *Relations Industrielles* XXI (July 1966), 332-55

WILLOUGHBY, W.F. 'Employers' Associations in the United States.' *Quarterly Journal of Economics* XX (November 1905), 110-50

WRIGLEY, G. WESTON. 'Socialism in Canada.' *International Socialist Review* I (May 1901), 685-9

BOOKS

AITKEN, HUGH G.J. *American Capital and Canadian Resources.* Cambridge, Mass.: Harvard University Press, 1961

AMERICAN FEDERATION OF LABOR. *List of Affiliated Organizations.* Volume I: 1902-1917. AFL-CIO Archives, Washington, DC

BENNETT, WILLIAM. *Builders of British Columbia.* Vancouver: Broadway Publishers, 1937

BERTHOFF, ROWLAND. *British Immigrants in Industrial America.* Cambridge, Mass.: Harvard University Press, 1963

BONNETT, CLARENCE E. *Employers' Associations in the United States: A Study of Typical Associations.* New York: Macmillan, 1922

CAVES, RICHARD E., and RICHARD H. HOLTON. *The Canadian Economy: Prospect and Retrospect.* Cambridge, Mass.: Harvard University Press, 1959

CHARPENTIER, ALFRED. *Ma conversion au syndicalisme catholique.* Montreal: Fides, 1946

CRISPO, JOHN H.G. *International Unionism: A Study in Canadian-American Relations.* Toronto: McGraw-Hill, 1967

DESPRÉS, JEAN-PIERRE. *Le Mouvement ouvrier canadien.* Montreal: Fides, 1947

DICK, WILLIAM. *Labor and Socialism in America: The Gompers Years.* Port Washington, NY: Kennikat Press, 1972

FIELD, FRED W. *Capital Investments in Canada.* Toronto: The Monetary Times of Canada, 1911

FORSEY, EUGENE A. *Economic and Social Aspects of the Nova Scotia Coal Industry.* McGill University Economic Studies no. 5. Toronto: Macmillan, 1926

GOMPERS, SAMUEL. *Seventy Years of Life and Labor.* 2 volumes. New York: E.P. Dutton, 1925

HANSEN, MARCUS, L. *The Mingling of the Canadian and American Peoples.* New Haven: Yale University Press, 1940

HOBSON, J.A. *Canada To-Day.* London: Fisher Irwin, 1906

HOFSTADTER, RICHARD. *Social Darwinism in American Thought.* Revised Edition. New York: George Brazillier, 1959

HOROWITZ, GAD. *Canadian Labour in Politics.* Toronto: University of Toronto Press, 1968

INNIS, HAROLD A. *Essays in Canadian Economic History.* Edited by Mary Q. Innis. Toronto: University of Toronto Press, 1956

– editor. *Labor in Canadian-American Relations.* Carnegie Foundation, The Relations of Canada and the United States. Toronto: Ryerson Press, 1937

JAMIESON, STUART. *Industrial Relations in Canada.* Ithaca: Cornell University Press, 1957

JENSEN, VERNON H. *Heritage of Conflict: Labor Relations in the Nonferrous Metals Industry Up to 1930.* Ithaca: Cornell University Press, 1950

KENNEDY, DOUGLAS R. *The Knights of Labor in Canada.* London: University of Western Ontario, 1956

LATHAM, ALLAN B. *The Catholic and National Trade Unions of Canada.* McGill University Economic Studies no. 10. Toronto: Macmillan, 1930

LEVITT, JOSEPH. *Henri Bourassa and the Golden Calf.* Ottawa: Les Editions de L'Université d'Ottawa, 1972

LEVITT, KARI. *Silent Surrender: The American Economic Empire in Canada.* New York: Liveright, 1971 [Toronto: Macmillan, 1970]

LIPTON, CHARLES. *The Trade-Union Movement of Canada, 1827-1959.* Montreal: Canadian Social Publications, 1967

LOGAN, H.A. *Trade Unions in Canada.* Toronto: Macmillan, 1948

LORWIN, LEWIS. *Labor and Internationalism.* Institute of Economics of the Brookings Institution no. 30. New York: Macmillan, 1929

MCNAUGHT, KENNETH W. *A Prophet in Politics.* Toronto: University of Toronto Press, 1959

MALTAIS, M-LUDOVIC. *Les Syndicats catholiques canadiens.* Washington, DC: Catholic University Press, 1925

MARSHALL, HERBERT, F.A. SOUTHARD, JR, and K.W. TAYLOR. *Canadian-American Industry.* Carnegie Foundation, The Relations of Canada and the United States. New Haven: Yale University Press, 1936

MASTERS, DONALD C. *The Winnipeg General Strike.* Toronto: University of Toronto Press, 1950

ORMSBY, MARGARET. *British Columbia: A History.* Vancouver: Macmillan, 1958

PERLMAN, MARK. *Labor Union Theories in America.* Evanston: Row, Peterson and Company, 1958

PHILLIPS, PAUL. *No Power Greater: A Century of Labour in B.C.* Vancouver: BC Federation of Labour and Boag Foundation, 1967

PORTER, JOHN. *The Vertical Mosaic.* Toronto: University of Toronto Press, 1965

ROBIN, MARTIN. *Radical Politics and Canadian Labour, 1880-1930.* Kingston: Industrial Relations Centre, Queen's University, 1968

SMITH, GOLDWIN. *A Selection from Goldwin Smith's Correspondence, 1846-1910.* Edited by Arnold Haultain. London: T.W. Laurie, 1913

TAFT, PHILIP. *The A.F. of L. in the Time of Gompers.* New York: Harper and Brothers, 1957

TRUDEAU, PIERRE ELLIOTT. *La Grève de l'amiante.* Montreal: Cité Libre, 1956

WARE, NORMAN J. *The Labor Movement in the United States, 1860-1890.* New York: Vintage paper edition, 1964

WARNER, DONALD F. *The Idea of Continental Union: Agitation for the Annexation of Canada to the United States, 1849-1893.* Lexington, Ky.: University of Kentucky Press, 1960

WEINBERG, ALBERT K. *Manifest Destiny: A Study of Nationalist Expansionism in American History.* Chicago: Quadrangle Books, 1963 (first published 1935)

WESSON, ROBERT G. *The Imperial Order.* Berkeley and Los Angeles: University of California Press, 1967

WILKINS, MIRA. *The Emergence of Multinational Enterprise.* Cambridge, Mass.: Harvard University Press, 1970

THESES

APPEL, JOHN C. 'The Relationship of American Labor to United States Imperialism, 1895-1905.' PHD thesis, University of Wisconsin, 1950

BARNES, SAMUEL H. 'The Ideologies and Policies of Canadian Labour Organizations.' PHD thesis, Duke University, 1957

CAHAN, JACQUELINE F. 'A Survey of Political Activities of the Ontario Labour Movement, 1850-1935.' MA thesis, University of Toronto, 1945

DAVIS, W. 'The History of the Early Labour Movement in London, Ontario.' MA thesis, University of Western Ontario, 1930

LOOSMORE, THOMAS R. 'The British Columbia Labor Movement and Political Action, 1879-1906.' MA thesis, University of British Columbia, 1954

TÉTU, MICHEL. 'Les premiers syndicats catholiques canadiens, 1900-1921.' PHD thesis, Université de Montréal, 1961

WILLIAMS, C. BRIAN. 'Canadian-American Trade Union Relations.' PHD thesis, Cornell University, 1964

BIBLIOGRAPHY

ISBESTER, FRANK, D. COATES, and C.B. WILLIAMS. *Industrial and Labour Relations in Canada: A Selected Bibliography.* Kingston: Queen's University Press, 1965

Index

AFL, *see* American Federation of
Labor
Ainey, Joseph 47n, 126-7, 151, 170,
177
Aitcheson, C.I. 197
Aitken, H.J.G. 32
Alberta 135, 146, 171, 174, 177, 202
Alien labour act
− American 17-18, 21, 24, 157, 211
− Canadian 114, 156-7
Allied Trades and Labor Association
(Ottawa) 20, 72, 198, 206
ALU, *see* American Labor Union
American Academy of Political and
Social Science 206-7
American Federation of Labor
− affiliates of in Canada 139-42
− and arbitration 82-3
− Bill of grievances of 165
− Boston convention (1902) of 99,
109,162,191
− Building trades dept. of 146
− and chartering issues 40, 47, 79-81,
99, 102-3, 186-9

− comparison of with TLC 12-15, 20,
83-4, 111-12, 210-11
− and dual unions 57-8, 63, 78,
109-10, 124, 136-40
− early history of 8-9, 13, 210
− expansion of beyond US borders
25, 36, 110, 210-16
− expenditures of in Canada 51-2,
108, 190-3, 196-9, 223-7
− grant to TLC 24-5, 65, 68, 75, 79,
99
− and immigration 115-16
− and International Secretariat 200-1
− and jurisdictional disputes 143-9
− labour politics of: and Knights of
Labor 14; and constitution 59, 94;
and socialists 59, 65, 70, 160-3,
168-9, 176; and US Congress 178;
and independent labour politics
165, 173-4, 179, 181-2
− and Lemieux act 204-9
− and Lougheed bill 4-6, 103-6,
108-9
− in Maritimes 46-7, 121-3

Fishermen's Union of Nova Scotia
  120
Fitzpatrick, J.S. 86, 88, 90
Fitzpatrick, T.H. 20
Flett, John A.
  — as AFL organizer 41-5, 51-2,
    117-19, 212-14
  — anti-Flett sentiment 82, 152-3
  — at Berlin convention of TLC 98
  — biographical data on 41-2
  — and city centrals 187-9
  — and dual unions 84, 109, 142,
    163-4
  — and Gompers 44, 74, 96, 100-3,
    118n, 184
  — on immigration 116
  — and jurisdictional problems 45, 82,
    144-5, 147
  — and labour politics: defends social-
    ists 59; endorses TLC referendum
    (1899) 64, 66; against Canadian
    Socialist League 68; lobbying acti-
    vities 68, 157; opposes labour
    party seating in TLC 95; and inde-
    pendent labour politics 158, 179;
    attacks socialists 161-2, 167, 172,
    180
  — and Lemieux act 202-4, 206, 208
  — and Lougheed bill 106-7, 109
  — in Maritimes 46-7, 81, 119-20
  — and mediation efforts 45
  — in New York State 118
  — and per-capita tax dues issue 20
  — in Quebec 48-50, 125-8
  — and secessions 149-51, 154
  — and James Simpson 161-2, 164,
    193
  — and TLC 74, 92, 162, 184
  — in Western Canada 136-9
Flint Glass Workers Union, American 11

Flynn, T.H. 99n
Foley, Chris 64
Fort William, Ontario, Trades and
  Labor Council 186
Foster, John W. 29
Francq, Gustave 131-2, 175, 180,
  200-1
Furuseth, Andrew 189

Galt, Ontario 149-50
Galt-Preston Trades and Labor Council
  81, 186
Garneau, A.L. 90
Garment Workers of America, United
  118, 128, 167, 197
George, Henry 56
Gervais, Joseph 197
Gibbons, Cardinal 130
Gibson, Senator William 4-6
Glace Bay, Nova Scotia 123
Glass Bottle Blowers' Association of
  the United States and Canada 144
Glockling, Robert 66n, 189
Glockling, William 178, 198
Goderich, Ontario 43
Gompers, Samuel
  — on arbitration 82-3, 96
  — and ASCJ-UBCJ dispute 147
  — and Berlin amendments 96, 98-100
  — and C.S.O. Boudreault 152
  — childhood of 6
  — and Cigarmakers' Union 7-8
  — and city central charters 40, 81,
    186-7
  — on CMA 106
  — continentalism of 25, 36-7, 54, 73,
    97, 209-15
  — and P.M. Draper 73-4
  — and dual unions: of metal miners
    57-8; of WFM and ALU 76-7; of

- and ASCJ-UBCJ dispute 147
- and city central charters 186-8,
  102n
- and dual unions 77, 140, 163-4,
  184
- and labour politics 181-2, 171,
  173, 214
- on Lemieux act 202-4
- in London, Ontario 41
- and Maritimes labour 119-20
- and Ontario labour 132-3
- on Oriental and immigrant labour
  116
- and Quebec labour 125-7, 130, 132
- on secessions 149-50, 151-4
- and James Simpson 163-4, 169,
  174-80
- on TLC as a state federation
  187-93, 197
- on TLC finances 191-2, 196-7
- and Western Canadian labour 133-9
Mosher, A.R. 117
Moulders' Union of North America,
  Int'l 10, 33, 43
Mowat, Sir Oliver 100
Mulholland, A.D. 108
Mulock, Sir William 66-7, 75, 93, 104,
  114n, 202
Musicians, American Federation of
  197

Nanaimo, British Columbia 47, 61,
  70, 77, 94, 100
National Association of Manufacturers
  30, 34, 161
National Civic Federation 35, 158,
  204, 206
National Founders' Association 33
National Metal Trades Association
  33-4, 107

National Policy 28, 30
National Trades and Labor Congress
  92, 116-17, 124, 143-4, 153, 170
Neilson, David 205
Nelson, British Columbia 63, 79, 137
Nesbitt, Wallace K. 204
New Brunswick 39-40, 46, 177
New Democratic Party 216
New York Merchants' Association 30
New Zealand 82-3, 93-4, 158, 175,
  201
Niagara Falls, Ontario 43, 118, 133,
  153
Norfolk, Virginia 174, 193-4
North West Territories 47, 51
Norwich, Ontario 47
Nova Scotia 39, 46-7, 119-23
Noyes, William 197
NTLC, see National Trades and Labor
  Congress

Obermeyer, Henry 89, 91
O'Dell, Ed A. 152n
O'Donoghue, Daniel J. 12, 14, 55-6,
  66, 88-90, 104, 107-8
O'Donoghue, John G. 107, 113,
  157-8, 180
Ontario
- independent labour politics in 64,
  171-4
- no. of international locals in 38-9,
  51-3, 139-42
- organizing in 47, 82, 100, 132-3,
  185, 213
- secessions in 153
- socialism in 163
Ontario Power Company 133
Ontario Reformer 108
Oriental labour 12, 101, 115-16, 134,
  136, 138

- platform of 25n
- and provincial federations of labour 177
- and PWA 120-3
- and Quebec labour 79-80, 124, 126-7, 130, 132
- Victoria convention of (1906) 136-7, 164-9, 181, 192, 214
Trades Union Congress 8, 16, 74, 185, 187, 197
Trotter, W.R. 166, 179, 193, 195, 205
Truro, Nova Scotia 122
Trusts 29, 31, 35, 37, 40
Twigg, T.H. 47n
Typographical Union, International
- at Berlin convention (1902) of TLC 89
- and first Canadian locals 11
- convention of in Toronto 12
- P.M. Draper a member of 72
- D.J. O'Donoghue a member of 88
- Arthur Puttee a member of 95
- James Simpson a member of 161, 163-4
- Hugh Stevenson a member of 86, 197
- 1905-6 strike 152-3
Typothetae of America, United 107

UBCJ, *see* Carpenters and Joiners, United Brot. of
UBRE, *see* Railway Employees, United Brot. of
UMW, *see* Mine Workers, United
United Kingdom
- immigration from 114-15
- independent labour politics in 65, 155, 158, 165, 171, 175
- and Lemieux act 208
United Socialist Labor party 62
Union labels 46, 88-9, 157

Valleyfield, Quebec 49
Vancouver, British Columbia
- ASCJ-UBCJ dispute in 145
- building trades council in 135
- building trades strike in 138-9
- chartering dispute in 186
- Gompers in 139
- independent labour politics in 177
- organizing in 137-8
- race riot (1907) in 115-16
- SLP in 58
- unemployment in 112
- Wrigleys move to 61
Vancouver Trades and Labor Council 19, 50-1, 61-2, 134, 146
Vazquez, Ricardo 99n
Verdon, D. 90
Vermont 207-8
Verville, Alphonse 157n, 162, 166, 170, 180, 184, 193, 203, 205
Victoria, British Columbia 47, 51, 78, 81, 134-6, 166
Victoria Trades and Labor Council 134, 148, 167, 186, 196
Voluntarism 76
Voluntary arbitration 93-4
Volunteer organizers 47-8, 50, 52, 99, 136

Waiters' FLU no. 36, Montreal 88
Walsh, Michael 127
Walters, Fred 20-1
War Eagle Mining Company 57
Warren, George 41, 47n, 48-9
Washington state 137
Waterloo, Ontario 43
Watson, J.H. 41, 47n, 50, 62-3, 78-9, 134
Watters, James W. 117, 147-9
Western Clarion 168

292 Index